In and Out of English
For Better, For Worse?

TRANSLATING EUROPE
Series Editors: Gunilla Anderman, *University of Surrey, UK*
Margaret Rogers, *University of Surrey, UK*

Other Books of Interest
Words, Words, Words. The Translator and the Language Learner
    Gunilla Anderman and Margaret Rogers
Translation, Power, Subversion
    Román Alvarez and M. Carmen-Africa Vidal (eds)
Culture Bumps: An Empirical Approach to the Translation of Allusions
    Ritva Leppihalme
Constructing Cultures: Essays on Literary Translation
    Susan Bassnett and André Lefevere
The Pragmatics of Translation
    Leo Hickey (ed.)
Time Sharing on Stage: Drama Translation in Theatre and Society
    Sirkku Aaltonen
Translation and Nation: A Cultural Politics of Englishness
    Roger Ellis and Liz Oakley-Brown (eds)
Contemporary Translation Theories (2nd Edition)
    Edwin Gentzler
Literary Translation: A Practical Guide
    Clifford E. Landers
Frae Ither Tongues: Essays on Modern Translations into Scots
    Bill Findlay (ed.)
Cultural Encounters in Translation from Arabic
    Said Faiq (ed.)
Identity, Insecurity and Image: France and Language
    Dennis Ager
Language and Society in a Changing Italy
    Arturo Tosi
The Other Languages of Europe
    Guus Extra and Durk Gorter (eds)
Multilingualism in Spain
    M. Teresa Turell (ed.)
Beyond Boundaries: Language and Identity in Contemporary Europe
    Paul Gubbins and Mike Holt (eds)
Bilingualism: Beyond Basic Principles
    Jean-Marc Dewaele, Alex Housen and Li Wei (eds)
Ideology and Image: Britain and Language
    Dennis Ager
Politeness in Europe
    Leo Hickey and Miranda Stewart (eds)
Urban Multilingualism in Europe
    Guus Extra and Kutlay Yagmur (eds)

For more details of these or any other of our publications, please contact:
Multilingual Matters, Frankfurt Lodge, Clevedon Hall,
Victoria Road, Clevedon, BS21 7HH, England
http://www.multilingual-matters.com

TRANSLATING EUROPE
Series Editors: Gunilla Anderman and Margaret Rogers
University of Surrey

In and Out of English: For Better, For Worse?

Edited by

Gunilla Anderman and Margaret Rogers

MULTILINGUAL MATTERS LTD
Clevedon • Buffalo • Toronto

Library of Congress Cataloging in Publication Data
In and Out of English: For Better, For Worse/Edited by Gunilla Anderman and
Margaret Rogers.
Translating Europe.
1. English language–Europe. 2. English language–Translating. 3. English language–
Influence on foreign languages. 4. Europe–Languages–Foreign words and phrases–
English. 5. Translating and interpreting–Europe. 6. Languages in contact–Europe.
I. Anderman, Gunilla M. II. Rogers, Margaret. III. Series.
PE2751.I5 2005
428'.02–dc22   2004016747

British Library Cataloguing in Publication Data
A catalogue entry for this book is available from the British Library.

ISBN 1-85359-788-0 (hbk)
ISBN 1-85359-787-2 (pbk)

Multilingual Matters Ltd
UK: Frankfurt Lodge, Clevedon Hall, Victoria Road, Clevedon BS21 7HH.
USA: UTP, 2250 Military Road, Tonawanda, NY 14150, USA.
Canada: UTP, 5201 Dufferin Street, North York, Ontario M3H 5T8, Canada.

Copyright © 2005 Gunilla Anderman, Margaret Rogers and the authors of individual
chapters.

Typeset by GCS Ltd.
Printed and bound in Great Britain by the Cromwell Press Ltd.

Contents

Preface

In the series *Translating Europe*, we aim to air topical subjects related to current linguistic and cultural developments in Europe of interest to linguists, translators and other language professionals. Each volume will centre around a chosen subject with major contributions from experts engaged in research in the area; further contributions on related themes from other subject specialists will also be included to provide a range of different perspectives. In this way we aim to capture the prevailing mood of thinking at a given time among academics and professionals on major topics which may in turn give rise to and shape new ideas, providing a stimulus for teaching and further research.

Work on the present volume developed as the result of the Enlargement of the European Union and the rapidly changing face of Europe. Growing interest among European nations in joining the European Union and the role of English as a *lingua franca* in long-standing member states naturally suggested further investigation into the influence of English on the languages of Europe. First, however, the wider context for these developments is set with a discussion of the now well acknowledged role of English as the global language. Looking beyond Europe, Stuart Campbell's 'English Translation and Linguistic Hegemony in the Global Era', discusses the role of English within the hotly debated framework of linguistic imperialism, an issue which is also the subject of discussion related to the role of English in an expanding Europe. Our second key contribution comes from Martin Gellerstam who takes as his subject the impact of English on Swedish: 'Fingerprints in Translation' raises a number of interesting questions about different kinds of language interference resulting from the process of translation which appears to be distinguished from traditionally-recognised patterns of transfer. In the remaining chapters, a wide range of issues related to the rapid growth of English and its influence in Europe are further examined.

The volume begins with an overview chapter – 'English in Europe: For Better, For Worse?' – in which a number of issues related to the European language situation are introduced, drawing on historical parallels and also looking ahead in anticipation of further growth in the use of English or 'Englishes'. The contribution on the imperial role of English from Stuart Campbell of the University of Western Sydney, Australia, follows in the second chapter. The argument focuses on the relationship between English and Lao, the language of Laos, a country less advanced technologically and economically than the smaller-sized

European nations at present subjected to the might of Anglo-American language and culture. There follow a number of chapters (3–13), which provide many contemporary examples of such influence across the European continent. Among the Romance languages, French, Spanish and Italian are discussed with a view to assessing the impact of English on individual national languages. Next, the Greek situation is examined, this time from a sociological angle. Two Slavonic languages, Polish and Russian, are also subjected to examination. In addition, Finnish, another language from northern Europe as well as a non-Indo-European language, provides further evidence of the influence of English. Attention too is focussed on a number of Germanic languages. Viewed from a linguistic perspective, the impact of English on German is not deemed to be far-reaching while in Danish, as well as in Norwegian, Anglicisms abound. This group of contributions concludes with the chapter by Martin Gellerstam of the University of Gothenburg, Sweden, in which the evocative metaphor of linguistic 'fingerprints' is used to characterise the nature of changes in the Swedish language, challenging us to accept that these differ from the type of interference traditionally known as *translationese*.

Whether English exerts its influence through translation or other more indirect forms of contact, in an extended Europe many texts are now being produced by non-native speakers of English. The suggestion that editing skills may therefore become as important as translation skills (Chapter 14) leads us to the key issue of the native speaker and the diminishing usefulness of this traditional concept in a modern European and global context (Chapters 15 to 17). In the penultimate chapter, we return to the question of power and language, but this time from a literary perspective in relation to the dominant Anglo-American tradition (Chapter 18). Finally, the volume concludes with a discussion of pragmalinguistics, the topical subject of intercultural communication in English between Europeans of different nationalities (Chapter 19).

The linguistic and cultural issues aired in *In and Out of English: For Better, For Worse?* should be of immediate concern to Europeans, increasingly combining a national and a European identity as well as to anyone with an interest in our multilingual world. Although many questions raised remain unanswered, we hope that this airing of topical issues will serve to generate further debate and research on the subject of English and the languages of Europe.

Gunilla Anderman
Margaret Rogers

Guildford, 2004

Acknowledgements

A number of people have helped us during the various stages of compiling this edited volume. A comprehensive overview of the influence of English on many of the languages of Europe required some diligence in tracking down language specialists in a number of different countries. As a result, speed of production unfortunately had to be sacrificed to other considerations and we are most grateful to the contributors for their forbearance. In addition, we owe a debt of gratitude to Multilingual Matters for allowing us the time to complete the volume in keeping with our original concept. We would also like to thank Høyskoleforlaget, Kristiansand, Norway for allowing us to reproduce, in English, a shortened version of Chapter 4, *Rocka hip og snacksy. Om engelsk i norsk språk og samfunn* by Stig Johansson and Anne-Line Graedler in Chapter 12. We are pleased that Rob Dickinson once again agreed to lend us his expert eye as copy editor, and that our former colleagues Nelly Chachibaia and Mick Colenso provided expert support in the early stages of preparation. Last, but certainly not least, our thanks as always go to Gillian James, not only for her attention to detail, persistence and patience but also for her enthusiastic co-operation and initiative in bringing the volume together.

Gunilla Anderman
Margaret Rogers

Guildford
May 2004

Contributors: A Short Profile

Beverley Adab is Senior Lecturer in Translation Studies and French at Aston University, UK, where she teaches on the undergraduate and post-graduate programmes in Translation Studies. Her publications in the field are primarily concerned with cross-cultural issues, particularly in the translation of advertising and in the use of corpora in the translation process.

Gunilla Anderman is Professor of Translation Studies at the University of Surrey, UK, where she teaches Translation Theory, Translation of Children's Literature and Translation of Drama on the undergraduate as well as postgraduate programmes in Translation Studies. A professional translator for the theatre, many of her publications have been in the field of drama translation.

Stephen Barbour teaches German and Linguistics at the University of East Anglia, where he is Head of the German Sector. His research and publications tend to focus on the sociolinguistics of German and on the role of language in the formation and promotion of national and ethic identities

Stuart Campbell is Professor and Head of the School of Languages and Linguistics at the University of Western Sydney, Australia. His publications in the field of Translation Studies have often focused on Translation and Interpreting Assessment as well as translation into the second language.

Nelly Chachibaia received her PhD in Translation Studies from Moscow State Linguistic University, Russia. She is the author of a number of articles on translation and interpretation and at present teaches on the MA in Bilingual Translation at the University of Westminster.

Władysław Chłopicki, PhD is Senior Lecturer at the Institute of English Philology, Jagiellonian University, Kraków, Poland where he teaches Linguistics, Translation and Cultural Studies. A co-organiser of biannual national conferences on 'Language of the Third Millennium', he has also written extensively on the language of humour, as well as on the influence of English on Polish, particularly in advertising.

Michael Colenso graduated from the University of Surrey with a degree in Russian and Law. He has taught specialised translation between Russian and English for a number of years and is currently working as a full-time professional translator.

Martin Gellerstam is Associate Professor and Director of Språkbanken (The Swedish Language Bank) at the University of Gothenburg, Sweden. As editor of the Swedish Academy Glossary, he is involved in the construction of the Swedish Morphology Database (SMDB).

Henrik Gottlieb is Associate Professsor of English at the Center for Translation Studies and Lexicography, University of Copenhagen, Denmark. He has published and lectured widely on different aspects of language transfer on the screen, including the translation of humour in subtitling.

Anne-Line Graedler, Associate Professor in Modern English, Institute of British and American Studies at the University of Oslo, Norway, wrote her PhD thesis on the incorporation of English borrowings into Norwegian. She is also the author of *Morphological, Semantic and Functional Aspects of English Lexical Borrowings in Norwegian.*

Stig Johansson is Professor of Modern English Language, Institute of British and American Studies at the University of Oslo, Norway. He is responsible for the project, *Engelsk i norsk språk og samfunn* (English in Norwegian Language and Society). In addition to his many publications and interest in the influence of English on Norwegian, his numerous publications are also concerned with studies in Corpus Linguistics.

Kate Moore is lecturer in English at the University of Technology in Tampere. In addition to the influence of English on Finnish, her research interests include Oral History and Speech Pathology.

Jeremy Munday is Senior Lecturer in Spanish Studies and Deputy Director of the Centre for Translation Studies at the University of Surrey. Specialising in Translation Theory and Corpus Linguistics, he is the author of articles as well as published and forthcoming books in the field of Translation Studies.

Maria Teresa Musacchio is an Associate Professor of English and Translation at the University of Padua. She also teaches specialist translation between English and Italian at the School for Interpreters and Translators of the University of Trieste, Italy. Her research is concerned with translation in the field of Economics.

Margaret Rogers, Reader in German, is the Director of the Centre for Translation Studies and teaches terminology, translation and text analysis on the undergraduate and postgraduate programmes in Translation Studies at the University of Surrey, UK. Her publications are in the field of Terminology, LSP and Translation.

Christopher Rollason obtained a First Class Honours in English Literature from Trinity College, Cambridge in 1975, and a PhD from York University in 1988. A former member of the Department of Anglo-American Studies at Coimbra University, Portugal, he is now an independent scholar and Language Editor for the Delhi-based Atlantic Literary Review. Research publications include articles in the field of Translation Studies.

Marcel Thelen is Senior Lecturer in the Department of Translation and Interpreting at the Maastricht School of International Communciation of Hogeschool Zuyd, Maastricht, The Netherlands. He is also editor–in-chief of the *Translation and Meaning* book series.

Polymnia Tsagouria studied Greek literature and Psychology at the University of Thessaloniki in Greece. She holds an MA in Classics and an MA in Ancient History, both from University College, London, where she is currently pursuing research in Ancient Greek Economic History. Since 1997 she has been working as a Greek language and Literature teacher in schools and universities in Greece as well as the UK.

Krista Varantola is Professor of English in the School of Modern Languages and Translation Studies and Rector of the University of Tampere, in Finland. Her research interests include the use of dictionaries and corpora in translation.

Chapter 1
English in Europe:
For Better, for Worse?

GUNILLA ANDERMAN AND MARGARET ROGERS

Introduction

When in 1977 the NASA spacecraft Voyager One blasted off on its historic unmanned mission to Jupiter and beyond, the capsule was equipped with greetings from the planet Earth, brief messages in 55 languages in preparation for the wide-ranging choice of languages that might be spoken in outer space. Preceding the individual language messages, however, was a lengthier statement from Kurt Waldheim speaking on behalf of the then 147 member states of the United Nations. Prophetically the statement made by the Secretary-General of the UN, himself an Austrian, was delivered in English. While, at the time, the use of English to ensure universal understanding of his message might not have been a foregone conclusion, at the present moment in history the choice of English as the language to represent the planet seems indisputable.[1]

For English to assume the role of global language is, however, not an altogether uncontroversial issue. While the availability of a *lingua franca* helps individual nation states to gain an increased international profile, the coexistence of a national and an international language is not always unproblematic; a number of major arguments have been raised related to retaining and promoting English in its present global role, and more particularly its role as European *lingua franca*. Six of these arguments are first presented in outline, then addressed in this introductory chapter.

Linguistic imperialism

The first argument concerns the hotly debated issue of linguistic hegemony, also known as 'linguistic imperialism' (see for example Phillipson, 1992 and Phillipson and Skutnabb-Kangas, 1999). Concern has been voiced that the needs of developing countries are better met through linguistic expertise used to help promote their own national languages than through the English-language programmes offered by Western, post-colonial powers. In a European context, as the use of English for cross-national communication makes inroads into an increasing number of specialist domains and activities, warning voices point to the risk of erosion of the European Union (EU) commitment to cultural and linguistic diversity of its member states (Phillipson, 2003).

A related issue resulting from the expanding use of English in many different spheres of activity – not only within the European Union – is its linguistic influence on many of the languages of the world. Given the tendency for languages with small numbers of speakers to be nudged out by languages spoken by many, it is estimated that in a hundred years' time about 3000 languages may have become extinct. According to some estimates, there are about 6500 languages in the world, about half of which are likely to cease to exist within that time period (Crystal, 2003, personal communication).[2] This means that on average, every two weeks, somewhere in the world, a language becomes extinct. Since 96% of the world's languages are spoken by only 4% of its people, it is hardly surprising that many of them may feel under threat.

Global English: Language change and language use

For speakers with English as their first language, the development of English as a means of international communication constitutes another, closely linked issue of concern. Signs of global English developing as a homogenised 'reduced standardised form of language for supra-cultural communication' (Barber, 1992, discussed in Snell-Hornby, 2000: 36) have made some mother tongue speakers fear that, in the process of becoming common property, their native tongue is turning into a 'hybrid' language, sometimes referred to as Eurospeak within the European Union and more broadly as 'McLanguage', reflecting the globalised nature of the modern commercial world (Snell-Hornby, 1999). Concern has also been expressed about the uniqueness and survival of some of the European languages spoken by small numbers of speakers. According to some, English is making visible inroads into their grammar and vocabulary and is therefore perceived as an accelerating force hastening their journey towards extinction to state the extreme case. Hence, linguistic developments in the context of global English constitute the second, topical issue to be addressed here in this volume.

English and translation

Closely linked to the linguistic problems developing in the wake of global English is the third issue: the need for non-mother tongue speakers to communicate and often translate into a language which is not their own (what Emma Wagner calls 'two-way translation', see this volume). This is already the case among first-generation immigrants in countries such as Australia (see Campbell, 1998); in Europe, the same situation pertains in countries such as Finland, where languages of limited diffusion are spoken (see Mackenzie, 1998: 15–19). The enlargement of the EU with its anticipated array of additional languages is likely to intensify even further discussions about the continuing usefulness of the concept of the 'native speaker'. Projections show that the balance between first-language and second-language speakers of English is changing. According to Graddol (1999), the number of second-language speakers will overtake that of first-language speakers within the next 50 years. Others maintain that this has already happened (Davies, 2003: 160; Jenkins, 2003: 2).

Any discussion about the language of a nation also needs to consider its literary traditions and its link with social identity; the influence of English on the languages of Europe also has important implications for translation. At the moment, the present linguistic stronghold of English is matched by the central position held by the Anglo-American literary tradition in Europe, sufficiently firmly established for translated literary works from other languages to be assigned more peripheral positions (see Even Zohar, 1978 and 1990). Hence, for European literature to travel successfully in translation into English, adjustments are often required in order to ensure that European literary imports fit the literary traditions prevailing in the receiving anglophone target culture, not infrequently at the cost of reducing the element of 'foreignness' in the original (see Venuti, 1995).

Language learning and teaching: Some implications of global English

The rapid spread of English has also been quoted as a possible factor underlining the present decline in interest among European students in the study of modern languages, a side effect of the use of an international language for purposes of cross-national communication. Nevertheless, there is evidence in the UK, for example, that graduates with a knowledge of modern-languages other than English are highly employable by industry. One account estimates that modern-language graduates have lower unemployment rates than those in Business/Administration, Engineering/Technology and Computing[3] but claims that not enough UK businesses are aware of the consequences of using only English. The development of English into the language in which many European citizens now tend to communicate with each other therefore raises the question of the way forward for modern-language teaching, not only in the UK but also elsewhere in Europe. While the approach which has most recently informed modern-language pedagogy places primary emphasis on listening comprehension and speaking the foreign language, with the emergence of a European *lingua franca*, a shift to the early development of reading and translation skills may more accurately reflect the needs of an enlarged Europe. Concentrating on the learning of a closely defined set of skills might help to ensure a continued supply of linguists with a knowledge of the less commonly known languages of Europe. A further step towards protecting such languages might be the introduction of a language policy following the precedents of Australia and South Africa (Phillipson, 2003).

The nature of the beast: What is International English?

For such a widespread and widely discussed phenomenon, it is surprisingly difficult to identify a commonly accepted definition of standard international English. According to McArthur, the term 'international English' stems from the 1980s and is also known as international standard English. He defines it as: 'the standard form of English conceived as an international language; international English in its standard form' (1992: 984). Similarly, in the case of English as the *lingua franca* of Europe, there appears to be little available data on the characteristics of this variety of English for purposes of cross-national communication (for details of an ongoing research project, see James, 2000). Hence the fifth and penultimate topic in the discussion of the present position of English includes some observations on the direction of this new variety of English now emerging.

Pragmalinguistics

As cross-national communication among European nationals increases, so does the need for greater understanding of social and cultural divides. In the act of communication, knowledge of a shared *lingua franca* may go a long way in the pursuit of mutually beneficial social intercourse; there are, however, additional factors that come into play, affecting the way speakers make use of a language other than their own and the way first-language interlocutors interact in such situations. Of considerable importance is an understanding of the prevailing social and cultural traditions which speakers, unwittingly, bring with them from their own language to a communicative situation. As a result, a successful cross-national exchange often requires pragmatic as well as linguistic competence, the sixth topic aired in this chapter, including a discussion of some of the factors concerned with the pragmatic competence required to use language appropriately in different contexts.

In the remainder of Chapter 1 we consider in greater detail these different issues in relation to the position of English as a global language and, in particular, its role as the *lingua franca* of Europe.

Linguistic Imperialism: Historical Precedents

Seen from the standpoint of linguistic imperialism (see for example Phillipson, 1999 and Skutnabb-Kangas and Phillipson, 1992), English in its present global role continues to serve as an instrument of colonial domination, reinforced after the end of World War II by the USA, the world's current superpower. As an argument in favour of a group of people being represented by a language of their own, the theory of linguistic imperialism points to the need to express group membership and the individual self as equal in importance to international communication (see also Seidlhofer 2002: 203). The debate further touches on the roles of specialists in Teaching English as a Second Language (TESOL) and Teaching English as a Foreign Language (TEFL) and the extent to which their expertise meets the needs of developing countries, many of them too small or too poor to draw on their own resources. Accordingly, moves in favour of expanding the use of English, based on claimed economic and technical advantages, should not be made without careful consideration of the educational and social inequality deriving from the use of English for official purposes (see Görlach, 1988).

In Europe, voices critical of this ideological perspective point to the increased use of English as a *lingua franca* in many aspects of the lives of Europeans, particularly in professional contexts. This is, for instance, the language in which academics are increasingly presenting and publishing their findings rather than the language of their own country. Fears of the member states of the EU that the commitment to linguistic diversity, confirmed in EU treaties and European Parliament resolutions, will not be respected are fuelled by official US statements that the most serious problem for the EU is that it has so many languages, 'this preventing real integration and development of the Union' (Phillipson and Skutnabb-Kangas, 1999: 22). Along with the geopolitical agenda, not infrequently attributed to the US government whose 'first grand objective [it is] of course, to keep America as a European power, not just for today but for the indefinite future' (Walker, 1997, discussed in Graddol, 1999: 22), such comments project a future European scenario in which political and economic supremacy are followed by linguistic hegemony. In this volume, the perspective adopted in Stuart Campbell's discussion of the role of English in Laos can be understood against this general background.

It is not the first time, however, that linguistic issues following in the wake of the establishment of a superpower have confronted Europeans; history furnishes ample evidence of powerful nations and their conquests, followed by political, economic and linguistic submission. This does, however, also provide illustrations of the continued use of two languages in a variety of different forms of coexistence. As historical models, these examples indicate a range of possible linguistic outcomes.

The ancient world

In the **Greece** of antiquity, where each separate state or *polis* pursued its own political interests, the **Greek** language varieties of the different areas ranked equal in prestige. But in the course of the fifth century BC the importance of Athens and, as a consequence, Attic, the dialect spoken by the Athenians, started to grow at the expense of the other states. When, a couple of decades before the middle of the third century BC the Macedonian Empire began to expand rapidly, conquering Greece and the countries around the eastern part of the Mediterranean, the influence of Greek culture and education was such that Alexander the Great, King of the Macedonians, made Greek the official language throughout the Empire. In a modified form, it became established as the written language, known as *koine*, meaning the common language. Gradually it ousted the traditional dialects which, after a few centuries, began to disappear from written records (Janson, 2000: 81). First used in what is now present-day Greece, the cultural and political power of Greece established Greek as the language of the region around the eastern Mediterranean for more than a millennium. Then, from the fifteenth to the eighteenth centuries, the period of time that Greece formed part of the Ottoman Empire, *koine* continued to be used as a spoken language, to re-emerge in the nineteenth century once more as a written, official language but with a political and linguistic legacy in the form of two competing language varieties: *Katharevousa*, the purified language containing words and forms from Classical Greek, and *Dimotiki*, the popularly used language which, in 1976, was announced as the official Greek language, mirroring a political shift following the fall of the junta. The current situation is one of diglossia.

While the use of Greek, once the language of a superpower, is now largely confined to its area of origin, the history of **Latin**, the language of the **Roman Empire**, tells a different story of political and linguistic conquest. During the first few centuries following its foundation, believed to be in 753 BC, Rome was the sole locus for the use of Latin, although smaller neighbouring states are likely to have been using similar languages (Janson, 2000: 90). Over the next 800 years or so, the Republic of Rome and then the Empire expanded to cover the area around the Mediterranean and vast regions beyond, its European boundary marked by the Rhine and the Danube. This enormous power remained largely intact until the fifth century AD when the invasion of Germanic tribes shattered the western part of the Empire.

Unlike Greek writers and Greek literature, from the very beginning Roman writers used one homogeneous language, the variety spoken in Rome. Mastery of the Latin language soon became the key to success in Rome, and this attention to language resulted in well-established language norms. Rules of grammar and rhetoric were formulated and scrupulously followed, including spelling and pronunciation, vocabulary and style (Janson, 2002: 92).

While at first Latin was spoken only in Rome, with time it spread, replacing not only the languages of the Italian regions but also a number of others, resulting in the emergence of the Romance language family. The use of Latin in school, in the army and in commercial life ensured that, within a few generations, urban populations shifted to using Latin, followed more slowly by speakers in rural areas. Also aiding the spread of Latin was the close link between Latin and Christianity, the new religion, the gospels and other texts having been translated earlier from Greek into Latin. However, while in its wake the Roman conquest was followed by linguistic submission, history also reveals less far-reaching social and cultural contact and, as a result, the continued coexistence of two languages.

More recent times

In 1494, the Treaty of Tordesillas between Portugal and Spain provided a blueprint for the two leading naval powers of the time to carve up the world outside Europe between them. For South America, the Treaty was decisive; while **Portugal** occupied the eastern part of the continent, the rest fell under the rule of **Spain**, resulting in **Portuguese** becoming the language of Brazil, while **Spanish** dominates in virtually all other states of the Americas south of what is now the USA. While, in South America, Portuguese developed into a native tongue, in Africa, where Portugal also seized extensive territory along the coast, including what are now the independent states of Angola, Guinea-Bissau and Mozambique, Portuguese, the official language, never became the first language for more than a very small percentage of the population, the majority of whom have continued to speak one of the many languages in use before the Portuguese arrived.

The need for a shared language to facilitate cross-national communication in Europe had long been filled by Latin when, in the late seventeenth century, **France** became the leading political and cultural force in Europe. This French dominance meant in turn that for Europeans of consequence it became imperative to know **French**. Not only did it become more important to have read Racine than to know Virgil by heart, in matters of social etiquette, French manners were also quickly adopted. To be able to converse in French became essential and French developed into the language of diplomacy and international contacts. While, in 1660, peace negotiations between Austria, Poland and Sweden were conducted in Latin, in Nijmegen in 1678 discussions between multilingual speakers including Frenchmen, Spaniards and Swedes, were held in French, with only the peace treaty itself drawn up in Latin; and, not long after, the agreement of Rastadt between Austria and France was recorded only in French (Janson, 2000: 178), setting a diplomatic model for times to come. The linguistic hegemony of French was not, however, achieved effortlessly. The Académie Française, vested with the task of cultivating and furthering the French language, was founded as early as 1635. As the national language of the successful nation state of France, French achieved linguistic supremacy in Europe, following political and cultural hegemony, thereby usurping the position of Latin as a means of international communication.

Throughout the nineteenth century, French retained its status as the favoured international language in Europe, remaining the language of diplomacy. Following the unification of Germany under Prussia and the Franco-German war of the early 1870s, the position of French met with competition from German, particularly in view of its dominance as the *lingua franca* in Central Europe. Politically dominant for a number of decades and making rapid scientific advances, the influence of **Germany** was for a time reflected in the use of **German** in the domains of science and technology. German was also the *lingua franca* across much of eastern Europe, enjoying its heyday in the nineteenth century (Russ, 1994: 3–4). Two world wars, however, left Germany in political and economic ruin, in turn reflected in diminished prospects for German to assume the role of an international language. The collapse of the Iron Curtain in 1990 also strengthened the position of English as a *lingua franca* at the cost of not only German, but also Russian.

For a while, however, it looked instead as if Russian might lay claim to the status of international language in part of Europe, and even beyond. As a superpower, the **Soviet Union** moved to manifest its political might through instruction of the **Russian** language within the educational systems of its satellite states. But, following its collapse in 1990, the speed with which the subject disappeared from the curriculum of many schools in eastern Europe serves as proof of the vagaries of power as reflected in language. Still, at a different point in history, the steps taken by Russia to impose its own language on speakers of other tongues had a different, lasting result. In the nineteenth century, it succeeded in turning many of the inhabitants of Siberia into speakers of Russian, bringing many of the original languages of the region to the verge of extinction.

As history shows, when languages coexist, the language of the superior power will inevitably leave its mark on the languages of those brought within its political and economic orbit. However, the extent of the linguistic impact of this asymmetry may vary. In the past, a number of scenarios have ensued as the result of the interplay of a number of different factors. One such factor is the degree of closeness between the languages and cultures concerned; one of the reasons cited for Latin failing to find a more permanent base in Britain, unlike in other parts of western Europe where the indigenous languages were suppressed, was the cultural divide between the rulers and the common man. To what extent then does the increasing use of English in present-day Europe also signal a growing change among Europeans to endorse the values and beliefs of today's superpower?

Global English: Language Change and Language Use

We have seen how the influence of a dominant language and culture can change over time, resulting in different outcomes. In modern-day Europe, in which English is increasingly functioning as the *lingua franca*, the question also arises, which or whose English? And to what extent does the increasing use of English signal a growing acceptance of the values of American mass culture with its closely linked commercial interests?

European culture and the language of the reigning superpower

There seems little doubt that most Europeans would not like to see their national language replaced by English. While a European Commission survey reported in 2001 (*Eurobarometer* 54, 15 February 2001), that 71% of Europeans felt that everyone in the EU should be able to speak one European language in addition to their mother tongue, and almost the same proportion agreed that this language should be English, 63% also believed that their own language needed to be safeguarded (cited in Phillipson, 2003: 61). There also seem to be valid arguments for believing that the increasing use of English among Europeans does not necessarily signal an equally rapid acceptance of values any more deep-rooted than the consumerism brought on by the so-called McDonaldisation not only of food but also of music and entertainment.

In his recent book, *The World We're In* (2003), the economic journalist and writer Will Hutton argues that Europeans are in fact more fundamentally different from Americans than is often assumed, as manifested in their attitudes towards property, equality, social solidarity and other public realms. At work here may be the shared use of English disguising more profound differences in values and attitudes, masked by formal lexical similarities. For example, a basic notion such as that of a *fair society* is, according to Hutton, interpreted radically differently in Europe and in the United States. In the United States, it stands for a concept that promotes opportunity for all but is indifferent to the consequential, unequal distribution of risks and rewards. In contrast, the European concept of a *fair society* assumes a large integrative role for the state as an actively conciliating social partner, providing public services and regulating business and society (Hutton, 2003: 45). Similarly, ownership and property rights differ in their meaning in the USA and in Europe. In the USA, the sanctity of ownership and the right of property spread from settler farmer to company; acquisition and holding of property was a private initiative, with the federal state policing and upholding it and acting as the arbitrator of the resulting private contracts between property holders (2003: 59). In Europe, on the other hand, attitudes are more complex. Here the notion persists that property is held in trust for all and only delegated to individuals for as long as they accept reciprocal social obligations, a contrasting legacy of the fact that, at the time when Europe was already settled, America's founding fathers operated in almost limitless, unsettled land.

For many Europeans, the war in Iraq also crystallised other, equally deep-rooted differences. While throughout Europe demonstrators opposed to military intervention in Iraq did not in all likelihood see themselves as citizens of the EU, Brussels being far from their minds, to many Europeans the war represented a transgression of deeply-held values. What united them was their repudiation of the geopolitics of the twentieth century and their concern that it should not continue into the new century. On 26 April 2003, in an article in the *Guardian* newspaper entitled 'Thanks, Mr President', the political columnist, Jeremy Rifkind, referred to the Iraq crisis as having 'united Europeans and armed them with a clear sense of shared values and future vision'. Ironically, therefore, the use of English, the language of the invading forces, has in a number of ways helped in the process of uniting many Europeans, who now use English in order to communicate with other European citizens. But at what linguistic cost has this ease of mutual access been established?

The influence of English on other European languages

We might want to start the discussion by asking whether it is in fact possible or even desirable to do without Anglicisms in matters relating to the contemporary world. This is the question posed by Christopher Rollason in relation to France in his contribution to this volume, 'Unequal Systems: On the Problem of Anglicisms in Contemporary French Usage', where he uses the framework of Even-Zohar's polysystem theory to capture the asymmetrical relationship between English as a global language, and contemporary French. One of the fields in which the impact of English is particularly strongly felt in France is that of information technology. As shown by Jeremy Munday in his contribution, '*E-mail, Emilio*, or *Mensaje de Correo Electrónico*? The Spanish Language Fight for Purity in the New Technologies', this is also the case in Spanish. Writing about another member of the Romance language family, in her chapter, 'The Influence of English on Italian: The Case of Translations of Economics Articles', Maria Teresa Musachio argues for a trend in modern Italian to borrow not only lexis, but also to reflect English textual and syntactic patterns in the register of economics. The contribution, 'The Influence of English on Greek: A Sociological Approach', by Polymnia Tsagouria, shows the situation in Greece to be somewhat different from that in other European countries, as the result of the use of English in the development of the tourist industry. It also stresses the difference Greeks tend to observe between spoken language, where the English influence abounds and the written mode, where efforts are made to keep the foreign impact at bay. Arguing along similar lines to Rollason, this time in relation to Danish, a cognate Germanic language, in 'Anglicisms and Translation' Henrik Gottlieb proposes that the adoption of Anglicisms brings with it a different cultural view. In 'Anglicisms in Norwegian: When and Where?', Stig Johansson and Anne-Line Graedler show the impact of English on Norwegian to be very influential in the case of vocabulary, particularly in relation to certain subject areas such as business, entertainment and information technology as well as certain social groups (Johansson & Graedler, 2002). Although it has been argued that German is particularly susceptible to the influence of English (Hoffman, 2000: 10), in his analysis of the English influences on German, 'Contemporary English Influence on German – A Perspective from Linguistics', Stephen Barbour similarly makes a clear case for its main linguistic impact also being on the lexicon. The two Slavonic languages discussed, Polish and Russian, also present similar findings in contributions by Wlalislav Chłopicki in 'Polish under Siege?' and Nellie Chachibaia and Michael Colenso in 'New Anglicisms in Russian', respectively. An interesting case of language contact between unrelated language families is presented by Kate Moore and Krista Varantola in 'Anglo-Finnish Contacts: Collisions and Collusions', a discussion of the influence of English as a Germanic language on Finnish, a member of the Finno-Ugric family with just over five million speakers. This genealogical difference seems, however, to offer few barriers to lexical borrowing (for more in depth examination of English influences on European languages see also Görlach, 2002).

The impact on English resulting from its present position

Due to its position as the language of global communication and the *lingua franca* of Europe, English may now be in the curious position of influencing itself. The type of English frequently found in international public places such as airports as well as in tourist brochures has been cited as putting English at peril and turning it into a 'free floating *lingua franca*' that has largely lost track of its cultural identity, its idioms, its hidden connotations, its grammatical subtleties and has become a reduced standardised form of language for supranational communication, the 'McLanguage' of our globalised 'McWorld', or the 'Eurospeak' of our multi-national continent'(Snell-Hornby, 1999). In 'Translation and/or Editing: The

Way Forward?', Emma Wagner's discussion of English as a *lingua franca* in the context of the EU, she presents counter-examples to the idea of a standardised impoverished variety of English, arguing instead that the quality of both translations and texts originally written in English (possibly by non-native speakers) should be judged according to their purpose and edited or revised accordingly. Her view is therefore one of a functionally specific variety, especially within an enlarged European Union.

English: A foreign or second language in Europe?

Outside the UK and the Irish Republic, English in Europe has traditionally been viewed as a foreign rather than a second language, the role it plays in India and other former British colonies. However, as the result of a new pattern emerging in Europe, the position of English now seems to be rapidly changing. According to surveys of the populations of European Union countries such as *Eurobarometer* 50, based on figures collected in 1998, almost one-third of the citizens of the 13 non-English-speaking countries of the EU feel that they can manage to hold their own in a conversation in English. In Denmark, 77% of the adult population stated that they can participate in a conversation in English, and in Sweden 75% felt equally confident that their mastery of English would allow them to converse in English; in The Netherlands the figure was 71% (reported in Graddol, 1999: 65).

The command that speakers of these European nations now have of spoken English has led Phillipson to refer to two groups of English-speaking countries (1992: 17). The term 'core English-speaking countries' includes countries where the dominant group are native speakers of English as in Britain, the USA, Australia, Canada and New Zealand. These countries correspond to Kachru's 'Inner Circle' of English speakers (1985: 12). In addition, there are so-called 'periphery English' countries, covering in Kachru's terminology both the 'Outer Circle' and the 'Expanding Circle' (1985: 12). The Outer Circle embraces those countries where English was imposed in colonial times and where it continues to serve a number of international functions; the Expanding Circle includes those countries where English is used as an international link language such as Scandinavia and Japan. However, as mastery of English continues to improve throughout Europe, membership of the periphery English category cannot be viewed as fixed, as Kachru's term Expanding Circle indicates. At present there are large variations between European countries in the use of English, with only 13% of Spanish adults feeling able to conduct a conversation in English in comparison with the much higher figures for northern Europe (Graddol, 1999: 65–6). As student exchange programmes facilitate easy movement between countries for younger generations of speakers, such variations are likely to diminish.

Moreover, it is already the case that English is used as a *lingua franca* between traditional English as a Foreign Language (EFL) countries such as Scandinavia and The Netherlands (see Jenkins, 2003: 34) and in some non-UK companies.

English and Translation

While English is changing in the modern world, at the same time, it is also leaving its 'fingerprints' on other languages, not only through its uses as a *lingua franca* but also through a particular type of language contact, namely translation. In 'Fingerprints in Translation', Martin Gellerstam demonstrates how not only English words and expressions have left their mark in translations into Swedish but also sentence constructions and rhetorical devices, more characteristic of an Anglo-American than a Swedish literary tradition. Conversely, the increasing volume of translation carried out by non-native speakers of English may also be having an effect on its own further development.

Translation into the second language

In the aftermath of colonialism, translation into the second language has long been unavoidable in some parts of the world, while in others the need to translate out of the mother tongue has of necessity developed in the wake of immigration. In Australia, for instance, the need for immigrants to gain access to social and communal services by means of their own language resulted in community interpreting and translation services developing in the early 1970s. In such a situation, the source of supply of translators and interpreters is inevitably the community itself. As a result, many translators need to work into English, their second language. By the 1990s, political, economic and cultural links between Australia and Asia added further international links, reflected in the development of a number of programmes in translator and interpreter training (Campbell, 1998: 23). However, the emergence of a second and a third generation of speakers gradually brought about a reduction in the need for such services. Parallel developments may be found in the Asian communities of the UK where younger generations of speakers have developed a mastery of English, sometimes as bilinguals, and translation and interpreting services are no longer required. In the USA, second-generation Armenian, Italian or Polish speakers make limited use of the language of their parents.

With the expansion of English as a *lingua franca*, the need for documents to be available in English also increases, thereby stimulating the translation market. Since demand outstrips the supply of native speaker translators, the need for translation into English as a second language becomes more acute. But when translating into a second language, however accomplished the English-language mastery of periphery speakers, the translator is normally 'by definition, on a developmental path with respect to that language' (Campbell, 1998: 12). From this follows a number of consequences with respect to translation competence, which Stuart Campbell discusses in his paper, 'English Translation and Linguistic Hegemony in the Global Era'. Campbell suggests these consequences may be considered in relation to the notion of Selinker's interlanguage (IL) (1998: 12). Among Selinker's observations, some are particularly pertinent to translation. In accordance with the IL hypothesis, first put forward by Selinker in 1969, learners create a partly separate linguistic system in which interlingual identifications and language transfer as well as a degree of fossilisation are featured (Campbell, 1998: 12–13).

The notion of interlanguage applied to translation provides Campbell with a framework for discussing translation competence that draws on related areas of research such as contrastive analysis, bilingualism and second-language acquisition. It may, for instance, explain the type of translation which Duff (1981: 10) describes as having been written in 'a third language', that is, translation into a language which is English 'but not quite'. It also provides an explanation of the observation, only too familiar to teachers marking translations into students' second language, that what is being achieved is frequently neither in the source nor in the target language (Campbell, 1998: 14). While not under time pressure, students are well aware of the specific differences between their own language and the one they are learning, but under the stress of examination conditions they tend to regress, drawing on structures familiar from their first language and projecting these onto the second language (Anderman, 1987). It is not uncommon for a teacher of translation to have to correct the same type of mistake repeatedly, the underlying first language of the student manifesting itself even in cases of anonymous marking.

The 'native speaker'

If the language learner is on a developmental path, as Campbell suggests, questions arise: can this learner become a native speaker? But what is a 'native speaker'? For monoglot English speakers, the concept of 'native speaker' is clear. For the majority of people around the world, however, multilingualism – most commonly found in the individual as a form of bilingualism – is the norm: with an estimated five to six thousand languages in the world and fewer than 200 countries, it could not be otherwise (Crystal, 1987: 360). Traditionally, teachers of modern languages and of translation have worked with the concepts of foreign language, second language and native language. As the result of modern communication systems and global mobility, the notion of locus as a geographical place has been weakened, opening up possibilities for rapid interchanges in a global *lingua franca* unconstrained by space and time, thereby blurring any neat distinctions between 'foreign' and 'second' language. Moreover, the range of terms for the 'native language' is already suggestive of differing perspectives which cloud the idealised notion of the native speaker: 'mother tongue', 'mother language', 'first language', 'L1', 'native tongue' (for further discussion, see Davies, 2003), and the closely-related but more use-oriented terms sometimes found in connection with translation or interpreting training: 'dominant language', 'A-language',[4] 'language of habitual use'. While this array of terms raises interesting theoretical issues, the notion of the 'native speaker' remains a cult concept which in the fullness of today's world of global communication needs to be questioned, as do the determining criteria linked to the type of speakers traditionally classified as speaking English as a foreign or second language.

It is generally accepted nowadays, at least among linguists, that there are a number of varieties of 'native' English, mainly in the UK, USA, Canada, Australia and New Zealand (see, for example, Jenkins, 2003: 14). But the status of the Englishes spoken and written in former British colonies and largely un-codified, such as India, Pakistan, Bangladesh, Nigeria and Singapore, is highly controversial. One widely held view, for instance, characterises deviations from a notional standard of native English as errors, rather than as locally-standardised features, firmly placing speakers of these Englishes in the second-language camp. This so-called 'deficit' approach (for recent discussion see Jenkins, 2003: 60–3) evokes traditional views of second language learning as error elimination on the path towards idealised native speakerdom, rather than as a developmental process towards a functionally appropriate means of communication with its own interlanguage features. Hence the question, whether second-language learners can become native speakers, can be re-framed in functional terms in accordance with fitness for purpose. So, for instance, if the variety of English used by the translator or interpreter is appropriate for the target audience, either ideologically as in the case of post-colonial translations into localised varieties of English (see Snell-Hornby, 2000: 41–3 for discussion), or functionally according to the type of text, then the native speaker issue becomes redundant. It also seems reasonable to assume that, as accomplished linguists, translators and interpreters who are speakers of 'Outer Circle' Englishes, would in any case be 'bilingual' or 'bidialectal', depending on your point of view.

In the context of *foreign*-language or 'Expanding Circle' learners, it seems unlikely, if we follow Davies's crucial criterion of early exposure to both language and culture (2000: 212), that such learners could become native speakers of the target language. But in translation and interpreting surely this is not the main point, as we have seen in the Outer Circle users. Genres which are functionally informative (see also Adab, 'Translation into a Second Language – Can We, should We?', Rogers, 'Native versus Non-Native Speaker Competence in German-English Translation: A Case Study' and Thelen, 'Translating into English as a Non-Native Language: The Dutch connection' in this volume), for example, highly-conventionalised texts such as instructions for use, lend themselves more to translation by non-native speakers than others which are operative or expressive, because they can be written in an English which is largely devoid of idioms and finer subtleties (Snell-Hornby, 2000: 38), bringing us back to 'International English'.

The idea of a culturally deracinated language devoid of idioms, humour and connotations sounds deeply unattractive. But it can also be viewed as a blank canvas on which can be painted many different colours. Or, in a more positive light, the canvas can be repainted many times in order to adapt to local situations – such is the case with the localisation, or customisation, of texts for particular readerships and situations in other languages. In these days of translation as a growing international business, often part of a document-management or even content-management enterprise (see, for instance, Göpferich, 2002: 343–8), costs are closely monitored and controlled. If a document is to be translated into 20 languages for a company which has a global operation, any culture-specific problems in the source text need to be solved 20 times. Hence a source text in which any potential problems of a culturally bound kind are neutralised, whether through editing or authoring, has clear cost advantages. Such 'internationalised' or simplified texts facilitate the process of localisation, and indeed translation, as writing guides pro-duced for that purpose demonstrate through recommendations on how to constrain variation in syntax and vocabulary.[5] An international variety of English, which is simplified in the ways described, may go some way to meeting this commercial requirement. On the other hand, instead of the blank canvas that may be adapted to localisation, in its role as an international *lingua franca*, the form of English used may also be painted with the strong tones of specific cultural assumptions and behaviours. If strange or unacceptable to other 'viewers' of the canvas, this may lead to communi-cation breakdowns, the type of problem to which we will return in the last section on Pragmalinguistics.

Asymmetry in translation

In matters related to literary translation between the less well known national languages of Europe and English, a further issue worthy of atten-tion is the difference in approach necessary for working out of and into English. In the former case, for a European readership, often familiar with the landmarks of Anglo-American history, geography and culture, major adjustments in translation to the source text are normally not required. In the latter case, however, limited knowledge about the everyday life and customs of many of the smaller nations in Europe on the part of English readers often necessitates explication in the form of added information. This asymmetry in translation may be viewed from the theoretical perspective advanced by Ithamar Even-Zohar's polysystem theory that has already been mentioned with reference to Rollason's discussion of the power relation between French and English and the resulting presence of Anglicisms in present day French. In her contribution, 'À l'anglaise or the Invisible European' Gunilla Anderman also draws on the framework of polysystem theory to substantiate her observations that translation from other European languages into English often requires adherence to the norms dictated by Anglo-American literary tradition, making the passage into English more difficult for works originating in other European languages and written in accordance with different national and literary dictates. Parallels are drawn with translation into French during the previous reign of French as the leading European language provider of cultural and literary models and the more recently established, dominant role of English/American linguistic and literary norms.

Language Learning and Teaching: Some Implications of Global English

Over the millennia, the relationship between language learning and translation has evolved in interesting ways (see Rogers, 2000). As a written language, Latin was not only the model for the writing and formulation of grammars, it also served as a blueprint for the teaching and learning of other languages, a pedagogical approach that was largely translation based.

In its present role as the *lingua franca* of Europe, English differs from Latin in that equal if not greater weight is given to the teaching of the spoken in preference to the written mode of the language. While for centuries language teaching focused on written modes of expression, the latter half of the twentieth century saw a move away from concentration on writing to emphasise spoken communicative competence. Hence, the role of English as a spoken *lingua franca* may have far-reaching effects on prevailing teaching objectives, and signs of changes in linguistic patterns are already making themselves known. A younger generation of Europeans is now conversant in English and, as a result, no longer feels as strong a need to learn to communicate in the other languages of the individual European nation states.

Language pedagogy: Changing role models

In the linguistic history of Europe, the continued use of Latin for about a millennium after the fall of the western Roman Empire is remarkable (Janson, 2000: 179). Even when competition started to rage with national languages, Latin remained the language used for official international communication up to the sixteenth century. In the educational sphere, however, its influence lasted even longer. The linguistic structure of Latin and its primary role as a written language came to leave traces in the teaching of other languages throughout Europe.

Following the rise of humanism and its reassessment of Latin, emphasis was placed on the teaching and pronunciation of Latin in its classical state. As Vulgar Latin, the spoken variety, was frowned upon, the language was effectively relegated to the position of a no longer living language (Baron, 2000: 115). This view of Latin as static and non-changing was in turn applied to other languages. Although William Lily's *A Shorte Introduction of Grammar* which appeared in 1542 was an early English grammar, it was in fact nothing but a grammar of Latin. In the sixteenth century the relationship between the two languages was characterised by English being considered 'a useful medium for teaching Latin and Latin . . . a good medium for learning English' (Baron, 2000: 116). In other words, English grammar as well as the grammar of other languages was perceived as much the same as Latin grammar. The end of the following century saw a change in that Latin was no longer viewed as the framework on which to drape English grammar, instead it had now become a normative model against which English was to be measured. The grammatical paradigms on which the description of English was based were provided by Latin, and if English was found to be different it had better be adjusted to achieve a closer fit (Baron, 2000: 116).

The learning of Latin as well as Greek included the study of grammar and the reading of texts with the help of a dictionary, a method usually involving the writing down of the translation of sentences and texts in English or vice versa. When applied to the teaching of modern languages, the method became known as the 'grammar translation' method and when, in 1858, its use was incorporated into the new public examinations in England, introduced and monitored by the universities of Oxford and Cambridge, the method was further sanctioned (Malmkjær, 1998: 3). However, during the latter part of the nineteenth century, through the attention attracted by the neo-grammarian movement centred around Leipzig, interest among linguists started to shift from the comparative and historical study of languages to living languages. After studying in Leipzig and Berlin, the father of modern linguistics, the Swiss linguist Ferdinand de Saussure, returned to teach at the University of Geneva. In his posthumous *A Course in General Linguistics* (1916) the distinction is drawn between diachronic and synchronic linguistics, endorsing the non-historical study of language in its spoken as well as written form.

The shift of interest in linguistics also brought about a change of attitude to language teaching. The reaction came in particular from members of the Reform Movement which included Henry Sweet and Otto Jespersen, who pointed to the importance of the primacy of speech and the priority of oral classroom methodology. With the first Department of Phonetics in the UK established at University College London in 1912 under the headship of Daniel Jones, spoken language became the subject of scientific study. It was not, however, until the opening up of Europe after two world wars and the renewed interest in linguistics in the late 1950s that linguists turned their serious attention to research into the interaction between language and society. Pioneering projects such as Labov's study of the interaction between language and social class among New Yorkers in 1972 and that by Trudgill in 1974 of the interaction between speech and social structure in Norwich set the stage for further, sociolinguistically-based research to come. By now, the Direct Method, later further developed into the Communicative Approach, had also shifted the emphasis from exclusive interest in the teaching of the written mode in Applied Linguistics to focus on spoken communication in the foreign language, seriously challenging the deeply entrenched methodology of previous centuries. As Phillipson's English periphery speakers, the present generation of European students are the products of a modern language teaching pedagogy which has placed primary emphasis on the spoken mode, prioritising the ability to communicate in speech in the foreign language. As early as the 1960s, the Swedish programme of 'rolling reform' in education placed the ability to communicate across national borders squarely at the top of linguistic priorities in language teaching (see Anderman, 1973). Reinforcing formal education in the English language, full-length feature films, television, pop music and computer games have further aided comprehension of the spoken language, leaving the development of writing skills as the poor cousin. Lack of stylistic awareness in written English often results in the use of contractions as well as other linguistic features characteristic of spoken language such as a preponderance of first and second person singular pronouns in more formal registers of written discourse. As a further force which tends to have established differences between written and spoken English, we need to note the pervasive use of e-mail, a form of electronic communication which has been viewed as a cross between speech and writing. (See, Collot & Belmore, 1996; Yates, 1996. Discussed in Baron 2000: 249–50.)

Changing linguistic needs

During the last few decades, the linguistic landscape of Europe has changed dramatically. It is likely to change even further during the years to come. While spoken mastery of the language of a nation unquestionably constitutes a linguistic asset, it would be unrealistic to hope that the speakers of languages such as Estonian, Latvian and Lithuanian, the languages of the nations of some of the smaller members of an enlarged Europe, are likely to be able to converse with many other European nationals in their own language. With English as the spoken *lingua franca*, knowledge of the spoken mode of many other European languages will be in limited demand, while on the other hand reading and translation skills are likely to be more sought after. This in turn suggests yet another swing of the pendulum and a reassessment of the linguistic skills to be prioritised in a Europe of the future, with the possibility of a refocusing on translation as a language skill in its own right, rather than as a means to language proficiency. For example *ab initio* courses in some of the less commonly known European languages have already been incorporated into some UK postgraduate programmes in translation with an early emphasis on translation into English as the target language, rather than exposure to the full spectrum of linguistic skills formerly deemed necessary to form part of a programme in Modern Language Studies. There is little doubt that the increasing use of English as a means of international communication has helped to establish contacts across linguistic and cultural borders as perhaps never before. Research, technology and business all benefit from the use of a common language and, in some respects, English would seem an ideal candidate to take on the role of the *lingua franca* of Europe. The speed of development of English for use in international communication has been helped by a variety of already existing Englishes. The existence of a large number of non-standard varieties and the impossibility of a purist approach, given the large number of words that have been incorporated into English over the centuries, has the effect that 'speakers of many other languages can recognise features which are not too dissimilar to characteristics of their own language' (Graddol, 1997: 14). And as access to English is open to speakers from widely diverse social backgrounds, its use cannot be viewed as a marker of social class and hence cannot be considered 'elite bilingualism' (Hoffman, 2000: 20). How long English will retain its present position is a question that remains open to discussion (see, for example Graddol, 1997) but there seems little doubt that if a change is to take place, it is not likely to occur overnight. 'For the immediate future, it is difficult to foresee any developments which could seriously reduce the stature of English on the information superhighway. The biggest potential setback to English as a global language, it has been said with more than a little irony, would have taken place a generation ago – if Bill Gates had grown up speaking Chinese' (Crystal, 1997: 112).

Looking to the future, the possibility of changing objectives in the approach to the teaching of modern languages is not the only factor that might need consideration in the era of English as the firmly established European language for purposes of cross-national communication. In order to plan for the avoidance of potential marginalisation of the national languages of Europe in the years to come, lessons might be learned from the management of multilingualism in other parts of the world. In Canada, the balance of power between English and French was redefined in a protracted process from the 1960s onwards. In South Africa, language policy has played an important part in the process of democratisation in the post-apartheid period, and, in Australia, language policy became a national need in the 1980s (Phillipson, 2003: 67–8). The guiding parameters in formulating language policy for Australia included enrichment (cultural and intellectual), for Europe economics (foreign trade and vocations), equality (social justice and overcoming disadvantages), external relations (Australia's role in the region and the world). In addition, Phillipson proposes a further 'E', standing for Europeanisation (2003: 68). Incorporated into such a policy may, for instance, be the suggestion put forward by Christopher Rollason in this volume that Anglicisms be confined to certain clearly specified areas of discourse, with writing professionals setting an example of good practice.

International English: The Nature of the Beast

International English as Language for Special Purposes (LSP)

Although frequent reference is made to the variety of English popularly known as International English, defining the characteristics that set this variety apart from Standard English is not likely to be an easy task, given the documented attempts to define even Standard English. According to Tom McArthur, Standard English is 'a widely used term that resists easy definition but is used as if most educated people nonetheless know what it refers to' (1992: 982). And, writing in 1989, Sidney Greenbaum considered 'Standard English' (by whatever name it is known) to be 'the variety of English that is manifestly recognised in our society as the prestigious variety' (1989, as reported in McArthur, 1992: 982). However, in 1995, David Crystal estimated that Received Pronunciation in its pure form, was spoken by less than 3% of the population (1995: 365). Henry Widdowson has suggested that 'English spreads as a virtual language which is, in the process, variously "actualised"' (1997: 139–40) (discussed in James, 2000). In some cases, this process of actualisation may manifest itself in the form of different dialects, determined by the region in which English is spoken. But it may also take the form of a variance in a register linked to special purposes which serves to hold International English in place and to maintain its global intelligibility. In his view of International English as English for Special Purposes, Widdowson has in mind international communication in quasi-institutionalised registers such as those of medicine, science and technology but, following Alan James, Widdowson's arguments apply equally to the *ad hoc* registers for more informal, international exchanges which also tend to 'regulate themselves in the interest of intelligibility and as actualisations of the virtual language serve thus as a brake on excessive diversity in the linguistic code' (James, 2000: 34). James draws on the Hallidayan notion of register as 'a variety according to the use', as 'what you are speaking (at the time), determined by what you are doing' (Halliday, 1978: 35). Thus James points to features of English as a *lingua franca* which closely fit the description of the characteristics of register with the principal controlling variables of *field* as type of interaction, *tenor* as role relationships, and *mode* the symbolic organisation. Controlled by these three variables, English as a *lingua franca* is a form of language which is characterised by the nature of the social activity, has a restricted special-purpose function, is semantically flexible and diverse, and shows typical features of spoken varieties of English (James, 2000: 33).

Higher degree of informality

The frequently quoted presence of spoken as opposed to written linguistic features in the emerging variety of English as a *lingua franca* may not only owe its origin to the mix of spoken and written styles used in electronic communication, as mentioned earlier, but may also be related to a more general move towards a higher degree of informality now prevalent in social intercourse. In Europe, the social and political upheaval of the 1960s and 1970s left its mark in changes in the mode of address in many European languages (see, for instance, Paulston, 1976 for a discussion of the so-called 'du' revolution in Swedish). The trend in some European languages towards increased use in writing of a more informal approach characteristic of spoken language is further reinforced by a growing American tendency for an overall more personal, less edited style of writing (Baron, 2003: 88–9).

In the USA, the years following the Vietnam era saw composition writing programmes switch their orientation from an emphasis on 'product' to 'process', to the more subjective 'I think', in preference to 'it may be argued'. Often taught as a form of conversational social interaction, now manifested in the marked speech-like character of much of contemporary American writing, these developments, deriving from transformations in American education, also owe their origin to social trends in the USA and the decline in concern about 'public face' (see

Baron, 2003: 89). For the last half century, American social preferences have changed to endorse a more casual style of behaviour whereby Americans no longer 'feel as driven as [they] once did to monitor what others see of [them]' (Baron, 2003: 92). This change in approach must, at least in some measure, be linked to the use of e-mail, a medium that demands less attention to the requirements of how we see each other.

These changes in American attitudes stem from a number of interacting factors: a reduced emphasis on established social stratification and on overt attention to upward mobility, a weakening of the link between education and rapid financial success made possible by information technology (IT) entrepreneurism, and a strong emphasis on youth culture. Steeped in the popular music, fashion and films promoted by the US entertainment industry since World War II, they have not failed to leave their marks on the everyday life and language of Europeans.

Pragmalinguistics

Although citizens of an immigrant country, Americans nevertheless belong to one and the same nation, while Europeans using English as a *lingua franca* are rooted in different cultural backgrounds, with their own traditions and notions of what constitutes their national understanding of 'public face'. As a result, when they function as participants in interactions in cross-national communication which requires the use of English as a *lingua franca*, other factors will come into play. Unless speakers are aware of cultural differences inherent in the use of language, wrong impressions can easily be formed, in the worst case leading to misunderstandings or national stereotyping. The aspect of linguistic competence lacking in such cases is pragmatic competence, which helps us to use language appropriately in different contexts. While 'pragmalinguistic' knowledge relates to the knowledge speakers have about how a particular language formulates speech acts such as requests, apologies and complaints, 'sociopragmatic' knowledge refers to the norms of a particular language for expressing politeness or for what constitutes suitable topics of conversation. Understanding these cross-cultural differences requires experience of other cultures which entails knowledge of other languages, yet another argument in favour of mother tongue English speakers studying other languages in spite of the present status of English as a global language. Thus the final chapter of this volume concludes with a contribution from Anne Ife on the linguistic dimension of intercultural communication under the title of 'Intercultural Dialogue: The Challenge of Communicating Across Language Boundaries'.

Conclusion

As membership of the EU grows to include more nation states, the use of English as the language in which Europeans can communicate cross-nationally is going to increase. Contributions to this volume seem to indicate that this development may be for better *and* for worse. In 'World English. A blessing or a curse?', Tom McArthur metaphorically draws on the polar opposites of yin and yang in order to describe the present situation:

> Like many things, English is at times a blessing and at times a curse – for individuals, for communities, for nations, and even for unions of nations. The East Asian symbol of yin and yang might serve well here. Although they are opposites, they belong together, in this instance within the circle of communication. Such symbolism suggests that that the users of the world's *lingua franca* should seek to benefit and as far as possible avoid invoking the curse. (McArthur, 2001: 61).

This, of course, leaves open the question of what constitutes a blessing and what a curse. We conclude, in full agreement with an equally tantalising statement, this time from David Crystal (1997: 114):

> In 500 years' time, will it be the case that everyone will automatically be introduced to English as soon as they are born (or, by then, very likely, as soon as they are conceived)? If this is part of a rich multilingual experience for our future newborns, this can only be a good thing. If it is by then the only language left to be learned, it will have been the greatest intellectual disaster that the planet has ever known.

Notes

1. Discussed in 'They're talking our language' by Robert McCrum in the *Observer*, Sunday 18 March 2001. Also in Pennycook, A. (1994) *The Cultural Politics of English as an International Language*, p. 1. London: Longman
2. Figures made available in a personal communication from David Crystal, December 2003.
3. Why Study Languages . . . When Everyone Speaks English? CD-ROM produced by the Subject Centre for Languages, Linguistics and Area Studies, University of Southampton, UK.
4. A-language is normally defined as the mother tongue or the language of education (see Snell-Hornby, 2000: 36).
5. See, for instance Simens Nixdorf's *Empfehlungen für Fachtexte: Verständlich und übersetzungsfreundlich schreiben*, produced by the SprachenDiesnt und Redaktionen, 1993; European Commission Translation Service 'How to write clearly' n.d.

References

Anderman, G.M. (1974) The Teaching of English within the Comprehensive School System in Sweden. *English Language Teaching Journal* Vol. XXVII (2), 150–9.

Anderman, G.M. (1987) The use of style and grammar in the work of advanced students of English. In I. Lindblad and M. Ljung (eds) *Proceedings from the Third Nordic Conference for English Studies.* Hässelby, 25–27 September, 1986. Vol. I. (pp. 21–9). Stockholm: Almqvist & Wiksell International.

Barber, B. (1992) Jihad vs McWorld. *The Atlantic Monthly* 3, 53–63.

Baron, N.S. (2000) *Alphabet to Email: How Written English Evolves and Where It's Heading.* London: Routledge.

Baron, N.S. (2003) Why email looks like speech: proof-reading, pedagogy and public face. In J. Aitchson, and D.M. Lewis (eds) *New Media Language* (pp. 85–94) London & New York: Routledge.

Campbell, S. (1998) *Translation into the Second Language.* London & New York: Longman.

Collot, M. and Belmore, N. (1996) Electronic Language: a new variety of English. In S. Herring (ed.) *Computer Mediated Communication: Social and Cross-Cultural Perspectives* (pp. 13-28) Amsterdam: Benjamins.

Crystal, D. (1995) *The Cambridge Encyclopaedia of Language.* Cambridge: Cambridge University Press.

Crystal, D. (1997) *English as a Global Language.* Cambridge: Cambridge University Press.

Davies, Alan (2003) *The Native Speaker: Myth and Reality.* Clevedon: Multilingual Matters.

Duff, Alan (1981) *The Third Language. Recurrent problems of translation into English.* Oxford: Pergamon.

Even Zohar, I. (1978 revised 1990) The position of translated literature within the literary polysystem. In L. Venuti (ed.) *The Translation Studies Reader* (pp. 192–7) London: Routledge.

Göpferich, Susanne (2002) *Textproduktion im Zeitalter der Globalisiering. Entwicklung einer Didaktik des Wissenstransfers.* Tübingen: Stauffenburg.

Görlach, M. (1988) English as a World Language – the state of the art. *English World-Wide* 9/1,1–32.

Görlach, M. (2002) *English in Europe.* Oxford: Oxford University Press.

Graddol, D. (1997) *The Future of English?* London: British Council.

Graddol, D. (1999) The decline of the native speaker. In D. Graddol and U. Meinhof (eds) *English in a Changing World. AILA Review* 13 (57–68). Also in G. Anderman and M. Rogers (eds) (2003) *Translation Today: Trends and Perspectives* (pp. 152–67) Clevedon: Multilingual Matters.

Greenbaum, S. (1989) Why should guidance be left to amateurs? *English Today* 5, 9–10.

Halliday, M.K. (1978) *Language as Social Semiotic.* London: Edward Arnold.

Hoffman, C. (2002) The spread of English and the growth of multilingualism in Europe. In J. Cenoz and U. Jessner (eds) *English in Europe. The Acquisition of a Third Language* (pp. 1–29) Clevedon: Multilingual Matters.

Hutton, W. (2003) *The World We're In.* London: Little Brown.

James, A.R. (2000) English as a European *Lingua franca*: Current realities and existing dichotomies. In J. Cenoz and U. Jessner (eds) *English in Europe. The Acquisition of a Third Language* (pp. 22–38) Clevedon: Multinlingual Matters.

Janson, R. (2000) *SPEAK, a short history of languages.* Oxford: Oxford University Press.

Jenkins, J. (2003) *World Englishes. A resource book for students.* London & New York: Routledge.

Johansson, S. and Graedler, A. (2002) *Rocka, Hipt og Snacksy. Om engelsk i norsk sprak og samfunn.* Norway: Norwegian Academic Press.

Kachru, B.B. (1985) Standards, codification and sociolinguistic realism. In R. Quirk and H. Widdowson (eds) *English in the World* (pp. 11–30) Cambridge: Cambridge University Press.

Labov, W. (1972a) *Sociolinguistic Patterns.* Philadephia: University of Pennsylvania Press and Oxford: Blackwell.

Labov, W. (1972b) *Language in the Inner City.* Philadephia: University of Pennsylavania Press and Oxford: Blackwell.

Mackenzie, R. (1998) The place of language teaching in a quality assured translators training programme. In K. Malmkjaer (ed.). *Translation and Language Teaching. Language Teaching and Translation* (pp. 15–19) Manchester: St Jerome.

Malmkjaer, K. (1998) Introduction: Translation and Language Teaching. In K. Malmkjaer (ed.) *Translation and Language Teaching. Language Teaching and Translation.* Manchester: St Jerome.

McArthur, T. (1992) *The Oxford Companion to the English Language.* Oxford: Oxford University Press.

McArthur, T. (2001) English Today. Discussed in *The Oxford Companion to the English Language.* Oxford: Oxford University Press.

Paulston, C.B. (1976) Pronouns of address in Swedish: social class, semantics and a changing system. *Language in Society* 5, 359–86.

Phillipson, R. (1992) *Linguistic Imperialism.* Oxford: Oxford University Press.

Phillipson, R. (2003) *English – Only Europe? Challenging Language Policy.* London: Routledge.

Phillipson, R. and Skutnabb-Kangas, T. (1999) Englishisation: one dimension of globalisation. In D. Graddol and U. Meinhof (eds) *English in a Changing World. AILA Review* 13 (pp. 19–36) Oxford: English Book Centre.

Rogers, M. (2000) Translation. In Michael Byram (ed.) *Routledge Encyclopedia of Language Teaching and Learning* (pp. 635–8) London & New York: Routledge.

Russ, Charles V.J. (1994) *The German Language Today.* London and New York: Routledge.

Seidlhofer, Barbara (2002) Habeus corpus and divide et impera: 'Global English' and applied linguistics. In K. Spelman-Miller and P. Thompson (eds) *Unity and Diversity in Language Use* (pp. 198–217) London: BAAL/Continuum.

Snell-Hornby, M. (1999) Communicating in the Global Village: on language, translation and global identity. In C. Schäffner (ed.) *Current Issues in Society,* Vol. 6(2), 103–19.

Snell-Hornby, M. (2000) 'McLanguage': The identity of English as an issue in translation today. In M. Grosman, M. Kadric, I. Kovačič,M. Snell-Hornby (eds) *Translation into Non-Mother Tongues. In Professional Practice and Training* (pp. 35–44) Tübingen: Stauffenburg.

The *Observer* (2003) Languages to bear brunt in schools crisis. 31 August 2003 (byline: Mark Townsend).

Trudgill, P. (1974) *Social Differentiation in Norwich.* Cambridge: Cambridge University Press.

Venuti, L. (1995) *The Translator's Invisibility.* London: Routledge.

Walker, M. (1997) *Guardian Weekly* 12 January 1997.

Yates, S.J. (1996) Oral and written linguistic aspects of computer conferencing. In S. Herring (ed.) *Computer Mediated Communication: Linguistic, Social and Cross-Cultural Perspectives.* Amsterdam: John Benjamins.

Chapter 2

English Translation and Linguistic Hegemony in the Global Era[1]

STUART CAMPBELL

The Illusion of Language Parity

The professional translation enterprise has largely ignored the implications of the most significant linguistic phenomenon of the last five
hundred years – the spread of English in the world. What is odd is that
there has been no lack of discussion about English in other fields such as
Sociolinguistics and Post-Colonial Studies; yet much of the translation
enterprise – and by this I mean the complex of theorists, educators and
practitioners – treats English as just another language. It seems to me that
at the centres of power in the professional translation enterprise there is
an illusion that English is just one of a set of replaceable codes of equal
value, a notion symbolised by the idea of the translation pair – the juxtaposition of two language names separated by a bland colon that, with its
implicit message of parity, masks the history of the global dominance of
one language.

I was tempted to entitle this paper *The Empire Translates Back*, because I
think that the root of the problem is a denial that English is no longer the
property of native speakers. But there are other subtler kinds of empire
besides the traditional sense – linguistic empires within developed multicultural states, the empire of the English teaching industry, and the imperial enterprise of the aid industry. All of these contexts pose serious
questions about English for the translation enterprise.

The role of English in the world has been extensively discussed by
sociolinguists and post-colonial theorists. Researchers in both these fields
recognise that English is not a value-neutral code, but the locus of power
leads to imbalance in a great range of human endeavours. Indeed, the
discipline of post-colonial literary studies is virtually defined by the prob-
lematising of the role of English, and a rich and complex debate continues
on the way in which the space occupied by writing in English is negotiated between the centre and the periphery. Gaurav Desai offers an elegant
metaphor for this debate in an account of the way that the annual bibli-
ography of the Modern Language Association gradually 'accommodated'

colonial writers. African literature in English first appears as one of the 'etceteras' under 'Australia, Canada, etc.'. We then get a new category of 'Oriental and African literature' in the fifties and sixties, until, as Desai writes, 'the storm burst [and] a whole new way of seeing emerged' with a detailed set of historically based categories of African literature (Desai, 2000: 528–9).

From the standpoint of Sociolinguistics, the power of English has been a key factor in the development of Robert Phillipson's theory of linguistic imperialism (Phillipson, 1992), and Tove Skutnabb-Kangas's notion of linguicism (Skutnabb–Kangas, 1988). A crucial factor in this sociolinguistic work is the problem of dealing with the fact that English is now used by more second-language users than mother tongue speakers. The best known framework for describing the spread of English in the world is Kachru's idea of the three concentric circles of English, with its Inner Circle of North America, Britain and Australasia, an Outer Circle of the ex-colonies, and the Expanding Circle of other countries that have adopted English as a second language (Kachru, 1985). Let us acknowledge, then, that for sociolinguists and post-colonial theorists, the dominance of English is a central issue. The question now arises: Is it an issue for translation theorists?

English Hegemony and Translation Studies

Where ideas about the hegemony of English have been taken up in Translation Theory, they tend to be at the intersection with Literary Theory or Cultural Studies. Lefevere (1990: 24), for example, speaks about the role of translation in bringing literary works in 'minor' languages into the ambit of 'world literature'. While I am not doubting that Latin, French, English and Russian can be considered 'languages of authority' that – to paraphrase Lefevere – have bestowed their inherent authority on works written in minor languages, it seems to me that the sheer volume and spread of English in this and the last century make it a special case. It is no coincidence that very interesting writing on the power role of English in translation comes from India: Ramakrishna (1997) plots the history of English translation in India from the conquest of Bengal in 1757, explaining that, while the translation endeavours of early British Orientalists played a key role in promoting the vernaculars, translation 'quickly came to serve as a tool in the domestication of the Orient. [It] helped to promote not only the commercial and legal interests of the British, but also their educational and linguistic needs as well, and thereby served as a major instrument in colonial domination' (1997: 445). The controversy over Tagore's translation of his own works from Bengali into English is symptomatic of this complex play of forces. Was Tagore 'tied to an ideology associated with colonialism and cultural domination' (Choudhuri,

1997: 442), or was he and his poetry 'lost in the politics of translation' as Western readers adopted him as a mystic who fulfilled their expectations of exotic India (Sengupta, 1995: 62)? A recent article by Prasenjit Gupta establishes a framework for interrogating the role of translation in India, and discusses the way that translators' strategies reflect the economic and political contexts of their work (Gupta, 1998).

I would like to suggest that we can extract three key issues for translation from the paradigms of Sociolinguistics, Post-Colonial Theory and Translation Studies.

- Translation into and from English must always be considered in the context of power relations among language communities and the reality of the spread of English in the world.
- Translation into and from English is not a technical linguistic issue that can be discussed in a value neutral way, but is inextricably linked to questions of culture and history.
- Translation into and from English outside the Inner Circle is not an aberration, but occupies a legitimate space in the translation enterprise.

While the interrogation of the role of English is second nature in post-colonial Translation Theory and Linguistics, and has tangentially occupied some translation theorists, it seems to me that the field of non-literary translation has managed to ignore this debate almost entirely. Take, for example, instruments concerned with the practice of translation into non-native languages. The Nairobi Declaration of 1976, for example, recommends that 'a translator should, as far as possible, translate into his own mother tongue or into a language of which he or she has a mastery equal to that of his or her mother tongue' (UNESCO). And the Charter of the International Federation of Translators stipulates that: 'The translator shall possess a sound knowledge of the language from which he/she translates and should, in particular, be a master of that into which he/she translates' (International Federation of Translators).

I would claim that stipulations such as these have been somewhat left behind in the wash of the spread of English. Consider that English is no longer the exclusive property of Inner Circle speakers; it is used by more non-native that native speakers; it is a multi-billion dollar educational commodity; it is – for now – the language of the Internet. In reality, I suspect that many people translating into English today are neither mother tongue speakers nor masters of it. I also suspect that the notion of 'mastery' of English is a simplistic Inner Circle construct. As Braj Kachru has recently written: 'The initiatives in planning, administration, acquisition and the spread of English in Asia are primarily in the hands of Asians (Kachru, 1997: 69)'. Spend an evening in Singapore at one of those karaoke functions where officials from various South East Asian countries sing ballads and pop songs in English, and ask the question 'Whose English?' and 'Whose mastery?'

Language Imbalance In Practice: Australia and Laos

During a career that has focused on teaching and researching non-literary translation mainly into English as a second language, I have become more and more uncomfortable with what I believe is a simplistic and unquestioning view about the role and status of English. It seems to me that the time is overdue for us to begin asking whether the preoccupations of post-colonial translation theorists are relevant to non-literary translation, and whether they can help us to interrogate our practices and beliefs about such translation into English. In the following sections, I will pursue this idea by looking at two contexts where non-native speakers are expected to translate into English, firstly in community translation in Australia, and then in the context of a regional organisation in South East Asia.

Training community translators in Australia

In countries like Australia large minorities of the population speak English as a second language, with profound effects on education and the delivery of government services. Mohan, Leung & Davison have recently reminded us that we can no longer think of second language learners of English in schools as an 'accidental, peripheral happening, a temporary local inconvenience, or an interruption in the normal course of affairs' (Mohan *et al.*, 2001: 2). The reality is that second language learners and speakers of English are a permanent feature of countries like Australia, and, as I have argued, an inevitable part of the translation scene given the imbalances in the language-learning market place (Campbell, 1998). I have also argued that in a country of recent high immigration like Australia , the very notions of first and second-language are hard to tease apart. Indeed, the notion of the second language speaker is constructed by stakeholders in the fields of education, employment and immigration policy. As Pennycook remarks: 'One of the most insidious constructions that has emerged from the glorification of English and the denigrations of other languages is the relationship between native speakers and non-native speakers. This is, of course, one of the classic dichotomies that result from cultural constructs of colonialism . . .' (Pennycook, 1998: 156). Schnitzer (1995: 231) argues that: 'If the theoretical model is the pure, unadulterated, monolingual, monocultural native speaker, this necessarily entails a view of all other speakers as "deviant" from the standard'. If this is the tacit belief in translation circles – enshrined in the maxim that one should translate into one's first language – then what is the standing of the many Outer Circle and Expanding Circle translators who routinely work into English as a second language out of sheer necessity? And what is their standing and the effect of translation practices in a country like Australia, where Inner Circle speakers generally hold the positions of authority? I will briefly discuss three areas where English exerts influence on translator education and credentialling, namely accreditation, terminology work and text types.

Firstly accreditation: in Australia, community translator and interpreter services were introduced in the late seventies, along with an ambitious system of accreditation which has expanded to include dozens of languages, all paired with English. I do not want to deal here with the technical strengths and weaknesses of the accreditation system itself – which is currently being reviewed – but to consider it as a gateway to privilege. The most obvious characteristic of candidates for accreditation is that they are mostly of migrant origin. For those destined to work in the area of community translation, their role will be to mediate between the institutions of the state and those citizens at its periphery – those who cannot function in the legal system, the health system and the welfare system because they cannot operate in its language. The otherness of the clientele of translators and interpreters is guaranteed by the role these clients play: they are for the most part seeking access to free government services, and they lack the facility to make their requests.

For many of the languages for which translators and interpreters are accredited in Australia there will be very few candidates who are Inner Circle English speakers. This fact is not explicitly recognised anywhere in the mechanism of the accreditation system; the criteria for gaining accreditation are identical for each language direction, and the illusion of parity is maintained. Far from being a value-free test of competence, the accreditation system can be seen to function as an entry point into the outer limits of the mainstream – a way by which bilingual migrants can move inwards from the periphery. The point at which an immigrant gains accreditation represents a door opening, where the world of otherness is left behind, and a kind of double agency lies ahead – a role where he or she has one foot in the domain of the institutions of the centre and one in the world of the periphery. The suspect status of the translator double agent is tacitly recognised in the mechanism that is set up to guard against treachery, namely an examination on a code of ethics. The questions asked to test prospective translators' understanding of impartiality are strongly flavoured by the fear of the other; translators are led into temptation by migrant clients, dishonest colleagues and unscrupulous translation agencies – but not by crooked doctors or lawyers. Thus to move from the periphery towards the centre, the candidate must pass a test of both mainstream values and mainstream language. It stretches the imagination to believe that the colon between English and Arabic, English and Italian, English and Vietnamese, etc. represents parity.

Terminology work in this context is especially loaded by the presence of English on one side of the colon, and I would like to cite as an example a failed research project that I undertook many years ago. A group of colleagues at our university were concerned with the problem of teaching students how to translate foreign educational qualifications. We obtained some funds to analyse a corpus of authentic documents from South America in order to come up with a set of English equivalents for hundreds of titles of qualifications, areas of study, and individual subject names. Armed with this list, all translators in Australia would produce exact equivalents, and the results would be consistent. What we did not understand was the importance of prior theoretical work. We failed to bear in mind that the ultimate purpose for translating such documents was to allow the authorities to assess the foreign qualifications against the local qualifications framework, and that in creating English equivalents we were simultaneously creating a qualifications assessment system. Each attempt at translating a term required us to ask not 'what does it mean?' but 'what does it mean to an Australian employer?' The question never asked was: 'what does the NSW [New South Wales] Higher School Certificate mean to a Uruguayan employer?' because the history of migration makes this a non-question. Needless to say, the research funds ran out before we had time to make even the most basic inroads. So much for language parity.

A third area of imbalance is the disparity of text types, and I will cite an example from my teaching of translation from Arabic to English. At our university – and at most others, I suspect – we like to imagine that equivalent text types are available in languages other than English (indeed this is an assumption of the translator accreditation mechanism in Australia). If we can teach the translation of technical texts from English this week, we can teach the translation of technical texts from Arabic next. The problem that arises for Arabic is that scientific texts are very hard to find; when they are found they are often translations or adaptations of English originals, containing English calques and unauthentic rhetorical strategies. So what does it mean to learn to translate such texts? Working into English (almost always as a second language) entails reconstructing the originals that generated the Arabic source text. The trick is to find English texts on the World Wide Web with similar content and style, and to plunder them for matches with words and phrases from the source text. Working in the other direction is much more problematic because of the lack of the authentic text models in Arabic. From the students' perspective, then, there are two quite different tasks: plundering the treasures of English one week, searching for Arabic needles in a haystack the next.

Clearly, the teaching of community translation in Australia is not immune to the concerns of post-colonial translation theorists and sociolinguists: its practices are shaped by the power imbalance between the mainstream and immigrant communities, and by the imbalance between English and the minority languages. Let me now move to a context where these forces are realised in different ways.

Translation development in Laos

I wrote the first draft of this paper in Laos, where I was undertaking an in-country consultancy for AusAID, the Australian development aid agency, to help establish a translation and interpreting unit in the Laos Ministry of Foreign Affairs. Development aid of any kind – whether it is concerned with animal vaccines, translation, or unexploded ordnance – places the donor and receiver in an unequal power relationship; to manage the relationship with dignity, donor and receiver need to adopt rules that allow them to meet as equals, or least to give appearance of doing so – hence the increasing use of the euphemism *development partner* instead of *donor* and *recipient*. In a translation-development project like this one, the donor-recipient relationship is especially complex because of the overwhelming issue of the second language – in this case English. The relationship is especially loaded by the power difference between English and Lao. Just as development aid casts the donor culture as the norm and the receiver culture as the other, so is English cast as the unmarked – the norm, the goal, the valued – and Lao as the marked – the alien, the point of departure, the less valued. A few comments on the Lao language drawn from Enfield (1999) will help to show why such an evaluation may be made: Lao, closely related to Thai, is characterised by wide variation and the lack of a recognised standard (Enfield, 1999: 262–4). Orthography is standardised – at least in Laos itself – this having come about by way of a number of reforms from the 1930s to the 1990s (Enfield, 1999: 264–5). The standardisation of grammar mostly concerns orthography 'leaving much about the overall grammar . . . the language undescribed and unexplored by Lao scholars . . . No Lao "reference grammar," in the descriptive linguist's sense, has so far been produced' (Enfield, 1999: 267).

Indeed perceptions about power difference in the aid context can hardly be doubted when one considers the massive infrastructure of the English instruction industry. Phillipson (1994) offers a penetrating account of the way that British and US agencies have promoted English as 'an instrument of state', spawning a vast English teaching industry and privileging English in foreign aid programmes. A language like Lao is like a distant and faint planet peering at the splendour of English. Consider that I bought almost every title in the Lao government bookshop for a few hundred dollars and had them posted home in a small carton; consider that there is barely one comprehensive Lao-English dictionary worthy of the name; even the donated computers now appearing in Lao government offices relegate Lao script to the bottom right corner of the screen

among the shields and trumpets, where it is activated by fiddling awk-
wardly with both buttons of the mouse. Lao is the *other* script, the marked,
the intruder that has been reluctantly admitted into Microsoftland. The
Lao language professional knows that the chance of Lao catching up with
the institutions of English-language publishing, language teaching, lexicography and information technology is as slim as Laos winning an
Olympic medal in skiing.

Let me now explore some of the practicalities of translation between
Lao and English as a second language. One of the key challenges faced by
Lao government translators is to develop a massive set of Lao technical
terms. The task seems insurmountable: a random sample of one of the
thousands of documents that will pass over their desks yielded this
handful of terms:

Agro-tourism
Aquaculture development
Artificial infestation
ASEAN Code of Practice
ASEAN Pesticide Database Network
ASEAN Sectoral Working Group on Livestock
bio-organic fertiliser
Confirmatory Test of Vapor Heat Treatment (VHT)
disease-free broodstock
Fisheries post-harvest technology centres
Foot-and-mouth disease
Good Manufacturing Practice
Harmonization of Phytosanitary Measures
Hazard Analysis and Critical Control Point (HACCP)
Institutional Development of Agricultural Cooperatives
Market Oriented Production
meat processing plants
phytosanitary legislation
poultry processing plants
serological examination
Symposium on Agricultural Cooperatives

Leaving aside the technical difficulty of finding equivalent Lao lexical
units, the underlying problem here is that to translate these terms is to
wrench terms out of the rich institutional environment that generated
them and to press them into an institutional wilderness. Laos is desper-
ately poor: Vientiane does not have a cinema; there are no trains; wealthy
foreigners who injure themselves go immediately to hospital in Thailand.
The scientific work that generates a *Confirmatory Test of Vapor Heat
Treatment (VHT)* is foreign; *Agro-tourism* is a fantasy thought up by
foreigners. Ironically, when I asked the Lao translators to produce Lao

equivalents for the terms above and to code each one for it reliability, they were only confident about *foot-and-mouth disease*; that at least is part of the Lao scene. So while the terms can be translated, the translations are like scenery on a film set. They are invented by people in other countries who have to give names for real things they are doing; my Lao translators have to *imagine* what those foreigners are doing and then find Lao words that pretend to describe things that are not yet done in Laos. The power imbalance is highlighted when the terms are translated back into English by these Expanding Circle users; they move from shaky to firm ground, from fantasy to reality, from the other to the norm, from East to West.

But the indignity does not end there. As a language of virtually no influence outside its borders, Lao is rarely learned by Inner Circle users. The upshot is clear; in nearly every case, people who translate from Lao to English will be the first language speakers of Lao. And even though my Lao translators are the cream of the Lao civil service, they will never pass themselves off as English native speakers. Under the prevailing – if unspoken – ideology of the translation profession, they are 'deviant', to borrow Schnitzer's term. Hence, the otherness of the second-language speaker is heaped onto the otherness of Lao.

There is a more subtle aspect to this power imbalance. The English that they are learning to translate from and into is in fact the English of the Association of South East Asian Nations (ASEAN), not of the US or Australia or Britain. It is a link language in an organisation of Outer Circle and Expanding Circle member countries. As a new and very poor member of ASEAN, Laos needs to prove its credentials against wealthy established members such as Singapore and Thailand, and developing a capacity to translate to and from English is seen as an essential strategy. Much of the English that is learnt for ASEAN purposes is already peripheral, having been created by skilled non-native writers of English in Outer Circle ASEAN countries. So, in a sense, the English of Lao translators is two steps removed from the Inner Circle; Expanding Circle learners must acquire the norms of Outer Circle experts.

These norms are a complex issue, which Jane Davies (2000) has begun to explore. Her analyses of prepared speeches delivered at formal ASEAN meeting reveal a pattern of highly formulaic expressions that contribute to a distinctly ASEAN mode of discourse. Perhaps it is not just in literature that 'post-colonial writing define[s] itself by seizing the language of the centre and re-placing it in a discourse fully adapted to the colonised place' (Ashcroft *et al.*, 1989: 39). In ASEAN discourse rhetorical functions such as *establishing common ground*, *exhortation* and *evaluating process* are coded by set formulae, for example *as we are all aware . . .*, *we must do our utmost to . . .*, *I wish to express profound satisfaction at the fact that we*. ASEAN English also appears to include quite rigid collocations such as *profound and rapid changes* and *living in harmony and co-operation*. While drafting a report on a visit to Laos, I was gently chided for using the unsuitable collocation *in peace and harmony*. Examining quite how these norms develop is beyond our task here, but the important thing is that they create a mode of discourse that conveys the principles of individual sovereignty, consensus and non-interference that ASEAN is founded on. One of the tasks of the Lao translator is to learn this ASEAN discourse (which is coded in English), to reinvent it in Lao, and then to translate it back into English. The effect is not just to inject new vocabulary and expressions into Lao, but to introduce a new mode of thought and action into the political and administrative practices of the Lao elite. Again, these practical issues resonate strongly with the concerns of post-colonial theory and sociolinguistics about power relations, culture, identity and the ownership of language.

A New Paradigm for English Translation

In summing up, I would like to suggest that we need a new paradigm for thinking about translation to and from English in a globalised world. I am not talking about a radical departure from standards and the acceptance of clearly poor English translations. But I do believe that we need to systematically question the notions that:

- Only a native speaker should translate into English;
- Standard English is a straightforward matter (that it is not is demonstrated in, for example Görlach (1994) and Bamgbose (1998);
- English has parity with other languages in a translation pair.

We need to refashion our practices in education and credentialling in the light of a rethinking of the role of English.

Alastair Pennycook, writing on critical views of English, has said:

> What I think is sorely lacking from the predominant paradigm of investigation into English as an international language is a broad range of social, historical cultural, and political relationships. There is a failure to problematize the notion of choice and an assumption that individuals and countries are somehow free of economic, political and ideological constraints. (1995: 38)

In a globalised world, we in the translation enterprise need to take heed of Pennycook's advice. The inhabitants of the colonial and economic empires are translating back into English in ever-increasing quantities, and we cannot sit back and pretend they will go away.

Notes

1. The research for this paper was funded by an Australian Research Council small grant and carried out at the University of Western Sydney. The research assistance of Adrian Weissen is acknowledged.

References

Ashcroft, B., Griffiths, G. And Tiffin, H. (1989) *The Empire Writes Back: Theory and Practice in Post-Colonial Literatures*. London & New York: Routledge.
Bamgbose, A. (1998) Torn between the norms: Innovations in World Englishes. *World Englishes* 17/1, 1–14.
Campbell, S. (1998) *Translation into the Second Language*. New York: Longman.
Choudhuri, I.N. (1997) The plurality of languages and literature in translation: The post-colonial context. *Meta* XLII, 439–43.
Davies, J. (2000) *Building Harmonious Relations the ASEAN English Way*. Paper presented at the 20th Thailand TESOL International Conference, 20–22 January 2000.
Desai, G. (2000) Rethinking English: Postcolonial English studies. In H. Schwarz and S. Ray (eds) *A Companion to Postcolonial Studies* (pp. 523–39) Malder & Oxford: Blackwell Publishers Ltd.
Enfield, N.J. (1999) Lao as a national language. In G. Evans (ed.) *Laos Culture and Society* (pp. 258–90) Chiang Mai: Silkworm Books.
Görlach, M. (1994) Innovations in World Englishes. *English World-Wide* 15(1), 101–26.
Gupta, P. (1998) Post or Neo-Colonial Translation? Linguistic Inequality and Translator's Resistance. *Translation and Literature* 7(2), 170–93.
International Federation of Translators. hhtp://www, fit-ift.org/english/charter.html
Kachru, B.B. (1985) Standards, codification and sociolinguistic realism; the English language in the Outer Circle. In R. Quirk and H. Widdowson (eds) *English in the World: Teaching and Learning and Literature* (pp. 11–30). Cambridge: Cambridge University Press.
Kachru, B.B. (1997) World Englishes and English-using communities. *Annual Review of Applied Linguistics* 17, 66–87.
Lefevere, A. (1995) Translation: Its Genealogy in the West. In S. Bassnett and A. Lefevere (eds) *Translation, History and Culture* (pp. 14–28) London & New York: Cassell.
Mohan, B., Leung, C. and Davison, C. (2001) *English as a Second Language in the Mainstream: Teaching, Learning and Identity*. Harlow: Longman.
Pennycook, A. (1995) English in the World/The World in English. In J.W. Tollefson (ed.) *Power and Inequality in Language Education* (pp. 34–58) Cambridge: Cambridge University Press.
Pennycook, A. (1998) *English and the Discourse of Colonialism*. London & New York: Routledge.
Phillipson, R. (1992) *Linguistic Imperialism*. Oxford: Oxford University Press.
Phillipson, R (1994) English Language spread policy. *International Journal of the Sociology of Languages* 107, 7–24.
Ramakrishna, S. (1997) Functions of translation in post-colonial India. *Meta* XLII/2, 444–9.
Schnitzer, E. (1995) English as an international language. Implications for interculturalists and language educators. *International Journal of Intercultural Relations* 227–36.

Sengupta, M. (1995) Translation, colonialism and poetics. Rabindranath Tagore in two worlds. In S. Bassnett and A. Lefevere (eds) *Translation, History and Culture* (pp. 56–63) London & New York: Cassell.

Skutnabb-Kangas, T. (1998) Multilingualism and the education of minority children. In T. Skutnabb-Kangas and J. Cummins (eds). *Minority Education: from Shame to Struggle* (pp. 9–44) Clevedon: Multilingual Matters.

UNESCO. http://www.unesco.org/human_rights/hrci.htm

Chapter 3

Unequal Systems: On the Problem of Anglicisms in Contemporary French Usage

CHRISTOPHER ROLLASON

Introduction

Anglicisms and pseudo-Anglicisms are scarcely a new phenomenon in French, as such long-established usages as *le dandy* and *le smoking* (for 'dinner jacket') attest. A degree of cross-linguistic contamination has always been inevitable between such close neighbours (or *frères ennemis*) as Britain and France, and until relatively recently the process has been a two-way one, with French enriching English with such usages as 'laissez-passer', 'maître d'hôtel', or, within living memory, 'cinéma-vérité' and 'nouvelle cuisine' – not to mention pseudo-Gallicisms such as 'duvet' (for the object known in French as a *couette*). In the last few decades, however, the question has taken on a clearly different dimension, as the prime source of Anglicisms in French – as in all other languages – is no longer Britain, a country with approximately the same population and political and economic weight as France, but the United States, since 1989 the planet's sole hegemonic power. The issue of Anglicisms now appears in France as an aspect of a much broader problem, namely the identity of Europe and its defence against perceived US domination in the economic, political and cultural fields.

The Scope of Anglicisms in French

Hostility to Americanisation is one of the recurrent themes in contemporary French journalism and polemical writing, and is a position to be found on both sides of the left-right divide. The charges typically laid at the door of the United States by French intellectuals include, in particular, an extreme free-market ideology, censorious neo-puritanism and mass-cultural domination. A number of examples of this tendency in France will now be quoted.

The journalist Ignacio Ramonet, editor-in-chief of *Le Monde Diplomatique*, writes in his book *La tyrannie de la communication* (1999:179):

'*Les États-Unis (premiers producteurs de technologies nouvelles et siège des principales firmes) ont, à la faveur de la mondialisation de l'économie, pesé de tout leur poids dans la bataille de la déréglementation: ouvrir les frontières du plus grand nombre de pays au "libre flux de l'information" revenait à favoriser les mastodontes américains des industries de communication et des loisirs.* (The United States, the main producer of new technology and the headquarters of the main companies [in the field], has, in the interests of economic globalisation, thrown all of its weight into the battle for deregulation, with the opening-up of the frontiers of as many countries as possible to the "free flow of information" being equivalent to favouring the US giants of the communications and leisure industries.)

Globalisation, deregulation, new technology and the ideology of 'entertainment' are all perceived, rightly or wrongly, as instruments in a strategy for US domination.[1] On the cultural front, the literary critic Guy Scarpetta criticises the trans-atlantic phenomenon known as 'political correctness' in the following terms:

Il y a, aux États-Unis, la tyrannie du "politically correct", qui fonctionne ouvertement comme une incitation à la censure et à l'autocensure, et qui vise à purifier la littérature de tout ce qui, en elle, pourrait donner une image "non conforme" de certains groupes (femmes, minorités): véritable police de la représentation, dont on ne voit guère, si ses normes venaient à s'imposer, ce qui pourrait rester d'oeuvres comme celles de Faulkner, d'Hemingway ou de Philip Roth' (1996: 29). ('In the US, there is the tyranny of the "politically correct", which functions quite openly as an incitement to censorship and self-censorship, with the aim of purifying literature of all elements which might give a "non-approved" image of certain groups (women, minorities): a full-blooded policing of representation, whose rules, should they prevail, would surely leave almost nothing intact of the works of Faulkner, Hemingway or Philip Roth.')

On a similar note, this time in the field of psychoanalysis, the authors of a respected work of reference, *Dictionnaire de la psychanalyse* (Elisabeth Roudinesco and Michel Plon), denounce '*un double mouvement de "correction politique" et de conservatisme qui fit des ravages à cette époque dans la partie anglophone du continent américain*' ('a two-pronged movement of "political correctness" and conservatism that spread like wildfire in this period through English-speaking America'), concluding that these tendencies have, as things stand, '*mis en danger, aux États-Unis comme au Canada, l'existence même du freudisme, une fois encore violemment attaqué dans un contexte puritain*' ('ended up threatening the very existence of Freudianism in the United States and Canada, such is the force of the present wave of attacks – not for the first time – in a context of puritanism') (1997: 166).

From the language viewpoint, it may already be noted that the above extracts themselves provide evidence for the existence of a certain terminological hesitation in French intellectual circles: where Scarpetta leaves the term 'politically correct' (used substantively) in English, Roudinesco and Plon, no doubt in order to demarcate themselves unambiguously from a value system which they reject, *translate* it, as *correction politique*. The hesitation over usage revealed by this divergence is – as we shall see later – in fact symptomatic of a general linguistic ambiguity that pervades contemporary French discourse. It has to be asked: is it possible – or even desirable – to avoid the use of Anglicisms when writing about the contemporary world in French?

The French intellectual milieux of which the above sources are representative are not alone in their critical stance towards the United States. The charges made by the likes of Roudinesco and Plon, Scarpetta and Ramonet against that country's multinationals, its entertainment business and its neo-puritanism of both left and right find their echo in the commentaries of a number of transatlantic social critics. Thus, in the area of globalisation, Noam Chomsky denounces the motives behind the US-led world trading system, as manifested in.the North American Free Trade Agreement (NAFTA) or in the General Agreement on Tariffs and Trade/World Trade Organisation (GATT/WTO) set-up.

> American companies stand to gain $61 billion a year from the Third World if US protectionist demands are satisfied at GATT (as they are in NAFTA), at a cost to the South that will dwarf the current huge flow of debt-service capital from South to North. Such measures are designed to ensure that US-based corporations control the technology of the future, including biotechnology, which, it is hoped, will allow protected private enterprise to control health, agriculture and the means of life generally, locking the poor into dependence and hopelessness. (1996, Internet article)

In parallel, Benjamin R. Barber, in his 1995 book *Jihad vs. McWorld: How Globalism and Tribalism are Reshaping the World*, attacks the tentacular global reach of Hollywood: 'Movies and videos are ever more unitary in content as they become ever more global in distribution. More and more people around the world watch films that are less and less varied. Nowhere is American monoculture more evident or more feared than in its movies and videos' (1995: 89). Elsewhere in the cultural field, Harold Bloom, possibly the best-known literary critic in today's US, repudiates both Christian fundamentalism *and* the 'politically correct' belief system that dominates his country's campuses, affirming the need to 'combat the cultural politics, both Left and Right, that are destroying criticism and consequently may destroy literature itself', and darkly predicts that 'we are only a decade or less away from the dawning of a new Theocratic Age'

(1995: 62), all in denunciatory tones that, if anything, exceed those of Scarpetta or Roudinesco and Plon.

If we return across the Atlantic to France, it may now be interesting to examine the text of *Non merci, Oncle Sam!*, a book published in 1999 by Noël Mamère, a Green politician and former Member of the European Parliament, and Olivier Warin, a journalist. This polemical volume brings together the various strands of anti-American critique, as manifested both inside and outside France – with Benjamin R. Barber cited as an authority – repeating the criticisms made in the examples quoted earlier (free-market economics, censorious neo-puritanism, mass-cultural domination) and making a number of further charges (obsessional use of the death penalty, rampant gun ownership, irresponsible promotion of GMOs, and even the export of Hallowe'en to France). The US is accused, above all, of *hégemonisme économique* ('economic hegemonism') and of promoting *la dictature du marché* ('the dictatorship of the market') (1994: 18-64).

However, the authors' general argument, though carefully document-ed, suffers from a curious contradiction in the specific field of language. On the role of English in the world, the authors note in passing that *la France . . . tente d'éradiquer les termes anglais de son vocabulaire* ('France . . . is trying to eradicate English terms from its vocabulary') (1994: 189) – a point which will be taken up later in this chapter. They also – if, again, only briefly – repeat the view, often heard in certain French intellectual milieux, that the Internet is essentially a medium for US cultural (and therefore, presumably, linguistic) domination: 'nous allons tout droit "vers un nouveau siècle d'impérialisme américain", par le truchement de la maîtrise des réseaux électroniques mondiaux' ('we are heading straight "towards a new century of US imperialism", via the mastery of the world-wide electronic networks'); the authors here, like so many others in France, fail to understand that the Internet is by its nature qualitatively different from earlier media such as television, since it allows its con-sumers to be producers too, and any user is free not just to take material off the network but to put material on – *in any language*, not only English. These points apart, however, Mamère and Warin scarcely touch on the phenomenon—surely relevant to their main argument – of the US-led global reach of English.

The text of *Non merci, Oncle Sam!* is, nonetheless, liberally – and some-what ironically, given its subject matter – sprinkled with Anglicisms. On the present writer's count, its 187 pages contain a total of 57 such words and phrases (excluding repetitions), which makes an average of almost one fresh Anglicism every three pages. Some of these usages might be jus-tifiable as tongue-in-cheek, while others could be explained by the specif-ic nature of the subjects discussed. Nonetheless, this book contains a large number of Anglicisms which seem quite simply unnecessary. These include: *les téléspectateurs zappent, [ils] surfent sur le Web, le lobby agroalimentaire, de confortables portefeuilles de stock-options, les gangs russes, un véritable 'boom' de l'industrie privée de l'emprisonnement, le record du monde des serial-killers, la publicité ou [le] marketing* (Mamère and Warin 1999: 10, 17, 42, 49, 89, 137, 185). There is no a priori reason why all the above Anglicisms – even where italicised or put in quotation marks – could not have been replaced by genuine French words or phrases: *sautent d'une chaîne à l'autre* for *zappent, naviguent sur la Toile* for *surfent sur le Web, les groupes de pression* for *le* lobby, *droits de souscription* for *stock-options, bandes de truands* for *gangs, essor* for *boom, plus grand nombre* for *record, tueurs en série* for *serial-killers, mercatique* for *marketing.* Arguably, the presence of these Anglicisms can only be understood as a manifestation, on an unconscious or semi-conscious level, of *precisely that submission to US mass-cultural hegemony* which, on a conscious level, the two authors reject, and *opposition to which* is actually the *raison d'être* of their book.

Anglicisms and Their Vicissitudes – Linguistic and Sociolinguistic Aspects

Having established, through the above telling examples, something of the persistence and extent of Anglicisms in French, we may now take a closer look at the characteristics of the phenomenon from a linguistic point of view. Words originating in English can pass through a whole series of vicissitudes in French, generating 'new' forms which no native speaker of English would recognise as genuine. The possible transformations are legion, and pseudo-English forms have come into being across the whole range of linguistic levels.

On the lexical level, modern French usage includes pseudo-Anglicisms in the form of words that are non-existent in English: these may be invented nouns, such as *le rugbyman, le tennisman, le recordman* (for 'rugby player', '[male] tennis player' and '[male] record holder'), or verbal nouns which scarcely exist in English as separate lexical items, such as *le lifting* (for facelift) or *le forcing* (approximately, an 'extra push'). On the semantic level, an English word may acquire a new meaning in French: *le spot* has come to designate what is known in Britain as a commercial. Indeed, lexical items can undergo both a semantic and a morphological shift, as in the curious case of *le pin's* (in English, 'badge'), where 'pin' has acquired the meaning of 'badge' by association, and, not content with that, has changed case to the genitive. A legitimate English noun such as *le snob* may generate a 'new' French verb: *snober* has established itself as an alternative to the native *bouder,* although no verb 'to snob' exists in English. Alternatively, the '-er' suffix may serve to naturalise an actually existing English verb, as in *shooter* ('to shoot' in the cinematic sense) or the dubious IT dyad *uploader/downloader;* another naturalisation strategy is to invent a French abbreviation for an English word, as in *le pull* for 'pullover', or, dare one add, *McDo* for the much-disliked yet much-patronised McDonald's. An English term may also be semi-assimilated by gallicising the spelling, as in *le bogue* ('computer bug'), a form which alternates in current usage with the more visibly alien *le bug*. For nouns, assimilation also requires the assignation of a gender; and, if the obvious temptation is to give semantically neutral Anglicisms masculine status (for example *le fax*), the goal of naturalisation has, in some cases, been better served by the choice of the feminine gender, as in the use – for a media personality of either sex – of *la star* (probably by analogy with the two grammatically feminine but semantically sex-neutral native terms, *la vedette* and *l'étoile*).

Pseudo-Anglicisms are, then, a quite widespread phenomenon in today's French, in line with a long-established tendency (after all, no native speaker of English would accept 'shampooing' as a synonym for 'shampoo', or 'self' on its own as meaning 'self-service restaurant'). The 'pseudo' nature of such forms may well not be recognised by native French speakers, who are likely to assume they are genuine English forms, and to be surprised if, say, a real live anglophone fails to understand *le baby-foot* ('bar football'). Indeed, even the experts may slip up: the *Dictionnaire des Difficultés du Français* (Robert, 1994), includes in its entry *Anglais (mots)* a reference to *le recordman* (recommended plural: *les recordmen*) which fails to specify that this term is actually not an English word at all – although, conversely, the *Petit Larousse illustré* for 2000 (hereinafter *Larousse 2000*) redeems Gallic lexicographical honour by correctly designating the same word as a *faux anglicisme*.

At all events, there is no doubt that contemporary French writing in the journalistic register (newspapers, magazines, topical non-fiction books) is strewn with words and phrases deriving from English, whether they are genuine British and/or American forms or pseudo-Anglicisms (as much is clear from our analysis above of Mamère and Warin's book). The phenomenon affects most areas of topical or public discourse, with the major exceptions of domestic politics and, above all, the law, where the difference of legal systems acts as an effective barrier to Anglicisms of any provenance.

It may now be interesting to consider briefly, from a sociolinguistic perspective, some of the possible motives for so widespread an employment of alien terms by writers and journalists, in what is, after all, a country that remains highly conscious of its specific cultural identity. Among the factors that may be identified are the following:

(a) *Terminological rigour*: an equivalent French word or phrase for the concept may not exist (or may exist only as a long-winded paraphrase). A French journalist writing on culturally or institutionally specific aspects of an English-speaking country would obviously be best advised not to translate terms which may have no exact equivalent. However, certain general subject areas, including some marked by a substantial Anglo-American conceptual input, have evolved their own terminology in French. This is particularly true of the computer/Internet field, which we shall look at in detail below.

(b) *Sectoral jargon*: in some subject areas, there is a whole arsenal of ready-made English-language terminology that is also highly specific. An example here is the world of non-classical musics, which has not evolved its own French terminology in the same way as the computer world has. Native French terms, such as *la chanson* and *les variétés*, do of course exist, but in the case of specific genres the tendency has long been simply to import the English term. This phenomenon goes back to the early twentieth century, with *le ragtime, le jazz* and *le blues*, and in recent years has been responsible for such usages as *le rap, la techno, le trip-hop*, etc. A curious case is provided by *la world* (for 'world music'), which might have seemed an unnecessary import since a native term, *les musiques du monde*, already existed; by now, however, in practice the French term has come to be reserved for 'genuine' ethnic music of the field-recording type, whereas *la world* usually denotes 'contemporary' ethnic music produced using modern studio techniques, or else music resulting from fusions between different ethnic genres or between such genres and mainstream Anglo-American popular forms.

(c) *Brevity*: *le flop* is shorter than *l'échec, le boom* than *l'essor, la star* than *la vedette*. This is, of course, a practical consideration in certain contexts, for example newspaper headlines.

(d) *Comprehensibility*: the 'approved' French word may not be readily understood. *Le fax/faxer* are likely to be understood where *la télécopie/le télécopieur/envoyer par télécopie* are not; the same applies to *scanner/le scanneur* as against *numériser/le numériseur*.

(e) *Unconscious pro-American reflexes*, as an expression of fashion or as a result of over-exposure to US media. Such reflexes may account for, say, the widespread contemporary use of *le kidnapping/kidnapper/le kidnappeur*, instead of the older *enlèvement/enlever/ravisseur*. Another factor here may be the naturalisation of transatlantic free-market values and the attendant mass-consumption lifestyle – hence *le management'* for *la gestion, le chewing-gum* for *la gomme à mâcher*, etc.

(f) (Conversely) *an ironic anti-Americanism*, which may dictate a conscious use of the English word, as a strategy to distance the French writer (and reader) from the US values being attacked. Possible examples here are *le business/le businessman* (with specifically American connotations, as opposed to the more general *les affaires/l'homme d'affaires*), and *le serial killer* (for *le tueur en série*), in contexts where certain US phenomena (the free-market system, endemic social violence) are being openly called in question.

The French writer is also free to choose not to use Anglicisms, and the deliberate selection of a French lexical item may be motivated by various factors, among them:

(a) *Officially organised hostility to Anglicisms.* The existence of this ten-dency in France and the French-speaking world generally, and the consequent attempts to reduce the use of Anglicisms, are well known. The special case of Quebec, the francophone territory which lies geographically closest to the US, falls outside the scope of the present study; the usual view, however, is that Québécois French has succeeded better than any other variant of the language in keeping Anglicisms down and out. In France, it is the official task of the *Académie française* to devise French equivalents for English neolo-gisms. This activity is typically derided by the British, as represent-ing the *dirigiste* antithesis to Britain's own empirical traditions; as the grammarian John Honey puts it, 'Britain has always resisted the idea of language management by an official body, especially an Academy' (1997: 144). Nonetheless, the French Academy's coinages have in some notable instances succeeded in imposing themselves, especial-ly in the computer field: *l'informatique* ('computer science'), *l'ordina-teur* ('computer'), *le matériel* ('hardware') and *le logiciel* ('software') have all become standard usage in France. Other officially approved concoctions (*le palmarès* for 'hit-parade', *la mercatique* for 'marketing') have been markedly less successful, although *Larousse 2000* dutifully lists such forms alongside the prevalent Anglicism, with the remark *recommandation officielle*.

(b) *The spontaneous generation of genuine French equivalents.* It occasionally happens that a genuine French counterpart to a US term springs up from the grassroots. A notable recent example, in the context of the WTO and the related controversies, is *la malbouffe* for 'junk food', a case of linguistic *bovéisme*? Another case in point is the fashionable phrase *dans tous ses états* (literally 'in all his/her/its states'; 'viewed from every side', also 'nervous, agitated'), as in *Le bogue dans tous ses états*, the headline given by *Le Monde* to its report of 22 December 1999 on the millennium bug.[2] This is an interesting case of reassimi-lation, since the vogue for this phrase actually derived from the French title of an American film, Woody Allen's *Deconstructing Harry*: the translator, instead of resorting to *déconstruction* – even though that is a true French intellectual term, deriving from the work of the eminently Gallic philosopher Jacques Derrida – came up with a totally different title, *Harry dans tous ses états*, thus giving a whole new lease of life to a native French phrase.

(c) *Conscious and systematic 'localisation' within a sector of activity*, leading to the creation of an entire terminological artillery in French. This has to a large extent happened in the computer/Internet field, where, for obvious operational reasons, a term has to have a specific and non-negotiable meaning.

In view of the particular importance – economic, cultural and linguistic – of the computer/Internet field, as highlighted at several points in the above discussion, we shall dedicate the next section to it.

Computer/Internet French

By now, a comprehensive arsenal of French computer terms exists – far more so than in other Romance languages. In the case of the basic terms *ordinateur* ('computer') and *logiciel* ('software'), French may be contrasted with Spanish, where *el ordenador* has established itself (at least in Spain) but *el software* is the norm, and, even more so, with Portuguese, which has not managed to improve on *o computador*, and Italian, in which, although *l'elaboratore* and the no longer very accurate *il calcolatore* are possible synonyms, in practice *il computer* rules. The entire lexicon of the world's most commonly used operating system has been laboriously translated into French, and it is those terms, not the English ones, that appear on the Gallic user's screen (*gestionnaire de fichiers* for 'file manager', *panneau de configuration* for 'control panel', etc.).

Even so, not all French IT coinages have succeeded, and those that do succeed do not do so all the time. *Le logiciel* and *le matériel* are certainly more frequent than *le software* and *le hardware*, but that does not prevent occasional blatant use of the English terms. Thus, on 26 June 2003 the daily newspaper *Libération* published an article on IT rivalry between India and China, entitled *Le partenariat obligé des deux géants rivaux* ('Forced partnership of two rival giants'), which quoted Zhu Rongji, a former Chinese deputy prime minister, as declaring on a visit to Bangalore: 'Vous êtes numéro 1 en termes de software, nous sommes numéro 1 en termes de hardware. Si nous combinons software et hardware, nous serons les numéros 1 mondiaux' ('You [i.e. India] are number one in terms of software, we [i.e. China] are number one in terms of hardware. If we combine software and hardware, we'll be the world's number ones'). While Mr Rongji may have been expressing himself in English, the failure to use the French terms might suggest that on some level, conscious or unconscious, the journalist is associating IT advances in Asia with global Americanisation (Ollivier, 2003: 8).

Meanwhile, *le shareware* and *le freeware* are far more likely to be found than *le partagiciel* and *le graticiel*, and the coinages *le fureteur* and *le butineur* have made little headway against *le browser*. In some cases, current usage hesitates between the French term and the Anglicism, as in *le fichier attaché* or *l'attachment*, *le lien* or *le link*, *la Toile* or *le Web*. In the last-named case,

French adds an alternative sense deriving from a compression that does not operate in English, for by now-established usage *le Web* can mean either 'the World Wide Web' or (often in lower case) 'an individual website'. Conversely, however, where a genuine French term is employed, there are cases where French has evolved greater sophistication than English in differentiating senses: for 'e-mail' (assuming the English word is not used), French has evolved *la messagerie* or *le courrier électronique* for the function, and *le courriel/le mél/le mail*, as alternative forms for an individual message. In addition, the French translations of '(Net)surf' and '(Net)surfer', *naviguer* and *le cybernaute/l'internaute*, may be considered rather more intelligent than the English originals, since their navigation and sailing images imply a purposive search, whereas 'surf', with its connotations of arbitrariness and superficiality, is actually based on a false analogy with 'channel-surfing', coming from a quite different medium, namely television. In practice, nonetheless, *surfer* and *le Netsurfeur* remain commoner than their ingeniously concocted French equivalents.

Similarly, attempts to signify the phenomenon of e-mail 'spam' in an authentically French fashion have been only moderately successful. The term 'spam' (meaning unsolicited and unwanted commercial e-mail) is an interesting case of IT terminology embodying 'Anglo-Saxon' mass-cultural contamination, as it is derived – as David Crystal explains in amusing detail in *Language and the Internet* (2001) – from a 1970 episode of a well-known British television show (2001: 53–4). Theoretically, there are two French coinages to choose from to translate 'spam'. Both are portmanteau words: *le publipostage* (from *publicité* (advertising) and *postage* (mailing)), and *le pourriel* (from *pourri* (rotten) and *courriel*, itself, as we have seen, a French term for 'e-mail'). However, in practice it is usually the Anglo-American usage that prevails, in *le spam*, *le spamming* and *le spammer* (sometimes morphologically naturalised to *spammeur*). Thus, in an article on the subject published in September 2003 in the business magazine *Capital*, *Rançon du succès, pirates et 'spammers' détournent le Net pour se livrer au cybercrime* ('The price of success: hackers and spammers abuse the Net to practise cybercrime') (Zarachowicz, 2003: 56), one at once notes the Anglicism in the title, its effect slightly attenuated by the self-consciousness of inverted commas. The text of this article contains the following revelatory sentence: *En Europe, une directive a été adoptée en 2002 pour interdire le publipostage (nom officiel des spams) sauf accord du destinataire* ('In Europe [i.e. the EU], a directive was adopted in 2002 outlawing "publipostage" (the official name for spam) except where the recipient has opted in'). The author admits the existence of a 'real', official French term (in parentheses), before nonetheless blithely going on to re-use the semi-naturalised English word: *Microsoft a déposé quinze plaintes, en juin dernier, contre des spammers qui auraient envoyé 2 milliards de mails sur MSN, le portail maison* ('Microsoft took out fifteen suits in June against spammers who had sent two billion e-mails to MSN, the company's house portal'), and to describe Bill Gates as *exaspéré par les spammers, qui polluent le Web avec leurs messages* ('exasperated by spammers who pollute the Web with their messages'). One may also note, in the title and the extracts quoted, the presence of other Anglicisms (*le Net, le Web*) and semi-Anglicisms ('mails'); and also, conversely, the genuine French terms *pirate* (hacker) and *portail* (portal).

It will now be interesting to look at the use of Anglicisms in a longer article in the IT field, taken from the 10–22 December 1999 issue of the magazine *Le Nouvel Économiste*. This text, entitled *La France bascule dans l'Internet* ('France moves on to the Internet') (Bertolus and Garigue, 1999: 24-30) exhibits – not unsurprisingly – a total of 25 Anglicisms. While the core terminology used displays a certain oscillation (*Internet* alternates with *le Réseau, le Web* with *la Toile*) and certain specifically French terms such as *internaute* do get a look-in, in many instances the authors visibly take the line of least resistance and borrow the English term nearest to hand. Thus, we find: *Ils sont des centaines de milliers . . . à échanger des e-mails, . . . à rechercher un job sur les sites d'emploi* ('In their hundreds of thousands . . . they exchange e-mails . . . and look for jobs on situations-vacant sites'); *ils veulent juste des snacks ouverts 24 heures sur 24* ('they just want snack bars open 24 hours a day'); *ce manager a créé Arbizon Multimédia* ('this manager set up Arbizon Multimédia'); *tee-shirt, haut débit et fun* ('T-shirt, high performance and fun'); *le directeur du marketing* ('the marketing director'); *cette start-up star de la Bourse* ('this start-up star of the Stock Exchange'); *leur business plan* ('their business plan'), etc. These examples reveal two more than arguably dangerous tendencies, both relating to the uncritical replication of transatlantic attitudes which are in reality highly ideological. One is the wholesale assimilation of American free-market values, as reflected in the use of 'business plan', 'manager', 'marketing', 'job', 'start-up star', etc. The other, equally insidious, is what might be called 'Disneyfication', the naturalisation of the 'entertainment' values of US mass culture, as manifested in usages like 'fun' (why not the native *divertissement*?), 'snack' (adapted from 'snack bar'; as if France did not have its *brasseries*), and, indeed, 'tee-shirt' (this spelling, all too common in French, is, to compound matters, a solecism creating a false etymology – as if the English word were a golfing term, when in fact it derives from the letter-T shape of the garment). While there is no doubt that greater French use of the Internet will increase the stock of francoph-one texts available on the network, lexical attitudes like these give reason to fear that the French sent out into cyberspace is likely to leave much to be desired in terms of authenticity.

The Language of Management

The lexicon of management, which in many contexts overlaps with that of IT, has come up in the last example, and will now be examined in its own right. Officially, the French words for 'management' and 'manager' are *gestion* and *gestionnaire*, but *le management* and (as just seen) *le/la manager* are also frequent. This is obviously a sensitive field in view of French reservations about 'Anglo-Saxon' free-market values, and the choice of English or French terminology may reflect a conscious ideological stance. There is meanwhile no doubt that management-related Anglicisms are creeping into French usage. *Le start-up* (again as just seen) is now virtually universal, whereas the official purist term, *la jeune pousse*, all but died at birth. Neologisms like 'benchmarking' or 'mainstreaming' are liable to be taken over straight from English into French, with only minimal attempts to ascertain what they might actually mean.

On 9 September 2003, the economics supplement of *Le Monde* carried a text entitled *Vous avez dit management de la performance?* ('Did you say "performance management"?') (Rollot, 2003: VIII) The reader will note the presence of two Anglicisms in a seven-word title, the second being the longer-established 'performance'. The article, which is about the extent to which management targets are being met in the French private sector, refers throughout to *les managers*, and also invokes *le coaching* (albeit in inverted commas): *À quoi servent les livres de management, les sessions de formation pour managers éclairés ou encore les séances 'de coaching'?* ('What is the use of management books, training courses for enlightened managers or, indeed, coaching sessions?') Nonetheless, a decidedly 'Anglo-Saxon' concept such as 'performance-related pay' appears here not in English but in a full-blown French version (*le système de rémunération variable*), while 'target setting' is, similarly, transposed as *la fixation des objectifs*. The picture is, then, a mixed one, and on the linguistic evidence the importation of transatlantic management ideas does not quite amount to a full-scale cultural colonisation.

The case of *le coaching* is particularly interesting, and may be further illuminated from an article of 14 April 2003, from the employment supplement of *Libération*, rather sceptically entitled *Ce coaching n'a servi à rien, sauf à rigoler* ('This coaching was only good for a laugh') (Millot, 2003: II–III). Here, the reader discovers that the imported terms *le coaching* and *le coach* have become morphologically productive in French, generating the verb *coacher* (to coach), the derived noun *le coaché* (coachee), and the non-English plural form *les coachs* (coaches): *'Le "coaching", à savoir "l'accompagnement de personnes ou d'équipes pour le développement de leurs potentiels et de leur savoir-faire dans le cadre d'objectifs professionnels" (définition de la Société française de coaching), est, sans conteste, la dernière marotte du management. Mais qui sont les coachs et les coachés?'* ('Coaching, that is, "the accompaniment of persons or teams for the development of their potential and expertise in the framework of professional objectives" (definition of the French Coaching Society), is, without any doubt, the latest management fad. But who are the coaches and the coachees?') The process of morphological naturalisation at work here suggests that the invasion of Anglicisms has its limits. The transatlantic term ends up absorbed into the grammatical logic of the recipient language, and the resultant linguistic acculturation suggests some degree of parallel adaptation of the foreign concept to French circumstances.

The Lexicon of World Trade

We shall now consider two articles on world trade, published in the wake of the 1999 WTO interministerial conference in Seattle and taken, again, from the 10–22 December 1999 issue of *Le Nouvel Économiste*. These are: an editorial, *Les leçons de Seattle* ('The lessons of Seattle') (Quatrepoint, 1999: 3) and a news feature, *Comment surmonter les divergences de Seattle* ('How to move beyond the disagreements of Seattle') (Plassart 1999: 32–5). The editorial pulls off the *tour de force* of discussing globalised trade while perpetrating only one solitary Anglicism. The author attacks US isolationism, declaring: *L'échec de la conférence de l'OMC n'est pas tant celui de la mondialisation que celui d'une certaine Amérique* ('The failure of the WTO summit is not so much that of globalisation as that of a certain America'). He concludes: *Et s'il est un slogan qui devrait survivre à Seattle, c'est bien que "le monde n'est pas un simple marchandise"* ('And if there's a slogan which deserves to survive Seattle, it's: "the world is not just a commodity" '), rather unfortunately marring his closing flourish with the article's sole Anglicism, *slogan* (rather than *devise*; to be fair, this is actually a word of Scottish Gaelic origin, but it is unlikely the author is aware of that). This lapse apart, across the article the editorialist skilfully manages to avoid the traps set by his subject matter: he employs *conférence*, not 'summit', *société informationnelle*, not 'information society', *libre-échange*, not 'free trade'. By contrast, however, the longer news feature on the WTO includes – despite the broadly critical slant of its content – no less than 15 Anglicisms, many of them avoidable. Its author opens his post-mortem with the laconic comment: *Flop* – rather than *échec* or even the Italian-derived *fiasco*, though both those words do, to be fair, crop up later in his text. Other Anglicisms employed include *les rounds de l'OMC* (despite the existence of *cycle* as an alternative to *round*), *le business yankee* (this may of course be ironic), *cet ex-hippie militant* (the French *soixante-huitard* – '68-er' – would have provided an approximate equivalent), *l'e-business américain* (why not *commerce électronique*?), *le dramatique crash du Boeing d'Egyptair* (*catastrophe* would perfectly well convey the meaning of 'crash'). The journalist's reading of the summit carefully avoids identification with any party, and is far from sycophantic to either the US administration or the American NGOs, suggesting, indeed, as regards the latter, that la *tour de Babel de la contestation anti-OMC n'en finissait pas d'aligner les contradictions de la société américaine* ('the Tower of Babel of the anti-WTO protests ceaselessly pointed up the contradictions of US society'). At the same time, his text, *considered in its linguistic dimension*, nonetheless leaves an ambivalent aftertaste similar to that produced by Mamère and Warin's anti-American tract.

Conclusion – Languages as Systems

From the examples we have looked at, the conclusion is inevitable that in numerous contexts – especially those directly relating to globalisation in its various aspects – contemporary French writing in the journalistic register is, as a matter of habit, liberally sprinkled with Anglicisms, the great majority of which originate in the United States.

There is no doubt that a similar analysis would come to similar conclusions for other major European languages such as Spanish, German and Italian – indeed, with the two last-named the process is considerably more advanced (if that is the word) than with French. Meanwhile, except in certain limited areas such as cuisine, very few words are today making it the other way, from any of the languages of mainland Europe, across the Atlantic (or even the English Channel): in other words, it is *not* a two-way process. The relationship between the languages of Europe and American English is not an equal one: it is predicated on the economic, military and mass-cultural power of the US.

In order to evaluate the impact of this process, it is here useful to make brief reference to certain theoretical perspectives. The concept of *languages as systems*, which has been gaining ground in recent years in critical linguistic circles, is advanced in the work of Itamar Even-Zohar, who, in his text *Polysystem Theory* (1990), states: 'The idea that socio-semiotic phenomena, i.e., sign-governed human patterns of communication (such as culture, language, literature), could more adequately be understood and studied if regarded as systems rather than conglomerates of disparate elements has become one of the leading ideas of our time.' From this vantage point, Even-Zohar considers that a given culture is a 'polysystem', or system of systems, while stressing that where cultures interact we are dealing with a dialogue between (poly)systems: '[the "culture" of one community] maintain[s] systemic relations with other systems organizing the "cultures" of other communities. In history, such "units" are by no means clear-cut or forever finalized. Rather, the opposite holds true, as the borders separating adjacent systems shift all the time, not only within systems, but between them.' By allowing for shifting boundaries between systems, this definition implicitly raises the question of the *power relations* between systems: one system may, at a given moment in history, be stronger than another. Hence, Even-Zohar argues, 'a certain culture may be interfered with by another culture, as a result of which repertoires are transferred from one polysystem to another' (1990, Internet article).

Even-Zohar's polysystemic model has been applied to translation issues by adherents to the 'Manipulation School'. Dora Sales Salvador explicates this application of polysystem theory to the practice of translation in the following terms: *'La traducción es una realidad del sistema literario y cultural. Traducir no es neutro. Desde esta asunción, nos parece importante que quienes practican la traducción sean conscientes de la necesidad de reflexionar crítica y auto-críticamente sobre este ejercicio.'* ('Translation is a reality of the literary and cultural system. To translate is not a neutral act. Starting from this assumption, we believe that those who practise translation have to be aware of the need to reflect on their act in a critical and self-critical fashion.') From this 'polysystemic' perspective, translation is a *dialogue between systems*; thus, in an ethically aware practice of translation, *'se presta atención tanto a las palabras como al sistema que se encarga de otorgarles sentido'* ('one pays equal attention to the words and to the system responsible for giving them sense') (2003, Internet article).

One may conclude that under an 'ideal' theoretical model, a particular pair of systems (here, French and English) would be perceived as being of equal value and importance; but in the real conditions currently obtaining, it is essential for the translator to be conscious, critically and self-critically, of the actually existing imbalances within such a pair. This theoretical perspective has a number of implications for the issue of Anglicisms. If the relationship between two languages is an encounter between two systems, what happens when one system permeates the other but not vice versa? The influence of US English on French is such that the stronger system is now seeping into, if not contaminating, its less powerful counterpart. The result can only be to undermine the creative and generative capacities of French *as system*, in a sapping operation whose objective impact cannot be denied, even if it is confined to certain lexical fields. It seems to be the case (certainly no obvious examples appear in the texts examined) that – in contrast to what is apparently happening to some other languages – the influence brought to bear by American English on the French of France is essentially lexical and not syntactic. French syntactic norms appear, for the moment, to be holding up well. However, a lexical contamination that affects a large and important group of semantic fields is enough on its own to impact strongly on both the theory and practice of interlanguage relations.

If one system dominates the other beyond a certain point, the risk arises that the second system will lose its autonomy and become a subsystem of the first. While things have certainly not gone that far between US English and French, Anglicisms already pose certain concrete problems for translation. When a French text is translated into English, should its Anglicisms be automatically transposed back into English? There will obviously be a strong temptation to do so, especially by the less linguistically aware, but context would suggest caution. As the French social and cultural macro-context is different from the American one, there is no guarantee that a term like 'mainstreaming' or 'coaching' will always, in all micro-contexts, mean exactly the same in (Anglicised) French as in English; yet it is highly likely to be retranslated back *tel quel* (as if translation were the 'neutral act' that Dora Sales Salvador warns us it is not). A provisional conclusion might be that while the invasion of Anglicisms does not *abolish* the status of French as a separate system, it is likely to *occlude* that status and render its perception by users more problematic. Certainly, more theoretical work in this field would usefully illuminate what is a new and growing – but insufficiently visible – problem for interlanguage relations.

Some might argue here that there is actually nothing to worry about, be it for French or for any other language, and claim that linguistic miscegenation could actually prove to be a cultural and communicational asset, improving writers' expressiveness by allowing them to draw on the resources of different cultures. This is a potentially interesting point – English itself was, after all, originally the product of a miscegenation between Anglo-Saxon and Latin/French elements – but a serious problem arises over defending Anglicisms in French on such grounds, namely the question of (in)equality. The situation between France and the US may be illuminated by comparison with the state of affairs in India.

In that country, two languages, English and Hindi, have de facto *lingua franca* status, while a total of 17 languages have official status at regional level, and the number of languages and dialects actually spoken is estimated in hundreds, if not thousands. English and Hindi, in particular, have cross-fertilised each other over time. Hindi has absorbed such terms as 'bank' and 'train', while any newspaper article in Indian English will feature, embedded into syntactically perfect English, such assimilated terms as 'lakh' (100,000), 'crore' (10 million), 'dacoit' (armed robber), 'chawl' (apartment block), etc. Half a century after independence, the continued use of English by now has little to do with colonialism and much to do with practicality: English is the only language used in the subcontinent in which educated speakers and writers from all language groups can understand each other. In the southern states, where the autochthonous languages are not Indo-European but Dravidian, Hindi is perceived as quite as 'alien' as English. Salman Rushdie wrote in 1983, in an essay entitled '"Commonwealth literature" does not exist':

> The children of independent India seem not to think of English as being irredeemably tainted by its colonial provenance. They use it as

an Indian language, as one of the tools they have to hand . . . In South India . . . the resentment of Hindi is far greater than of English . . . English is an essential language in India, not only because of its technical vocabularies and the international communication which it makes possible, but also simply to permit two Indians to talk together in a tongue which neither party hates. (Rushdie, 1991 [1983]: 65-6)

In these circumstances, with Indian English established as a home-grown language variant, it is quite possible for English and Hindi to compete on equal terms, and therefore to influence each other on a reciprocal basis.

However, such is not the case in present circumstances in the relationship between US English and French. Reciprocal influence, while theoretically a possibility, is simply not happening. Those concerned about the survival of the unique expressive character of French (or any other language) may wish to conclude that Anglicisms in French (and all other languages) could usefully be confined to the absolute minimum (to phenomena specific to anglophone countries, and to technical terms where a reasonably concise local equivalent has not emerged) – and that writing professionals could set an example here. It is well enough known that France is the member state spearheading the European Union's position at the WTO in favour of preserving 'cultural diversity'. This policy applies in the first place to the audiovisual sector, but cultural diversity also implies linguistic diversity. The price of linguistic diversity is, however, eternal vigilance; and those who preach diversity in international forums could usefully remember that vigilance begins at home.

Notes

1. All translation into English are my own.
2. 'Le bogue dans tous ses états', *Le Monde*, 22 December 1999 (supplement: *Le Monde Informatique:* VI).

Special note

This text is a modified and updated version of an article originally published in 2003, under the title 'The Use of Anglicisms in Contemporary French', in: *Crossing Barriers and Bridging Cultures: The Challenges of Multilingual Translation for the European Union*, ed. Arturo Tosi (Clevedon, UK: Multilingual Matters).

References

Barber, B.R. (1996 [1995]) *Jihad vs. McWorld: How Globalism and Tribalism are Reshaping the World*. New York: Ballantine.
Bloom, Harold (1995 [1994]) *The Western Canon: The Books and School of the Ages*. London: Macmillan.

Chomsky, N. (1996) Notes on NAFTA: The Masters of Mankind. <http://www.cs.unb.ca/~alopez-o/politics/chomnafta.html>.
Crystal, D. (2001) *Language and the Internet*. Cambridge: Cambridge University Press.
Even-Zohar, I. (1990) Polysystem Theory. *Poetics Today* 11:1, 9–6. Reproduced at: <http://www.tau.ac.il/~itamarez/papers/ps-th-r.htm>.
Honey, J. (1997) *Language Is Power: The Story of Standard English and its Enemies.* London: Faber and Faber.
Mamère, N. and Warin, O. (1999) *Non merci, Oncle Sam!* Paris: Ramsay.
Millot, O. (2003) 'Ce coaching n'a servi à rien, sauf à rigoler'. *Libération*, 14 April 2003 (supplement: *Emploi*: II–III).
Ollivier, S. (2003) 'Le partenariat obligé des deux géants rivaux'. *Libération*, 26 June 2003: 8.
Plassart, P. (1999) 'Comment surmonter les divergences de Seattle'. *Le Nouvel Économiste*, 10–22 December 1999: 32–35.
Quatrepoint, J. (1999) 'Les leçons de Seattle'. *Le Nouvel Économiste*, 10–22 December 1999: 3.
Ramonet, I. (1999) *La tyrannie de la communication*. Paris: Éditions Galilée.
Rollot, C. (2003) 'Vous avez dit "management de la performance"?' *Le Monde*, 9 September 2003 (supplement: *Économie*: VIII).
Roudinesco, E. and Plon, M. (1997) *Dictionnaire de la psychanalyse*. Paris: Fayard.
Rushdie, S. (1991 [1983]). '"Commonwealth literature" does not exist'. In *Imaginary Homelands Essays and Criticism 1981–1991*. London: Granta.
Sales Salvador, D. (2003) 'La relevancia de la documentación en teoría literaria y literatura comparada para los estudios de traducción'. *Translation Journal* 7:3 (July 2003): <http://accurapid.com/journal/25documents.htm>.
Scarpetta, G. (1996) 'La littérature en procès.' *La Règle du Jeu* No. 18 (January 1996).
Zarachowicz, W. (2003) 'Rançon du succès, pirates et "spammers" détournent le Net pour se livrer au cybercrime'. *Capital*, No 144, September 2003: 5

Dictionnaire des Difficultés du Français (1994). Paris: Robert.
Petit Larousse illustré 2000 (1999). Paris: Larousse.

Chapter 4

E-mail, Emilio or Mensaje de Correo Electrónico?
The Spanish Language Fight for Purity in the New Technologies

JEREMY MUNDAY

Introduction

This chapter sets out to summarise briefly some of the ways in which the Spanish language and its institutions are reacting to the worldwide spread of English. The Spanish-English interface is of great interest: Spanish is a major world language, an official language of the United Nations and the European Union, and itself has experienced a noticeable growth in the past decade; most interestingly, the number of speakers of Spanish in the United States has risen rapidly with immigration from Mexico and Central and South America. Although Spanish has therefore increased in prominence in the United States, it is also under pressure from English, which has given rise to a hybrid form, sometimes called 'Spanglish' or 'espanglish', that is fraught with controversy. A major focus of this chapter will be an attempt to relate how the institutions charged with protecting the Spanish language are reacting to the situation. In particular, an analysis will be provided of the battlefield of information technology, where technical terms and 'netspeak' show the increasing influence of English but where electronic corpora have been set up by the Spanish Royal Academy of the language to try and protect and maintain the unity of Spanish.[1]

The Development of Spanish as a First Language

Although there is some debate about the number of first-language speakers of different varieties of Spanish in the world, the generally accepted figure is upwards of 320 million. The largest number (more than 90 million) live in Mexico, followed by Spain (nearly 40 million). In total, Spanish is the first or main language in 23 countries, including the countries of Spanish America, one African state (Equatorial Guinea, with 400,000 speakers) and the Philippines (at least 1.8 million speakers).[2] In addition, Spanish is becoming increasingly popular as a second language in countries such as Japan, which has more than 60,000 university students registered on Spanish courses (López, 2000). Meanwhile, in the European Union it is calculated that 16% of the population know some Spanish as a foreign language, behind only English (70%), French (37%) and German (23%) (Pozzi, 2000). Such a geographical spread confirms the strength of Spanish worldwide.

Several factors have assisted the rise of Spanish, one of the most important of which was the creation in 1991 of the Mercosur (Mercado Común del Cono Sur, 'Common Market of the Southern Cone'), a trading association of four South American states along the lines of the North American Free Trade Association and the European Union. The key players in the Mercosur are Argentina and Brazil and both Spanish and Portuguese are the working languages within the association. This has had positive consequences for the learning of Spanish, since Brazil, a country of over 150 million inhabitants where the first language is Portuguese, made Spanish a compulsory subject in secondary schools from 2000 onwards. Investment in Brazil and Iberoamerica in general by large Spanish companies such as Telefónica has both strengthened economic links between Spain and the countries of the region and provided an additional impulse for the Spanish language and culture.

However, the most contentious and exciting development in the growth of Spanish concerns the situation in North America. The *Anuario 2000* of the Instituto Cervantes showed that Spanish had become the second language in the United States. Based on the US census figures in 1999, there were 31.3 million Hispanics living in the country. This represented 11.5% of the total population and a 35% increase on 1990. It is very likely, therefore, that the United States will soon overtake Spain as the second largest Spanish-speaking community in the world. The *Anuario* also confirmed that Spanish is by far the most popular foreign language at all levels of schooling in the United States, with more than 60% of university students studying some element of Spanish in their courses.

The controversy around the interface of Spanish and English is a political issue that has been raging for years. In 1998, California passed a ban on bilingual schooling as part of an 'English for Children' campaign. Arizona followed suit in November 2000. Yet Spanish has continued to grow in the United States. Its importance, or rather the importance of the electorate which uses it, was illustrated during the 2000 and 2004 presidential elections when the websites of George Bush, Al Gore and John Kerry all produced Spanish versions. Bush in particular stressed his ability to converse in Spanish, which helped him win an estimated 35% of the Hispanic vote in 2000, surpassing expectations.

Spanish and English

Yet hand in hand with this increase in Spanish has been the emergence of a hybrid of Spanish and English, sometimes known as 'Spanglish', that has become a source of great concern for many Spanish institutions. The phenomenon is illustrated by the appearance in US Spanish of expressions such as comprar groserías ('to buy groceries'), vacunar la carpeta ('to vacuum the carpet') and la rufa ('roof'). These are not only literal adaptations from American English. They are also amusing because they challenge the conventional sense of the Spanish word; the conventional dictionary sense of groserías is 'swear words', vacunar is 'to vaccinate', carpeta is a 'folder', and so on. Furthermore, they are used in place of an established Spanish expression. In the case of the three examples given above, these would be comprar comestibles, pasar el aspirador/la aspiradora por la alfombra and el tejado (Stavans, 2001b).

There has been considerable work in the United States on language contact and bilingualism (for example Roca 2000, Silva Corvalán, 1994, 1995). One important factor stressed by Silva Corvalán (2000) is that there are in fact many different varieties of Spanish spoken in the United States. She sees a greater variety among first-generation immigrants and relative homogeneity among the later generations. Clearly, the product of this language contact will also vary according to the frequency of use and the communicative function of the Spanish spoken, but Silva Corvalán does identify certain categories of influence of English on Spanish. These include, but are not restricted to, lexical borrowings and technical vocabulary. In addition, she discusses such phenomena as the simplification of grammatical categories such as verb tenses and mood and calquing of pragmatic forms such as Cuídate and Te veo, mimicking the function of the English 'Take care' and 'See you'.

Such is the prevalence of this mix of the two languages that in September 2000 the University of Massachusetts inaugurated the first ever chair in Spanglish. The new incumbent, Professor Ilán Stavans, has listed 6000 entries in his *The Sounds of Spanglish* (Stavans, 2001a), collected from among nuyorriqueños, that is, Puerto Ricans living in New York, chicanos, that is, Mexicans living in the United States, and Cuban-Americans living in Miami. Stavans sees it as 'a dialect that is being formed, a dialect born of the meeting of the Hispanic and Anglo-Saxon cultures in the US since the nineteenth century and which has spread as a result of the influence of TV, rap and salsa music and, finally, the Internet' (Stavans, 2001b, see also Stavans, 2003).

The Fight for Purity

While Spanglish was once a source of amusement, it is now taken very seriously by the establishment, some of whom consider it to represent a potential dilution of Spanish by the importation of American English terms (Alonso Piñeiro, 2001). At the forefront of the reaction against the trend is the Real Academia de la Lengua, Spain's Royal Academy of the Language, and the Instituto Cervantes. The Academy was founded in 1713, principally to defend Spanish against the invasion of Gallicisms, and now functions in partnership with its counterparts in 21 other countries, including the North American Academy, founded in 1973.

For its part, the Instituto Cervantes was set up in 1991 along the lines of the British Council and Goethe Institut. It is a non-profit-making institution devoted to promoting the Spanish language and culture worldwide. With centres currently in 25 countries, it delivers Spanish language courses as well as promoting and co-ordinating a range of activities from teacher training to theatrical productions and author tours. According to its then director in Spain, Fernando Rodríguez Lafuente, the main challenge facing Spanish 'is to consolidate itself, in the first years of the twenty-first century, as the second international language',[3] with its future being determined by its presence in Brazil, the United States and the Internet (*El País (Digital)*, 2000).

To cite the virtual world alongside the real is to emphasise that it has become the testing ground for the Spanish language. In September 2003, Spanish was calculated to be the fourth language of the Internet after English, Japanese and Chinese (http://www.glreach.com/globstats/index.php3). In the eyes of Francisco Marcos Marín, the academic director of the Instituto Cervantes from 1999–2001 and co-ordinator of the Real Academia's electronic corpora project (see below), the consolidation of the language depends on increasing its use on the web. This has become the great 'obsession' of the Institute, which wishes to see an increase in the use of Spanish from the 5% in 2000 to 15–20% of total Internet traffic (López, 2000). In order to achieve this, the Instituto is working with the government to support Spanish American companies offering electronic language tools and services and is implementing a plan to 'update' the use of Spanish on the web. One method of achieving this, driven by Andrés Elhazaz Molina, the director of the Institute's virtual learning centre, the Centro Virtual Cervantes (cvc.cervantes.es), is the creation of a powerful Internet search engine designed to locate cultural resources in Spanish. The project has received funding from the Spanish government amounting to approximately 900,000 euros and the collaboration of the Spanish telecommunications company Telefónica (López, 2000). This has resulted in a series of tools based around the virtual learning centre. These tools include, principally, the 'Oteador' search engine, which seeks links to pages in Spanish, and the 'atril del traductor' ('translator's work-bench'), with activities updated daily.

The implementation of the 'Oteador' project has even promoted debate about the status of Spanish worldwide. Following on from the first international congress of the Spanish language held in Zacatecas, Mexico, in 1997, October 2001 saw the second congress, held in Valladolid, Spain, bringing together more than 400 experts from across the world to discuss the present and future of Spanish. Significantly, two of the main conference themes were Spanish and its relation to other languages and Spanish and the Internet. In keeping with the new technology angle, the papers from this conference have been made available on the Centro Virtual Cervantes (cvc.cervantes.es/obref/congresos/valladolid). Similarly, the 2002 Symposium on contact between English and Spanish, held in New York by the Instituto Cervantes, is also readily available (http://cvc.cervantes.es/obref/espanol_eeuu).

However, the rapid growth of the new technologies has at the same time brought with it an expansion in the use of English and the borrowing of English terms. It is calculated that around 1000 words related to information technology are coined each year. An article on 4 January 2001 in the IT supplement of the prestigious Spanish daily *El País* described this phenomenon in the following terms (author's translation):

> Linguists warn that the current invasion is greater and more infectious than ever because of its rapid spread via the Internet. The new language brought by the Anglo-Saxon world from the hand of technology and the new economy is being augmented by the growth of mobile telephony. Signs greatly outnumber letters and there are more consonants than vowels. While in years gone by we learnt English through the Beatles, now it is through e-mail and webpages, although, unlike the past, it is no longer certain whether the English we read is correct. The concern of the Royal Academy of the [Spanish] Language for the purity of the language equals that of Anglo-Saxon linguists for the resilience of their own language.[4]

Several points stand out here: the strongly emotive and negative vocabulary, which considers the new technology terms to be an 'invasion' and 'infectious'; the related view of the situation as a kind of war between Spanish, defended by the Real Academia de la Lengua, and English, championed by 'Anglo-Saxon linguists'; and the concern for the 'correctness' of the new form of writing. The focus on linguistic 'purity' is one which marks Spain's view of language, and the Real Academia's in particular. After all, the motto of the Academy is *limpiar, fijar y dar esplendor* ('to clean, fix and give splendour' to the language), and its recent work has been targeted at defending the unity of the language across its many countries. The unity is also proclaimed by Jon Juaristi, the director of the Instituto Cervantes from 2001 to 2004, who was outraged at the fact that <u>Harry Potter and the Order of the Phoenix</u> was to be published in different editions in Spanish, incorporating local regionalisms in Mexico, Argentina and other Spanish-speaking countries: 'This type of linguistic fragmentation is unnecessary', he is quoted as saying (García Yebra, 2003).[5]

An organisation that aims to prevent the break-up of its language in the face of such a fluid linguistic and cultural phenomenon as Spanglish is clearly going to be worried by the abundant examples of hybrid Spanish/English terms in the new technologies, a field known as 'ciberspanglish'. The new forms include <u>chatear</u> ('to chat') instead of the established <u>charlar</u> and <u>forwardear</u> in place of <u>reenviar</u> ('re-send'), where the typical Spanish <u>-ear</u> suffix, for example <u>golpear</u> ('to hit') from <u>golpe</u> ('a blow'), is attached to an English term. These new hybrids are displacing established Spanish terms as illustrated in Table 4.1.

This type of shift is even being seen in the case of basic elements of computer hardware. Thus, the mouse, which was always the literal translation <u>el ratón</u>, is now challenged by the borrowing <u>mouse</u> or <u>maus</u>, and <u>laptop</u> is beginning to be used in place of <u>portátil</u>. Even the terms <u>palmtop</u> and <u>pocket PC</u> are competing against <u>ordenador de bolsillo</u> on some webpages (for example.www.procuno.com/hardware/palmtop.htm).

There are other instances where Spanish seems to be playing with words and sounds in an attempt to imitate English. <u>El correo electrónico</u> now faces competition from <u>el e-mail</u>, and a message is far less likely to be a <u>mensaje electrónico</u> and more probably a <u>mail</u>, <u>emilio</u> (also a proper name) or <u>imilio</u>. The word <u>Internet</u> itself has been borrowed from English, yet it has taken some time for its grammatical status to be decided. Current usage appears to prefer the omission of a definite or indefinite article, for example <u>en Internet</u> ('on the Internet'). In the case of other terms, Spanish continues to waver, both between a Spanish and English

Table 4.1 Ciberspanglish adaptations of English IT terms

Ciberspanglish	Established Spanish term	*Literal translation of established Spanish term*
Attachar/attachear	Adjuntar	to attach
Downloadear	Descargar	to unload
Printear	Imprimir	to print
Resetear	volver a encender	to switch on again
Taipear	escribir a máquina	to write by machine

form such as Spanish <u>Red</u> or English <u>Web</u>, and over the gender of the foreign form. The English import <u>Web</u> seems to have predominated thanks to its currency in ready adaptations such as <u>página web</u> ('web page') and <u>sitio web</u> ('website'). Both <u>el</u> and <u>la</u> <u>Web</u> are seen, the masculine being the default for such neologisms while the feminine is used by association with <u>la Red</u> ('the net'). <u>El Web</u> is also often used in place of <u>sitio web</u>. As further evidence of the power of the English terminology, <u>el World Wide Web</u> is sometimes seen as an alternative to <u>el/la Web</u> or <u>la Red</u> or even <u>la malla mundial</u>, perhaps propelled by the ubiquitous and catchy 'www' abbreviation in website addresses.

In a fascinating development to the battle, the Real Academia has enlisted the use of technology to try and defend the Spanish language. In the autumn of 1998, the first large-scale corpus of the Real Academia went on-line on the organisation's website (www.rae.es). The fruit of six years' preparatory work, and an ongoing project that was updated in 2003, it consists of two large-scale corpora:

(1) The CREA or Corpus de Referencia del Español Actual (Reference Corpus of Current Spanish), currently consisting of upwards of 140 million entries compiled from sources published between 1995 and 2003. It is intended that this corpus, based on newspapers, magazines, books, radio, TV and recorded interviews, will increase to 160 million words by the end of 2004 and that at least 50% of its sources will be from Hispanoamerica. Each year new entries will be added while those of the earliest year will be transferred to the CORDE.

(2) The CORDE or Corpus Diacrónico del Español (Diachronic Corpus of Spanish). This corpus was originally set up to provide a sample of texts in Spanish over the centuries up to the year 1975. It is now being progressively increased from 15 million entries in 2001 to, eventually, an anticipated 180 million word forms.

These corpora are used in the compilation of the prestigious *Diccionario de la Real Academia Española*. Such an approach represents an important shift in Spanish lexicography and brings it more in line with countries such as the United Kingdom which has a long history of corpus use, dating back to the Cobuild Bank of English in the 1980s (most recent version available at http://titania.cobuild.collins.co.uk/pages/boe.aspx) and the 1990s British National Corpus (http://thetis.bl.uk/). It is also of extreme interest in that the Real Academia perceives this kind of technology to be a tool in fixing the language and preventing penetration from English at exactly the same time as Spanish is being threatened by the growth of a global English Internet terminology.

The corpora are consulted by the Academia to assist in decisions regarding the inclusion of new words. The following two examples, given by Joaquín Segura (1998), a member of the North American Academy of the

Spanish Language, are indicative of the formal problems that arise when a word is imported from English. The borrowing of the English word <u>alkyl</u>, a term used in chemistry, necessitated a choice between two possible spellings in Spanish: <u>alquilo</u> or <u>alcohílo</u>. Yet the verb <u>alkylise</u> and past participle <u>alkylised</u> also needed to be borrowed, and the spelling <u>alquilar</u> and <u>alquilado</u> would have presented confusion with their everyday meaning ('to rent') and ('rented') in Spanish. For this reason, <u>alcohílo</u>, <u>alcohilar</u> and <u>alcohilado</u> were suggested as the preferred options. Yet, on other occasions, the English form and spelling impose themselves, even where this creates grammatical complications in Spanish. Thus, the IT term <u>byte</u> has been borrowed into Spanish, almost to the exclusion of any adaptation such as <u>bitio</u>, which would allow the normal plural to have been formed more easily (<u>bytes</u> presents pronunciation difficulties in Spanish because of the final sound cluster). On neither occasion, however, is there any suggestion that Spanish could find a term unconnected to the English. This to a large extent reflects the economic and technological power of American English, which has created the need for the word in the first place, and the fact that many Spanish speakers may initially encounter the terms through their study, research or work in English environments.

This is not always true for neologisms. An update of new terms for the English-Spanish bilingual dictionary of one of the major British publishers, prepared in the summer of 2001 from a list of new English entries, reveals several trends in the choice of Spanish equivalents:

(1) IT terms which borrow an English term: <u>el chat</u> ('chat room'), <u>el lector (de) DVD</u> ('DVD player'), <u>el URL</u> ('URL');
(2) Terms which are calqued from English: <u>aldea global</u> ('global village'), <u>buzón de voz</u> ('voice mail'), <u>comercio electrónico</u> ('e-business'), <u>corrector de ortografía</u> ('spell-checker'), <u>generado por ordenador</u> ('computer-generated'), <u>hiperenlace</u> ('hyperlink'), <u>mostrador de ayuda</u> ('help desk'), <u>proveedor de acceso a Internet</u> ('Internet Service Provider'), <u>teléfono celular</u>, or simply <u>celular</u> ('cell phone');
(3) Some technical terms where Spanish has preferred its own root forms: <u>acceder al sistema</u> (for 'to log on'), <u>buscador</u> ('search engine'), <u>codificar</u> ('to encrypt'), <u>el busca/el localizador</u> ('pager'), <u>ecológico</u> ('ecological', 'organic', 'environmental'), <u>navegador</u> ('browser') and <u>transgénico</u> ('genetically modified');
(4) More abstract terms which are currently glossed in Spanish: <u>competente en el uso de ordenadores</u> ('computer–literate'), <u>que respeta el medio ambiente</u> ('eco-friendly').

This list shows that the majority, but by no means all, of the terms are borrowed or calqued from English. The interesting point, and one where the corpora may assist the compiler or bilingual lexicographer, is to gauge the evolution of a term and/or of competing terms. Table 4.2 provides a

Table 4.2 Frequencies of competing terms in the Real Academia corpora and Google

	CORDE (27.11.03)	*CRAE (27.11.03)*	*Google (3.11.01)*	*Google (27.11.03)*
Browsing	0	1	777	33,400
Curiosear ('to browse')	92	108 (all senses)	2,960 (all senses)	12,500 (all senses)
Email	0	40	897,000	2.94 million
e-mail	0	295	1.4 million	4 million
Mail	12	24 (sense of 'e-mail')	50,000	130,000
Correo electrónico ('electronic mail')	0	1035	240,000	1.11 million
Mensaje electónico ('electronic message')	0	5	5,270	8,310

brief examination of some findings for two such pairs of terms in the dictionary update in cases where the Spanish equivalent of the English term was undecided:

curiosear vs. hacer browsing and mensaje electrónico/correo electrónico vs. email/e-mail/mail

Four searches were made for the frequency of each item:

(1) In the older and smaller CORDE corpus;
(2) In the up-to-date CRAE database;
(3) Using the popular Google search engine (www.google.com) to search Spanish language texts on the web in November 2001; and
(4) Repeating the Google search in November 2003.

Clearly there are many variables that affect these figures, with the corpora differing vastly in size and composition. Nevertheless, such a search does suggest some hypotheses. First of all, it is unsurprising that the older CORDE corpus contains few instances of these new terms. Indeed, the 92 instances of curiosear are all with its older sense of browsing books, shops, and so on. There are 108 instances in the CRAE, but only four in the information technology domain. Of these four, only one (curiosear en un archivo 'to browse a folder') is actually used in relation to computing. Strangely, there is only one example of browsing in the CRAE, from a Colombian computing magazine of January 2003. However, using Google and the web as a kind of albeit disorganised supercorpus, 777 instances of browsing were found in Spanish texts in November 2001, including hacer offline browsing and the application of the term to other domains (hacer browsing en el dominio temporal). A trawl for <u>curiosear</u> brought up 2960 examples. Although some are the older 'browse a book/shop' category, many are related to websurfing (for example <u>curiosear en la WWW</u>). By 2003, the numbers had shot up hugely, with <u>browsing</u> far exceeding <u>curiosear</u>, though it should be noted that a good number of the documents are English-language texts. A far more detailed study needs to be undertaken before firm conclusions can be drawn, but even these very simple findings point to a competition between the two terms not registered by CRAE.

Similar conclusions can be drawn from the other search words. <u>Mail</u> does appear in the older CORDE corpus, but closer examination reveals it to be the compound <u>mail coach</u>. The updated 2003 CRAE shows 24 instances of <u>mail</u>. Of these ten are from 2003 and only six in total are from Spain. There are 295 examples of <u>e-mail</u> and 40 cases of the spelling <u>email</u>. Fourteen of the latter occur in a single work of fiction, Edmundo Paz Soldán's <u>La materia del deseo</u>, published in Bolivia in 2002, which illustrates how results based on very low numbers can be skewed by just one text. Interestingly enough, <u>correo electrónico</u> is much more common overall than <u>e-mail/email</u> or <u>mail</u> combined, with 1035 instances.

On the other hand, Google results paint a different overall picture, with <u>e-mail/email</u> being ten times more frequent than <u>correo electrónico</u> in 2001 and seven times more frequent in 2003. However, <u>correo electrónico</u> still has a strong and perhaps even increasing presence of some 1.11 million instances, including on more formal instructional websites, as is demonstrated in the following example on the US Robotics site for Spain:

> Envíe un mensaje por correo electrónico a un técnico del Departamento de Asistencia Técnica (http://www.usr-emea.com/ support/s-email-techie-span.asp?loc=span.
> 'Send a message by electronic mail to a technician in the Technical Assistance Department.'

Some evolution of the different terms is noticeable from the CRAE. One early instance, in an introductory computing book from 1993, introduces the English term in brackets after the Spanish:

> los servicios de correo electrónico (E-mail, en inglés)

Two years later, in an article about the global village ('<u>aldea global</u>') in the Madrid daily, *El Mundo*, we find '<u>e-mail</u>', in inverted commas, with no gloss in Spanish, an indication that it has gained currency.[6] On the other hand, in the same article the lesser-known term <u>chats</u> is added in brackets after the Spanish form <u>charlas</u> since it had yet to establish itself among the general public.

Because of the complexity of constructing and updating a representative corpus, not to mention the issues of the selection of texts and the inclusion of less formal language, it is perhaps not so surprising that the

CRAE is struggling to reflect some of the most recent developments at the IT interface. What is rather more concerning is that the Real Academia uses the corpus when deciding which new terms to include in its dictionary. It is therefore not focusing on some interesting neologisms, such as correo-e. This term occurs 45 times in the CRAE but around 393,000 times when using Google (up from 110,000 times in 2001). It retains the Spanish form, but imitates the creativity and flexibility of the English abbreviated form (cf. Crystal, 2001: 21). It will be interesting to continue to examine its progress to see if it becomes a competitor, first to correo electrónico and then to e-mail/email.

For some, of course, the fear is that the older established terms will be progressively eliminated by the new forms. Some academicians believe it is possible to arrest the flow of these changes. Thus, Odón Betanzos Palacios, director of the North American Academy in New York, attempts to locate current trends within an ongoing history of Spanish speaking in the southern states from the time of the conquest and colonisation. He considers the Spanish-speaking nations as 'illuminating lights' (focos iluminadores) for Spanish speakers in the United States (Agosto, 2001). Betanzos Palacios is particularly riled by the 'unnecessary' use of Anglicisms in new science. The reasons he gives for this use are affectedness, trendiness and plain silliness: 'people resort to the foreign language when we have the word in Spanish, better and more complete'.[7] Such opinions must surely be due more to political views than to a serious analysis of the phenomenon. The reference to 'better and more complete', in particular, is indicative of an attitude of linguistic cleansing which does not take into account the fluid and living organisms which languages are. In the contrary view of Ilán Stavans, 'fighting Spanglish under the guise of fighting 'gringo' imperialism is to fight a reality that is already inevitable'. Language change is evident in the related area of text messaging, where shortened forms are common, as is illustrated in the sample in Table 4.3:

Table 4.3 Examples of text message abbreviations in Spanish

full expression	*text message form*	*sense*
adiós	a2	good-bye
el	l	the
en	n	in
esto	sto	this
¡no tengo ni idea!	n tngo ni ida!	I've no idea
por	x	by, through, for
que	k or q	what, which, that
¿qué tal?	k tl? or q tal?	how are things?

These abbreviations reflect similar tendencies in other languages, namely the reduction in characters, especially vowels, and the creative use of the sounds of the letters and numbers where these can represent full words (Crystal, 2001: 230). The motives for these changes are money- and effort-oriented in that there are fewer characters to key in and send. But they also relate to the construction of a jargon that is inclusive to the group and exclusive to those who do not understand it. The result is an increased group identity but also a potentially huge shift in linguistic conventions. Diacritic marks along with many vowels are omitted. So too are initial exclamation and interrogation marks which are characteristic of Spanish, as, for example, in ¿qué tal? or ¡no tengo ni idea!

This kind of trend, where users are actively creating a language that is frowned upon by other users,[8] is likely to outstrip any government countermeasures. Yet there are political attempts in many countries to protect the Spanish language using legislation. Thus, castellano is protected as the official language of State in Spain's 1978 Constitution which also protects regional languages. In addition, there is legislation regarding advertising and dubbing in Argentina (Vázquez Villanueva & Vitale, 2001). The Argentine Broadcasting Bill of 1980 included an article 23 specific to the protection of castellano, requiring, for instance, that adverts be produced in Argentina, in castellano, with all foreign words translated unless they were brand names or 'in universal use'. Changes proposed in the 2001 Bill removed these restrictions, but required 75% of advertising to be produced in Argentina, and 100% whenever the national unemployment rate was 10% or higher. Interestingly enough, the Bill also attempts to protect the national film-dubbing industry by reducing duties paid on films and TV programmes where the soundtracks are professionally dubbed in Argentina. As Vázquez Villanueva & Vitale point out, this also serves to protect the Argentine variety of Spanish, an important consideration, since the fight is not only against English but also between competing varieties of Spanish.[9]

Globalisation has also presented Spain with new challenges that link language and economic power. The rise of the Spanish-speaking community around Miami is the prime example. Overriding the traditional rivalries between the two major cities in Spain, there are calls for Madrid to ally itself with Barcelona to defeat Miami in the war to be the capital of the Hispanic world (quoted in Romero & Valls, 2001). This is the war which looms over the current battle as the Spanish language seeks to defend itself against American English 'invasion' and Spanglish 'infection'. Yet the opportunities are also vast since Spanish is likely to become ever more prominent on the Internet; figures from Global Reach at March 2004 show Spanish to have overtaken German and to be almost on a par with Japanese with 9% of Internet traffic, with its creative users taking it beyond the protective confines of the Academies. In the end, the new technologies, far from 'fixing' the identity of the language, may well enable it to evolve and expand in ways unforeseen by its guardians.

Notes

1. In Spanish both español and castellano refer to the language, castellano ('Castilian') reflecting its origin as the variety spoken in Castile, the driving economic and military force in medieval Spain. However, Penny (1991: 24–5) and Mar-Molinero (2000: 35–9) discuss the differences implied by these terms in certain political and cultural contexts.
2. These are official figures used by the Instituto Cervantes in its publicity material in the UK.
3. In the original Spanish *es consolidarse, en las primeras décadas del siglo XXI, como segunda lengua internacional*.
4. 'Los lingüistas advierten de que la invasión actual es mayor y más infecciosa que nunca por su rápida expansión a través de Intenet. Al nuevo lenguaje que trae el mundo anglosajón de la mano de la tecnología y la nueva economía se une el fomento de la telefonía móvil. Abundan más signos que letras y más consonantes que vocales. Si antaño se aprendía inglés con los Beatles, ahora es con el *e-mail* y las *webs*, aunque, a diferencia de entonces, ahora no es seguro siquiera que ese inglés sea el correcto. La preocupación de la Real Academia de la Lengua por la pureza del idioma no es menor a la que tienen los lingüistas anglosajones por la dureza de la suya.'
5. 'Este tipo de fragmentaciones lingüísticas son innecesarias.'
6. Miravalls, J. La aldea global, El Mundo 27 December 1995.
7. 'Se recurre a la lengua extranjera cuando tenemos la voz en español, mejor y más completa.'
8. One of the most eagerly joined on-line debates at the Valladolid congress concerned the disappearance of the Spanish ñ character from the new technologies. Most respondents were dismayed at this, considering the ñ to be almost a symbol of Hispanic identity. See Trejo Delarbe (2001).
9. In Spain, castellano is of course competing with other languages too. The post-Franco Constitution of December 1978 designated Spain as an Estado de autonomías ('State of Autonomous regions') and the languages of the autonomous regions of Catalonia, Euskadi (the Basque Country) and Galicia enjoy equal status with castellano in their respective regions. In Hispanoamerica, Amerindian languages are struggling for recognition in a context where castellano is generally the prestige language.

References

Agosto, S.E. (2001) España e Hispanoamérica son focos iluminadores para los hispanos de EE.UU. www.unidaden/adiversidad.com/actualidad/ actualidad_ant/2001/octubre_01/actualidad_311001_01.htm, accessed 23 July 2004.

Alonso Piñeiro, A. (2001) Pobreza y riqueza del español en el tercer milenio, paper presented at the II Congreso Internacional de la Lengua Española, Valladolid.

Crystal, D. (2001) *Language and the Internet*. Cambridge: Cambridge University Press.

El español en el mundo: Anuario del Instituto Cervantes 2000. Madrid: Círculo de Lectores, Plaza & Janés, online at http://cvc.cervantes.es/obref/anuario/ anuario_00/

El País (Digital) Premio al patrimonio común de 400 millones de personas, www.elpais.es, 7 September 2000.

El País (Digital) Directores de 31 diarios discuten sobre el futuro del castellano, www.elpais.es, 15 November 2000.

El País (Digital) (2001) Internet y los móviles aceleran los cambios en el lenguaje, *Ciberpaís, www.elpais.es*, 4 January 2001.

García Yebra, T. (2003) Jon Juaristi rechaza las distintas versiones en español del próximo libro de Harry Potter. *Heraldo de Aragón* 17 October 2003.

López, J.M. (2000) Español: Nuestro idioma todavía suspende. *El Mundo (suplemento Ariadna)* 26 October 2000.

Marcos Marín, F. (2001) El español, segunda lengua internacional. *La Razón*, 12 January 2001.

Mar-Molinero, C. (2000) *The Politics of Language in the Spanish-Speaking World*. London and New York: Routledge.

Mora, M. (2000) El Cervantes certifica que el español avanza como segunda lengua en EE.UU. *El País (Digital), www.elpais.es* 6 July 2000.

Penny, R. (1991) *A History of the Spanish Language*. Cambridge: Cambridge University Press.

Pozzi, S. (2000) Los europeos ven el español como una de las lenguas más útiles. *El País (Digital)* 9 July 2000.

Roca, A. (ed.) (2000) Research on Spanish in the United States: Linguistic Issues and Challenges. Somerville, MA: Cascadilla.

Romero, J.M. and Valls, F. (2001) Madrid y Cataluña, frente a frente, *El País (Digital)* 13 May 2001.

Segura, J. (1998), El DRAE y obras recientes de la Academia Española de la Lengua, *Apuntes*, www.intrades.org/translation/articles/artvol6no3.draeobrasrae.htm accessed 23 July 2004.

Silva Corvalán, C. (1994) *Language Contact and Change: Spanish in Los Angeles*. Clarendon: Oxford.

Silva Corvalán, C. (ed.) (1995) *Spanish in Four Continents: Studies in language. contact and bilingualism*. Washington D.C.: Georgetown Univ. Press.

Silva Corvalán, C. (2000) La situación del español en Estados Unidos. In *El español en el mundo: Anuario del Instituto Cervantes 2000*, cvc.cervantes.es/obref/anuario/anuario_00/silva/, accessed 23 July 2004.

Stavans, I. (2001a) *The Sounds of Spanglish: an illustrated lexicon*. New York: Basic Books.

Stavans, I. (2001b) Webeando, *www.cuadernoscervantes.com/art_33_webeando.html*, accessed 23 July 2004.

Stavans, I. (2003) 'Spanglish: The making of a new American language'. New York: Rayo.

Trejo Delarbe, R. (2001) La 'ñ' en la Sociedad de la Información: Internet y el español. Tendencias y preocupaciones, paper presented at the II Congreso Internacional de la Lengua Española, Valladolid, *cvc.cervantes.es/obref/congresos/valladolid/ponencias/el_espanol_en_la_sociedad/4_internet_en_espanol/trejo_r.htm*, accessed 24 July 2004.

Valenzuela, J. (2000) Una Universidad de Massachusetts crea la primera cátedra mundial de 'spanglish'. *El País (Digital)*, www.elpais.es 3 September 2000.

Vázquez Villanueva, G. and Vitale, M.A. (2001) La(s) lengua(s) y el fomento de la industria cultural: el Proyecto de Ley de Radiodifusión 2001, Argentina, *www.comfer.gov.ar/publi/pdf/laslenguas.pdf,* accessed 23 July 2004.

Chapter 5
The Influence of English on Italian: The Case of Translations of Economics Articles

MARIA TERESA MUSACCHIO

In linguistics the influence of one language over another language is generally studied with reference to borrowing, a term used to designate both the process of incorporation of units from another language and its result. Borrowings range from stems and words – or loan words – to phrases and as such involve aspects of linguistic structures like phonetics and/or phonology, morphology and lexical semantics (Heath, 1994: 383). But it is perhaps as part of lexis that borrowings are more noticeable when they make their way into a language. In the last fifty years English has replaced French as the most widely known and most influential foreign language in Italy. In particular, it has influenced Italian lexis in fields such as business and economics, science, technology and more generally in popular culture (Dardano, 1993: 350–1). The influence of a language in terms of syntax is more difficult to trace (Stammerjohann, 2003: 78–9) because syntactic loans often consist of words which are bound in a fixed phrase whereas real syntactic borrowing implies the transfer of 'productive' constructs. As to syntactic loans in Italian, a general consensus seems to have been reached among linguists that on close inspection syntactic loan constructs often turn out to be pre-existing Italian constructs which become more widely used as a consequence of contact with a foreign language. In Italian typical examples are cleft sentences such as *è con grande piacere che* . . . (it is with great pleasure that . . .), which are traditionally regarded as syntactic loans from French, though their usage has expanded because they rely on already existing Italian constructs (Benincà, 1993: 284–5).

In translation a broader influence of a language over another is encountered as it extends beyond lexical borrowing and syntactic loan. Investigations into the complex process of discourse transfer in translation have led researchers to hypothesise that translating goes as far as to create a 'third code' having its own standards, though derived from source and target languages (Frawley, 1984: 169). On a more positive note,

Baker (1993: 232–3) stresses the value of translations as genuine communicative events which shape our experience of life and our view of the
world in the most diverse fields of language use ranging from politics to
art and literature. The existence of features considered common to all
types of translated texts has been tentatively suggested. These by-
products of the process of translating are often referred to as 'translation
universals'. Baker (1993: 243–5) indicates six features which might belong
to this category:

(1) explicitation, i.e. a rise in the level of explicitness compared to
     specific source texts and to original texts in general;
(2) a tendency towards disambiguation and simplification;
(3) normalisation as preference for conventional 'grammaticality';
(4) a tendency to avoid repetition through rephrasing;
(5) naturalisation as a tendency to exaggerate features of the target
     language;
(6) a specific distribution of certain features in target texts compared to
     source texts and original texts in the target language.

Pursuing the idea of translation universals, Toury (1995: 275) has gone
even further, suggesting that translators tend to produce a target text not
by retrieving the target language through their own knowledge of the language, but directly from the source text. Based on this intuition, Toury has
posited the existence of two probabilistic laws of translation, the law of
growing standardisation and the law of source-language interference.
Discussion about these laws (Toury, 1995: 267–79) provides valuable
insights into the process of translating, especially as it helps to explore the
boundaries of acceptability of translations as naturally sounding target-
language originals. Though in translation they are used to describe rather
than evaluate, terms such as 'interference' or 'third code' have inherently
negative connotations. In this respect influence seems a more appropriate
designation of what happens during discourse transfer from one language to another as it can include cases in which translation enriches the
target language and culture.

Method

A parallel/comparable corpus of articles has been specially collected[1]
to investigate the influence of English on Italian in the field of business
and economics. The corpus therefore comprises original English texts,
their translations (i.e. parallel texts), and original Italian texts (i.e. comparable texts). In building the corpus an attempt has been made to reconcile
two conflicting aims – choice of a special language for its more easily
identifiable terminology and phraseology, and selection of texts directed
at as wide a readership as possible within the field of business and

economics. As noted above, English is said to influence Italian especially in business and economics, science, technology, popular culture and their special languages. Texts to be included in the corpus have been selected from one of these areas, business and economics. A further consideration in corpus development concerns what translations are most suitable for this kind of investigation within the range of genres that are actually translated. Though evaluation in this area may be problematic as no industry-wide studies are available, journal articles have been excluded since Italian economists mainly write in English nowadays and address a more limited number of readers. University textbooks have also been ruled out because they, too, are aimed at a restricted readership. In the end, translations of English economics articles published in an Italian magazine and in a special supplement of an Italian daily have been selected for inclusion in the corpus. Fifteen articles were taken from *The World in 2001, 2002* and *2003*, publications issued by *The Economist* towards the end of each year and containing forecasts of the economic situation in the following year. Since 2000, a selection of *The World in . . .* publications has been issued in a special supplement of the Italian daily *La Stampa*. Eight more articles were taken from various issues of *The Economist* as their translation was published in a new Italian business weekly, *Economy*. Besides these parallel texts, the corpus also includes a comparable component consisting of twenty business and economics articles taken from the Italian daily *Corriere della Sera*, its business and economics supplement *CorrierEconomia* and the financial newspaper *Sole 24 Ore*. Nine other articles whose contents were similar to the translated ones have been taken from the magazine *Economy*. The original English component of the corpus is 32,579 tokens, the parallel Italian component is 35,386 tokens and the comparable Italian one is 34,580. Corpus composition is summarised in Table 5.1 below.

General corpus features such as text and sentence length are first analysed to identify a possible influence of English over Italian at macro level. Then the corpus is studied at micro level to detect the influence of English with reference to lexis, syntax and the categories identified by Baker – except for naturalisation, which by definition excludes the possibility of the influence of a foreign language. The hypothesis to be tested is to what extent language contact in translating affects target text production beyond lexical borrowing to take the form of the transfer of patterns such as syntactic constructs, reproduction of source text repetition and cohesion.

First, considering that Italian is generally regarded as a language using longer sentences and a more complex, hypotactic sentence structure than English, the parallel/comparable texts have been analysed using *WordSmith Tools* software to investigate the length in relation to the number of words or tokens, as well as sentence length and to extract loan words. Secondly, borrowing from English is studied in the parallel texts and contrasted with the comparable texts to trace not only loan words, but also the influence on word formation through compounding and derivation. Thirdly, categories identified by Baker are investigated by comparing source and target texts and contrasting them with Italian originals. Categories such as repetitions and cohesive devices which were partly amenable to machine analysis have been investigated using the *WordSmith Tools* concordancer. Results are also compared with data from a corpus of economics jointly developed by the University of Surrey and the University of Trieste comprising different genres from the corpus discussed here.[2] Finally, some conclusions on the influence of English on Italian are drawn on the basis of the quantitative and qualitative analysis outlined.

Analysis

An analysis of text and sentence length can give an idea of the influence of the source language on the target language as translations can attempt to reproduce source-language structure (Baumgarten et al., 2004). General data emerging from the corpus in Table 5.1 suggest that translations into Italian tend to be longer than English originals. In the case of the *Economy* magazine, translations are approximately 15% longer than the source texts despite occasional deletions of sentences in the translations. Translations in the *La Stampa* supplement are only marginally longer (0.6%), partly as a result of more substantial deletions and partly as a consequence of a closer rendering of originals.

Table 5.1 A parallel/comparable corpus of economics articles (English/Italian)

	Parallel sub-corpus				*Comparable sub-corpus*	
	English originals	*Italian translations*	*English originals*	*Italian translations*	*Italian originals*	
	The Economist 2003	Economy translated articles 2003	The World in 2001, 2002, 2003	Il mondo nel 2001, 2002, 2003 LaStampa	Comparable Economy articles	Comparable newspaper articles
No. of articles	8	8	15	15	9	20
Tokens	16,902	19,605	15,677	15,781	15,691	18,889
Sentence length	23.11	22.74	20.09	24.87	22.03	30.25

Analysis of sentence length provides even more mixed results. Contrary to expectations, translated texts in *Economy* have slightly shorter sentences than English. Comparisons between source texts and target texts show, however, that the original English sentences are frequently joined in Italian translation by coordination or subordination to reflect the Italian preference for longer and more complex sentences. Sentence length in the Italian press has reduced from an average of 35 words in the 1950s to 20 to 25 in the last decade (Bonomi, 2002: 249). Analysis is confirmed by sentence length in the comparable *Economy* corpus (a 22-word average per sentence). It could be argued that this trend in the Italian press is at least partly a result of the success of British and American journalism as a model for news reporting, and that translations in the corpus reflect this trend. Furthermore, translations alternate longer, complex sentences with short ones to achieve marked effects of contrast that are typical of news reporting. Another distinctive feature of the press that is reproduced in the translations is the introduction of short headings summarising contents of article sections (Bonomi, 2002: 228). Table 5.1 also shows that sentences are longer than their corresponding originals in the Italian translations of articles from *The World in 2001*, *The World in 2002* and *The World in 2003* – 24.87 compared to 20.09 – though not as long as in comparable Italian newspaper articles (30.25). This may indicate a more marked influence of the source texts. Analysis of the Surrey-Trieste corpus of economics shows that the average sentence length is 37, pointing to a completely different concept in text composition of official reports and speeches.

In conclusion, quantitative analysis of the corpus indicates that there may be some kind of influence of English originals on Italian translations which may be worth investigating further.

Lexis

In terms of influence of one language over another, Italian can be regarded as one of the main transformations of Latin. Its lexis largely derives from Latin (66.8%) though over the centuries Italian has been influenced by other European languages, most notably French in the eighteenth century. With regard to lexis, the contribution of English to Italian was only 0.7% in the 1990s – compared to 7.8% from French (Marazzini, 1994: 418). In twentieth century Italian, however, English replaced French as the source of the majority of foreign words. A comparison of word origins in two recent Italian general language dictionaries, DISC (1997) and De Mauro (2000), shows that the rise of English parallels the demise of Latin – and later French – as a source of new words in Italian. Similar data are found by comparing the origins of economic vocabulary in the two dictionaries (Table 5.2) over the last three centuries.[3] Though the number of loans in the two dictionaries varies as a function of the number of terms each of them included for the fields of business and economics, the increase in English economic terms coincides with the decrease in the number of terms of French origin. In these fields the influence of other languages has always been negligible, as the example of German in Table 5.2 clearly shows.

Table 5.2　Loan words in the domain of economics according to two Italian dictionaries, DISC and De Mauro

Language	*English*		*French*		*German*		*Latin*	
Period	DISC	DeM	DISC	DeM	DISC	DeM	DISC	DeM
1901–2000	133	52	27	32	1	1	12	8
1801–1900	8	16	27	45	1	2	20	16
1701–1800	4	5	12	18	0	0	10	7

Legend: DeM = De Mauro

In the parallel and comparable texts, the highest number of borrowings is to be found in the comparable *Economy* sub-corpus (Table 5.3). Today, most English words enter the Italian language as loan words rather than loan translations (Dardano, 1993: 351). However, in the parallel component of the corpus the percentage of borrowings is lower than in the comparable component. In the Surrey-Trieste corpus the percentage of borrowings is lowest as the policy of both the Bank of Italy and ISTAT is to avoid loan words in economic reports and speeches unless there are no equivalents in Italian.

Table 5.3　Occurrences of English borrowings (economic terms)

	Economy translations 2003	*Il mondo nel* 2001–3 *La Stampa*	Comparable *Economy* articles	Comparable newspaper articles	Surrey-Trieste corpus
Tokens	19,605	15,781	15,691	18,889	187,680
Occurrences	59	43	134	68	202
Percentage	0.301%	0.272%	0.854%	0.360%	0.108%

In both parallel and comparable parts of the corpus and in the Surrey-Trieste corpus most borrowings are either single-word or compound terms. Occurrences of hybrids, that is compounds formed by Italian and English components, show that in business and economics traditional Italian word formation consisting of word + preposition + word still prevails over the English model based on the juxtaposition of words: *agenzie di rating, società di outsourcing, trading dei derivati, bond a tasso variabile, duration del portafoglio.* Whenever juxtaposition is used, it takes the typical Italian form of post-modification rather than the English pre-modification pattern: *direttore marketing, personale off-shore.* Greater productivity of borrowings can be seen in noun + adjective compound terms where one or more components are Italian and the other ones are English: *leasing finanziari, obbligazioni corporate, bond governativi, depositi overnight, centri finanziari off-shore, depositi bancari cross-border.*

In the parallel component of the corpus another direct influence of English can be seen in loan translations ranging from single words to phraseology. In the example below the English adjective *global* is translated as *globale* in Italian. However, *globale* in Italian means (1) general, cumulative, or (2) relating to the whole globe (DISC, 1997: 1088) seen as a sphere and not 'relating to the whole world' as *global* in English. This additional meaning has made its way into Italian, as *globale* is now also regarded as an adjective deriving from *globalisation* ⟶ *globalizzazione.* It should be noted, though, that *globalizzazione* is another loan translation from English; in French the term was 'Frenchified' as *mondialisation* using a Latin stem for word formation.

Deflation is a *global concern*. (*The Economist, 28* June 2003: 26)
La deflazione è una *preoccupazione globale*. (*Economy,* 17 luglio 2003: 58)[4]

Other loan translations are translations of false friends. In the following sentence the adverb *virtually* is rendered as *virtualmente* in Italian. In English *virtually* is defined as 'in effect though not in fact; practically; nearly' (Collins, 1994: 1714) whereas in Italian *virtualmente* has two meanings: (a) theoretically, hypothetically; (b) almost certainly (DISC, 1997: 2938). In economics, hedges – divided into the two categories of approximators and shields – play a central role as they highlight degrees of certainty (approximators) or speaker's commitment to the truth value of statements (shields) (Bloor & Bloor, 1993: 153–4). As can be seen, the loan translation alters the meaning of the sentence because *virtually* is used as an approximator-type of hedge in English, whereas in Italian *virtualmente* is a shield-type of hedge. In economic argumentation these are major changes, especially – as is the case in the sentence below – when they alter economic forecasts, an area in which economists are extremely careful in their wording of sentences lest they put their reputation at risk (Merlini Barbaresi, 1996: 82):

> Its [Germany's] growth over the past three years has been even slower than Japan's, and it is tipped to see *virtually* no growth this year. (*The Economist*, 28 June 2003: 26)

> . . . il suo sviluppo negli ultimi tre anni è stato addirittura più lento di quello del Giappone, e quest'anno è *virtualmente* destinata a non avere alcuna crescita . . . (*Economy*, 17 luglio 2003: 58)

Loan translations of sub-technical vocabulary, i.e. vocabulary that is common to more than one special language (Trimble, 1985: 129), are also found in the parallel component of the corpus. In the example below, the verb *supportare* is a loan translation from English:

> One reason for hoping that America will avoid deflation is a weaker dollar, which will *support exports* and boost import prices. (*The Economist*, 28 June 2003: 26)

> La speranza che l'America possa evitare la deflazione è legata a un dollaro più debole, che *supporti le esportazioni* e aumenti i prezzi di importazione. (*Economy*, 17 luglio 2003: 58)

Collocations of sub-technical vocabulary can also give rise to loan translations. In the example below, the collocation *evidence suggests* belongs to the language of scientific argumentation which cuts across disciplines. Increasingly, this type of language is rendered in Italian through loan translations:

> China's growth may be patchy, localised and exaggerated. But all *evidence of the senses suggests* that it is far faster than India's. (*The Economist*, 21 June 2003: 59)

> La crescita cinese potrà sembrare incoerente, localizzata ed esagerata, ma l'*evidenza suggerisce* che è di gran lunga più rapida rispetto a quella dei vicini. (*Economy*, 10 luglio 2003: 71)

The examples show that similar words exist in Italian though they have different meanings. As a consequence of loan translation, Italian words take on new meanings and give rise to new collocations when used in combination. However, the process can only be tested over long periods of time; in individual translations the value of innovations of this kind has to be measured against considerations of intelligibility and pragmatic effect.

Explicitation

Research in explicitation has been extensive in Translation Studies since the 1960s. According to Nida (1964) explicitation is part of the adjustments that occur in translating and takes the form of additions of which several categories can be identified: filling out elliptical expressions, obligatory specification, addition required because of grammatical restructuring, amplification from implicit to explicit status, answers to rhetorical questions, classifiers, connectives, categories of the target language which do not exist in the source language, and doublets. In the parallel component of the corpus, addition of information can be a consequence of foreign terms or words being used in the text and for which an explanation is felt to be necessary. This is the case in the following sentence, where *core rate* is borrowed in the Italian translation, but an explanation of the term is considered necessary:

> Preliminary figures suggest that Germany's inflation rate rose to 1.0% in June, but its core rate is still falling. (*The Economist*, 28 June 2003: 26)

> Secondo i primi dati, a Berlino il tasso d'inflazione ha raggiunto l'1% in giugno, ma il *'core rate' – ovvero il tasso al netto di alimentari ed energia* – continua a diminuire. (*Economy*, 17 luglio 2003: 58)

Even when a term is literally translated, an explanation may be considered advisable, as in the following example, in which *repeat sales* is translated as *vendite ripetute*:

> They found, by logging *repeat sales* of almost 5,000 paintings sold at public auctions from 1875 to now, that in the very long term equities outperform art. (*The Economist*, 23 August 2003: 51)

> Studiando *le vendite ripetute (cioè ogni dipinto inserito nell'indice era stato ceduto almeno un'altra volta in precedenza)* di quasi 5 mila quadri collocati tramite aste pubbliche dal 1875 a oggi, Moses e Mei hanno scoperto che, nel lunghissimo termine, le azioni hanno rese migliori dell'arte. (*Economy*, 11 settembre 2003: 57)

Discourse-level explicitation was studied by Blum-Kulka (1986) with reference to shifts of cohesion and coherence. Shifts of cohesion can be dictated by different grammatical systems of languages and different text-building strategies; they include shifts in the level of explicitness of cohesive relationships and differences in stylistic preferences for types of cohesive markers. Shifts of coherence can be reader focused and text focused. Reader focused shifts reflect changes in the possible world evoked and/or presupposed by the text and as such will be dealt with under disambiguation. Text focused shifts are linked to the process of translating and are the underlying theme of this chapter.

English frequently uses juxtaposition of sentences while Italian prefers a more Latinate prose where links between sentences are explicit:

> Many economists predict that growth will rebound to 3.5–4% in the second half. The Fed's latest cut is simply insurance against the risk of deflation. (*The Economist*, 28 June 2003: 25)

Molti economisti prevedono che la ripresa raggiungerà il 3,5–4% nella seconda metà. L'ultimo taglio della Fed, *quindi*, rappresenta solo una garanzia contro il rischio della deflazione. (*Economy*, 17 luglio 2003: 57)

In the last decade, shorter sentences in the Italian press have meant that juxtaposition of sentences is more common and that implicit subordinate clauses are preferred to explicit ones whenever possible (Bonomi, 2002: 252). Again, it can be argued that this development is at least partly a reflection of the influence of the English and American press as models coming from what are considered highly prestigious cultures especially as regards business and economics.

As Table 5.4 shows, the influence of English in the parallel component of the corpus can be traced in the different frequencies of some subordinating and coordinating conjunctions when they are contrasted with data from the comparable component. Translations make more extensive use of coordinators such as *ma* ('but') or *tuttavia* ('however, yet, still') or *così* ('so, thus') than comparable original Italian texts. Some coordinators such as the adversative *invece* ('whereas, instead, on the contrary, conversely, but') and the conclusive *dunque* and *infatti* ('hence, therefore, as a matter of fact') are more frequent in the comparable component. The causal subordinator *perché* ('because') is used much less extensively in the translations than in the original Italian texts, while the concessive *per quanto* ('however, no matter') is more frequent. Some particular examples are discussed below.

Table 5.4 Occurrences of coordinating and subordinating conjunctions creating cohesion in Italian translations (parallel texts) and original texts (comparable texts)

	Italian Translations		*Italian Original Texts*	
	Economy 2003	*Il mondo nel 2001, 2002, 2003 La Stampa*	*Economy articles*	*Newspaper articles*
ma	97	83	68	68
tuttavia	24	22	3	8
dunque	3	1	10	10
infatti	13	1	20	26
invece	16	8	19	25
così	28	14	39	26
perché	13	15	39	26
per quanto	5	12	1	0

Cohesive devices can be introduced in translation to summarise what was outlined in the previous part of the text or sentence and before proceeding with the argument. This is the function of *a questo proposito* ('with regard to this') in the following example:

> There is some evidence to show that these institutions are worse at evaluating and managing credit risk: in the three years to 2003, non-bank financial instititutions took an increasing share of syndicated bank loans. (*The Economist*, 16 August 2003: 51)

> *A questo proposito,* alcuni dati dimostrano che le istituzioni finanziarie non bancarie hanno minori capacità di valutazione e di gestione del rischio creditizio: alla fine del 2002, queste società avevano in portafoglio il 10% dei mutui sindacati negli Stati Uniti. (*Economy*, 4 settembre 2003: 63)

Similarly, a phrase can be added to give the reason behind a fact (*e per questo* ⟶ and this is why):

> Some of the world's top bankers are currently asking regulators to look again at the potentially perverse consequences of these new capital rules. (*The Economist*, 16 August 2003: 52)

> *E per questo* alcuni dei più importanti banchieri internazionali hanno chiesto ai legislatori di riconsiderare le conseguenze potenzialmente inique delle nuove norme sul capitale. (*Economy*, 4 settembre 2003: 64)

The traditionally long, complex structure of Italian sentences is reinstated when *mentre* ('while', 'whilst') is used and an English phrase ('China's twice as fast') is turned into an explicit subordinate clause:

> In the ten years from 1992, India's GDP per head grew at 4.3% a year, *China's twice as fast*. (*The Economist*, 21 June 2003: 57)

> Nei dieci anni successivi al 1992, il Prodotto interno lordo (Pil) pro capite in India è aumentato del 4,3% annuo, *mentre il tasso di crescita in Cina è stato il doppio*. (*Economy*, 10 luglio 2003: 68)

A link can be introduced even after paragraphing has been altered in the translation to add a heading, as is the case with *intanto* ('in the meantime') in the example below:

> American consumer spending has outpaced the rest by an even bigger margin, growing at an annual rate of 3%, compared with 0.8% in Germany and 1.3% in Japan. *Europe* is on the brink of recession. (*The Economist*, 28 June 2003: 26)

> Le spese dei consumatori americani hanno superato quelle degli altri Paesi di un margine anche maggiore, con un incremento pari a a un

> tasso annuo del 3%, contro lo 0,8% della Germania e l'1,3% del Giappone. **La Germania è bloccata.** _Intanto_ l'Europa è sull'orlo della recessione. (_Economy_, 17 luglio 2003: 58)

A trade-off between explicitation – which is said to be typical of translation – and conciseness demanded by current Italian news reporting is achieved by replacing English parataxis with Italian hypotaxis where the subordinating clause is made implicit using the gerund _portando_. Genre conventions are also complied with in the use of a multi-purpose verb, _portare_ (here: 'lead to'), and nominalisation – the verb _slow_ is rendered by the noun _rallentamento_ ('slowdown').

> Much of the recent run-up in share prices appears to be betting on a sharp recovery in corporate profits. If that fails to happen, share prices may slump _and the pace of mergers slow_. (The _Economist_, 12 July 2003: 58)

> Gran parte dell'impulso alla crescita dei listini azionari sembra basarsi su una netta ripresa degli utili societari, ma se la previsione verrà smentita, i titoli potrebbero crollare, _portando a un rallentamento dell'ondata di fusioni_. (_Economy_, 31 luglio 2003: 54)

In short, with regard to explicitation, the influence of English can be traced directly in a different use of some cohesive markers compared to their use in original Italian articles and indirectly in the notion that English is more concise and prefers juxtaposition of sentences – a problem that somehow needs to be 'remedied' in Italian translations. A limit on the use of cohesive markers in English-Italian translation of business and economics can be found in the translators' reluctance to introduce linkages between sentences that might lead to an incorrect interpretation of the text when they are not sure what the best cohesive marker is and cannot check with an expert.

Disambiguation and simplification

Disambiguation and simplification are strategies used in translation to clarify possibly ambiguous references or when syntax is deemed to be too complex to be rendered smoothly in the target language. The need for disambiguation can also originate from differences between cultures and as such constitutes a shift of coherence in Blum-Kulka's sense (1986). In the following example _Richemont_ is supposed to be part of shared knowledge in English, but not in Italian where the name of a famous subsidiary – Cartier – was added. On the contrary, Cerruti is supposed to be known to the Italian readership whereas the parent company is not – this is therefore the information that is made explicit in the translation:

Switzerland's _Richemont_ recently gave warning that, after a one-fifth fall in profits in the year to March, sales in April and May had fallen by over 20%. The auditing firm KPMG recently refused to certify the accounts of _the parent of Cerruti, an Italian label,_ due to mounting losses and crippling debts. (*The Economist,* 5 July 2003: 63)

La svizzera _Richemont, nota per il marchio di gioielleria Cartier,_ ha appena annunciato che, dopo un calo di un quinto negli utili dell'esercizio chiuso a marzo, le vendite di aprile e maggio sono scese ancora di oltre il 20%. La società di revisione Kpmg qualche tempo fa ha negato la certificazione dei conti alla _Finpart, che controlla anche Cerruti,_ a causa delle crescenti perdite e del pesante indebitamento. (*Economy,* 24 luglio 2003: 58)

The easiest form of simplification in the process of translating is omission. Clearly, cuts in published translations are often the result of editorial decisions taken on grounds of required text length. However, omission can sometimes be the consequence of a translator's choice on the basis of pragmatic considerations. It can be argued that in such cases omission is the product of an indirect influence of the source language and culture. The excerpt below is one of many examples in the translations published by the Italian magazine *Economy* where the omission seems to follow from the pragmatic consideration that – particularly in business – English is a slightly 'lower context culture' than Italian (Victor, 1992: 183). Thus in English arguments are provided and conclusions are drawn; in this case, in Italian, conclusions are deemed to be obvious and as such are omitted to avoid information redundancy:

A report commissioned by the Confederation of Indian Industry, a national lobby organisation, sought to explode what it said were five widespread Indian myths about China: that its growth stems entirely from investment, not improvements in productivity; that manufacturing is driven primarily by exports; that low Chinese prices are the result of flawed accounting; that exports are priced more or less at cost; and that Chinese products are shoddy. _Indian industry, it seems, suffers from a curious mixture of panic and complacency about China._

The report found that neither is justified. It explains lower Chinese prices largely in terms of a tedious accumulation of minor cost disadvantages borne by Indian industry (see chart 2 on previous page). (*The Economist,* 21 June 2003: 59)

Un rapporto commissionato dalla Confindustria indiana, una lobby a livello nazionale, ha cercato di distruggere quelli che considerava i cinque miti sulla Cina: la crescita cinese ha origine interamente dagli investimenti, non dall'ottimizzazione della produttività; l'industria manifatturiera è alimentata soprattutto dalle esportazioni; i prezzi bassi sono il risultato di una contabilità carente; il valore dell'esportazione è pressoché equivalente ai costi; i prodotti cinesi sono scadenti.

Il rapporto ha però rilevato che nessuno di questi fattori è sufficiente e spiega, in larga misura, i prezzi più contenuti della Cina adducendo una serie di condizioni sfavorevoli nei costi secondari che penalizzano l'industria indiana. (*Economy*, 10 luglio 2003: 71)

Similarly, English hedging can be altered or eliminated in translation – apparently because in English there is a tendency to understate, in Italian to overstate (Katan, 1999: 223–6). In a way, this amounts to simplification as it implies the alteration or omission of parts of the original text. In the following example *have done much less* is rendered rather bluntly as *non hanno voluto* ('did not want'):

Households *have done much less* than firms to repair their balance sheets. (*The Economist*, 28 June 2003: 26)

I nuclei familiari *non hanno voluto* riassestare i loro bilanci. (*Economy*, 17 luglio 2003: 58)

From a pragmatic point of view, though, hedging is an important feature of special languages as it is used to modify claims. As such hedges cannot be altered or omitted without subtly changing the meaning of the message.[5] In the example below, the shield *may* is translated, but *appear* is rendered as *essere* ('be'), and the sentence between dashes which serves to qualify the statement – and is thus a sort of extended hedge – is omitted altogether. As a consequence, the careful hedging of the original is lost in translation and the original author's speculation is turned into fact:

The official 2.25% to 2.75% growth range which the Treasury uses for budget planning – *and will shade down only slightly in its 2002 forecasts* – *may*, for a while, *appear* to be out of sight. (Kaletsky, 2001: 40)

Il tasso del 2,25%–2,75% che il Cancelliere dello Scacchiere utilizza per la pianificazione del bilancio *potrebbe* per il momento *essere* fuori portata. (Kaletsky, 27 dicembre 2001: 14)

The opposite strategy is often adopted in the translation of informative texts such as magazine articles from English into Italian when the original English structure is considered too simple to sound natural in Italian. However, the trend towards shorter sentences in the Italian press has meant that an increasing number of short English sentences are more closely rendered in Italian – in many cases to create a sharp contrast between two different sections of a text as in the example below:

The fund sold most of its art portfolio in the late 1980s, doing reasonably well with a return on its investment of 11.3% compound to December 1999.

That was then. Because information and transparency are the stuff of liquid markets, today's investors may not have to invest for quite so long a term. (*The Economist*, 23 August 2003: 51)

Dalla vendita di questo patrimonio, avvenuta alla fine degli anni 80, il fondo ha tratto un buon ritorno, pari all'11,3% composto annuo.

Quelli, tuttavia, erano altri tempi. Dato che informazione e trasparenza sono l'essenza dei mercati liquidi, gli investitori attuali possono evitare gli investimenti così a lungo termine, . . . (*Economy*, 11 settembre 2003: 57)

Changing conventions in the press (Bonomi, 2002) are beginning to affect strategies for disambiguation and simplification in English-Italian translation.

Normalisation

Normalisation is the tendency to stick to conventional grammar and standard language in translation. Linguistic research shows that the representation of information is language-specific and that there are language-specific focus-attributing positions within the syntactic structure of sentences (Doherty, 1997a; 1997b). In English, right-branching clauses are easiest to comprehend, whereas extensive clause embedding renders sentences awkward if the clauses are in initial position, where their length and complexity may go against the principle of end-weight (Quirk *et al.*, 1985: 49–52). In Italian this principle also applies, as the most important information is usually found at the end of the sentence (Benincà *et al.*, 1991: 121). However, sentence constituents can also be extracted and moved to the initial position of the sentence in a sort of 'free zone' (Benincà, 1993: 255) in order to reduce structural weight. Pragmatically, normalisation of syntax is useful when it balances sentence structure and enhances sentence flow without affecting focus. Another form of normalisation is lexical in that translators – especially in technical and scientific texts – tend to normalise creative language. However, the opposite strategy may also be applied to replicate syntactic structure or render standard phraseology closely. Again, the viability of this strategy can best be assessed in terms of pragmatic effect.

In the following example, the Italian translation is normalised in the sense that peripheral information (*in a speech in May*) is placed at the beginning of the sentence. The structural weight of the sentence is also balanced by promoting *financial sector* to subject in Italian, so that the long

English subject can be moved to the free zone on the left of the sentence and act as peripheral information (*this spreading of the banks' risks* —▶ *grazie alla ripartizione dei rischi delle banche*). The theme appearing in a non-sentence-initial position is occurring with increasing frequency in the Italian press (Bonomi, 2002: 238).

> Alan Greenspan, chairman of America's Federal Reserve, said *in a speech in May* that *this spreading of the banks' risks* has made the financial sector more resilient, and individual institutions within it less vulnerable to shocks. (*The Economist*, 16 August 2003: 51)

> *E in occasione di un discorso tenuto lo scorso maggio*, Alan Greenspan, presidente della Federal reserve, ha dichiarato che, *grazie alla ripartizione dei rischi delle banche*, il settore finanziario è diventato più forte e le singole istituzioni che lo compongono ora sono meno vulnerabili agli choc. (*Economy*, 4 settembre 2003: 62)

English juxtaposition of sentences or clauses – parataxis – can be normalised in Italian as hypotaxis:

> Foreign observers have tended to view weak GNP growth as evidence of *stagnation; they have not seen* the many welcome changes in the economy, whose benign first effects are to cause it to contract. (Tasker, 2001: 59)

> Gli osservatori stranieri hanno visto nella debole crescita del Pil la prova della *stagnazione economica del paese, senza considerare* i numerosi e positivi cambiamenti che hanno come primo effetto una contrazione dell'economia. (Tasker, 27 dicembre 2001: 22)

Further, normalisation in Italian frequently entails subject-verb inversion (*the dollar needs . . .* —▶ *è necessaria una svalutazione . . .; as many manufactures have learned* —▶ *come hanno imparato molti produttori*) thus creating a marked structure which, however, is more usual in Italian, and enhances sentence flow and rhythm:

> To correct America's massive current-account deficit, *the dollar needs* to become cheaper still; because many of its biggest trading partners, such as Japan and China, are resisting a rise in their currencies, this means it will have to fall further against the euro. (*The Economist*, 28 June 2003: 26)

> Per rettificare il forte deficit delle partite correnti esistente in America, *è necessaria* un'ulteriore svalutazione del dollaro. Poiché molti dei maggiori partner commerciali degli Stati Uniti, come il Giappone e la Cina, resistono a un rialzo delle proprie valute, sarà necessario che il dollaro venga svalutato ancora rispetto all'euro. (*Economy*, 24 luglio 2003: 60)

Then:

> In a world of benign deflation companies can remain profitable, as *many manufacturers* have learned over the past decade. (McRae, 2002 : 123)

> In un mondo di deflazione benigna, le aziende possono continuare ad essere redditizie, come hanno imparato *molti produttori* nello scorso decennio. (McRae, 23 dicembre 2002: 35)

In other cases, the build-up of suspense created in English by placing peripheral information at the beginning of the sentence is normalised to the standard subject-verb-object sentence order in Italian. As a consequence, most peripheral information is placed in an unnatural position in Italian, that is in mid-sentence. Structural balance is impaired and the sentence does not flow:

> *For a company that once seemed more resilient, more international in outlook and readier to embrace new manufacturing techniques than its Detroit neighbours, General Motors (GM) and Chrysler*, Ford is caught in a tight spot. (*The Economist*, 14 June 2003: 65)

> La Ford, *che una volta sembrava avere più capacità di recupero, più prospettive su scala internazionale e più prontezza nella scelta di nuove tecniche di produzione rispetto ai suoi vicini di Detroit, la General Motors (Gm) e la Chrysler*, è in difficoltà. (*Economy*, 26 giugno 2003: 45)

Close rendering of the English syntax can increase structural weight and/or shift focus. In the following sentence the information placed at the end in the English original (*in terms of international purchasing power*) should take mid-position in Italian (*di superare – in termini di potere di acquisto internazionale – l'Italia, la Francia e nel 2003 probabilmente anche la Germania*) to enable readers to find the intended meaning without unnecessary effort:

> The strength of the pound may have been unwelcome to manufacturers and exporters, but it has allowed the British to overtake the Italians, the French and in 2003 probably the Germans *in terms of international purchasing power*. (Kaletsky, 2002: 46)

> Tanta forza può non essere stata bene accolta dagli industriali e dagli esportatori, ma ha permesso alla Gran Bretagna di superare l'Italia, la Francia e nel 2003 probabilmente anche la Germania *in termini di potere di acquisto internazionale*. (Kaletsky, 23 dicembre 2002: 12)

In the following two examples creative language is normalised. In the first sentence the metaphor is taken from the weather and physical world – frequent sources of figurative language in economics. In Italian the metaphor refers to medicine, another source of figurative language in economics, though tremor as an image is probably more powerful than *ne hanno appena risentito* ('they have hardly been affected').

> The glut of corporate bankruptcies in 2001 and 2002 – including the two biggest of all time – Enron and WorldCom – have not had the devastating effect on the big banks' balance sheets that might have been expected. The two biggest banks in America, for instance, *have hardly registered a tremor*. (*The Economist*, 16 August 2003: 51)

> I numerosi fallimenti societari avvenuti nel 2001 e 2002 – compresi quelli di Enron e WorldCom, i maggiori di tutti i tempi in Usa – infatti non hanno avuto l'effetto devastante sui bilanci delle grandi banche che molti prevedevano. I due principali istituti americani *ne hanno appena risentito*. (*Economy*, 4 settembre 2003: 62)

In the second example, the idea of loyalty combined with resilience and ethical behaviour, that is projected by the image of the Japanese samurai, is lost as only *salaryman* is translated.

> As in western countries, the rise of the service economy has profound cultural implications. The era of the *samurai salaryman*, who gave absolute loyalty in return for permanent job security, is over. (Tasker, 2001: 59)

> Come nei paesi occidentali, anche in Giappone l'affermazione dell'economia dei servizi ha profonde implicazioni culturali. L'era del *lavoratore salariato*, che offre fedeltà assoluta al datore di lavoro in cambio del posto a vita, è finita. (Tasker, 27 dicembre 2001: 22)

The influence of English can be seen in the literal translation of a standard figure of speech which gives rise to an unusual metaphor in Italian. The standard equivalent of *ride a wave* is *cavalcare l'onda*, as Italian, unlike English, distinguishes between product (*onda*) and process (*ondata*):

> In its heyday in the 1980s and 1990s, the supersonic jet was full of investment bankers and advisers criss-crossing the Atlantic as *they rode successive waves* of mergers and takeovers. (*The Economist*, 12 July 2003: 57)

> Nel fulgore degli anni Ottanta e Novanta, il jet supersonico era stipato di banchieri e consulenti di investimento che attraversavano l'Atlantico, *cavalcando ondate* di fusioni e di acquisizioni. (*Economy*, 31 luglio 2003: 52)

Examples show that striking a balance between normalisation and influence of the source language can be a difficult process. Syntactic constructs should be carefully assessed to ensure optimal distribution of information and structural balance. Normalisation of lexis calls into question considerations of standard versus original phraseology and figures of speech in the fields of business and economics.

Rephrasing of repetition

The issue of repetition is particularly relevant for translation into languages such as Italian where it is normally avoided for stylistic reasons unless it gives rise to ambiguity – a major problem in technical and scientific communication. According to Halliday & Hasan (1976) repetition is a kind of reiteration, that is lexical cohesion created by the same word repeated. Other types of reiteration identified by Halliday & Hasan are used in translating to rephrase repetitions: synonyms or near-synonyms, superordinates or general words. Preferred methods to avoid repetition are language-specific. In Italian repetition can be avoided using the forms of reiteration outlined above and by ellipsis, paraphrase, metonym and the like.

In the example below, the repetition of *losses* is avoided in translation by using an explicit relative clause introduced by *che*:

> In addition, European investors financed much of America's boom and have since suffered _big losses_. As the dollar falls, *those losses* will swell. (*The Economist*, 28 June 2003: 28)

> Inoltre, gli europei hanno finanziato gran parte del boom americano, soffrendo poi _notevoli perdite, che_ sono aumentate e aumenteranno con la caduta del dollaro. (*Economy*, 17 luglio 2003: 59)

In the following sentence, repetition takes the form of a shorter variant of the term (*Bank of England* ➤ *the Bank*); in Italian, anaphoric reference is achieved by means of a superordinate term in shortened form – *istituto* as a short form of *istituto di credito* ('credit institution'):

> Starting with policy, the _Bank of England_ is under a legal obligation to pursue an activist approach to managing demand. Britain's symmetrical monetary policy target – inflation must neither exceed nor undershoot the 1.5% to 3.5% target range – means that the _Bank_ treats economic weakness and inflationary overheating as equally threatening. (Kaletsky, 2001: 40)

> Per quanto riguarda la politica, la _Banca d'Inghilterra_ ha l'obbligo legale di un approccio attivo nella gestione della domanda. Il target di politica monetaria di tipo simmetrico – l'inflazione non deve mai superare né scendere sotto l'intervallo dell'1,5%–3,5% – significa che l'_istituto_ considera una minaccia sia la debolezza economica che le spinte inflazionistiche. (Kaletsky, 27 dicembre 2001: 14)

Repetition can also be avoided by paraphrase. In the following example, the specification *Japan's* is first rendered as *del Giappone* and then as a paraphrase, *del paese nipponico* (literally 'of the Nipponese country').

> In other words, *Japan's* economy continues to shrink in nominal terms, making it harder for firms to work off their excessive debts. The rise in the yen over the past year, though a lot smaller than the rise in the euro, may also damage *Japan's* recovery. (*The Economist*, 28 June 2003: 28)

> In altre parole, l'economia *del Giappone* continua a contrarsi in termini nominali, rendendo più difficile per le imprese liberarsi dei propri debiti in eccesso. Anche la crescita dello yen nel corso dell'ultimo anno, sebbene molto più limitata rispetto all'aumento dell'euro, potrebbe danneggiare la ripresa *del Paese nipponico*. (*Economy*, 17 luglio 2003: 60)

The influence of English is to be found when repetition is reproduced in Italian even when it could be avoided. In the following example the same term (*dollar*) occurs at the end of the first sentence and at the beginning of the next one. Another repetition is the term *currency* ('moneta') for which there are two synonyms in Italian, *valuta* and *divisa*, which could have been used in this case:

> Of the five countries worst-affected then – Thailand, Malaysia, Indonesia, the Philippines and South Korea – only Malaysia now pegs its *currency*, the ringgit, rigidly to the *dollar*. If the *dollar* depreciates in 2002, there will be sharp downward pressure on Asian *currencies* too. (Long, 2001: 61)

> Dei cinque paesi allora più colpiti – Tailandia, Malesia, Indonesia, Filippine e Corea del Sud – solo la Malesia mantiene la propria *moneta*, il ringgit, rigidamente legata al *dollaro*. Se il *dollaro* si indebolirà nel 2002, anche le *monete* asiatiche perderanno terreno. (Long, 27 dicembre 2001: 25)

The influence of English on Italian is also felt in the translation of possessive adjectives or demonstrative determiners. In many cases, where English uses a possessive determiner, Italian prefers the definite or nil article when the reference is clear enough. In the following example, the cohesive *its* is used twice and in one instance it is also combined with *own*, while the cohesive *their* is also used once. In Italian *its* is translated literally, even though in the first case the definite article would be more natural (*i tassi di interesse*); where it occurs again, a nil article would be more appropriate in economic jargon (*in recessione*):

Often over the past decade Japan's central bank has even neutralised *its own low interest rates* with countervailing 'guidance' to banks on lending. The course of policy in Japan over the past ten years would be easier to understand if it had actually been a goal of the authorities to keep the economy *in its slump*. It still seems to be *their intention* in 2003. (Crook, 2002: 21)

Spesso, nel corso degli ultimi dieci anni, la banca centrale giapponese ha persino neutralizzato *i suoi propri tassi d'interesse* con 'disposizioni' di compensazione alle banche sulla concessione di prestiti. Il corso della politica in Giappone negli ultimi dieci anni sarebbe stato più facile da comprendere se l'obiettivo reale delle autorità fosse stato quello di mantenere l'economia *nella sua recessione*. Sembra che questa sarà ancora *la sua intenzione* per il 2003. (Crook, 23 dicembre 2002: 3)

In this example, repetition of the possessive determiner is even more marked in Italian as *their* is translated as if it referred to Japan's policy and not to Japanese authorities in what appears an unlikely personification in Italian. As a consequence of repetition, the flow of the sentences in Italian is impaired. The wider use of possessive determiners in English compared to Italian is confirmed by data in Table 5.5. Occurrences of *its* and *their* per thousand words are two to three times higher than the

Table 5.5 Occurrences of possessive determiners (per 1000 words) in the parallel and comparable components of the corpus (Figures in italics and bold indicate data that are directly comparable, i.e. *Economy* translations with original Italian *Economy* articles and *Il mondo in 2001, 2002, 2003* translations with original Italian newspaper articles)

	Parallel sub-corpus				Comparable sub-corpus	
Language	English originals	Italian translations	English originals	Italian translations	Italian originals	
Source	The Economist 2003	Economy 2003	The World in 2001, 2002, 2003	Il mondo nel 2001, 2002, 2003	Economy articles	Newspaper articles
Tokens	16,902	19,605	15,677	15,781	15,691	18,889
its ➤ suo/ a-suoi/ sue	6.4	2.8	3.5	**2.1**	*1.7*	**1.5**
their ➤ loro	4.9	*1.4*	4.0	**1.4**	*0.6*	**1.8**

corresponding Italian possessive determiners, *suo/a-suoi/sue* and *loro* in the translations. Still, in all cases but one – *loro* in the comparable newspaper component of the corpus – the frequency of *suo/a-suoi/sue* and *loro* is higher in the translations than in the comparable Italian sub-corpus.

As can be seen, repetition is one of the issues in translating where there is clear evidence of direct influence of the source language.

Specific distribution of certain features in target texts

With regard to the influence of English on Italian translations, the specific distribution of certain target-text features can be seen as a tendency to produce certain features with a frequency of occurrence that is more typical of the source than the target language. For example, the demonstrative pronouns *this* and *that* are commonly used for textual linkage in English to refer to an extensive piece of text. In Italian translating, a standard strategy to render them consists in using a demonstrative determiner plus a general word as in the example below (*this* —► *questa situazione*):

> This would be fine *if* there were risk-takers *elsewhere in the financial system* equipped to evaluate, take on and manage credit risk. But there aren't. (*The Economist*, 16 August 2003: 53)

> *Questa situazione* sarebbe positiva *se, nel sistema finanziario*, esistessero altri operatori disposti ad assumersi il rischio creditizio e con a disposizione gli strumenti necessari per valutare, accettare e gestire tale rischio. Purtroppo, non è così. (*Economy*, 4 settembre 2003: 65)

Quite apart from English influence in translation, however, demonstrative pronouns are increasingly rendered by means of Italian equivalents (*questo, quello, ciò*):

> If sound banks are not performing their lending function, what economic use are they? *This* has been a particular dilemma in central Europe, where banks were cleaned up at vast expense, often ending up in foreign hands (*The Economist*, 16 August 2003: 53)

> Se le banche più solide non assolvono la propria funzione di prestare soldi, che utilità economica hanno? *Questo* ha rappresentato un dilemma particolarmente importante nell'Europa centrale, dove si è avuta una dispendiosa riorganizzazione di istituti bancari finiti spesso in mani straniere. (*Economy*, 4 settembre 2003: 66)

This trend is confirmed by a comparison of the two components of the corpus (see Table 5.6). Frequency of demonstrative pronouns is lower than in English both in the parallel and in the comparable texts. Yet, frequency in the Italian translations is double that in the comparable Italian original texts.

Table 5.6 A comparison of anaphoric reference using *this/that* in the English component and *questo/quello/ciò* in the parallel and comparable Italian components of
the corpus. Frequencies are given in number of occurrences and per 1000 words
(Figures in italics and bold indicate data that are directly comparable, i.e. *Economy*
translations with original Italian *Economy* articles and *Il mondo in 2001, 2002, 2003*
translations with original Italian newspaper articles)

	Parallel sub-corpus				Comparable sub-corpus	
Language	English originals	Italian translations	English originals	Italian translations	Italian originals	
Source	The Economist 2003	Economy 2003	The World in 2001, 2002, 2003	Il mondo nel 2001, 2002, 2003	Economy articles	Newspaper articles
Tokens	16,902	19,605	15,677	15,781	15,691	18,889
This/that ⟶ questo/ quello/ciò	44	26	60	**33**	12	**20**
X 1,000 words	2.6	1.3	3.8	**2.09**	0.76	**1.05**

The higher frequency of possessive determiners in translations than in
comparable articles in the corpus as shown in Table 5.6 can be seen as
another example of the tendency to produce certain features with a frequency of occurrence that is more typical of the source than the target
language. Further analysis of features of this kind could make corpus
parsing and tagging essential if reliable results are to be obtained and thus
goes beyond the scope of this chapter.

Conclusions

Corpus analysis suggests that in translating economics articles, the
influence of English on Italian is not restricted to lexical borrowing, but
extends to pattern transfer. The influence on lexis can be traced in loan
words, loan translations, formation of compound terms, phraseology and
figurative language. The influence on syntax can be found in the close
rendering of syntactic constructs, in repetition, in the higher frequency of
cohesive links such as coordinators, subordinators, possessive determiners, and demonstrative pronouns. An indirect influence may also be
detected when features of English such as conciseness, preference for juxtaposition and parataxis or repetition are deemed to be so different from
those of Italian writing that strategies like explicitation, disambiguation,

simplification, normalisation, use of long and complex sentences, and rephrasing of repetitions are regarded as a necessary translators' response to the source text if translations that read naturally like originals are to be produced. Though results should be validated by comparison with a larger corpus of texts, translation is a special case of language contact – and trends emerging in translation may affect the target language over time. Indeed, English-Italian translation is slowly but subtly influencing the conventions governing some genres, for instance university manuals for students. Corpus analysis indicates that Italian as used in the economics press is slowly moving away from long sentences and linguistically connected syntactic, grammatical and lexical constructs.

Translated texts in the corpus show that the influence of the source language is probably unavoidable, especially if the source culture is regarded as highly prestigious in the target community. Influence is not necessarily positive or negative per se. Ultimately, the test case for translation in specialised fields is quality, that is the extent to which it meets the pragmatic principle of optimal relevance, enabling readers to find the intended meaning without unnecessary effort and providing the kind of meaning that is worth the readers' effort (Gutt, 1998: 43). In the translation of economics articles into Italian this equals adequate distribution of information, balanced structural weight of sentences, and cohesion and coherence suited to text and genre.

Notes

1. Sources from which examples are cited are not listed in the references.
2. The Surrey-Trieste corpus has 187,680 tokens and consists of economic reports and speeches published by the Bank of Italy and ISTAT, the Italian National Institute of Statistics (Musacchio, 2002: 781).
3. The two dictionaries were consulted in electronic form. Investigation of business and economic terms is limited to the last three centuries because the establishment of economics as an independent discipline is traditionally regarded as dating from the publication of Adam Smith's *Wealth of Nations*. Stammerjohann (2003: 88) gives a percentage of 2% for English loan words in Italian and cites De Mauro's percentage of 0.2% for spoken Italian which is taken from data in the *Lessico di frequenza dell'italiano parlato* (frequency lexicon of spoken Italian).
4. As no indications of authors are given in *The Economist* and consequently in its *Economy* translations, quotations from these sources are followed by short references consisting of the name of the magazine, the date of publication and the page. Articles from *The World in 2001*, *The World in 2002*, *The World in 2003* and their corresponding translations published by *La Stampa* are followed by short references using the traditional author-date-page system. It should be noted, however, that date of publication is always the year before the one to which the title of the collection *The World in* refers, i.e. Crook 2000 indicates an article by Crook which appeared in *The World in 2001*. Underlined sections of text highlight parts on which the following or preceding analysis focuses.
5. See also explicitation above.

References

Baker, M. (1993) Corpus linguistics and Translation Studies. In M. Baker, G. Francis and E. Tognini-Bonelli (eds) *Text and Technology. In Honour of John Sinclair* (pp. 233–50). Amsterdam/Philadelphia: Benjamins.

Baumgarten, N., House, J. and Probst, J. (2004) English as *Lingua Franca* in Covert Translation Processes. *The Translator*, 10(1) pp. 83–108.

Benincà, P. (1993) Sintassi. In A.A. Sobrero (ed.) *Introduzione all'italiano contemporaneo. Le strutture* (pp. 247–90) Roma-Bari: Laterza.

Benincà, P., Salvi, G.P. and Frison, L. (1991) L'ordine degli elementi della frase e le costruzioni marcate. In L. Renzi and G.P. Salvi (eds) *Grande grammatica italiana di consultazione* (Vol. 1) (pp. 115–225) Bologna: Il Mulino.

Bloor, M. and Bloor, T. (1993) How economists modify propositions. In W. Henderson, T. Dudley-Evans and R. Backhouse (eds) *Economics and Language* (pp. 153–69) London: Routledge.

Blum-Kulka, S. (1986) Shift of cohesion and coherence in translation. In J. House and S. Blum-Kulka (eds) *Interlingual and Intercultural Communication: Discourse and Cognition in Translation and Second Language Acquisition Studies* (pp. 17–35) Tübingen: Gunter Narr.

Bonomi, I. (2002) *L'italiano giornalistico. Dall'inizio del'900 ai quotidiani on line*. Firenze: Franco Cesati Editore.

Collins (1994) *Collins English Dictionary* (3rd edn). Glasgow: HarperCollins Publishers.

Dardano, M. (1993) Lessico e semantica. In A.A. Sobrero (ed.) *Introduzione all'italiano contemporaneo. Le strutture* (pp. 291–370) Roma-Bari: Laterza.

De Mauro, T. (2000) *Dizionario della lingua italiana*. Torino: Paravia.

DISC (1997) *Dizionario italiano Sabatini-Coletti*. Firenze: Giunti.

Doherty, M. (1997a) 'Acceptability' and language-specific preference in the distribution of information. *Target* 9:1, 1–24.

Doherty, M. (1997b) Textual garden paths – parametrized obstacles to target language adequate translations. In C. Hauenschild and S. Heizmann (eds) *Machine Translation and Translation Theory* (pp. 68–89) Berlin/New York: Mouton de Gruyter.

Frawley, W. (1984) Prelegomenon to a theory of translation. In W. Frawley (ed.) *Translation: Literary, Linguistic, and Philosophical Perspectives* (pp. 159–175) London/Toronto: Associated University Presses.

Gutt, E.A. (1998) Pragmatic aspects of translation: Some relevance-theory observations. In L. Hickey (ed.) *The Pragmatics of Translation* (pp. 41–53) Clevedon: Multilingual Matters.

Halliday, M.A.K. and Hasan, R. (1976) *Cohesion in English*. Harlow, Longman.

Heath, J. (1994) Borrowing. In R.E. Asher (ed.) *The Enclycopedia of Language and Linguistics* (Vol.1) (pp. 383–94) Oxford: Pergamon Press.

Katan, D. (1999) *Translating Cultures. An Introduction for Translators, Interpreters and Mediators*. Manchester: St Jerome.

Marazzini, C. (1994) *La lingua italiana. Profilo storico*. Bologna: Il Mulino.

Merlini Barbaresi, L. (1996) Traduzione e pragmatica del discorso. In G. Cortese (ed.) *Tradurre i linguaggi settoriali* (pp. 73–85) Torino: Edizioni Libreria Cortina.

Musacchio, M.T. (2002) The search for technical collocations and subtechnical vocabulary in native-language corpora as an aid to LSP translation. In M. Koskela, C. Laurén, M. Nordman and N. Pilke (eds) *Porta Scientiae* (Vol. 2) (pp. 778–92) Vaasa: University of Vaasa.

Nida, E. (1964) *Towards a Science of Translating*. Leiden: E.J. Brill.

Quirk, R., Greenbaum, S., Leech, G. and Svartvik, J. (1985) *A Comprehensive Grammar of the English Language.* Harlow: Longman.

Stammerjohann, H. (2003) L'italiano e altre lingue di fronte all'anglicizzazione. In N. Meraschio e T. Poggi Salami (eds) *Italia linguistica anno mille. Italia linguistica anno duemila* (pp. 77–101) Roma: Bulzoni.

Toury, G. (1995) *Descriptive Translation Studies and Beyond.* Amsterdam/ Philadelphia: Benjamins.

Trimble, L. (1985) *English for Science and Technology. A Discourse Approach.* Cambridge: Cambridge University Press.

Victor, D.A. (1992) *International Business Communication.* London: HarperCollins.

Chapter 6

The Influence of English on Greek: A Sociological Approach

POLYMNIA TSAGOURIA

Introduction

The influence of English on other languages is a well-attested phenomenon and the literature concerning the widespread use of English in many European languages is prolific. As has often been pointed out, the influence of English in the field of technology has been particularly noticeable, including the borrowing of English words for use as tech-nological terms. This applies equally to Modern Greek. For instance, Greeks now refer to 'e-mail' instead of *electroniko tachydromeio* (ηλεκτρονικό ταχυδρομείο), while the Greek word for 'fax', *teleomoiotypia* (τηλεομοιοτυπία), is hardly used by Greek speakers, let alone found in dictionaries. A word such as 'e-mail' is not only used in spoken Greek but has also entered the administrative language and found its way into official documents written, in most cases, in the Greek not the Roman alphabet. But then who is going to use the Greek word *'teleomoiotypia'* when the word 'fax' is understood globally by speakers of different languages? In today's hurried world, people seek to simplify and abbreviate wherever possible, seizing opportunities available to Greek speakers through the use of English words.

In this chapter I shall concentrate on the sociological aspects of the lexical influence of English on Greek and the influx of English words into the Greek language. More specifically, in the first part I shall outline those factors operative in Greek society which, in my opinion, have given rise to the widespread use of English words. In the second part, I shall discuss some attitudes among Greeks towards their own language and their reaction to the increasing use of English words. Finally, I shall focus on the influence of English on spoken and written Greek as the outcome of these attitudes to Greek and English respectively.

Greek Society – Past and Present

The development of Greek society during the last decades has created fertile ground for the widespread use of English in oral and written

Greek. The following parameters may be viewed as having affected the introduction of many English words into Greek.

First, an important factor was the emigration of a large number of Greek speakers to the United States. The first large wave of migration to North America took place during the period 1890–1920 when many parts of Greece were still under Ottoman occupation, resulting in the US government introducing a quota system limiting the number of Greek immigrants to 100 a year. Then in the aftermath of World War II, which had left Greece poverty-stricken as well as politically unstable, civil war raged (1945–9). The political turmoil that ensued resulted in a massive migration of political and economic refugees to many European countries, most frequently to Germany, and across the Atlantic primarily to North America. By the end of the 1960s and the early 1970s, the Greek immigrants to America and their descendants started to visit Greece, bringing back not only riches but a new 'language' in which Greek and American English now fused. Returning to Greece for a period of time, a few to settle permanently, these speakers introduced into Greek a new accent, reflecting traces of their acquired American English. As a result, American-Greeks – at least the first generation of returnees – started to speak a form of idiomatic Greek using many English words and idioms. In addition, many American-Greek English words were adapted and made to fit Greek grammatical categories, resulting in English words entering the vocabulary of Greek as spoken in the Greek diaspora particularly in North America and Australia. Words such as *hospital-i* (usually found in spoken rather than written language and meaning 'hospital'), where the Greek suffix *-i* is used for nouns of neuter gender, came to be used by Greek speakers.

If the Greek-Americans were at least partly responsible for the introduction of English words into spoken Greek, an important consequence was that a large number of English words were introduced into Greek in an idiosyncratic or, more specifically, irregular form. The majority of the first Greek immigrants to America were not very well educated nor did they receive adequate education in their new home country. Hence, an uncertain grasp of English and Greek, or at least the use of non-standard English and non-standard Greek as spoken by Greek-Americans, gave rise to the use of English words by other Greek speakers but, in most cases, in new versions adapted to achieve a closer fit with the Greek grammatical system (for a detailed discussion, see Seaman, 1972). The use of so-called Greco-American became the butt of many jokes; during the 1960s and 1970s, the 'Golden Age' of Greek cinema, the use of recently introduced American English was lampooned in many Greek films (see, for example, Mickelides, 1997; Triantaphyllides, 2000).

Secondly, in the late 1960s, Greece started to be viewed as a popular place for tourists. An increasing number of visitors, attracted by the natural beauty of the country, would go for their holidays every year. Many of them also purchased land, resulting in some becoming inhabitants of parts of the Greek peninsula for certain periods of the year. Since the tourism industry developed and became important financially for Greece, a well-organised system now provides many services for the influx of visitors. As a result, English is used in order to cater for the needs of non-Greek speakers. As Greeks speak English, as well as other languages, in particular German and Italian, they gave English names to their restaurants, their shops and to their ships; menus were written in English; information was provided in English and places and products were advertised in English. Moreover, as time went on, Greeks involved in the tourist industry became increasingly more professional in their work, and the initially somewhat elementary English which they spoke started to become more sophisticated. This in turn influenced the Greek language which became affected by the knowledge and widespread use of English in everyday transactions. In fact, English words and expressions have become incorporated into Modern Greek, in certain cases replacing the original Greek.

Thirdly, during the last few decades education has increased in importance in Greece. Many Greeks study abroad and a considerable number of young Greeks are awarded their degrees from UK universities. A growing number of Greek students are also involved in postgraduate studies, the majority of them at British and US universities. Nowadays, the old established and prestigious tradition of German and French universities has been overtaken by the status of British and American ones. As a result, many Greeks who have studied at English-speaking universities draw on English when they speak as well as write. Most of them go out for 'a drink' instead of the Greek *poto* (ποτό) or they *'kathontai se exetaseis'* (κάθονται σε εξετάσεις – sit an exam) instead of the Greek *'pigaino se (gia) exetaseis'* or *'grafo exetaseis'* (πηγαίνω σε (για) εξετάσεις or γράψω εξετάσεις – go to exams or write exams). Here, the influence of English on Greek is on the one hand direct, since English words are used by Greek speakers, and on the other hand indirect, since the system of Greek idiomatic expressions is affected as a result of calquing colloquial English.

Fourthly, the global industry of cinema and music plays an important role in the extensive use of English words and phrases by Greek speakers, and it is, in passing interesting to note that the practice of subtitling rather than dubbing is employed in Greece for non-Greek films mainly due to the fact that the percentage of illiterate Greeks is low. It is well known that, to a considerable degree, Greeks are influenced by the American English of Hollywood films. English slang has become part of Greek slang, or 'argot' (αργκώ), although in certain contexts the Greek term *chydaia glossa* (χυδαία γλώσσα), originally meaning the language of the common people and thus bad language, is often used. Similarly, pop and rock music affect the way young people speak. Young Greeks flavour their language with English words derived mainly from the world of music. Hence, many Greeks say 'I love House' or 'I like Hard Rock' and, very rarely, 'I like *to sklero rock*' using the Greek word *sklero* (σκληρό) for hard. Also, to a large extent, Greek pop music employs English for commercial reasons; in the refrain of many Greek pop songs, the Greek '*S*' *agapo*' (Σ' αγαπώ) is replaced by the English 'I love you'. A similar approach is used by many magazines specialising in the field of cinema and music, where the reader is more likely to find English expressions, such as 'ab fab' instead of a Greek word, for instance, *yperochos* (υπέροχος – fabulous) or *theamatikos* (θεαματικός – spectacular). Finally, the same attitude is reflected in the choice of names given to commercially run leisure venues; Greeks may spend their leisure time at places called 'Rock Cafe', 'Ministry of Sound', 'Velvet', etc. The most amazing aspect of the Greek approach is that sometimes, out of concern for their own language, they sometimes add a flavour of 'Greekness' to otherwise English names, resulting in a form of 'Greek-English' such as 'Βέλβετ' for 'Velvet' or 'Σάντουιτς Λαντ' for 'Sandwich Land'.

Fifthly, the Greek system of public and private education gives ample opportunity for the use of English in general contexts by a growing Greek-speaking population. The teaching of English as a foreign language became compulsory in the curriculum of non-private primary schools in the early 1990s. Greek pupils are taught English in a systematic fashion from the fourth to the sixth year of primary school, on average for three hours per week. English is also taught as the first foreign language in secondary education at the Greek *Gymnasion* and *Lyceion*, while French and German are taught as second foreign languages of the students' choice. In addition, English, French, German and Italian are taught at Greek universities, requiring four years of compulsory study. While English is a subject on the curriculum of state schools, the tuition of English is also offered by many private schools teaching foreign languages where English may be studied at various levels of proficiency. As a result, the majority of Greek schoolchildren attend English classes in state or private schools, and, since young people are familiar with English from an early age, they frequently incorporate English words into their everyday speech either as a matter of course or as a form of showmanship.

Greek and the Use of English

We have argued that the structure of Modern Greek has created a template on which the English language operates. It is clear that a large number of English words are used by Greek speakers and that English influences the way the language is spoken in Greece. However, many English loan words are subject to certain constraints due to the structure of the Greek language. In essence, loan words – usually nouns – are assigned a particular gender and one of the articles ο, η, το in accordance with the gender selected. (For a discussion of the gender of loan words in Greek, see Anastasiade-Simeonide, 1990: 155–77.) For instance, the English word 'film' in Greek, *to film* (το φιλμ), has been assigned the neuter gender and the same form is usually used in the singular and plural. The gender and the plural form may also be variable. The English word 'pub' can be neuter in Greek as in το παμπ, or feminine as in η παμπ, in the plural it is τα παμπ(ς), οι παμπ(ς) respectively, with the final 's' left to the speaker's discretion. Also, it is possible for a Greek suffix which requires a particular gender to be added to loanwords, resulting in the new word created following a specified declension. For example, the English word 'motor' appears in the Greek of some speakers as *motor* and with the ending i(l) as *motor-i* (το μοτόρ–ι). The first form is indeclinable but the second can be declined. Thus the form for the nominative and accusative plural is *(ta) motor-ia* (τα μοτόρ–ια) (for the gender of indeclinable loan words see King, 1982). Moreover, many English words are used by Greek speakers according to individual preference. For example, for many Greek speakers, 'computer' is the plural as well as the singular form. Sometimes they take it a step further and add a Greek suffix to the word giving, in some cases, a new meaning to the original word, such as computer-*aki* (κομπιουτεράκι) when referring to a calculator.

The idiosyncratic way in which the Greeks use English words manifests itself even more clearly in the case of pronunciation. For those less familiar with English, the pronunciation of 'Microsoft' is *M-i-crosoft* and not *M-a-i-crosoft*, reflecting also the fact that 'Microsoft' is partly formed by a Greek word, the Greek adjective *mikros* (μικρός – small). A number of English words containing Ancient Greek words are introduced into Modern Greek in this way, at the same time acquiring a new meaning. The new meaning of the word is adopted by Modern Greek but, at the same time, the Greek pronunciation is preserved (for an early discussion of English loan words in Modern Greek, see Swanson, 1958). It is also worth pointing out that, before the present influence of English on Greek, French had a similar strong hold. More specifically, until very recently it was a matter of prestige for Greeks to adopt the French pronunciation of words used in French and English. Nowadays, more Greeks prefer the English version to the French one. They prefer to say κολέξιου (collection) with the stress on -e- rather than κολεξιόυ with the stress on -o- as in French, although some variation between English and French modes of pronunciation is still evident. The prestigious position of French in Greek society for many decades becomes clear from the practice of reporting on many social events in French as well as in Greek. In the early twentieth century, a good example of this practice was the publicity for the release of *Golfo* (1915), one of the early Greek films. In the publicity material, we can see the Greek 'η πρώτη ταινία Ελληνικής παραγωγής' ('the first Greek film production') along with the French 'le premier film hellenique' (see Delveroude, 2001: 397). The prestige of French was predominant within the upper strata of Greek society until very recently, when it was over-taken by English, a change triggered by business needs.

Varieties and Modes of Greek

Conscious of the strong influence of English on Modern Greek, Greeks have reacted to the situation in a number of ways. But before I come to this, it is necessary to discuss briefly the status of the Greek language in present-day Greece. Modern Greek is the outcome of a process of development of Ancient Greek (spoken on mainland Greece, on the islands of the Aegean and in the Greek colonies in Asia, Africa and Italy) throughout time[1] and, more specifically, of the so-called *Koine* spoken in the *Hellenistic* kingdoms, within a geographical area extending from the Adriatic Sea to Eastern Iran and from Euxine to the Persian Gulf, from 300 BC onwards. *Koine* was the common language facilitating communication across cultures (see Brixhe, 1993 and *The Oxford Classical Dictionary*, 1996). Greek became the *lingua franca* for centuries in antiquity[2] and, moreover, it provided words which are now found in other languages. In addition, an outstanding literature has been written in Greek from antiquity to modern times. The Greek language is related to classical civilisation and, as a result, many people all over the world study Greek. However, it is the very long history of the Greek language which has given rise to problems in Greek society from the time of Greek Independence in 1830 until today. This very fact affects the attitude of Greeks towards their own language and towards the influence of other languages on Modern Greek. The so-called Language Question, namely the linguistic, educational, political and social debate concerning the establishment of either *Katharevousa* or *Demotiki* as the official language of the nation dominated the political scene of the independent state until the 1970s.[3] Only in 1974 was *Demotiki* recognised as the official language and an end was put to the issue of 'Diglossia'.[4]

In 1983 innovations were introduced into Modern Greek, mainly the result of governmental policy. The aspiration of vowels and of diphthongs was abolished and only one accent instead of the previous two was preserved. It was in essence an attempt to achieve a simplification of the Greek grammatical system in response to demands from politicians and intellectuals. In many cases the innovations which were introduced into Modern Greek have resulted in new forms of expression even beyond *Demotiki*. Such changes do not appear, however, to be embraced by all Greeks and language remains a political issue.

In their reaction to the increasing influence of English on their language, a distinction can be drawn between those Greeks who are motivated by xenophobia and those motivated by xenophilia. Some Greeks adopt a hostile attitude towards the widespread use of English words in many sectors of private and public life. They feel that the Greek language is rich and flexible, that it offers Greek speakers precise and functional words for even the most recent technological innovations. This reaction owes its origin to a broader moral attitude according to which Greek tradition and Greek civilisation are the victims of a destruction brought about by the European cultural 'invasion' of Greece. The notion of the importance of Greek to European languages is deeply rooted among Greeks even today. That Greek offers material for the formation of new scientific terms in many languages is, to a degree, true. Nevertheless, many Greeks when speaking and writing use English words even when there is a well-established Greek word in existence. Sometimes this attitude reflects a sense of cosmopolitanism but, in most cases, it reflects only the vanity of the speaker who likes to demonstrate his/her knowledge of foreign languages.

This ambivalent attitude towards the increasing influence of English shown by Greek speakers has stimulated a lively debate in Greece. There are a number of institutions whose main concern it is to safeguard the Greek language, and to maintain and disseminate it all over the world. The Academy of Athens was established in 1926, the main concerns of which are the appropriate use of the Greek language, the further development of Modern Greek and the promotion of a high standard of oral and written Greek. One of the projects undertaken by the Academy is the edition of a new dictionary of Modern Greek. Also, the Foundation *Manolis Triantaphyllides* (Τδρυμα Μανώλη Τριανταφυλλίδη), linked to the Aristotle University of Thessaloniki, is a very important institution for the development of Modern Greek. The Foundation is responsible for the most recent pronouncement on the standardisation of the morphology and syntax of Modern Greek. In addition, a number of publications dealing with issues related to the Greek language owe their origin to this Foundation. Finally, it has responsibility for mainstream policy with respect to morphology, grammar, syntax, the orthography of loan words and the academic status of the Greek language. As a result, the standard book on the grammar of Modern Greek taught in schools is the work of this Foundation. The Centre of Greek Language (Κέντρο Ελληνικής Γλώσσας) is concerned with similar issues and co-operates with the Triantaphyllides Foundation on certain projects related to the Greek language.

The promotion of the Modern Greek language and culture is the main aim of the Foundation for Hellenic Culture (Τδρυμα Ελληνικού Πολιτισμού), which has drawn up plans for the establishment of branches in several European capitals, including London, Paris, Berlin, Moscow, Sofia and Tirana, as well as in Odessa, Alexandria and New York (*Iris* 1–2, 1993). According to the statutes of the Foundation for Hellenic Culture, its aim is to support the systematic development, promotion and propagation of Hellenic culture abroad and, as a corollary, the promotion of the Greek language (*Iris* 3–4, 1994). To this end, the Foundation for Hellenic Culture offers Modern Greek lessons through its various branches, supports Modern Greek teaching programmes in universities outside Greece, and helps speakers of Greek descent living abroad to learn colloquial Greek as it is spoken today.[5] Hence the Greek government finances language programmes in Modern Greek in schools and at universities abroad. To a considerable degree, this initiative helps to meet the needs of Greeks who have lived abroad for many generations – the Greeks of the so-called diaspora.[6] Many Greeks living abroad learn Greek as a second language in schools run by the Greek State and the Orthodox Church.

The institutions working for the maintenance and promotion of Modern Greek are also responsible for drawing up policies to implement changes and innovations. Similarly, they are responsible for managing the influence of English on Greek, the morphology of loan words, their frequency of use and the coinage of Greek words for new technological concepts. However, the status and the use of English in Modern Greek is still an issue of political and intellectual debate among Greeks. The effects of the rapid spread of English go hand in hand with the concern for the maintenance of the Greek language, and thus more cautious use of English, an attitude reflected by the difference in the use of English between spoken and written Greek. While English is used extensively in the spoken mode of language, in written Greek, and then mainly in academic Greek, there is a tendency to use a Greek word rather than an English word where both possibilities exist. This practice is established in Greek schools where the use of 'pure' Greek in written essays is mandatory, pointing to a form of subconscious 'defence' of the Greek language by the Greeks themselves. For example, while a majority of Greeks would use the word κομπιούτερ ('computer') in spoken Greek, the expression *(ηλεκτρονικός) υπολογιστής* or '(electronic) computer' is favoured in written Greek. Again, some Computer Centres are advertised as 'Computers Centers' while others are advertised as centres *'υπολογιστών'*. In the telephone directory, computers are listed as υπολογιστές. Another example is the word for 'cinema'. In spoken Greek, the word σινεμά ('cinema') is used more often than the Greek word *kinematografos* (κινηματογράφος) but, in the written language, it is the Greek word which is mostly found. Thus the history of Greek cinema is the history of *kinematografos* (not of σινεμά) and, similarly, a film festival is known as *Kinematografou* (Φεστιβάλ Κινηματογράφου). In everyday life the Greeks say that they suffer from 'stress' (στρες) but in written Greek stress is expressed through the use of the Greek word *agchos* (άγχος) and anti-stress pills are called *agcholitika* (αγχολυτικά). Many Greeks love basketball (μπάσκετ) but they prefer to write *kalathosferise* (καλαθοσφαίριση) instead of 'basket'. Nowadays many Greeks have their lunch at *Fast Foods*, used in both spoken and written Greek. The Greek word *tachufagadika* (ταχυψαγάδικα) was coined on the English pattern for *Fast Food* but is not really used. Probably, the concept of fast food does not correspond to the Greek notion of social behaviour. In Greek society, eating and drinking are a means of communication and social contact. Thus, even at American-style *Fast Food* restaurants, modern Greeks enjoy leisurely meals. However, in spoken and often in written Greek, a form of the English 'fast food' with the Greek suffix – *adiko*, i.e. *fast food adiko* (φαστφουντάδικο), indicates places where fast food might be found.

Conclusion

The above examples illustrate some Greek attitudes towards the influence of English on Greek. While English is used extensively in the spoken language serving many of the linguistic needs of modern Greeks, in written Greek there is a systematic effort to use Greek words in all contexts. But this practice is not employed by newspapers and magazines reporting on fashion and music, where English is used, in many cases even in the Roman alphabet, as we have discussed earlier. Also, in Modern Greek literature, a variety of practices are employed since literary language is subject to variation in style and register.

To conclude, the influence of English on Greek is significant. For many decades French was the language of prestige in Greek society, a role now clearly taken over by English. Developments in Greek society make the use of some English words inevitable and, in their everyday transactions, Greeks make extensive use of English words. However, they are concerned about the future of the Greek language and fear substantial replacement of Greek words by English in spoken and written discourse. In written language, the use of Greek instead of current English words is the preferred choice. In fact, the spread of English is a controversial issue in many spheres of Greek society, the question having been a political and social issue from early on in the independent Greek State. In my personal opinion, a constructive reaction to the widespread use of English words and expressions in Greek could impose restrictions on the use of English to apply to new technological concepts and recent terminology related to 'globalisation'. At the same time, the dynamics of the Greek language should be further explored and continue to be developed by Greek speakers.

Notes

1. Greek is the Indo-European language with the longest attested history; the first documents belong to the second half of the second millennium BC and arguably there is very little break between ancient Greek and the modern language of Greece. Regarding the Greek language we distinguish an early

ancient period from the first attestation of Mycenaean Greek (in *Linear B*, circa 13th c. BC) to circa 3rd c. AD, a Byzantine and medieval period (until circa 1650), and a modern period.

2. It is interesting that, even within the Roman Empire, Greek was the established administrative language in the eastern provinces of the Empire. Moreover, the imperial decrees written in Latin were translated into Greek to meet the needs of Roman subjects of the Eastern Empire (see Kyrtatas, 2001). It is worth noting, that under the Romans religious Jewish texts were translated into Greek.

3. Katharevousa ('Purist' Greek) is 'a somewhat stiff form of language by means of which Greek scholars tried in the 19th c. to "cleanse" and enrich the "low life" demotic vernacular spoken by mostly illiterate Greeks under Ottoman rule'. Demotiki is 'a form of Greek based on the vernacular used by the mostly illiterate Greeks in their speech, poetry and songs during the 400 years of Ottoman occupation' (circa 1453–1830) (Veremis & Dragoumis, 1995).

4. There is an extensive literature on the subject of diglossia in Greece (see Ferguson, 1959; Householder, 1962; Rotolo, 1965; Petrounias, 1978; Warburton-Philippaki, 1980; Alexiou, 1982; Babiniotes, 1979; Mackridge, 1985).

5. Many foundations in Greece, such as the Foundation *Alexandros Onasis*, the Foundation *Goulandres*, the Foundation *Ouranes* are concerned with the promotion of Greek language and culture, and thus Hellenic Studies (Classical and Modern) are promoted through scholarships and other funding.

6. According to the archives of the Greek Foreign Ministry 5,000,000 people are considered to be ethnic Greeks. 700,000 live in Europe, 700,000 in Australia, 130,000 in Africa, 40,000 in Asia while the Greek-Americans amount to some 3,000,000.

References

Alexiou, M. (1982) Diglossia in Greece. In W. Haas (ed.) *Standard Languages, Spoken and Written* (pp. 156–92) Manchester: Manchester University Press.

Anastasiade-Simeonide, A. (1990) Το γένος των σύγχρονων δανείων της ΝΕ. *Studies in Greek linguistics* 10, 155–77.

Babiniotes, G. (1979) A linguistic approach to the 'Language Question' in Greece, *Byzantine and Modern Greek Studies* 5, 1–16. Νεοελληνική Κοινή. Πέραν της καθαρευούσης και της δημοτικής, Athens: Nancy.

Brixhe, C. (ed.) (1994) *La Koine grecque antique: Une langue introuvable?* Presses Universitaires de Nancy: Nancy.

Delveroude E-A. (2001) Κινηματογράφος. In C. Chatzeiosif (ed.) Ιστορία της Ελλάδας του 20ου αι. Οι Απαρχές *1900–1922* [History of 20th century Greece. The Beginning 1900–1922] Tom. A. Part II (pp. 389–99) Athens: Vivliorama.

Ferguson, C.A. (1959) Diglossia. *Word* 15, pp. 325–40.

Hornblower, S. and Spawforth, A. (eds) (1996) *The Oxford Classical Dictionary* (3rd edn). Oxford: Oxford University Press.

Householder, F.W. jun. (1962) Greek diglossia. *Georgetown Monographs* 15, 109–32.

King P. (1982) Notes on the gender of indeclinable loan nouns in Modern Greek. *Orbis* 31, 253–62.

Kyrtatas, D.I. (ed.) (2001) Ο ελληνικός κόσμος την εποχή της ρωμαικής αυτοκρατορίας [The Hellenic world at the time of the Roman Empire]. In A.F. Christides, Ιστορία της ελληνικής γλώσσας. Από τις αρχές έως την ύστερη αρχαιότητα [History of the Greek Language. From its Origins to Later

Antiquity] (pp. 261–7) Thessaloniki: Centre for the Greek Language and Institute for Modern Greek Studies.

Mackridge, P. (1985) *The Modern Greek Language*. Oxford: Oxford University Press.

Mikelides, N.F. (1997) Ιστορία του κινηματογράψου: *100 χρόνια ελληνικές ταινίες, από το 1897 μέχρι σήμερα* [History of Cinema: 100 Years of Greek Films from 1897 until the Present] Vol. 3. Athens: Maniatea.

Petrounias, E. (1978) The Modern Greek Language and diglossia. In S.Vryonis (ed.) *The 'Past' in Medieval and Modern Greek culture* (pp. 193–220) Malibu: Undena Publications

Rotolo, V. A. (1965) *A Korais e la questione della lingua in Grecia*. Palermo: Presso L'Academia.

Seaman, P.D. (1972) *Modern Greek and American English in contact*. The Hague: Mouton.

Swanson, D.C. (1958) English loanwords in Modern Greek. *Word* 14, 26–46.

Triantaphyllides, I. (2000) Ταινίες για φίλημα [Films to Love]. Athens: Exandas.

Veremis, T.M. and Dragoumis, M. (1995) *Historical Dictionary of Greece, European Historical Dictionaries* 5. Metuchen, NJ, London: Scarecrow Press.

Warburton-Philippaki, I. (1980) Greek diglossia and the true aspects of the phonology of Common Modern Greek. *Journal of Linguistics* 13, 45–54.

Chapter 7

Polish Under Siege?

W. CHŁOPICKI

Introduction

Polish is used by some 40 million citizens of Poland, including circa 3% ethnic and national minorities (see Kajtoch 1999), as well as 10 to 15 million native Poles or speakers of Polish origin residing abroad in approximately 100 countries, the North American minority being by far the largest group (almost seven million; see Miodunka 1999: 309). Polish cannot compete with Arabic, Chinese, English, French, German, Russian or Spanish in their worldwide roles, but it has a firm anchor in its population living in the independent state of Poland. For them Polish is their first, native language, a vibrant instrument used in the mainstream of public life, a sign of national identity and a value in its own right. The political history of Poland, including long periods of foreign occupation and the partition of its territory between neighbouring states, has made the Polish language synonymous with nationality. Attitudes have developed which make loyalty to the language a patriotic duty; hence its vitality and autonomy as well as a normative approach to correctness have been matters of public concern for some time (see Gajda, 1999: 180). Recently, the Polish Language Act has been passed to protect the position of the language in the public sphere in the face of the increased influence of foreign languages in areas such as official communication, business and company names, as well as legal contracts.

Polish can be compared with French and Russian in the size of its vocabulary (125,000 lexical entries in the largest available dictionary published in 1969, compared with 100,000 in French and 130,000 in Russian), but its vocabulary is considerably smaller than German (185,000) and much smaller than that of English (615,000 items in the *Oxford English Dictionary*) (data from Serejska Olszer, 2001: 26). Interestingly, in the larger vocabulary of English, as much as 70% of lexical items are made up of older or more recent imports from foreign languages (Serejska Olszer, 2001: 27); by contrast, only 7% of the Polish vocabulary system are international cognates (technical and specialist terminology is excluded from the count; Maćkiewicz, 2000: 55).

History and Background

In cross-linguistic research, Polish is considered a 'borderline language' (*język pograniczny*), with strong features typical of both western- and eastern-European language groups, or 'language leagues' (Maćkiewicz, 2000). Borrowings from English go a long way back, although in the past the influence of English on Polish has been weaker than that of Latin, Czech, German, Italian or French, due to the lack of extensive trade or cultural links between Poland and England – later Great Britain – in contrast to the ties with neighbouring countries, as well as with Italy or France (Mańczak-Wohlfeld, 1994: 7). The situation changed in the eighteenth and even more so in the nineteenth and twentieth centuries when political and economic ties with Great Britain and the US intensified (see Mańczak-Wohlfeld, 1994: 7–8).

The first English words to be borrowed into Polish, such as 'cutter', 'catch', 'yacht', 'budget', 'bill', 'gallon', 'club', 'rum' and 'punch', date back to the eighteenth and early nineteenth centuries. Then, throughout the nineteenth century, they kept increasing in number and in the twentieth century the process continued. In the 1920s and 1930s a few English loan words started to appear in newspaper adverts in the press of the newly independent Poland. Examples include: 'sedan', 'shampoo', 'extra', 'cleansing cream', 'vanishing cream', 'vacuum' (see Chłopicki & Świątek, 2000: 592–601). In 1961, over 700 English borrowings had already been registered by lexicographers, in 1985 there were over 1000, and in 1994 Mańczak-Wohfeld published a dictionary comprising some 1600 loans not including internationalisms (defined as words belonging to at least three languages), hybrids and calques (data from Mańczak-Wohlfeld, 1994: 9).

By 2002, the number of lexical items borrowed from English can be estimated to be about 2000. This is a large number, especially compared with the basic Polish vocabulary of 6000 to 7000 words which constitute the 'non-expressive, non-specialist, non-erudite' core of the spoken language. But overall, the total number of loans, mostly from English, Russian and German, does not exceed 20% of the entire vocabulary (Dunaj *et al.*, 1999: 238, 241). Furthermore, many foreign lexical items are short-lived and quickly forgotten, for example *obdżektor*, in the early 1990s referring to a conscientious objector in the post-totalitarian Polish army, was soon replaced by its descriptive Polish equivalent (see Serejska Olszer, 2001: 38). Some also have a limited range of use as specialist vocabulary, and others are ousted by native lexical items; 'mouse' related to computers was soon replaced by the Polish translation 'mysz' (see Dunaj, 2000: 30). All in all, no more than 400 English borrowings appear to function regularly in contemporary Polish, and the impression created of their importance is due to their frequency of use, especially in the media (Serejska Olszer, 2001: 192). Dunaj argues that the expansion of foreign vocabulary in Polish was even larger during the thirteenth, fourteenth and fifteenth centuries, German borrowings being even more numerous than are English borrowings today, but not causing any linguistic disasters. The loans that remain in Polish are the ones that are needed (Dunaj, 2000: 30–31). Nevertheless, Polish linguists have written prolifically about the influence of American English as shown by the list of references following this chapter (in particular Ożóg, 2001: 224–38). This is evidence of their own concern as well as of the concern of the average native speaker of Polish about the present state and the future of the language. Visions of diglossia in Poland even started to emerge in some writings (see Smułkowa, 2002), with English as the dominant language in the public sphere and Polish being limited to the private sphere.

In fact, the linguistic situation in Poland is far from that which would make diglossia a likely future scenario. According to data published by *The Economist* in October 1997, 11% of Poles professed at least average knowledge of English, while in a similar survey in 2000 the number was closer to 20%, consisting in particular of young Poles learning English intensively: at state run and private schools of primary and secondary level, language schools, teacher training colleges, universities, British Council courses, summer schools, language courses abroad – everywhere they could. The English language is now considered by Poles their main window on Europe. The Poles still have a long way to go, compared to the Dutch or the Swedes, who showed the highest score in the same survey with 70–80% claiming knowledge of English (data reprinted by the daily *Gazeta Wyborcza* in 1997 and 2000).

The 1990s was a period of transition for Poland, when it faced a huge influx of international words, mostly from American English, which was connected with the economic and political transformation, following adoption of the capitalist system after Communism had collapsed. As a result, speakers started feeling confused as previously comparatively stable language patterns started to become affected, as evidenced by the new 1999 edition of *Słownik poprawnej polszczyzny* ('A Dictionary of Correct Polish'), an official publication, prescriptive in its approach and authorised by the Polish Language Council (*Rada Języka Polskiego*). For the first time in history, it recognised the existence of two language norms in Poland: the variety that is the colloquial norm, and the model that is the official norm. The former is less strict and recognises a series of usages which have recently come into widespread use in colloquial spoken Polish, including a number of English loan words. The official norm comprises the recommended forms which should be used in written language and for purposes such as public speeches, official presentations, lectures, sermons, debates, etc. Further evidence of the fact that Polish is a language in transition and that norms have become less rigid is the size of the new edition of the Dictionary: 1785 pages, compared with 1055 pages of the former edition from 1973. One of the reasons for the adoption of the double norm was the expansion of colloquialisms into standard Polish, previously rather stilted in official situations; the trend is particularly marked in the media (Majkowska & Satkiewicz, 1999: 195).

The impact of English on Polish has been uneven, certain semantic fields having been influenced more than others. However, in the main, traces where Polish yields to other languages, mostly English, are noticeable only in the language of science and technology in the public sphere (Pisarek, 1999: 9): English has dominated international conferences in the natural sciences as well as published articles in most journals. In other instances, Polish holds a very strong grasp on public life in Poland, although under the influence of English it has turned over a new leaf in the 15 years that have passed since the change of the political and economic system.

Lexical Influence of English on Polish in Poland and in the US

In 1989, Poland saw a new system that made the American lifestyle highly popular; a new social class of so-called yuppies appeared, bringing along a new vocabulary in which Americanisms feature prominently. Now young *businessmen* call themselves either *salesmen* (Polish *sprzedawca* – 'shop assistant' – fell into disgrace) or *art directors*, or introduce themselves as *PRs* of their company. They deal with *leasing, consulting* or *dealer sales* (Polish *dealerstwo*). When they want to get a job, they go for *interviews*, having their *CVs* in their pockets, written in accordance with the American *how-to* manuals. They use *billboards*, they are *creative*, they have *clients, bosses*, they run around town talking on their *mobile phones*, at noon they go for *lunch*, in the evening they go to a *bar* for a *drink*. Once every ten minutes they say *sorry, OK, oops, wow*. They exchange *handshakes*, they are *cool*, and they enjoy swearing in English. At work they keep using English terminology, not even trying to find Polish equivalents, and when talking, they constantly insert direct translations of English phrases (adapted from Serejska Olszer, 2001: 41–2)

Newspapers and magazines poke fun at this new social group and their language as evidenced by the publication of spoof conversations. In the imagined exchange below, the account manager Basia and the copy-writer Piotrek talk in the Creative Department of a Polish company:

B: Ten *spot* ma być *stargetowany* na *teenagerów*. Postępuj zgodnie z *briefem* i postaraj się w *selling linie zfocusować* na *benefitach* całego *rangu produktów*.'

P: Jaki jest *deadline* na *prezentację story boardu?*

B: *Skanselowaliśmy* jeden termin i następny jest do *zdeterminowania*. Potrzebne są kolorowe *layouty printów* – najlepiej *spready, wyrenderowane billboardy* i *story board. Copy* po polsku z *back translation, OK?*
(Serejska Olszer, 2001: 219; after *Polityka* magazine)

The kind of linguistic pressure exerted by American English on Polish spoken in Poland puts the similar pressure felt by Americans of Polish origin, the users of so-called 'pidgin Polish' in America, in a different perspective. Naturally, the influence of American English on their native language is much stronger, Polish being confined to their homes, while most public life is the domain of American English. Serejska Olszer (2001) discusses the typically 'polonised' loan words used by Poles in America, most of them not justified by existing lexical gaps in Polish, but acquired through the influence of the American environment (see also Polymnia Tsagouria, this volume for Greek in the US): *bejzment* ('basement'), *offic* ('office'), *trock* ('truck'), *wena* ('van'), *subkontraktor* (subcontractor), *hauskiper* ('housekeeper'), *łykend* ('weekend'), *lancz* ('lunch'), *gabeć* ('garbage'), *egzyt* ('exit'). Other expressions, which would be difficult to express in Polish through the use of single words, are also borrowed by Poles in America, in order to express specific meanings absent in related Polish terms, for example *graduacja* ('graduation'), *tenura* ('tenure'), *karpety* ('carpeting'), *dean, chancellor* (Serejska Olszer, 2001: 150–52). Poles in Poland adopted unfamiliar American terms, such as 'dealer' or 'marketing', in much the same way. There are differences though: while, for instance, 'interview' was replaced in Poland by *rozmowa kwalifikacyjna*, following the initial omnipresence of the English loan word, this did not happen in America (Serejska Olszer, 2001: 155). The pidgin sentence *lukuj, lukuj, czy ta kara jeszcze stoi przy kornerze, bo tykietuja i tołuja* ('look, look if the car is still at the corner, as they are giving tickets and tow cars away') has become proverbial and was known in a similar form as far back as the late nineteenth century when the writer and Nobel prize winner Henryk Sienkiewicz wrote for Polish newspapers, discussing oddities of the Polish-American language in letters from America. The pidgin has developed to such an extent that a Polish-pidgin dictionary is being compiled for use by Polish tourists in the US.

In our discussion of lexical borrowings, it is worth mentioning research by Anisimowicz (2001), who examined contexts in which unassimilated English loan words or expressions appeared in newspaper articles in Poland. In many cases, the cohesion of the texts was disturbed, as explanations were largely absent, so that the meaning of the loanwords had to be inferred. For example:

- *A ja jestem dobrej myśli, bo teraz z Polsce „business is busines".* Mamy *dowody na to, 'że jest popyt na muzykę środka.* ('I am optimistic, as now in Poland business is business. We have proofs of the demand for mid-market music.) (Anisimowicz, 2001: 16).
- *Zanim „Killer" został skierowany do produkcji, przeszedł tzw. script doktoring. – Machulski zmienił typ humoru, a co za tym idzie dialogi. Wypadły też kosztowne pościgi samochodowe – wylicza Piotr Wereśniak.*

('Before *Killer* was cleared for production it went through "script doctoring". Machulski changed the type of humour, and, consequently, the style of dialogue. The expensive car chases were dropped too, explains Piotr Wereśniak.') (Anisimowicz, 2001: 20).

As is shown by the above examples, the new vocabulary points to the influence of English, which is prominent and readily noticeable. There are two basic reasons for the expansion of Polish vocabulary in this way:

(1) the Poles need to name new concepts, new elements of their world which were absent before (particularly in some semantic fields, such as electronics, cosmetics, banking, economy, trade and tourism);
(2) they also need to expand on their expressive vocabulary in order to be able to convey their attitudes towards the physical or mental aspects of the world (this is particularly salient in the area of word formation: new, expressive affixes abound – see next section).

Transformations in vocabulary take place in two ways:

(1) new lexical items, syntactic and semantic neologisms and loan words are introduced;
(2) the range of the use and status of some words, limited by register, changes with words moving between varieties, particularly from colloquial, regional and professional varieties to the standard language (Dunaj, 2000: 28–9).

Power of expression and economy

The development towards internationalisation coincides with the tendency towards economy of expression, with abbreviated forms rapidly spreading in Polish, for example *autokomis, automyjnia, speckomisja* for 'second-hand car dealer', 'car wash' or 'special commission' respectively (Dunaj, 2000: 30). This latter tendency, as well as the need for self-expression, is reflected in a huge influx of creative prefixes, largely Latin and Greek in origin but mediated through English, for example *super-, re-, de-, pro-, anty-, post-, mega-, hiper-, extra-, pseudo-, mini-, mikro-, euro-, tele-, wideo-, neo-, eko-, agro-, bio-, cyber-, eks-, krypto-, multi-, narko-, para-, porno-, quasi-, seks-* (Dunaj, 2000: 29–30), as well as the loaned suffixes: for example *–izacja, -ing* and *-ant* (see Serejska, 2001: 39). The prefixes help to form nouns, adjectives or participles, such as *subnotebook, superwykładzina, ultracienkie, extraprogram, preinstalowany, multiwkrętak* (Chłopicki & Świątek, 2000: 373-8), which are used mostly in the language of advertising, where their expressive function makes them highly desirable loans.

The need to fulfil this function is probably also the reason for the spread of such forms as the adverb *dokładnie* ('exactly'), which has nearly supplanted the native contextual synonym *właśnie*, a less expressive reply to a statement with which we agree. Other emotive words are imported directly from English, for example 'wow', 'oops', 'hi', 'hello', 'sorry', and have spread mostly among young people, influenced by English-language films as well as by the speech used by native speakers of English to express their reactions. Relatively formal phrases find their way into informal conversations too, another sign of the language deregulation mentioned above. For instance, the expression *z tej strony* is being used with increasing frequency as an opening to private telephone conversations: *Cześć, Maciek z tej strony* ('Hi, it's Maciek at this end') replacing the more idiomatic phrase: *Cześć, mówi Maciek* ('Hi, Maciek speaking'). It could be argued that the reason is the transfer of polite but foreign telephone manners which are required from employees in many international companies based in Poland to informal, private conversations, a testimony to the fact that many Poles are not linguistically sensitive to the crucial difference between official and unofficial registers in their own language.

Unjustified loan words and calques

A striking feature of the recent expansion of Polish vocabulary is the great number of unjustified loan words which have good native equivalents ('shop' – *sklep*, 'top' – *bluzka*), while many others can be considered justified as fillers of lexical gaps, mainly in the field of electronics, banking, cosmetics or marketing, such as 'market', 'dealer', 'T-shirt', or 'gadget'. In some cases, it could be argued that the advantage of these new lexical items over the established terms such as *sklep*, *sprzedawca* ('seller'), *koszulka* ('shirt/blouse') or *urządzenie* ('device') is their universal applicability. Such is the case with 'sponsor', which now tends to replace *mecenas* and 'patron', referring to private and public sponsorship respectively; other examples include *kreować* ('create') and *kreatywność* ('creativity'), which are considered more attractive than *pomysłowość* ('ingenuity') and *inwencja* ('inventiveness'), and have been used extensively in particular in the media. The newly formed position of the Creative Director in foreign-owned advertising companies operating in Poland has been rendered into Polish as *Dyrektor Kreatywny*, which sounds odd in Polish as *kreatywny* can describe a trait of an individual person and not of anyone who happens to fill the post. Furthermore, according to the Polish perspective, the *dyrektor* should first of all follow the rules, and not 'create' them as the title seems to suggest. In fact, the cultural clash is epitomised in the nature of this new position more than in anything else.

A very characteristic feature of the influence of English is semantic shifts among existing Polish lexical items which often acquire new meanings. *Promocja*, which used to refer to a school certificate and employee promotion in a company, now (owing to the influence of English) refers primarily to a marketing strategy aiming at selling something. Moreover, the noun *promotor*, which traditionally meant a thesis supervisor in a university context, now also refers to a sales representative who will come to your house, demonstrate a product and try to sell it to you (see Chłopicki & Świątek, 2000: 121–5; Chłopicki & Świątek, 2001: 319). *Rozwój*, which used to mean primarily the process of being developed, now refers to creating, for example business, team, operations, links, friendship, programme, traditions, showing the very clear influence of American usage (see Chłopicki & Świątek, 2000: 253–5). *Lojalność*, which used to refer only to interpersonal relations, can now be employed in the phrase 'loyalty to brand names' as in American marketing jargon (Bralczyk, 2001: 57). A similar case is that of *agresywność* ('aggressiveness'), which in its new marketing meaning can have a positive connotation and describe active and successful salesmanship (Chłopicki & Świątek, 2000: 286).

A related development is new collocations, since new meanings are usually developed by or expressed through new phrases and expressions. These occur mostly in advertising and the media, which use them as attention catchers. And so we can hear of *inteligentny proszek* ('intelligent detergent'), *sprytne pranie* ('clever laundry'), or *pielęgnacja samochodu* ('nursing the car' – meaning 'maintenance'), the phrases which typically expand the hitherto accepted scope of personification in Polish (Bralczyk, 2001: 64–69). If you want to sell your product, make it sound as if it were a human being, the advertisers seem to be saying. New collocations also appear to gain in expressive strength, for example in one radio commercial for a supermarket chain, prices spoke in high-pitched childish voices and said *jesteśmy takie małe* ('we are so small'). The billboards which followed up on the campaign also boasted of *małe ceny* (literally 'small' prices, instead of 'low' prices), which was naturally the reference to the imagined children from the commercial.

Sometimes certain advertising keywords are used so frequently that, to express all the required meanings, they start occurring in a number of previously unknown collocations. 'Successful' is a case in point. It appears in quite a range of collocations in English, for example in reference to a person, company, party, career, attempt, or even life. As a result of the influence of English on Polish, these collocations entered Polish which had originally dealt with the same contexts in varied, non-uniform ways: on the one hand, a person could *odnieść sukces w życiu* ('be successful in life'), a company could *odnosić sukcesy na rynku* ('be successful on the market'), but on the other, a party, attempt or life may be *udane* ('successful') while a career may be *błyskotliwa* ('brilliant'). 'A success-oriented man' is more idiomatically rendered as *człowiek ambitny* ('ambitious man'), and 'a success-oriented company' as *prężna/dynamiczna firma* ('resilient, dynamic company'). Furthermore, 'a record of success in . . .', the expression frequently used in adverts of headhunting companies, cannot be directly translated into Polish except with the word *doświadcze-nie* ('experience'). Advertisers, however, seem to ignore these linguistic habits of the Poles, and indeed insert direct translations of English phrases into the copy they produce. For instance, companies look for partners who are *nastawieni na success* ('success-oriented'), they require experience *z udokumentowanym sukcesem* ('with a record of success') or *doświadczenie w udanej sprzedaży* ('successful sales experience') (see Chłopicki & Świątek, 2000: 246–8).

What advertisers do then is produce calques of handy English phrases, which sound odd in Polish even though they consist of Polish words. Calques abound everywhere in the media. A recent example is *pogotowie bezpieczeństwa*, the expression used on the Polish radio on 9 September 2002 to refer to the 'safety alert' introduced in the US prior to the anniversary of the 9/11 attacks. This direct translation would more precisely be rendered with *stan pogotowia* ('state of alert'). Calques are found in private conversations too – *Jest mi potwornie przykro* sounds like a translation of 'I am terribly sorry' introduced to boost the expressive power of *Jest mi bardzo przykro* ('I am very sorry') – as well as in sports commentaries: *idealny remis* ('a perfect tie'; see Bralczyk, 2001: 86) seems to express an emotional attitude towards the result, rather than the 'ideal' nature of the tie. Calques are present in large numbers also in video camera instruction manuals (Roszko, 2001), for example *szybkość migawki* ('shutter speed'). What Roszko stresses is the lack of linguistic and professional preparation in the writing of instruction manuals, which results in careless and incoherent texts.

The parallel evolution of Polish and other languages

An interesting aspect of the recent development of Polish, often ignored by Polish researchers, is that it is, at least to some extent, parallel to the contemporary development of other languages, including English, sometimes faster, sometimes slower. Let us then briefly look at some recent, largely lexical developments in Polish and English in that respect. An obvious example is the growth of political correctness (PC), which is slowly penetrating into Polish. On the one hand, in Polish grammar there is special plural sub-gender called *męskoosobowy*, which always requires that two or more males as well as a male and a female be referred to using a male plural pronoun *oni* and its related forms. On the other hand, 'Everybody should mind his/her/their business' may very easily be expressed through the use of the neutral pronoun *swój*, which can cover all those cases. Polish is rich in inflections and can naturally distinguish genders as in *Nauczycielka zrobiła* ('A female teacher did') and *Nauczyciel zrobił* ('A male teacher did'). Some non-grammatical elements of political correctness have filtered through, however, for example persons with a disability are no longer referred to as *upośledzeni* ('handicapped'), but as *niepełnosprawni* ('disabled'), or even *sprawni inaczej'* ('differently abled'), although this last expression can have humourous connotations.

Some lexical items acquire new meanings in both languages, for example the noun 'alternative' seems to have passed along a similar route in Polish as in English. Originating in Latin, it referred to 'one of two possibilities', but in popular usage in the two languages it has become synonymous with 'option' or 'possibility', as in the phrases 'We have several alternatives to choose from' or *Są inne alternatywy*, which is still considered inappropriate by some users (see *Longman Dictionary of English Language and Culture* and Bralczyk, 2001: 85). Similarly, the noun 'couple' (but not 'pair') is used in English to refer not only to 'two things', but also to 'a few, several things', and in Polish the noun *para* ('pair') has also been used in both the senses for some time now (Bralczyk, 2001: 75). In English, the distinction 'number/amount' is rather strict, although as dictionaries acknowledge 'amount is used when talking about goods which are handled in large quantities: *The shopkeeper had a large amount of oranges in his storeroom'* (*Longman Dictionary of English Language and Culture*). Poles have the problem of distinguishing between *liczba* ('number') and *ilość* ('amount'), perhaps because the countable/uncountable distinction is not so vital in Polish as it is in English, to such an extent that Bralczyk even argues that usages such as *ilość ludzi'* ('amount of people') or *ilość dzieci* ('amount of children') will have to be accepted as part of the standard (i.e. colloquial) norm (2001: 80).

Some new developments, however, are typical of Polish, for example the expansion of diminutives as a way of reducing the distance from the interlocutor, as if 'taming' the often hostile environment (*pieniażki, domek, kotlecik, kiełbaska* for *pieniądze, dom, kotlet, kiełbasa*). Some Poles have a strong reaction to this tendency and treat it as linguistic manipulation, particularly when used by shop assistants, waiters or interviewees; it can be compared to the habit of American salesmen frequently adding the phrase 'for you' when speaking to their customers. On the other hand, informal variants of people's first names are typically used in American English, including for public figures (President Bill Clinton). Here Polish is highly conservative, and the current fashion for American-style informal names (Olek Kwaśniewski for President Aleksander Kwaśniewski) is considered highly inappropriate by many Poles. The same goes for the habit among lorry drivers of displaying their first names in the diminutive form on the windshield of their lorries – this is directly contrary to the Polish tradition, which requires strangers to address one another with their full names first before they can use first names and then their shortened forms. Therefore, in this context the full first name and surname would be required, although in fact the best option for many Poles would be no name at all.

Direct forms of address

A certain tendency towards the use of first names and their shortened variants where tradition requires full names is in line with another pronounced trend, namely frequent and inappropriate use of the second person singular. This is clearly the result of the influence of English with its universal 'you' form, which fits both formal and informal contexts. Polish has a range of forms of address, including the impersonal (for example *trzeba, należy*; 'one should') and the third person singular (*Pan/Pani*) and plural (*Państwo*) for official, public contexts, and the second person singular (*ty*) and plural (*wy*) for unofficial, private contexts, although mixed forms exist as well, especially in print, including the first person plural (*my*) referring to you, the second person, the third person *Pan/i* and *Państwo* used with the second person verb forms, and *Państwo* and *wy* forms combined in one text (most of the mixed forms are used to reduce the distance typical of official forms, at the same time avoiding the very direct second person singular form) (see Chłopicki, 2000: 190; Chłopicki & Świątek, 2000: 322–31). The expansion of the '*ty* convention' and the confusion in the range of forms of address is characteristic of advertising and the electronic media. Radio audiences are particularly exposed since some commercial radio stations make it their policy to use direct forms to address their listeners, regardless of their age, which is a violation of the traditional system. Under American influence, radio presenters use very colloquial language and address their audiences informally, saying for example *Powinniście już wstawać* ('You should now get up'; Bralczyk, 2001: 24). Bralczyk even noticed symptomatic mistakes made, probably under the influence of English, by people who introduced themselves saying: *Nazywam się Maria* ('My name is Maria'). This is inappropriate in Polish as the form *nazywam się* calls for the use of the surname, while first names should be given using the form: *Mam na imię Maria* ('My first name is Maria'). Alternatively, the form could be followed by both the first name and the surname, for example *Nazywam się (Maria) Kowalska* (Bralczyk, 2001: 26).

Non-Lexical Influences

Now a few remarks are in order about the non-lexical influence of English, which is quite varied and includes reduction of inflections, copying the English use of capitalisation and possessive pronouns, of English structures and idioms, as well as expansion of English metaphors and personification. All these and other phenomena have been analysed in detail in Chłopicki & Świątek (2000). A few examples are discussed here.

The spread of capitalisation is very characteristic of the influence of English as Polish normally capitalises fewer nouns and other lexical items than English, and the sudden tendency to extend capitalisation of important items in the text is rather striking, especially since traditionally Poles use capital letters in titles and proper names only for the first word of the name. Here are some examples of modern capitalisation patterns (Chłopicki & Świątek, 2000: 211–9).

- *Rozwiążemy Każdy Fotograficzny Problem* ('We will solve all your photographic problems'; advertising slogan).
- *SIPS – System Ochrony Przed Uderzeniami Bocznymi* ('Side Impact Protection System'; concept in car technology).
- *Podstawowe zasady: Jakość, Odpowiedzialność, Wzajemność, Wydajność i Wolność, stanowią o tożsamości naszej firmy* ('The fundamental principles of Quality, Responsibility, Mutuality, Efficiency and Freedom mark the identity of our company'; job advert).
- *Program Pomocy Pracownikom Naukowym w Wyjazdach na Konferencje Zagraniczne* ('Programme for Funding Trips of Academics to International Conferences'; foundation flyer).

Furthermore, the core of the Polish linguistic system, inflections, tend to become reduced, in particular in nominal phrases (see Handke, 1994). Lack of inflections is very typical of advertising discourse where foreign names tend not to be inflected, for instance, *modele Fiat* for *modele Fiata*, or *Kodak Produkty* for *Produkty Kodaka*. This latter slogan is characteristic of the expansion of the use of English nominal structures: *Komputer Świat* ('Computer World'), *Tenis nauka* ('Tennis lessons') or *Opony serwis* ('Tyre Service'), instead of the inflected Polish structures: *Świat komputerów, Nauka tenisa* or *Serwis opon*, respectively.

The increased use of possessive adjectives is another very clear example of the influence of English, with expressions such as *mydło nawilża Twoją skórę* ('the soap moisturises your skin') replacing the idiomatic *mydło nawilża skórę* ('zero pronoun') or *mydło nawilża Ci skórę* ('dative pronoun') (see Chłopicki & Świątek, 2000: 336–8).

The compactness of English nominal structures is very attractive to the media and to advertisers, as it allows an expression of the message in the most succinct way, such as the translation of 'land mines ban' as *zakaz min przeciwpiechotnych* instead of the more natural and idiomatic *zakaz stosowania min przeciwpiechotnych* ('ban on the use of land mines'; Bralczyk, 2001: 80–2). Similarly, the expression 'front-seat passenger' has sometimes been translated as *pasażer przedniego siedzenia* (Chłopicki & Świątek, 2000: 358), instead of the natural *pasażer siedzący obok kierowcy'* ('passenger sitting next to the driver'). Other English-style nominal structures also typically involve adjectives replacing prepositional phrases, for example *wanny masażowe* ('tub massaging') for *wanny do masażu'* ('tubs serving to massage') or *rozwiązania informatyczne* ('information solutions') for *rozwiązania z zakresu informatyki* ('solutions from the field of computer science'). Other syntactic aspects of English influence include the use in broadcasting of sentence openers such as *Ja myślę* ('I think'), *Ja sądzę* ('I believe'), *Ja przypuszczam* ('I suppose'), where the personal pronoun is unnecessary for syntactic reasons (the inflected verbal form presupposes the first person pronoun) and can only be used to emphasise that what follows is the speaker's opinion (especially when it is controversial). In this context, the expression *Jestem przekonany* ('I am convinced') is more acceptable because here some issue appears to be in dispute (see Bralczyk, 2001: 31).

To complete this overview, let us look at some metaphorical expressions which bear witness to a less obvious, but more far-reaching influence. Examples are taken mostly from advertising as this is the kind of discourse for which new metaphors are sought in order to enhance the persuasive element. Apart from the expansion of the scope of personification these examples illustrate the clashes of the abstract and the concrete (Polish seems unwilling to accept their juxtaposition), compact metaphors alien to Polish, and other foreign-sounding expressions.

- *Magnetowidy oferują najwyższy poziom jakości* ('The video recorders offer best quality levels') instead of 'Producers offer . . .' or 'Video recorders have . . .' which would reduce personification.
- *Światowy lider w produkcji herbatników* ('World leader in biscuit production'); 'world' (abstract) versus 'biscuit' (concrete).
- *Opony pozwolą Ci przejechać przez każdą zimę* ('The tyres will allow you to drive through the winter') – compact metaphor meaning 'the tyres will allow you to drive safely in winter'.
- *Prawdziwy diament wśród papierów ksero* ('The real diamond among papers') – abstract/concrete clash, 'The real pearl among papers' would be more idiomatic in Polish, although the clash would still remain.
- *Rodzina papierów do kopiowania* ('The family of copy papers') – a typical advertising metaphor, very odd in this context (abstract versus concrete).
- *Siła profesjonalnego obrazu na usługach Twojej firmy* ('The power of professional image in the service of your company') – this sounds rather far-fetched and abstract. The less metaphorical expression 'high printing quality in your company' would sound more convincing. (cf Chłopicki & Świątek, 2000: 510–544).

Conclusion

In this overview, I have tried to show the extent to which English has influenced Polish during the last decade. It can be concluded that, although the influence is considerable and very strong in some areas such as electronics or advertising, Polish has shown a great deal of resilience. According to some commentators, the quality of the resulting language leaves a lot to be desired, but it has certainly been enriched lexically by new concepts and collocations. Therefore, there seems to be no need to panic, as did one of the journalists from *Polityka* (1996) who wrote in desperation: 'Poles are not even willing to look for Polish equivalents for English terms or even simply translate them . . . Our language is dying.'

Notes
1.   All original translations by W. Chłopicki.

References
Anisimowicz, A. (2001) Spójnościowe aspekty zapożyczeń angielskich we współczesnej prasie polskiej. In G. Habrajska (ed.) *Język w komunikacji* (Vol. 3) (pp. 13–23) Łódź: Wyższa Szkoła Humanistyczno-Ekonomiczna.

Bralczyk, J. (2001) *Mówi się: Porady językowe profesora Bralczyka*. Warszawa: PWN.

Chłopicki, W. (2000) Język angielski w polskiej reklamie. In G. Szpila (ed.) *Język a komunikacja 1: Zbiór referatów z konferencji „Język trzeciego tysiąclecia"* (pp. 187–96) Kraków: Tertium.

Chłopicki, W. and Świątek, J. (2000) *Angielski w polskiej reklamie*. Kraków: PWN.

Chłopicki, W. and Świątek, J. (2001) Wpływ języka angielskiego na współczesny język polskiej reklamy. In G. Habrajska (ed.) *Język w komunikacji* (Vol. 1) (pp. 319–26) Łódź: Wyższa Szkoła Humanistyczno-Ekonomiczna.

Dunaj, B. (2000) O stanie współczesnej polszczyzny. In G. Szpila (ed.) *Język a komunikacja 1: Zbiór referatów z konferencji „Język trzeciego tysiąclecia"* (pp. 25–34) Kraków: Tertium.

Dunaj, B., Przybylska, R. and Sikora, K. (1999) Język na co dzień. In Rada Języka Polskiego przy Prezydium PAN and W. Pisarek (eds) *Polszczyzna 2000: Orędzie o stanie języka na przełomie tysiącleci* (pp. 227–51) Kraków: Ośrodek Badań Prasoznawczych UJ.

Gajda, S. (1999) Program polskiej polityki językowej. In J. Mazur (ed.) *Polska polityka językowa na przełomie tysiącleci* (pp. 179–88) Lublin: UMCS.

Handke, K. (1994) Przyczyny ograniczania fleksji nominalnej we współczesnej polszczyźnie. In K. Handke and H. Dalewska-Greń (eds) *Polszczyzna a/i Polacy u schyłku XX wieku: Zbiór studiów* (pp. 73–84) Warszawa: Slawistyczny Ośrodek Wydawniczy.

Kajtoch, W. (1999) Język mniejszości narodowych w Polsce. In Rada Języka Polskiego przy Prezydium PAN and W. Pisarek (eds) *Polszczyzna 2000: Orędzie o stanie języka na przełomie tysiącleci* (pp. 279–301) Kraków: Ośrodek Badań Prasoznawczych UJ.

Maćkiewicz, J. (2000) Czy Polska jest częścią Europy? Polszczyzna w europejskiej lidze językowej. In G. Szpila (ed.) *Język a komunikacja 1: Zbiór referatów z konferencji „Język trzeciego tysiąclecia"* (pp. 49–56) Kraków: Tertium.

Majkowska, G. and Satkiewicz H. (1999) Język w mediach. In Rada Języka Polskiego przy Prezydium PAN and W. Pisarek (eds) *Polszczyzna 2000: Orędzie o stanie języka na przełomie tysiącleci* (pp. 181–96) Kraków: Ośrodek Badań Prasoznawczych UJ.

Mańczak-Wohlfeld, E. (1994) *Angielskie elementy leksykalne w języku polskim.* Kraków: Universitas.

Miodunka, W.T. (1999) Język polski poza Polską. In Rada Języka Polskiego przy Prezydium PAN and W. Pisarek (eds) *Polszczyzna 2000: Orędzie o stanie języka na przełomie tysiącleci* (pp. 306–25) Kraków: Ośrodek Badań Prasoznawczych UJ.

Ożóg, K. (2001) *Polszczyzna przełomu XX i XXI wieku: Wybrane zagadnienia.* Rzeszów: Fraza.

Pisarek, W. (1999) Wprowadzenie. In Rada Języka Polskiego przy Prezydium PAN and W. Pisarek (eds) *Polszczyzna 2000: Orędzie o stanie języka na przełomie tysiącleci* (pp. 5–11) Kraków: Ośrodek Badań Prasoznawczych UJ.

Roszko, R. (2001) Język polskojęzycznych instrukcji obsługi kamer wideo. In G. Habrajska (ed.) *Język w komunikacji* (Vol. 3) (pp. 134–40) Łódź: Wyższa Szkoła Humanistyczno-Ekonomiczna.

Serejska Olszer, K. (2001) *Polszczyzna z oddali: Język polski w anglojęzycznym świecie.* Poznań: Media Rodzina.

Smułkowa, E. (2002) Language, Identity, Nationality in Social and Political Change – Poland and the East. In E. Jeleń *et al.* (eds). *Language Dynamics and Linguistic Identity in the Context of European Integration.* (pp. 79–88) Kraków: Księgarnia Akademicka.

Chapter 8

New Anglicisms in Russian

NELLY G. CHACHIBAIA and MICHAEL R. COLENSO

Introduction

The radical changes in Russian life during the last decade of the twentieth century – the sudden increased exposure to Western influence, and the introduction of large numbers of new institutions, habits and concepts – have led to the inundation of the Russian language with neologisms, in particular Anglicisms, due to the global use of English. These neologisms relate in particular to the ideology of democratic change in Russia, in the economy and its management, social problems, scientific and technological progress, education and culture, law and order, international and inter-ethnic relations.

Many well-established words in the Russian lexicon are loan words from various languages. A large number of them have entered Russian from non-Slavonic peoples and languages at various times in Russia's history: for example, from the Turkic nomads who inhabited the southern steppes in the early Middle Ages (for example *loshad'* – 'horse'); from Greek around the time of Russia's conversion to Christianity in the tenth century (for example *angel* – 'angel'; *evangelie* – 'the Gospels'); from the Tatars, who ruled over Russia from the thirteenth to the fifteenth century (for example *den'gi* – 'money'; *tamozhnya* – 'Customs'; *yarlyk* – 'label', and many others); from German, from the time of Peter the Great at the beginning of the eighteenth century (for example *bank* – 'bank'; *universitet* – 'university'); and from French, from the mid-eighteenth century (*p'esa* – 'play'; *teatr* – 'theatre').

The status of many loan words in Russian is very unstable. We should distinguish between:

(1) those for which there appears a genuine need inasmuch as they denote a new concept which an existing Russian word does not convey, or at least does not convey with the appropriate flavour;
(2) those which seem modish and which are used more for the sake of their resonance, being up-to-date and exotic, than because they convey essentially new meaning.

The fact that such loanwords have become so fully absorbed into the Russian word stock has left little room for suspicion in people's minds that they are anything other than Russian words.

In this chapter we consider Anglicisms in Russian[1] – particularly over the last two decades – exclusively on the lexical and semantic level. The reason for so doing is that the grammatical system of Russian is less susceptible to influence from foreign words and stricter in making foreign words conform to its grammatical rules than some other languages. All English words which enter the Russian language fall into Russian grammatical categories irrespective of the existence or absence of such categories in the grammatical system of English (see Aristova, 1978).

Russian is a flexible language with a wide range of derivational means. It assimilates borrowings easily by giving them certain morphological characteristics (gender, number, type of declension or conjugation, prefixation, suffixation, etc.), and by forming a derivational paradigm on the basis of a single borrowed word (for example *universitet* – borrowed noun [n.] > *universitetskii* – derived adjective [adj.]; *sport* [n.] > *sportivnyi* [adj.]; *eksperiment* [n.] > *eksperimental'nyi* [adj.]; *kriminal* [n.] > *kriminal'nyi* [adj.]; *al'ternativa* [borrowed noun] > *bezal'ternativnost'* – lack of alternative – [derived abstract noun using prefix *bez-* 'without' and suffix *-nost'* – '-ness']; *lobbi* [n.] > *lobbirovat'* [v.] – 'to lobby', and *lobbirovanie* – 'lobbying' – [derived abstract noun].

A borrowing may be used in a narrower or wider sense than its equivalent in the language from which it is borrowed (Offord, 1996), for example the Russian borrowing *okaziya* ('an opportunity', or 'unexpected happening') is narrower than English 'occasion'; *obligatsiya* means 'a bond', in the specialised economic sense, and not 'an obligation' in the general sense. Divergences of this kind may become so great that substantial differences of meaning arise, for example *replika*, in Russian, is a cue or response in speech, and not an exact copy of something. The loan word *ambitsiya*, and the derived adjective *ambitsioznyi*, express only proud and arrogant ambition, and not healthy, positive aspiration. Borrowings like these have become the *faux amis* of the translator, which are an interesting and important topic in itself, but we shall not be considering them in this chapter.

It is relevant to mention here the fact that borrowings may also undergo changes of stress as they enter the receptor language, for example (English) *marketing* > (Russian) mar**ke**ting; (E) *monitoring* > (R) moni**to**ring; (E) *football* > (R) fut**bol**; (E) *goalkeeper* > (R) gol**ki**per.

In considering the phenomenon of lexical borrowing as an outcome of language adaptation to changing environments, we must first address the question of economic, political and cultural globalisation as a major cause of the globalisation of English and of the enormous impact of English upon other languages.

Globalisation

Globalisation is one of today's main preoccupations. To some, it means something that will improve our lives in all kinds of ways; to others it represents something vague and menacing, something bound to create unhappiness and disorientation. For everyone, however, globalisation is the intractable fate of the world, an irreversible process (Bauman, 1998).

The study of globalisation, initiated by economists and other social scientists, developed as a response to the emergence of a global economy grounded in modernisation and fuelled by the expansion of Western capitalism. Initially, attention was focused on how the growth of capital production had, by the 1960s, become increasingly tied to the rise of transnational corporations and the proliferation of markets that regularly crossed nation state boundaries.

Globalisation is not a new phenomenon; it has a long history. Its evolution embraces a series of life-changing events, such as the schism in Christianity, the development of maps and maritime travel, the rise of the nation state, global exploration, colonialism, the creation of citizenship and passports, diplomacy and the entire paraphernalia of international relations, the rise of international communication and mass migration, the founding of international organisations like the League of Nations (replaced in 1945 by the United Nations), the outbreak of world wars, space exploration, and a developing sense that communities based on race, ethnicity, gender, sexual preference and so on cut across national and state boundaries (Jay, 2001).

Globalisation studies have gradually moved from an initial interest in the emergence of a global economy towards an interest in globalisation as a cultural phenomenon. This process is certainly at work in the global spread of English, which is increasingly influenced by various cultural traditions specific to diaspora communities in the USA (Asian, Puerto Rican, South Asian, African, Latin American, etc.). The culture of English is so thoroughly hybridised, so inexorably based on complex exchanges among these different cultures, that it is becoming ever more difficult to identify a dominant Western discourse that is not being subordinated to, and shaped by, this accelerating mix of sources and discourses from outside Britain and the USA.

So, why a global language? There is the closest connection between language dominance and cultural power. Without a strong power base, whether political, military or economic, no language can make progress as an international medium of communication. Language has no independent existence, living in some sort of mystical space apart from the people who speak it. When people succeed on the international stage, their language succeeds; when they fail, their language fails (Crystal, 1997a).

Industry and commerce in the USA, that nation's post-World War II emergence as a technological leader, and the worldwide network of communication – which is now an established fact of modern life – have all combined to ensure that English is in use in almost every part of the world (Marckwardt, 1980). English is becoming the *lingua franca* of the world. It is used as the official or semi-official language in over 60 countries. It is either dominant or well established in all six continents. It is the main language of books, newspapers, airports and air traffic control, international business and academic conferences, science,[2] technology, medicine, diplomacy, sport, international competitions, pop music and advertising (Crystal, 1997b).

We use English for our international contacts, and we believe that, at the beginning of the twenty-first century, we need to make a programmatic commitment to the study of English in a newer, global framework, one that recognises the transnational character of English in the past, and the global context in which it will function in the future.

The idea of inventing an international language is not new. In the past 200 years a number of attempts have been made to invent an international language which would be easy to learn and equitable to many national language groups. There are more than a dozen of these invented languages, including Kosmos, Monoglottica, Neo-Latine, Mundolingue, Esperanto[3] and so on, all dedicated to the idea of establishing one international language for the entire planet (Berlitz, 1984).

Due to its past, modern English is an assimilated mixture of a number of languages. To the original crucible of Celtic, Anglo-Saxon and Norman French thousands of other words have been added from Dutch, the Scandinavian languages, German, modern French, Italian, Spanish, Portuguese, Arabic, Hindi, Hebrew, Malay, Chinese, Japanese and the Amerindian tongues (Berlitz, 1984). Russian too has contributed to its present-day vocabulary. For example: *vodka* ('little water'), *samovar* ('self-boiler'), *pogrom* ('massacre'), *sputnik* ('fellow-traveller; satellite').

Whereas English was formerly enriched by borrowing from other languages, a reverse process may now be observed, namely the enrichment of other languages by English. Our focus in this chapter is on the influence of English on Russian over the last 20 years, i.e. since *Perestroika* (economic and political reconstruction) in Russia.

The disintegration of the Soviet Union and its political system opened the country's borders to foreign influence and provided access to the global economy and culture, including the media. People were presented with new opportunities for broad international interaction and communication. These environmental changes have accelerated the process of borrowing.

There are three main reasons for borrowing:

(1) lack of an equivalent word in the receptor language;
(2) the establishment of some positive or negative connotation which the equivalent word in the receptor language lacks;
(3) the establishment of stylistic or emphatic effect.

We shall discuss these in turn in relation to Russian, before presenting some examples of recent borrowings.

Lack of an Equivalent Word in the Receptor Language

The first, and most obvious, reason for borrowing is to represent a phenomenon for which there is no exact equivalent in the receptor language. These borrowings arise because of societal differences (political, economic, technical and cultural), for example:

seil ('cut-price sale')
peidzher ('pager')
spiker ('parliamentary Speaker')
diler ('dealer')

Examples from recent press articles:

*Pervichnyi **reiting** na vtorichnom rynke* ('Prime **rating** on a secondary market').

***Lizing** khotyat lishit' investitsionnoi privlekatel'nosti* ('Plans to remove the investment attractiveness of **leasing**').

In some cases borrowed words are found in newspapers given directly in English, for example

***Windows** – ne instrument monopolii na rynke brauzerov* ('**Windows** is not an instrument of monopoly in the browser market').

It may be noted that *instrument, monopolii* and *brauzer* are also borrowings, *brauzer* being a very new addition from computing terminology.

Imperiya **Microsoft** ustoyala na sude *('The **Microsoft** empire wins the case')*.

Establishing Positive or Negative Connotations Which the Equivalent Word in the Receptor Language Lacks

It has always been fashionable in certain circles in Russia to believe that foreign technology is more advanced, foreign economies are more successful, foreign food is tastier, foreign banks are more reliable, and foreign goods are of higher quality than their Russian equivalents. These views are widely exploited in advertising, in which borrowings are used in place of Russian synonyms to provide positive connotations, for example:

Novyi **bestseller** ('New bestseller'), instead of the Russian word *boevik* ('a hit').

While borrowing is a perfectly natural process in language enrichment, borrowings of this kind – which proliferate in the Russian press – impose on Russian readers a need to know English as well as their own language in order to understand what is being said. This is a cause of great frustration for many readers.

Establishing Stylistic or Emphatic Effect

Borrowings are widely used in the media for achieving stylistic effect, for example in news headlines:

Satisfaktsiya *Hakkinena* ('Hakkinen's **satisfaction**'),

where a borrowed word has been substituted for the usual Russian word *udovletvorenie* to produce an emotional effect. Another example (from a newspaper advertisement):

. . . **eksklyuzivnaya** villa *('exclusive* villa').

A Russian word (or an older – and therefore more widely understood – borrowing) could have expressed 'exclusive' equally well; the word used here, however, lends the phrase a certain *cachet*. In an advertisement, it would have a greater impact on a potential buyer. A third example:

Ona **trudogolik**. ('She's a **workaholic**'); *trudogolik* substitutes for Russian *rabotyaga*.

The effect of the hybrid (Russian *trud* – 'labour' – plus borrowed suffix – 'holic') is to add a touch of humour and affection, which is lacking in *rabotyaga*.

Modern Borrowings

Recent loans are predominantly Anglicisms, mostly from American English. These borrowings cover the following semantic fields:

(1) **social and political life**, for example *oppozitsiya* ('opposition'); *konfrontatsiya* ('confrontation'); *lobbi* ('lobby'); *prezident* ('President'); *spiker* ('Speaker'); *lider* ('leader'); *impichment* ('impeachment'), *reiting* ('rating'); *spich-raiter* ('speechwriter'); *imidzh-meiker* ('image-maker'); *n'yusmeiker* ('news maker'); *plyuralizm* ('pluralism'); *killer* ('hired killer'); *autsaider* ('outsider'); *piarshchik* ('public relations officer'); *krieitor* ('creator'); *sponsor* ('sponsor'); *prezentatsiya* ('presentation'); *platforma* ('political platform); *reket/-ir* ('racket/-eer'); elektorat ('electorate'); *brifing* ('briefing'); *globalizatsiya* ('globalisation'); *sammit* ('summit'); *pablisiti* ('publicity');

(2) **finance, economy and trade**, for example *biznesmen* ('businessman'); *nou-khau* ('know-how'); *vaucher* ('voucher'); *broker* ('broker'); *marketing* ('marketing'); *monitoring* ('monitoring'); *lizing* ('leasing'); *taimsher* ('timeshare'); *menedzher* ('manager'); *logistika* ('logistics'); *banknot* ('banknote'); *baksy* ('bucks, $'); *investor* ('investor'); *sekvestr* ('sequestration'); *transfer* ('transfer'); *oferta* ('offer'); *transh* ('tranche'); *audit* ('audit'); *tender* ('tender'); *shokovaya terapiya* ('shock therapy'); *kholding-kompaniya* ('holding company'); *giperinflyatsiya* ('hyperinflation');

(3) **information and communication technology**, for example *komp'yuter* ('computer'); *Internet* ('Internet'); *printer* ('printer); *i meil* ('e-mail'); *skaner* ('scanner'); *noutbook* ('electronic notebook', i.e. 'palmtop'); *defolt* ('default); *sait* ('site'); *veb* ('web'); *fail* ('file'); *deskriptor* ('descriptor') *khaker* ('hacker'); *chat* ('chat'); *modem* ('modem'); *klaster* ('cluster'); *freim* ('frame'); *khosting* ('hosting'); *gipertekst* ('hypertext'); *brauzer* ('browser'); *navigatsiya* ('navigation'); *kibrarian* ('cybrarian'); *peidzher* ('pager); *khends-fri* ('hands-free'); *kopirait* ('copyright'); <u>*mobil'nyi* telefon</u> ('<u>mobile</u> phone');

(4) **education, culture and arts**, for example *kolledzh* ('college'); *spelling* ('spelling'); *test* ('test'); *sertifikat* ('certificate'); *roud-muvi* ('road-movie'); *triller* ('thriller');

(5) **travel and tourism**, for example *shop-tur* ('shopping trip'); *motel* ('motel'); *kommunikatsiya* ('communication'); *informatsiya* ('information'); *tranzit* ('transit'); *charternyi reis* ('charter flight');

(6) **food and drink**, for example *sendvich* ('sandwich'); *lanch* ('lunch'); *chizburger* ('cheeseburger'); *kokteil'* ('cocktail'); *barbek'yu* ('barbecue'); *drink* ('drink'); *fast food – sic* ('fast food');

(7) **clothes and fashion**, for example *feshnshou* ('fashion show'); *pampersy* ('Pampers'); *shuzy* ('shoes'); *snikersy* ('sneakers');

(8) **sport**, for example *sheiping* ('shaping'); *fristail* ('freestyle'); *pleiof* ('play-off'); *skeitbord* ('skateboard').
    (Note: Sport in Russia has always drawn heavily on words and terms borrowed from English – *start, finish, match, offside, penalty, goalkeeper,* etc. They are too numerous, and also too well established, to merit extensive listing here)

(9) **pop music and entertainment**, for example blyuz ('the Blues'); *shoubiznes* ('show business'); *di-dzhei* ('DJ'); *SiDi-pleier* ('CD player'); *kompakt-disk* ('CD'); *rok-klub* ('rock club'); *rep* ('rap'); *klip* ('clip, short TV item');

(10) **standard forms of communication**, for example *khai!* ('Hi!'); *bai-bai* ('bye-bye'); *o'kei* ('OK'); *olrait* ('all right').

Borrowings of these kinds are to be found everywhere in the media (press, radio, television, advertising, etc.); they are intended to produce a calculated effect on the reader, listener or viewer, for example:

Reiting populyarnosti importnykh skrepok
Rating the popularity of imported paper clips
                              [*reiting* was preferred to *otsenka*]

*Rossiiskoe **shou** s angliiskim aktsentom*
A Russian **show** with an English accent
                              [*shou* was preferred to *predstavlenie*]

*Chemodanchik s **banknotami***
A briefcase full of **banknotes**
                              [*banknoty* was preferred to *den'gi*]

*. . . spetsial'no zagotovil **spich** ob antiglobalizme*
. . . specially prepared a **speech** on anti-globalism
                              [*spich* was preferred to *rech'*]

*A eto kak romantika dlya **tineidzhera***
And this is like a romance for a **teenager**
                              [*tineidzher* was preferred to *podrostok*]

*. . . edet na rabotu v **ofis***
. . . travels to the **office**
                              [*ofis* was preferred to *kontora*][4]

In every area of science and technology, Russian has always used borrowings from other languages, not least from English. The following examples show how collaboration with foreign companies (in Oil and Gas exploration, in this case) has led to increased lexical transfer from English into Russian:

gazoil'	gas oil
kavitatsiya	cavitation
konversiya	conversion
kontsessiya	concession
kreking	cracking
barrel'	barrel
offshornyi	offshore (adj.)
bar	bar (unit of pressure)
optsion	option
platforma-terminal	terminal platform
riskovoi kapital	risk capital
ekstraktsiya	extraction
elevator	elevator
lumpsum-frakht	lump-sum freight

All the examples in this chapter show how language in general, and especially the process of lexical borrowing, is influenced by various extralinguistic factors, such as social, political and economic change.

The influence of English on other languages has often been severely criticised. France has legislated against its use in certain public domains; there have been anti-English movements in Spain, Germany, Mexico, India and elsewhere. One often finds anti-English articles in the Russian press.[5] The Russian Language Institute insists that Russian must still be spoken correctly, and that includes the huge vocabulary of neologisms. But, unlike France, Russia has no prestigious academy to police its language.

The Institute, founded in 1958 by Sergei Ozhegov, Russia's most famous lexicographer, is part of the Russian Academy of Sciences. In the Communist period, it brought together a group of linguists who insisted that, however stultifying government decrees, official documents and political speeches might be, they must be properly written, including use of the right cases, correct spelling, etc.; for the purpose of negotiations, correct stress is also an important issue.

Conclusion

An upsurge of interest in the issue of neologisms occurred in the early 1990s, with the post-Communist turmoil. Many questions have been prompted by the change from the command economy to a market-based economy, and Russians needed to know how to set out business letters correctly, and what standard greetings, conventions and etiquette were applicable. The Russian media were suddenly awash with Westernisms, particularly Anglicisms.

New words are the biggest challenge to the older generation, which was brought up on a Russian language much less tainted by Anglicisms. The vocabulary of the 'New Russians' is peppered with these wholesale imports from every area of Western media and market language. The older generation is, understandably, bewildered by the jargon used by DJs on private radio stations or splashed across advertising hoardings – some of which is displayed in Roman, not Cyrillic, characters. Many neologisms are incomprehensible to large numbers of Russians themselves, particularly if poorly educated and unfamiliar with Western languages and societies from which the new words and concepts are drawn.

Globalisation as a phenomenon is a protracted historical process that has dramatically accelerated in recent years and the globalisation of English is a simple fact of modern life.

Notes

1. While the global impact of English is nowadays attributed to the economic might of the USA, Anglicisms began to be imported into Russian in the 16th century, when a ship of King Edward VI's fleet first anchored in St Nicholas's Harbour in the Northern Dvina estuary on 24 August 1553 (Aristova, 1978); a second, more intense, wave of English influence came later, in the nineteenth century, as England's international prestige increased. After the defeat of Napoleon, England gained dominance in world trade, and her political and military influence on the world stage began to expand. Having a large number of colonies in her possession, England was able to develop her industry rapidly. In turn, industrialisation fuelled new developments in science and technology. Major advances such as the industrial loom and the steam locomotive led to the publication of technical literature which was read throughout Europe, including Russia. This produced a new influx of English words into Russian. These achievements were regularly covered in newspaper articles (for example in *Moskovskii Telegraf* 1813, No 1, p. 403; *Moskovskii Telegraf* 1831, No 13, p. 116, etc.).
2. Linguistic history shows us repeatedly that it is wise to be cautious when making predictions about the future of a language. Nobody in the Middle Ages could have predicted the death of Latin, which was used as a medium of education and science. As for French, it was used as the language of international diplomacy from the 17th to the 20th century.
3. The most persistent of these invented languages has been Esperanto. It was invented in 1887 by Dr L.L. Zamenhof.
4. Although *kontora* is itself a borrowing in Russian, it is neither recent nor English, and does not have the same resonance as *ofis*.
5. As reported from Moscow by Nick Paton Walsh in the *Guardian* newspaper (7 February 2003), the Russian parliament passed a new law which provides for the imposition of community service as a penalty for using profanity, slang and Westernisms in speech.

References

Aristova V.M. (1978) *Anglo-Russkie Yazykovye Kontakty: Anglizmy v Russkom Yazyke.* Leningrad: Leningrad University Press (in Russian).

Bauman, Z. (1998) *Globalization. The Human Consequences.* Oxford: Polity Press.

Berlitz, C. (1983) *Native Tongues.* London: Granada.

Crystal, D. (1997a) *English as a Global Language.* Cambridge: Cambridge University Press.

Crystal, D. (1997b) *The Cambridge Encyclopedia of Language* (2nd edn). Cambridge: Cambridge University Press.

Jay, P. (2001) Beyond Discipline? Globalisation and the Future of English. *Publications of the Modern Language Association of America. Special Issue Globalizing Literary Study.* Volume 116 No 1, pp. 32–47.

Marckwardt, A.H. (1980) *American English* (2nd edn). New York and Oxford: Oxford University Press.

Offord, D. (1996) *Using Russian. A Guide to Contemporary Usage.* Cambridge: Cambridge University Press.

Robertson, R. (1992) *Globalisation.* London: Sage.

Chapter 9
Anglo-Finnish Contacts: Collisions and Collusions

KATE MOORE and KRISTA VARANTOLA

It is Beginning to Look a Lot Like English – Almost Everywhere

An incontestable fact of life is that English is now the international *lingua franca* and the main means of communicating across cultures and borders, this being evidenced in Finland. For example, more than 80% of Finnish schoolchildren currently choose English as their first foreign language. Another reflection of the Finns' frequent use of English was recently reported in the largest Finnish daily newspaper, *Helsingin Sanomat* (2 April 2002): a study conducted by the Research Institute for the Languages of Finland (KOTUS) revealed that the most common word in the Finnish domain of the web (.fi) is the English word *the*. Of course, this does not imply that *the* has entered and conquered the article-less Finnish language, but it does reflect the pervasive nature of English in Finnish websites. The position of English is thus strengthening day by day, partly fuelled by the Internet and globalisation, and partly by an increased co-operation that is political, economic, intellectual and even military. Yet what does actually happen when a Germanic, analytic language like English meets a non-Indo-European, Finno-Ugric synthetic language such as Finnish?[1]

In this chapter, we will examine some aspects of this meeting of minds. We will not only explore the different types of linguistic and cultural contacts – the head-on linguistic collisions when the two tongues get tied – but we will also mention some of the ingenious clever, creative collusions that occur when English and Finnish mix. In other words, we are most interested in the amalgam and mutual influence of English and Finnish. This means the impact of English on the Finnish spoken in Finland and the impact of Finnish on the English produced by native and non-native speakers of English living in Finland. Indeed, we will address the issue of how Finnish might actually influence global English by looking at the transformation of English within Finland. We will note the varieties of English that are used in that country and also discuss the worries English predominance evokes.

The quest for a universal *lingua franca* – the need for an unambiguous means of expression – has occupied scholars for centuries. Well-known attempts include the 1668 project report to the Royal Society by Bishop Wilkins, *Essay towards a Real Character, and a Philosophical Language*. At the turn of the twentieth century, movements emerged to support other international solutions, such as Esperanto and Basic English, a simplified form of English developed in the 1930s. Even though Britannia no longer rules the mighty waves, the English language continues to prevail on land, sea and air. *Airspeak*, and to a certain extent *Seaspeak*, are the controlled radio telephony phraseologies for air and sea traffic. Simplified forms also flourish as company languages and as writing rules for technical communication. In short, we can surmise that for the time being English is the pragmatic solution to the quest for a universal language. English assumed this role aided by the rise of the British Empire in the nineteenth century; the result is the unrivalled emergence of English as the de facto *lingua franca* at the beginning of the twenty-first century.

If we review the historical background of the present situation, we observe that in the early seventeenth century there were only about five million English speakers in the world, the overwhelming majority residing in England. Compare this to the present state of affairs in Finland, where there are also only five million speakers of Finnish. Since Finland is not yet in a position to become a colonial power and to leave one of the colonies to keep up the good work, we are not suggesting that Finnish will be a world language in the foreseeable future. Yet, we do maintain that English has in a sense become world property, indelibly influenced by the languages with which it comes into contact, including Finnish. A global language has thus to accept a David and Goliath situation with respect to the languages with which it comes into contact or attempts to replace.

The Contemporary Situation: What is happening in Finland today?

Streetwise English in Tampere, Finland

As for the effect of English, it is very difficult to walk through the largest cities of Finland without being visibly bombarded by English on billboards and signs. The smaller towns and villages, attempting to reflect this trend, also feature English words in their advertisements, sometimes with disastrous results, as will be discussed later. What is offered here is a glimpse of this streetwise English together with an attempt to analyse some of the types encountered. One data-gathering exercise involved driving along the main street of Tampere, the second-largest city in Finland, recording all the English and quasi-English words observed along the way. In addition, yellow pages, job advertisements, personal adverts, were consulted in an attempt to determine the range and frequency of English being used as the main part of advertisements, as an amalgam with Finnish, as well as embedded in texts.

Not everyone in Finland, however, is caught in the web of globalisation: homespun crafts and customs that have a domestic audience refrain from the use of trendy English. Time-honoured tradesmen such as local shoemakers and bakers are not necessarily blinded by the glamour of English. Consequently we had difficulty finding a shoemaker with a business name in English. Furthermore, professions such as undertakers and funeral parlours retain their signs in Finnish only; dying in English is not as yet fashionable in Finland.

Beauty, breasts, bingo, booze, dancing and data technology

Certain sectors of Finnish society are particularly fond of using English as an alluring advertising strategy. Mainly because of the glamorous foreign factor it purports to portray – a certain crowd in Finland thinks that the use of English makes establishments sound sexier, cooler and more attractive. In other words, the more a particular business hopes to entice people to buy their products, the more likely it is that English is used. It is noticeable that enterprises associated with beauty enhancement, sex, gambling, alcohol, music and information technology are more inclined to use English in their names. These Finnish-meets-English contacts have been successful to a varying degree. Whereas some newly coined words are very productive and playful as the result of Finnish/English collusion, others involve minor accidents – small semantic dents created in the mixture of the two languages. Still others are like head-on collisions, where the attempt to use English somehow goes grotesquely awry.

In the retail beauty industry, salons often use the English word *hair* plus another English word, such as *shop, place, team, city, point*, and we also ran across the inventive *HairStory*. Very few combinations use the Finnish word for 'hair', *hius*, combined with English words, except for *Hiusland*. English word boundaries were often ignored in these combinations, but not always. Small dents included names such as *Tophair*, *Wo'Men*, and *Rainbow Style*. Some less attractive, ambiguous English collisions such as *Hair Garage*, *Head Makers*, and the unfortunate, *Kirsin Beauty Illusions* were found. This last example is reminiscent of one hairdresser's ingenious but threatening sign that was encountered in the western Finnish city of Turku, *Veija Chop*, which developed because *Chop* and *Shop* are interchangeable in spoken Finnish.

Sex shops in particular seem to exploit English in order to attract customers. Prominent in Tampere is the rather subtle *Erotic Restaurant, Big Tits Show*, with others being the predictable *Red Lights, Pussy Cat Erotic*

Bar, Fantasy World, the *Erotic Showroom* and the dangerous sounding, *No Limits*. While these are obviously deliberately naughty, sometimes Finnish advertisers unwittingly bump into English allusions. A prize example of the misuse of English is by the Finnish women's choir who had the Finnish bird, *tiaiset* in their name. The choir requested an English-language programme for their forthcoming concert. Their own suggestion for their name in English was the rather unfortunate *Swinging Tits*.

Gambling in Tampere is not very apparent on billboards or advertisements. One rather large sign, however, offered the mind-boggling promise of *Boxing Bingo*. Bars, pubs and restaurants seem nevertheless to be doing thriving business, with the help of English names such as *Bar Dog's Home Pub, Streetbar, Golden Unicorn, Golden Rose, Manhattan Steak House, Ly's Garden, Pup Stop, Crazy Horse*, and *Nite Train Cocktails Bar Dance Restaurant*. Another sign that is frequently seen in restaurant windows or displayed on doors is the inviting but ambiguous, even Neo-Chomskyan, *For Eating Customers Only*, presumably to dissuade the tourist crowd from only purchasing drinks. Perhaps the most disconcerting find, reminiscent of old horror films, was the *Non-Stop Hamburger Restaurant*, possibly something for the more obsessive-compulsive. This type of ambiguity is frequent in Finland, with all sectors participating. One further example we came across was *Free Record Shop*.

Head-on linguistic collisions sometimes occur in Finland because of English spelling errors, so that *Crazy Horse* can be misspelled as *Grazy Hors*. We also found 'Easter Menus' occasionally advertised in hotel windows as 'Eastern' menus, and *Finnish Design* frequently written as *Finnish Desing*. Sometimes mixtures of Finnish and English are transparent to Finns, but opaque to English speakers. The use of the Finnish word for market, *tori*, plus the word *burger* – *toriburger* – refers not to a burger with a political bent but to a kiosk in the local market place that serves hamburgers, something that is far from obvious to a monolingual English speaker. The most ingenious combinations of Finnish and English are parodies of English usage in Finland, the comprehension of which is for Finns only. For instance, the playfulness of a department store advertisement displayed at Helsinki tram stops reading *Kevät on Hinnat off*, which literally states 'spring is on – prices off', referring to the spring sales where the prices are 'off', meaning lower. This advertisement is designed for a minimally bilingual audience. Likewise, the western city of Turku hosts an annual music festival with the name, *Down by the Laituri*, presumably taken from the song title 'Down by the Riverside' with *laituri* meaning 'jetty' or 'dock'. In spoken language, young Finns will sometimes refer to restaurants with English names by a Finnish play on sounds. Thus, a pub called *Lost and Found*, is locally referred to as *lastenvaunut*, which means 'baby prams', but sounds like the English wording.

However, occasionally clever English wordplays are similarly lost on many Finns: one example is the Finnish National Railways' roadside advertisement of some years ago, *2fast4U*. It appears that many Finns perceived this as an English word sandwiched between Finnish numbers and a letter. There may also be a generation gap in comprehending such abbreviations, as younger Finns who are more upwardly-mobile (phoned) can decipher such messages because they send text messages in English. Other billboards in the Finnish countryside try to be clever but somehow grossly miss their mark. On the road to the Finnish seaside resort Naantali is the town of Raisio which used to proudly present itself as *Town of Today*, while a few kilometres away is the giant billboard of the seaside spa welcoming us reassuringly to *The Fountains of Feeling Good!*

Connecting People

In the case of Information Technology (IT) existing English vocabulary is imported into Finnish as the result of the global dimension of this phenomenon. Here the global and virtual community uses English words as a necessity and by doing so reflects a real-time net community that is constantly in contact and updating each other. This IT English is therefore an insider's language for those 'in the know', and this has created an information-age class or generation distinction, which is evident in Finland. Localisation and nationalisation of this global variety is only just beginning in this sector. The problem of localisation is that sometimes we need to be bilingual in Finnish and English to comprehend the signs. For instance, one Helsinki company is called *Datatie*, which in English would possibly be a new form of wired apparel, but instead the loanword *data* is combined with the Finnish word *tie*, which here has the connotation of 'highway' to communicate the concept of a 'Data/Information highway'.

Sometimes the humour in the combinations depends on which is your native language. For example, as authors, one of us has English as her native language, while the other is native Finnish speaking. When we looked at certain company names, for instance, *Ars Golf*, our interpretations were very different; the native English speaker found this amusing while the Finnish speaker held tight to the Latin association. The native English speaker thought the company name *Fani-Trade* was in the sex industry category until the Finnish co-author pointed out that this was actually a translation loan from the English word *fan*. *Fan*, in turn, has become assimilated in spoken Finnish with the Finnish ending *–i*.

The cases of head-on-collisions cited are quite simply instances in which the users of English as a *lingua franca* had no awareness of the impact or implications of the words they were using; this can be an occupational hazard in any second-language situation. In this sense, users feel that a global English can be changed, adapted or even mutilated, since it falls within the user's individual property rights. Thus, one can be 'dangerous at any speed' in English – take liberties – and national Englishes have to pay the price. Perhaps this is the penalty of being both a global and a national language.

As mentioned earlier, the effects of globalisation and internationalisation are readily apparent in Finland: in newspapers, some job titles and descriptions are no longer translated into Finnish, some are only partially in English, while others remain in English but are adapted to Finnish with case endings. Sometimes whole English phrases are incorporated into Finnish advertisements. For instance, a recruitment ad for the Finnish Air Force appearing in a newspaper was entirely in Finnish, except for the slogan, *Feel the Force*, which was followed by the Finnish-language equivalent to 'Join the Air Force'. Another newspaper recruitment advertisement from a company with the name *FinnConsult* published their ad entirely in Finnish, with the exception of *Reliable Partner in Development*. In company names, the prefix *Finn* is not surprisingly one of the most frequently used. We have *Finnair, Finnpublishers, Finntours, Finnforest, Finngear, Finnwear, Finnsights, Finnspice*, etc.

However, those who are linguistically aware can sometimes feel alienated and marginalised by this trend, finding the mixing to be strange. A western Finnish poet describes her linguistic disorientation when coming to the metropolitan Helsinki area and seeing all kinds of non-Finnish titles advertised in the vacancies sections. So she converts the job titles, such as *Director, AD, Sales Manager, Test Lab Engineer* to the following, imitating her own local dialect and pronunciation:

/ . . . /
TIREKTÖR
AAREE
SALES MANAKER
TEST LAP ENKINER
/ . . . /
(From Heli Laaksonen, 2001: 12)

Indeed, job advertisements are particularly rich and baffling examples of bilingual coexistence. When studying the situations vacant section in *Helsingin Sanomat*, all possible combinations were observed. The pages include many smaller advertisements in Finnish, some larger ones in English only, with the others being advertisements that are partly in Finnish and partly in English. Full integration of the two languages takes place when the English terms are assimilated into the Finnish sentence structure. The result is an intriguing mixture of language use and global image building.

This image building becomes apparent in the sections of the Helsinki daily where appointments are announced: the name of the person is followed by the Finnish *on nimitetty* ('has been appointed as'), but then the position itself has an English name with the appropriate Finnish case ending, the translative affix, *-ksi*. Thus we find examples such as:

X on nimitetty   *AD:ksi*
copywriteriksi
controlleriksi
portfolio analystiksi
senior expatriate representativeksi
country manageriksi

The embedding of English in Finnish clauses can be further illustrated as follows:

- Toteuta ideasi *Accenture Sap Centerissä* . . .
- Haemme markkinointiosastollemme *Brand Manageria*
- Etsimme *Investment Manageria*

A monolingual English speaker will only understand the above as indecipherable Finnish words appearing before a mutilated English job title. On the other hand, the Finns who do not understand the concepts behind the English titles are also in trouble, and should certainly not apply.

For those sceptical of the marriage of analytic and synthetic languages, ample evidence can be provided to demonstrate that this interchange occurs in other contexts as well. For instance, in 1990, a European Standard recommended that product specifications should be printed on packages 'in an international language' and 'in a language that can be understood by everybody'. This recommendation was often interpreted to mean English. A manufacturer of perfumes and toiletries using the word *fragrance* in their product specification was later asked whether they really thought that this word would be known to most Finnish consumers. The reply was something along these lines:

- Well maybe it is something that will become clear to the consumers in the course of time when everybody starts using words like this in their product specifications.
- We thought that words like *water* and *fragrance* would anyway be words that the majority already understands.
- The idea is that everybody would start using such words as *urea, fragrance* and *fosfate* [sic!], etc. with the same spelling all over Europe.

(From an interview in *Helsingin Sanomat*, August 1990)

Whereas we have commented on the eager use of English by many Finns, acronyms constitute an area that really tests the Finns' flexibility to adopt and adapt English. Acronyms are difficult enough in one's own language, let alone in a foreign language. Of course, some acronyms become household words and the references then become commonplace. Still, the Finns have the ingenious habit of localising English acronyms to sound more Finnish. Examples again involve computer technology and the universal use of English. Here English acronyms such as GSM (Global System for Mobile Communication) in spoken language become 'Finnicised' as *gesmi* (pronounced as 'guess me'). Wireless Application Protocol – WAP is adopted wholesale as *Vappi*, without querying what is behind the letters in the acronym. Certain prefixes and affixes are also extremely productive in Finnish, such as *digi-, bio-, data-, time-, -soft, net-.*

Many English expressions have been more or less fully assimilated at least into spoken Finnish. *Data, hand-out, brändi, trendi, city- veppi, netti, surffata* (verb) and *draivi* are examples of relatively recent imports. A Finnish word exists for most of these terms but at the moment many of them still sound odd and artificial. These words are also typical loan words and exemplify traditional ways of borrowing. However, there do not appear to be any 'English' expressions prevalent in the Finnish-language community only, which would be comparable to the German *Handy* ('mobile phone') or the Swedish *free-style* ('Walkman').

In the same vein, the Finnish Postal Service has just changed its logo and, following the general trend, considered changing its name, *POSTI* – among the suggestions shortlisted were the following: *Amos, Fidelia, Insignia, Ovella Group, Postia*. These coinages reveal the latest tendency of inventing 'Anglo-Latinate' names for companies that wish to revitalise their image. Fortunately, in the above case *POSTI* was in the end considered modern enough to look after letters in the future (*Helsingin Sanomat*, 7 April 2002).

Another development in Finland is that English proper names and titles are rarely translated any more. Thus film titles and proper names in literature tend to remain intact. However, exceptions are made to accommodate children who may not comprehend English wordplay. Presumably this may be one of the reasons why, in *Harry Potter* books, words such as *Quidditch, Hogwarts, Muggle*, etc. have been translated into their Finnish equivalents: *huispaus, Tylypahka, jästi*. These Finnish words have also become household words among local Harry Potter enthusiasts.

English on Television

Finns who watch English programmes on Finnish television absorb the cultural references and the English phrases. Since subtitling is the norm and dubbing is common only in children's programmes, most Finns watching TV on a regular basis are subjected to several hours of spoken English per week. The benefit is, of course, that the younger population has a clear incentive to learn English and becomes fluent in English at a very early age. The Internet further reinforces this need to learn and to use English later on.

Both American English and British English are commonly heard on television. We will return to the issue of British versus American English later. In this context we would mention that television must be the main channel through which new and fashionable English expressions enter Finland and consequently spread into the spoken 'teenager' Finnish, only to be finally picked up by their trendier parents. Cultural consciousness may also be subliminally affected by TV English: a Finnish policeman was heard commenting on juvenile delinquency, saying that these days, young offenders when apprehended often ask first to be read their Miranda rights or to make one phone call to their lawyer. These habits are obviously copied from American law enforcement programmes. In emergencies some people are also dialling the American 911 instead of 112, the general European emergency number.

Mutual Interference and Translationese

English into Finnish

So many originally English texts appear today in Finland as translations or adaptations that there is bound to be a profound effect on Finnish itself (see also Gellerstam, this volume, for Swedish). Where interference occurs, the resulting form of the target language is often called 'translationese'. The most obvious manifestations of linguistic interference occur in the vocabulary of the translated texts for which we have already provided many examples. We will now look at some more implicit effects.

Grammatical and textual 'translationese' was first discussed by Martin Gellerstam (1985, 1989) when, on the basis of corpus evidence, he demonstrated that clear statistical differences existed between translated Swedish and 'authentic' Swedish. Certain structures and expressions were far more frequent in the translations than in authentic Swedish texts. Inkeri Vehmas-Lehto (1989) discussed the same phenomenon in a Russian-Finnish context, showing that the Finnish appearing in newspaper texts translated from Russian differed remarkably from authentic Finnish newspaper texts. She is now studying the same phenomenon in EU translations and maintains that EU translations and translations of political Soviet texts share certain characteristics. Vehmas-Lehto states:

> Both types of text are mostly written in abstract language with long sentences containing numerous foreign terms and concepts. Additionally, not only translations of Soviet texts, but often also EU translations are characterised by a certain political pomposity. These characteristics render the translations rather 'alien' and more or less difficult to understand.

. . .

On closer inspection, however, the similarities between the translations of Soviet texts and EU texts are less astonishing. The literalness
of the translations is imposed on the translators by those who commission them, in both cases institutions or organisations representing
a powerful political system and a strong ideology.
(Vehmas-Lehto, 2001)

Kaisa Koskinen (2000) also focuses on the literalness of EU translations
in her doctoral thesis on the ethics of translation. She discusses what
effects the official EU language policies have on the translations. By insist-
ing on the equal status of all language versions, the EU actually traps the
translators into producing practically impenetrable prose. The prose style
results from an illusion of sameness, a kind of Emperor's-new-clothes-
type credo, which is based on structural similarity rather than idiomatic
and natural language use. We can therefore only hope that EU Finnish is
and remains so alien to genuine Finnish that it will not have a lasting
impact on the administrative and legal genre of authentic Finnish. The
examples below are, however, not based on EU usage but on academic
writing and current journalism.

Many English conventions have found their way into academic Finnish,
because a great proportion of the academic literature to which Finnish students and researchers are exposed is in English. So, for example, cohesive
textual organisers such as *in this country, today* are often rendered literally
in Finnish *tässä maassa, tänään* whereas a more idiomatic way of expressing
the same ideas would be *Suomessa* ('in Finland') and *nykyään*
('nowadays'). *Billion* is a word that has entered into Finnish newspaper
translations in its American English sense of 1000 million. This is actually
similar to the development that has taken place in British English. The
problem, of course, is that the reader no longer has any clue as to whether
billion means one million million or one thousand million.

How would present-day colloquial Finnish survive without *yes, please,
well, OK, whatever, sorry, thanks, anyway, about* and *f*** off*? Easily no doubt
in the language of the older generation, while the younger generation
would have a hard time thinking of suitable domestic replacements.
English words such as *OK, sorry* and *please* are also particularly apt additions that fill a real gap in Finnish. The adaptation of English 'yes' to *Jees*
or *jess* has evolved, resulting in these forms now having gone on to lead
their independent lexical lives. In addition to the ordinary affirmative
sense of *jees* and the exhilarated *jess, jees* is used in an adjectival sense,
more or less as a synonym of <u>OK</u> – somebody or something can be *ihan
jees* ('quite OK'/'very OK') – or *ihan jees tyyppi* ('quite an OK guy').

Finnish word order has also often been affected. *X proudly presents . . .*
probably began as a conscious joke in Finnish as *X ylpeänä esittää* (adverb

+ verb instead of the normal verb + adverb), but has since been adopted by promoters, entertainment presenters, etc. on such a scale that its origins are hardly recognised any longer. The adverb + verb order is also spreading to other contexts in promotional texts, newspapers and academic writing. In present-day Finnish, it can frequently be noticed how *discuss* is literally mistranslated from English as *keskustella* in contexts where Finnish would require a very different verb, for example *käsitellä* ('to handle'). Combinations of non-idiomatic adjective + noun are also typical examples of interference in translated texts. *Weak coffee* remains 'weak' in Finnish, whereas the normal Finnish collocation would be with the equivalent of 'thin coffee'.

An interesting development has taken place with *in the long run*. This was happily imported into Finnish in the mid-nineties and was translated literally as *pitkässä juoksussa* where the meaning of *juoksu, run* was much more clearly associated with running than the English 'run'. *In the long run* is thus taken literally instead of meaning 'over a period of time' or 'in the future'. It has become a cliché and we have even heard it used in Finnish in the context of 'the plan being still *in the long run*'.

Punctuation also often goes haywire because the principles governing punctuation rules in Finnish and English differ dramatically. In Finnish, punctuation is basically grammatically determined and has less to do with communicative emphases. Another orthographic feature is that English clearly inspires the spelling of Finnish compounds as separate words.

Finnish influence on English

In this section we present a kaleidoscope of views and patterns starting with the types of problems Finnish speakers have when they express their ideas in English. Most examples come from the archives of experienced teachers of translation.[2] The rationale of this discussion is that if semi-professional students of English have these problems, then they are likely to multiply in the nation at large, forming part of Finland's contribution to global English. Under this heading we will also look at how Finnish affects the language of native English speakers having lived in Finland for a prolonged period of time.

From Finnish into English

At first sight it would seem unlikely that any false friend-type cognates exist between English and Finnish because of their very different linguistic parentage. Nevertheless, they do occur. The examples in Table 9.1 first give the English word, then its Finnish equivalent and finally the word that is common in the English of Finnish speakers.

Table 9.1 False friends in the English of Finnish speakers

English term	Finnish equivalent	English false friend
car battery	akku	accumulator
label	etiketti	etiquette
cardboard	kartonki	carton
criticism	kritiikki	critic
radiator	patteri	battery
paraffin	petrooli	petrol
prescription	resepti	recipe
censorship	sensuuri	censure
technique	tekniikka	technics

A number of lexical clashes occur between the two languages which are very problematic for bilingual lexicography, because the exact shade of meaning is so difficult to capture in the few lines of the dictionary entry. Finns wrestle with the differences because there is one general Finnish word that could cover all the options. The list below gives an idea of the types of nightmarish words for lexicographers:

- business, affair
- civilisation, education, training culture
- event, incident, happening
- journey, trip, voyage, excursion, cruise, distance, travels
- judge, referee
- nature, environment, countryside, scenery, landscape
- researcher, research worker, scientist, scholar, academic technique, technology, technics
- thing, object, fact
- thought, idea

- approve, approve of, agree to, pass, adopt
- arrange, organise, look after
- deny, forbid, prohibit, refuse
- discover, find, invent
- divide, share, distribute
- function, work, act, carry out, put into effect, practise, realise, accomplish, fulfil
- notice, note, take note of, pay attention to, observe

- common, usual, customary, normal, general, ordinary

- considerable, significant, important, major, remarkable
- ill, sick, sore
- legal, lawful, legitimate
- spiritual, mental, intellectual, cultural

- besides, in addition to, as well, versus except, apart from
- just, exactly, in particular
- obviously, clearly, evidently
- quite, pretty, somewhat, rather, fairly
- till, until versus up to, as far as
- undoubtedly, no doubt

Borrow versus *lend* are confused because one Finnish verb – *lainata* – is used for both senses. The same is true of *roof* and *ceiling* which can both be rendered in Finnish as *katto*. Similarly Finnish does not have a he/she pronoun distinction but instead has only one form *hän*, irrespective of the gender of the person and, as a result, Finns often make mistakes in assigning gender when talking.

Experienced teachers report that Finnish writing conventions affect the English written by Finns in a number of ways. For instance, Finns have difficulty in shifting from the 'higher' register used in Finnish brochures to the 'lower' more dramatic, adjective-rich register English speakers use. Furthermore, students prefer to stick to their Finnish identity when writing in English for a non-Finnish audience. They therefore forget to explain what non-Finns do not know, such as Finnish names and surnames and culture-specific information in general.

The lack of explicit cohesive elements in the text is a phenomenon that English editors often comment on when revising the English of Finnish academics (cf. Ventola & Mauranen, 1990, 1991). Finns are not too fond of connectors such as *furthermore, in addition, nevertheless* and *moreover*, etc., but tend to overuse and sometimes misuse *also, in other words* and *on the other hand* while completely forgetting the 'first hand' – *on the one hand* – as a text-structuring element. The general reason is most likely that Finnish is so rich in word-ending particles that the cohesive elements can be added as signals to the meaningful words in the text without a need for separate 'cohesion words or expressions'.

Anna Mauranen (1993: 168–71) states in her study on *Cultural Differences in Academic Rhetoric* that connectors do not seem to improve the readability of texts, but that they certainly contribute to the rhetorical effect of texts. She also argues that, although Finnish writers use fewer cohesive elements in their English, no comparative studies exist showing that the same is true of academic Finnish. Mauranen (1993: 252 ff.) summarises her major findings about cultural differences between Finnish and Anglo-American academic writing as follows:

- Finnish writers use fewer text references than native speakers of English and 'may therefore miss opportunities of making their argument appear connected to English audiences' (1993: 253).
- Furthermore, Finns do not seem to regularly make a clear statement of what their main point is. 'Finns tend to start with referents which are not central to the text as a whole, and move on to the central referents only later' (1993: 253–4).
- Finns tend to use less metatext in their writing to navigate the readers through the text. This reflects the more implicit writing styles prevailing in Finnish. It has also been claimed that Finnish writers are worried about underestimating their readers and therefore avoid saying what they think is obvious.
- 'Finnish rhetoric is thus in many ways more implicit than Anglo-American rhetoric, and it also favours the placement of the main content towards the end of the text' (1993: 255).

These findings underscore the dramatic differences between Anglo-Finnish and Anglo-American writing styles that frequently result in misunderstanding of the various communicative intents and emphases.

Native English speakers in Finland

A native English speaker who regularly uses Finnish extensively inevitably faces the wear and tear of Finnish on native English expressions. This lapsing into a capricious 'Finglish' depends on many factors, ranging from code switching for word concepts that are typically Finnish to calque translations. For instance, since mobile (cell) phones are now an intrinsic part of Finnish life, English-speaking expatriates sometimes use the Finnish *kännykkä* in English. So a bilingual expatriate could say in English, 'You know, I left my *kännykkä* at home yesterday.' Sometimes English speakers also use Finnish words for professions. The person at the university who sits in a small office is not referred to as a porter/caretaker/superintendent, but as a *vahtimestari*. We have heard our American, Canadian and British colleagues saying, 'Well, go ask the *vahtimestari*!' Similarly, the notion of job permanency in state-funded employment (tenure) is called *virka* in Finnish. English speakers in Finland can ask each other, 'Do you have a *virka*?'

Perhaps the most disturbing indication that it is indeed the moment to spend some time in an English-speaking country is when a native English speaker thinks of a Finnish verb, translates it back into English and uses it out of context in English. Thus, if we 'take medicine' in English, a stranded native English speaker would say the very distressing sentence, 'I need to *eat my medicine*', which is not an overdose, just transferring the use of the Finnish verb. For the same reasons, some expatriates '*close the TV*' and '*close the lights off*'. Matters of pronoun gender also die hard for English speakers. If a native English speaker speaks Finnish and repeats a dialogue between a man and a woman in Finnish, he/she can refer to both speakers with *hän* forgetting that the Finnish pronoun means both male and female. In English the he/she would be sufficient but in Finnish the listener needs more information. The problem is that some English speakers maintain the he/she distinction tacitly but forget to disambiguate in Finnish and simply say *hän* and utterly confuse the Finnish listener.

On the other hand, it is difficult for English speakers to practise their Finnish in Finland. Finns are unfortunately not always very tolerant towards foreigners learning Finnish and prefer to switch over to English as soon as they realise that the person they are speaking to is an English learner of Finnish. One reason for this behaviour is the persistently maintained myth that Finnish is impossible to learn, a myth that has by now been proven wrong by many fluent Finnish-speaking non-Finns. Another reason is that this type of relative intolerance is typical of native speakers of smaller languages because of the default expectation that speakers of lesser-used languages always have to use a major international language when talking to foreigners. And finally, Finns are just not yet used to having their language mutilated by foreigners or used as a *lingua franca* between multicultural groups.

Another intriguing aspect related to linguistic attitudes in Finland is the superior status often associated with the British English variety. The reasons may be partly historical and partly geographical, because the majority of older-generation English teachers in Finland were taught English by British university teachers and often went to the UK to learn to speak English. In addition, the myths of Oxford English and the elegance of BBC English are still ingrained in the minds of non-linguists. A factor that has helped to foster prejudiced attitudes is that the British have a longer history in exporting language and culture. However, one cannot help thinking that the Americans themselves perpetuate the myth by deferring to the inherent superiority of British English as the 'original' variety. Fortunately, attitudes are changing and the younger generations in particular show a much more global and balanced attitude towards the varieties of English.

Global English

Whose property is global English? It may be claimed that global English does not belong to anyone but is everyone's property. And yet it is important to make sure that it remains comprehensible and thus fulfils the basic requirement of a *lingua franca*. The purpose of global English is purely pragmatic. It is also noteworthy that the scholarly interest in global English is of mainly British origin. The British seem to be much more aware than, say, the Americans of the necessity of somehow overseeing the development of global English. They have also fully realised its economic potential and its role in the UK export market. In recent years *The Economist* has, for example, published a number of articles about the 'triumph of English' in the world, and in Europe in particular, as well as in national contexts in Britain and Canada. (see, for instance, the issues of 23 October 1997, 16 July 1998, 12 July 2001, 20 September 2001, 20 December 2001). Comments range from how English is on its way to becoming the de facto *lingua franca* of the European Union, how the Internet has further consolidated the position of English in the world and how indisputable its role is in the present and future.

In certain contexts, the *lingua franca* role of English changes into an interlingual role. One example is technical communication. Today the localisation of product documentation often starts with an internationalisation of the documentation, i.e. by providing an English version that is then used as the basis for localising it into all the other languages. Moreover, the idea of internationalisation-cum-localisation is often combined with the concept of the simplified and structurally-controlled use of English. However, the success of these processes, and how well the interlingua concept works in this context is a matter of opinion and will not be discussed here. What is somewhat worrying, though, is that implicit in this thinking is the notion of language as a code, which is devoid of all cultural associations and which can be reproduced in other languages by means of a conversion table.

The idea of English as the interlingua sometimes also crops up in multilingual lexicography, most recently in the contexts of electronic semibilingualised dictionaries, where the source dictionary is the same monolingual English dictionary in all cases. This monolingual dictionary has then been bilingualised into a number of languages by adding the target language glosses to explain the English entries. It is thus theoretically possible to look for a word in Swedish, Norwegian, Czech, etc., by entering a Finnish search word and obtaining the answer by way of English. The method is, however, by no means foolproof. The user must be fluent in English and be aware of all the possible pitfalls that may result from translation equivalents that have not been intended for multilingual comparisons.

Global Multinational English in Finland and in a Nordic context

English is the leading academic language in the world and thus in Finland as well. Finnish universities inform their potential international students that a number of courses will be offered to them in an international language. This international language is unmistakably always interpreted as English. Researchers are required to submit their national project proposals in English for the sake of potential international reviewers. The extreme view frequently promoted today is that Finnish academics should stop writing in Finnish altogether and resort exclusively to English to make sure that their research becomes generally accessible.

The academic context is, however, not where global English is most visible in Finland. Instead, global English is probably best manifested in the variants of English used by companies in Finland. These corporate Englishes, a type of multinational English, will certainly develop their own characteristic features depending on what the majority native language is in any particular context. They are also very susceptible to changes when ownership structures change. A Finnish employee working for a Japanese-owned company in Finland recently expressed her concern as to what would happen to their international communication when the company had sold out their American plants. This meant that they would lose their main source and input of authentic English texts since they no longer had any native English-speaking subsidiaries in their corporation. The communications that had originated in the US had been used by everybody else as a model to follow in their own English text production.

Nokia probably provides a fairly typical case of the language policy of a global multinational company. The official language is (global) English with multinational overtones. In practice this means that, in Finland, the documentation process adheres to British English conventions. The source language of Nokia's terminology database is thus British English, whereas marketing material mainly uses American English. Minutes of meetings are kept in English even if the meeting is held in another language.

English is also the unofficial *lingua franca* in the Nordic context, although the official policy in Nordic co-operation is to use a Nordic language as the language of communication. With a little modification and consideration for the other, Danish, Norwegian and Swedish are 'Nordically' comprehensible but Finnish and Icelandic are not. This means that, in Nordic contexts, Finns typically try to speak Swedish while Icelanders use Danish. In unofficial contexts, English has replaced both Swedish in Finland and Danish in Iceland. Finnish-speaking Finns usually prefer English to Swedish even though they have all learned Swedish at school.[3] The same is true of most Nordic academic contexts involving all the Nordic countries. English is today the prevailing *lingua franca*. In a different context, Krista Varantola asked the question whether a Nordic *lingua franca* is necessarily a language and suggested that the feeling of unity is based more on cultural and historical ties, as well as on political beliefs, than on unifying linguistic practices (Varantola, 2000).

The study of global English, its trends and developments will certainly become a major interest area in English Studies in the future. Therefore, there will also be a growing demand for global English corpora originating in different countries and in different contexts. The global English corpora will in a sense be the mirror images of translation corpora, since they will display the implicit effect of the source languages on the international non-native target language. As mentioned above, translation corpora are, in contrast, normally used to study the effect of the source language, typically English, on the native target language.

Concluding remarks

So far nothing has been said about the Finnish reaction to the 'Triumph of English'. Is it worrying, is it a dangerous development for a lesser-used language like Finnish? In other words, are 'small' languages an endangered species today that are threatened by linguistic imperialism? We personally feel that there is no need for doomsday predictions, nor for counter-productive linguistic policies that would try to restrain the spread of English in Finland. We think that for now Finns will happily concede 'the territory of beauty, breasts, bingo, booze, dancing and data technology'. As long as a language can assimilate the linguistic loan, play with it and mould it to fit its own patterns, there is no danger. On the contrary, the changes are normal developments in language contact. What would be worrying, however, is if Finnish speakers began to underestimate the status of the language spoken in their own country and instead began to overestimate their skills in English.

If Finnish academics were to stop writing in Finnish and intentionally deprecate the role of Finnish in higher education then our language would be in trouble. This is, however, not the case today. Finnish students prefer to have their teachers teach them in Finnish. Finnish newspapers appear in Finnish and Finnish-speaking writers express their thoughts in Finnish and prefer their narratives to travel as translations rather than as works written originally in a global *lingua franca*. A global *lingua franca* is a pragmatic and useful solution for multinational co-operation and time has shown that it is better to adapt a natural language for this purpose than to create an artificial language with no back-up culture to be used as the means of international communication. Whatever happens in Finland we will be sure to keep English as some sort of Finnish Design, if not Desing.

Notes

1. The impact and influence of English in Finland has been systematically studied since the 1980s when the results of the first large-scale project were reported (Sajavaara & Lehtonen 1981). New work is now in progress on a number of fronts, with the focus on the use of English in media, educational and professional settings (see for example, Sirpa Leppänen, University of Jyväskylä at http://www.jyu.fi) and the effect of English on translated texts (Anna Mauranen, University of Tampere at http://www.joensuu.fi/slnkvl/sivut/tutkimus/supisuomi.htm). The present article is

more impressionistic– based on observations, cross-sections and glimpses of Anglo-Finnish linguistic encounters in present-day Finland.
2. We would like to thank our colleagues who have provided us with these examples, particularly Gerard McAlester and Dr. Carl Wieck, the University of Tampere who over the years have systematically kept track of the pitfalls Finns fall into.
3. As a matter of fact, *The Economist* claims in one of its articles about the spread of English that 'Now that its members also include Denmark, Finland and Sweden, whose people often speak better English than the British, English is the EU's dominant tongue. Indeed, over 85% of all international organisations use English as one of their official languages' (20 December 2001, *The Triumph of English. A world empire by other means*).

References

Arnola, H., Hyvönen, K., Juntunen, J-P., Linnavirta, T. and Suoranta, P. (1996) Kielikone Finnish-English MT System 'TranSmart' in Practical Use. *Translating and the Computer* 18. Proceedings of the Eighteenth International Conference on Translating and the Computer, London: Aslib.

Crystal, D. (1997) *English as a global language.* Cambridge: Cambridge University Press.

Gellerstam, M. (1985) Translationese in Swedish novels translated from English. In L. Wollin and H. Lindquist (eds) *Proceedings of the Scandinavian Symposium on Translation Theory (SSOTT)* (pp. 105–17) Malmö: Liber förlag.

Gellerstam, M. (1989) Om svenskan i översättningar. In S. Allén, M. Gellerstam and S.G. Malmgren (eds) *Orden speglar samhället* (pp. 107–115) Stockholm: Allmänna Förlaget.

Graddol, D. (1997) *The Future of English.* London: British Council.

Kachru, B.B. (1997), World Englishes and English-using communities. *Annual Review of Applied Linguistics* 17, 66–87.

Koskinen, K. (2000) *Beyond Ambivalence: Postmodernity and the Ethics of Translation.* Acta Universitatis Tamperensis 774/Acta Electronica universitatis Tamperensis 65. Tampere (academic dissertation).

Laaksonen H. (2001) *Pulu uis.* Turku: Runoja.

Mauranen, A. (1993) *Cultural Differences in Academic Rhetoric.* Frankurt am Main: Peter Lang.

Moore, K. (1993) To speak or not to speak? *Nordicum*, (Scandinavian Business Magazine. Helsinki), 7.

Sajavaara, K. (1986) Aspects on English influence on Finnish. In W. Viereck, and N. Bald (eds.) *English in Contact with other languages* (pp. 65–77) Budapest: Académiai Kiadó.

Sajavaara, K. and Lehtonen, J. (1981) Anglismit nykysuomessa (Anglicisms in modern Finnish). *Virittäjä* 4, 289–304.

Varantola, K. (2000) Is the Nordic *lingua franca* necessarily a language? Paper given at the SASS 2000 (Society for the Advancement of Scandinavian Study) Conference in Madison, Wisconsin.

Vehmas-Lehto, I. (1989) *Quasi-correctness. A critical study of Finnish translations of Russian journalistic texts.* Neuvostoliittoinstituutin vuosikirja 31. Helsinki: Neuvostoliittoinstituutti.

Vehmas-Lehto, I. (2001) Do Political Translation Universals Exist? Translations of EU and Soviet texts. Paper given at a Symposium on 'Translation Universals – Do They Exist' at Savonlinna, 19–20 October.

Ventola, E. and Mauranen, A. (1990) *Tutkijat ja englanniksi kirjoittaminen* [Researchers and Writing in English]. Helsinki: Helsinki University Press.

Ventola, E. and Mauranen, A. (1991) Non-native writing and native revising of scientific articles. In E. Ventola (ed.) *Functional and Systemic Linguistics. Approaches and Uses (Trends in Linguistics. Studies and Monographs* 55) (pp. 457–92). Berlin: Mouton de Gruyter.

Chapter 10

Contemporary English Influence on German – A Perspective from Linguistics

STEPHEN BARBOUR

Introduction

There is a widespread perception that contemporary German is subject to intense influence from English. There is also probably a consensus that this consists of a large number of 'English words' entering the language; more controversial is the claim by some, notably the journalist Dieter E. Zimmer, that English influence is disrupting the grammatical system of German, and transforming it into a different entity, possibly a Creole language, no longer identifiable with 'German/*Deutsch*' as this has been traditionally understood (see Zimmer, 1997: especially 7–85). There are even public action groups dedicated to preserving the language in the face of this perceived threat to its very substance, notably the *Verein Deutsche Sprache* (http://www.vds-ev.de).

In contrast to this perspective, which seems to be espoused particularly by those concerned with language who are not trained linguists, the view from linguistics seems generally not to be one of massive overall influence of English on German; the influence is largely confined to the lexicon, and is striking only in certain registers, such as those of advertising and computing (see Eisenberg, 1999; Eisenberg, 2001; Ruhnkehl, *et al.*, 1998). Linguists are rightly concerned, however, about quite a distinct problem, that of the reduced role of German as an international medium of communication (see Ammon, 1998). The replacement of German by English in this role is most unhelpfully linked in some popular discussions with the very different phenomenon of the influence of English on the German lexicon.

It is not easy to explain the contrasting differences of view between linguists and other groups interested in language. They can be partially accounted for by the relatively widespread acquaintance among the German-speaking public with some of the categories of historical linguistics, so that terms such as *nicht-germanisch*, 'non-Germanic', and *Lehnwort*, 'loan word', mean something to the average person in the street. This is reinforced by the lexicological practice of publishing *Fremdwörterbücher*, literally 'dictionaries of foreign words', such as Duden (1997), which would however be more accurately described as 'dictionaries of German words clearly of ultimately non-German origin'. The pedagogical or informational value of such dictionaries is unclear, but they seem to accord with the linguistic purism of a certain section of society, which lexicographers are happy to cater for, and to which some may even subscribe themselves. Such purism can only be understood against the background of a German (and Austrian) national identity in which the German language is a 'core value' (see Barbour, 2000; for a full discussion of core values see Smolicz, 1981).

The view, then, that German is subject to massive, even destructive, influence from English is, from the linguistic point of view, not well founded. However, it is unlikely to have developed out of thin air; there must be phenomena in the language which lead certain groups to espouse such a view.

English Influence of the German Lexicon – A Threat?

One such phenomenon is the presence in the German vocabulary of lexical subsets, an extremely widespread, perhaps even universal, characteristic of languages (see, for example, Itô & Mester, 1995). A lexical subset is a group of words, or more precisely lexical items, which share certain phonological or morphological properties not shared by other lexical items. For example, in English the adjective *legal* belongs to a subset which we might wish to label 'learned', in the sense of being characteristic of usage by speakers of the language with greater formal education. The subset is characterised by rather complex derivational morphology, with *legal* being morphologically connected to other items of related meaning, such as *legalise, legality, legislate, legislation, legislature,* by processes of affixation. Although related, *legal, legalise, legality,* etc. show in their phonology differing stress patterns and differing pronunciation of vowels and consonants, a characteristic typical of the 'learned' lexicon. Also typical is the rather complex formation of negatives, as shown by the forms *illegal* and *illegality*. In addition we may note that although *legal* contains the suffix *–al*, often added to nouns to form adjectives, there is in this case no noun *leg* (the noun *leg* meaning '(lower) limb of the body' is clearly unconnected). In contrast the related[1] lexical item *law* belongs to the 'non-learned' subset of the lexicon; apart from the adjective *lawful*, its derivational morphology is otherwise characterised by compounds of transparent structure, such as *lawbreaker, lawmaker,* and the adjective *lawful* forms a negative with the invariant suffix *un-*.

Although speakers of English can be made aware of such subsets of the lexicon, and labels such as 'hard words' for the learned subset are used, they are not a matter of common public discussion, and no subset is popularly labelled 'foreign'. Although a very high proportion of English lexical items, particularly 'learned' items, are demonstrably of ultimately foreign origin, this seems to be a matter of total indifference to most speakers of the language; it is perhaps only the rather small group of items, such as *savoir faire, joie de vivre, sang froid*, which demonstrate, at least in intention, a 'French' pronunciation, which is perceived as 'foreign', although even here the label 'affected' is probably equally likely to be applied.[2] I shall leave open the question of how many subsets one would wish to delimit in English, and what the most appropriate designations for them should be.

It is important to note that the subsets of the English lexicon discussed here are delimited from each other on purely synchronic criteria, on the basis of morphological and phonological properties in the contemporary language. On the basis of synchronic considerations we can also delimit at least four subsets of the German lexicon, which I shall label 'core', 'Eurolatin', 'French-derived' and 'English-derived'.

The core lexicon

The core lexicon, which contains a high proportion of the most common lexical items, is characterised by taking stress on the initial syllable of words, unless the first syllable is one of a small set of unstressed prefixes, such as *be-, ge-, ent-, emp-, ver-, zer-*. In unstressed syllables, particularly those following the stressed syllable, the syllable centre is almost always a central vowel or a syllabic nasal or lateral consonant. Typical core lexical items are *Lauf* ('run') (noun), *laufen* ('run, walk') (verb), *entlaufen* ('run away'). Such core lexical items, particularly nouns, enter rather freely into compounds, such as *Leerlauf* ('neutral gear'), or *weglaufen* ('run away'), which generally, but not always, have primary stress on the first element of the compound. Derivational morphology in the core lexicon is mainly characterised by suffixes; nouns can be seen as being formed from other parts of speech by the addition of *-schaft, -ung, -heit, -keit, -tum, -nis*, among others, adjectives by the addition of *-ig, -lich, -isch*, and verb stems by the addition of *-er-, -el-*. This core lexicon is popularly termed *Deutsche Wörter*, 'German words', a misleading designation, since many of the items in question are known to have their origins in other languages; for example *Mauer*, 'wall', and many others are known to derive from Latin (*Mauer* from Latin *murus*). Some, like *Sport* from English, are of quite recent foreign origin. It is important to note that words like *Mauer* and *Sport* conform entirely to the phonological and morphological patterns of the core lexical subset.

Eurolatin

The second subset I shall label 'Eurolatin' following Alan Kirkness and Horst Haider Munske (see Munske, 1996). The Eurolatin subset of the lexicon is characterised by more complex derivational morphology than the core subset, but vowels and consonants are identical to those found in the core lexicon, although the unstressed syllables differ from those of the core lexicon by exhibiting a full range of vowel contrasts. In polysyllabic items stress is usually not on the first syllable and, unlike core lexical items, Eurolatin items consisting of elements of Latin and Ancient Greek origin shared by other European languages often show changes of stress between derivationally linked items, and even between different items in the same inflectional paradigm, such as singulars and plurals. Complexity in derivational morphology can be illustrated by comparing, on the one hand, the noun *Fiktion*, 'fiction', and its related adjective *fiktiv*, with, on the other, a noun-adjective pair in the core lexicon such as *Sport* and *sportlich*. A stress shift in derivational morphology is illustrated by the noun-adjective pair *Nation*, with stress on the second syllable, and *national*, with stress on the third syllable; these should be compared with the core noun-adjective pair *Staat* (the state) and *staatlich*, both with initial stress. Stress shift between singular and plural is illustrated by *Professor* with stress on the second syllable, and its plural *Professoren* with stress on the third syllable.

The German Eurolatin lexicon can be seen as being constructed from a set of elements, most of which are ultimately of Latin and Ancient Greek origin, and which are largely shared by languages that developed in western Europe, and others from further afield, although often with pronunciation differences between the languages which can obscure the connections. In German, the words in question form the largest proportion of the so-called *Fremdwörter* ('foreign words'). The application of the label 'foreign' to them is highly misleading; they exhibit no vowels and consonants not found in the core lexicon and generally exhibit the same inflectional patterns as the core lexicon (although they may show singular-plural shifts in stress placement). Most importantly, they are frequently indispensable to the German language; for example the 'foreign' *Professor* has no 'native' German equivalent (*Hochschullehrer* is of rather wider meaning). In addition they are often not present in any meaningful sense in the 'donor' language: *Telefon*, a 'foreign word' composed of elements from Ancient Greek, was not used by fifth century BC Athenians (modern Greek *tilefono* is a nineteenth-century formation and does not derive directly from an ancient form). However, German publishers, no doubt responding to public demand, insist on relegating the Eurolatin lexicon to dictionaries of *Fremdwörter*. Not only is this term altogether misleading, but it also obscures the fact that, as we have seen, many words of known foreign origin today conform to the patterns of the core lexicon; there are even some words of native German origin, such as *lebendig* ('lively, alive') and *Forelle* ('trout'), which show stress patterns typical of the Eurolatin lexicon. Eurolatin and core items enter freely into compounds with each other, such as *Telefonbuch* ('telephone book'), and derivational affixes from either part of the lexicon can be used with roots from the other part; core lexical *-isch* freely forms adjectives with Eurolatin roots, and the Eurolatin suffix *–ier-* is the verb-forming suffix par excellence in the contemporary language, combining with roots from all parts of the lexicon, such as the core lexical *Haus* ('house'), with which it forms *hausieren* ('sell from door to door, peddle').

French-Derived

Words of perceived French and perceived English origin form two further subsets of the lexicon, which also appear in *Fremdwörterbücher*. The designation 'foreign' is slightly more justified here, as speakers of German will attempt to reproduce the phonetics and phonology of the 'donor' languages. Degrees of success in the 'foreign' pronunciation are highly variable, related to speakers' proficiency in the supposed source language. As I have argued elsewhere in a paper that pursues many of the issues raised here from a different perspective (Barbour, 2001), objections to these words arise partly, I believe, from the fact that they are socially divisive; they are intimidating for those with poor knowledge of French or English, particularly as they may involve attempts to produce vowels and consonants not foundin the speaker's variety of German, such as the vowel in the second element of *City Call* ('local telephone call'). In principle, 'foreign words' showing such attempted phonetic and phonological transfers are possible from other source languages; their virtual restriction to English and French 'loans' reflects the past and present status of these languages as by far the most widespread foreign languages learnt by German speakers.[3]

English-Derived

To focus now on the 'English' subset of the German lexicon, I would like to answer the questions: 'Are the items in question disrupting the patterns of the German language?' and 'Are they English?' My answer to the first question is that they show behaviour closely comparable to the Eurolatin lexicon, which has represented a large and growing subset of the German lexicon for centuries, without turning German into Latin or Greek, or into some other non-German entity, wrenched from its German heritage. The 'English' lexicon does, as we have seen, exhibit exotic phonetics and phonology, but not in the mouths of those who know little English. It could be claimed that the *–s* plural suffix used with 'English' nouns is an alien intrusion into German inflectional morphology, but then its arrival is partly independent of English influence, as it is also found in words like *Jungs* ('lads') originating in the Low German language of North Germany. It is also the most common plural suffix in nouns of any origin ending in vowels other than the central schwa vowel (corresponding to written *–e*), such as *Autos* ('cars'), and is now a productive suffix in the core lexicon added to newly coined monosyllables like *Treffs* ('meeting places'). Most 'English' nouns ending in *-er* follow the general German pattern for such nouns of not taking plural suffixes, and, if they refer to people, they take the German feminine suffix *–in*; hence the noun *Manager* is invariant in the plural, and has a feminine equivalent *Managerin*. Contrary to the assertions of Zimmer (1997: especially 70–5), adjectives of English origin, such as *pink* and *cool*, do seem able to take German adjective endings (David Yeandle, personal communication). 'English' words also enter into compounds with elements of other subsets of the lexicon, with forms like *Managerkrankheit* ('executive disease, stress-related illness').

Influence of English Vocabulary on German

Do the items in the 'English' subset of the German lexicon represent English words in any simple or intelligible sense? Contrary to apparent widespread public perception (see again the website of the *Verein Deutsche Sprache* at http://www.vds-ev.de), my answer to this question is also negative. Except occasionally when used by some German speakers who are highly fluent in English, their phonetics and phonology is noticeably German, with the German word *Manager,* for example, sounding to English speakers like a non-existent English word *'menetcher'*. We have already discussed the ways in which these are integrated into German morphology. As with loan words generally, they are used to fill perceived gaps in the lexicon, which arise, almost by definition, in more specialised registers; for example, while the British English noun 'shop' is found in the most everyday varieties of the language, the German noun *Shop* has a rather specialised usage, denoting retail outlets providing exciting or unusual wares such as expensive clothes, in fact denoting the kind of establishment which in British English is often termed a *boutique* (another common use is in the term *Sex Shop*). German *Manager* tends to be a manager of a specialised or senior kind, and equates more to the English 'executive' than to 'manager'.

A disturbing and puzzling aspect of loan words is that they quite frequently do not actually exist in the supposed source language. The 'English' loan words in German are no exception here, with such items as *City Call* ('local telephone call'), *Showmaster* ('presenter of television programme') and *Handy* ('mobile phone, cellphone') clearly perceived by

German speakers as 'English words', being unknown to those who see English as their first language.

Conclusion

As the German language has the status of a core value for many of its speakers, political movements are able to use defence of the language as a source of mobilisation, and I would argue that an organisation such as *Verein Deutsche Sprache* is, despite its apparent linguistic focus, a political movement using defence of the language to enlist support. Its website uses rhetoric of 'threat' and 'defence' in a fashion commonly found in the usage of political movements. In this world-view the English language or even English speakers are attacking German through their words. The fact that so many of the 'English' words in German differ appreciably in one way or another from their supposed sources, or may not even be present in English, gives the lie to this view. A much more helpful view is to regard these so-called English words as part of the German lexicon, albeit a subset exhibiting particular phonetic, phonological and ortho-graphic phenomena not found in other subsets. A sure sign that this is a subset of the German lexicon, and not an alien intrusion, is demonstrated by the fact that the items concerned are used by German speakers in novel constructions, such as *City Call,* not paralleled in English, and that some supposedly English items have no obvious source in English at all. Just as the Eurolatin subset of the German lexicon is a creation of German speak-ers within their own language, so is the 'English' subset. The label *fremd* ('foreign') for both subsets is a misleading distraction from their true nature.

It would, however, be a mistake to claim that use of the 'English' subset is unproblematic; its phonetics, phonology and orthography are difficult for many German speakers. The English subset of the German lexicon represents 'hard words' for some people. The problems could, however, be much more effectively tackled if they were seen as problems of social-ly divisive usage, and not of alien intrusion. Avoidance of unnecessary use of the English subset could then be presented as a democratisation of usage, and be removed from its current highly unfortunate tone of xenophobia.

A realisation that the English language is not destroying or taking over the German language could also allow a clearer focus on a real problem facing the language and its speakers, the reduction in its use as an inter-national medium of communication.

Notes

1. *Law* and *legal* are of rather distinct historical origin in English, but are probably felt to be related by speakers of the contemporary language. Labelling them as 'non-learned' and 'learned' does not necessarily imply that these particular words belong to informal and formal registers respectively (in fact *lawful* is probably a more formal term than *legal*); these are in principle simply labels designating subsets of the lexicon, which are distinguished from each other morphologically and phonologically.
2. To these 'French' words we could add, for some speakers, a small number of 'German' words, such as *Schadenfreude*. Perhaps some items, including *fortissimo* and other musical terms, are 'Italian'. Maybe some phrases found particularly in legal registers, such as *ultra vires*, belong to a 'Latin' subset, distinct from the very large entirely assimilated 'learned' subset of Latin origin.
3. The virtual restriction to French of attempted pronunciation transfers into English is a clearly parallel case.

References

Ammon, U. (1998) *Ist Deutsch noch internationale Wissenschaftssprache?* Berlin: de Gruyter.

Barbour, S. (2000) Germany, Austria, Switzerland, Luxembourg: the total coincidence of nations and speech communities? In S. Barbour, and C. Carmichael (eds) *Language and Nationalism in Europe* (pp. 151–67) Oxford: Oxford University Press.

Barbour, S. (2001) Defending languages and defending nations: some perspectives on the use of 'foreign words' in German. In M.C. Davies, J. L. Flood and D.N. Yeandle (eds) *'Proper Words in Proper Places'. Studies in Lexicology and Lexicography in Honour of William Jervis Jones* (pp. 361–74). Stuttgart: Heinz.

Duden (1997) *Duden Fremdwörterbuch* (6th edn). Mannheim: Dudenverlag.

Eisenberg, P. (1999) Stirbt das Deutsche an den Internationalismen? *Der Deutschunterricht* 3, 17–24.

Eisenberg, P. (2001) Die grammatische Integration von Fremdwörtern – was fängt das Deutsche mit seinen Latinismen an? In G. Stickel (ed.) *Neues und Fremdes im Deutschen Wortschatz. Jahrbuch 2000 des Instituts für Deutsche Sprache* (pp. 183–209) Berlin: de Gruyter.

Itô, J. and Mester, R.A. (1996) Japanese phonology. In J.A. Goldsmith (ed.) *The Handbook of Phonological Theory* (pp. 817–38). Oxford: Blackwell.

Munske, H. H. (1997) Eurolatein im Deutschen. Überlegungen und Beobachtungen. In H.H. Munske and A. Kirkness (eds) *Eurolatein. Das griechische und lateinische Erbe in den europäischen Sprachen* (pp. 82–105) Tübingen: Max Niemeyer Verlag.

Ruhnkehl, J., Schlobinski, P. and Siever, T. (1998) *Sprache und Kommunikation im Internet*. Opladen: Westdeutscher Verlag.

Smolicz, J. (1981) Core values and cultural identity. *Ethnic & Racial Studies* 4, 75–90.

Zimmer, D.E. (1997) *Deutsch und anders: die Sprache im Modernisierungsfieber*. Reinbek bei Hamburg: Rowohlt.

Chapter 11

Anglicisms and Translation

HENRIK GOTTLIEB

The Impact of English

As other linguistic *–isms*, such as Gallicisms and Germanisms, Anglicisms are signs of language contact. This meeting of languages may be established either directly – through interpersonal contacts – or indirectly, mediated by cultural artefacts ranging from literary works, including translations, to technical inventions. The notion of 'Anglicisms' is part and parcel of what is sometimes referred to as 'non-English-speaking cultures' but which should rather be referred to as 'cultures in which English is not the language of habitual use'. In such cultures, English is used less than the local or national language(s), if used publicly at all. By this definition, one even encounters non-English-speaking cultures inside predominantly anglophone countries like the UK (Welsh-speaking parts of Wales, for instance) and Canada (Quebec, in particular). Even the Hispanic speech community in the United States may be considered a non-English-speaking culture, yet a very Anglicism-prone one.

In this chapter I will focus on my own speech community, Denmark, without losing the international perspective, since today Anglicisms constitute perhaps the strongest unifying factor among the world's languages. As a modern *lingua franca,* English is unrivalled, and an increasing part of the language in the media worldwide has been translated from English: best-selling books, as well as more 'anonymous' material (news bulletins on the radio, computer manuals, etc.), not to mention innumerable films and TV programmes.[1]

The success of English is not new; ever since the infancy of the former British Empire, and especially since the birth of the Hollywood-based American media dominance in the first half of the twentieth century, English has been in a no-lose situation. Interestingly, the increasing use of English must be seen against a backdrop of relative stagnation in the numbers of native English speakers. Today, native – or rather, first-language – speakers of English make up a smaller percentage of the world's population than a generation ago. In 1975, about 310 million people out of the global population of 3.9 billion lived in anglophone countries, amounting to 7.95%, against the 1999 figure of some 380 million people out of 6.1 billion, only 6.23%. Thus, the native English speakers' share of the global population decreased by 21.6% over the years 1975 to 1999.[2]

So, in terms of 'market shares', the real victory for English lies in its importance as a second language. After the demise of the Soviet Union, and with China's de facto capitalist, non-self-reliance policies, the number of people on this planet for whom the first *foreign* language is not English, is historically low.[3] Today, most of those who (are able to) speak English are mother tongue speakers of some other language. In fact, the majority of the world's population are (at least) bilinguals, and most of them are exposed to English every day – via American brand names, ads and commercials, through subtitled anglophone TV, film and DVD productions, and through anglophone lyrics and titles of all kinds. In addition, a growing international elite access English-language websites, read technical documentation, books, and, last but not least, communicate in English – often with other non-native speakers.

The increasing growth and importance of English as a second language has several communicative and language-political implications, one of which will be dealt with here: the impact of English on other languages.

The Concept of Anglicism: A Paradigm Shift

Anglicisms not only reflect how the world looks, tastes, or sounds (cf. *website, burger* or *hiphop*), they also dictate how it is viewed, what 'good taste' is, and what 'sounds right' in other languages. Still, Anglicisms are not merely vehicles of some Anglo-American mental imperialism; they are the offspring of other languages' voluntary intercourse with English. Having been conceived this way, Anglicisms are prone to being considered bastards by purists, whereas more eclectic observers may see them as exotic pictures on the walls of the world's national language galleries.

The standard terminology when discussing language contacts – and the resulting Gallicisms, Anglicisms, etc. – operates with notions of 'loan words' or 'linguistic borrowing'. Although it is difficult to avoid such terms altogether, they should not be taken at face value, since neither individual words nor other linguistic features are ever handed back to the 'lending' language, in this case English. More than the simile of a lending library, with a limited amount of copies available for temporary borrowing, the concept of Anglicisms can be compared to a cyberspace public-domain catalogue of linguistic features that may be downloaded by anybody and used, abused or discarded ad infinitum. No deposit, no return, but a major impact on the languages which are hooked up.

In mixing blood with different mother tongues, the English donor language fosters children that are only half-sisters and -brothers. Only partly English, raised by their respective mother languages – and thus not always mutually comprehensible – these Anglicisms have become the epitome of the so-called 'globalisation'.

Unfortunately, not even among linguists does the term 'Anglicism' have a fixed, unambiguous meaning.[4] Connotations vary, according to context and user. In witnessing discussions on language contacts today, one meets unbiased etymological definitions alongside very emotional views on the subject, expressed in dramatic language.

Translation scholars and lexicographers, however, tend to stay neutral in such debates, and an example of a strictly technical definition of 'Anglicism' based on traditional linguistic views is the one cited by Slovenian lexicologist Eva Sicherl (1999: 12): 'a word borrowed from the English language which is adapted with respect to the linguistic system of the *receptor language* and integrated into it'. This definition has the merit of emphasising the point that, once borrowed, the 'loans' may remain forever with the borrowing language and may in that process change both pronunciation, spelling and meaning, etc. However, two serious objections may be raised to this definition:

- It is too narrow. It only looks at the most conspicuous elements of language: the individual lexical items. Morphological, syntactic and other features are ignored.
- It expresses a naive integrational paradigm which is no longer generally valid – that of stable domestic language structures which eventually 'digest' and integrate all (English) loans. In this day and age, what happens between English and other languages points to a paradigm of systemic influence. In an increasing number of speech communities, especially Germanic ones, the threshold of integration has been exceeded and English linguistic features – even grammatical ones – are now adopted, rather than adapted, by the domestic language.[5]

In a Danish context, this systemic influence has been convincingly demonstrated by Fritz Larsen (1994). Therefore, based on my own research and inspired by other contemporary authors (Gellerstam, 1986; Picone, 1996; Carstensen & Busse, 1993–96; Sørensen, 1997; and Graedler & Johansson, 1997), I suggest a wider definition of 'Anglicism', namely *'any individual or systemic language feature adapted or adopted from English, or inspired or boosted by English models, used in intralingual communication in a language other than English'*.

Classifying Anglicisms

A structural classification of Anglicisms

Based on the above definition, the taxonomy outlined in Table 11.1 can be established:

Table 11.1 A typology of Anglicisms

I.   Active Anglicisms

(A)   *Overt lexical borrowings* (sometimes with naturalised spelling), constituting:

   (i)   a new word: Danish *jeep,* Icelandic *jeppi,* Croatian *džip; kompjuter* in Slovene; *doping* in French
   (ii)   a new morpheme: *anti-* in German; *mega-* in Danish
   (iii) a new multi-word unit: *grand old man* in Swedish; *on the rocks* in Norwegian

(B)   *Covert lexical borrowings,* the English origin not obvious to the native speaker:

   (i)   Spanish *elepé* (English: LP); Swedish *teve* (TV)
   (ii)   Danish *strejke* (pronounced in two syllables, from *strike*)

(C)   *Loan translations:*

   (i)   *Compound substitutes*: Dutch *luidspreker* (from English *loudspeaker*)
   (ii)   *Multi-word substitutes*: Danish *være oppe imod* (= *be up against*)

(D)   *Hybrids*:

   (i)   *Partial borrowings*: Danish *speedbåd* (from English *speedboat*); Danish *hårspray* (from English *hairspray*)
   (ii)   *Expanded borrowings*: German *Cockpitmitte; Schaltjoystick*

(E)   *Pseudo-Anglicisms*, including:

   (i)   *Archaisms* derived from English expressions now obsolete: Russian смокинг ('smoking', via German, from *smoking jacket,* now *dinner jacket* or *tuxedo*)
   (ii)   *Semantic slides* where an English word is used 'wrongly': Swedish *babysitter* (for English *baby bouncer,* as *barnvakt* already covers the notion of English *babysitter*)
   (iii) *Conversions* of existing English words, for example adjective into noun: German *Handy* (for *mobile phone* or *cellular phone*)
   (iv)   *Recombinations,* reshuffling existing English lexical units: Italian *slowfood* (as opposed to American *fast food*); Danish *cottoncoat* (= trenchcoat), Swedish *fit for fight* (for *fighting fit*)

(F)   *Morphosyntactic calques*:

   Danish plural -s in for example *interviews* (correct plural: *interview* or *interviewer*);[6]
   Spanish 'Es *un* maestro de escuela' instead of 'Es maestro de escuela' (from English 'He is *a* school teacher');
   German 'Mein Leben war in Gefahr' instead of 'Ich war in Lebensgefahr' (from English 'My life was in danger')

II.   Reactive Anglicisms

(G)   *Semantic loans* (existing words acquiring new meanings or new homonyms):

(i)   *Extensions*: Danish *massiv* (traditional meaning: 'solid')
      (metaphorical meaning added via *massive*)
(ii) *Reversions*: Danish *overhøre* (traditional meaning: 'fail to hear')
      (opposite meaning introduced via *overhear*)
(iii) *Doubles*: Danish *misse* (from English *to miss*)[7]
      (puts pressure on existing homonym: = *to blink*)

(H)   Isolated or systemic ***changes in the spelling of existing words***:
      Danish *resource* (correct spelling *ressource* or *resurse*);
      Danish *Lena's købmands kiosk* (Lena's grocery store)
      (correct spelling: *Lenas købmandskiosk*)

(I)   Isolated or systemic ***changes in punctuation***, for example
      inserted 'English' commas in 'determiner + NP + name', as in Danish
      'Den svenske sangerinde, Monica Zetterlund, . . .' (the Swedish
      singer, Monica Zetterlund, . . .), which, according to Danish punctuation
      rules, means that M.Z. is the only singer in Sweden

(J)   ***Changes in the pronunciation of existing words***:
      Danish *unik* (from French),
          pronounced with an initial (English) 'you' sound;
      Danish *backfisch* (from German),
          pronounced with a 'flat' initial English vowel
      Danish *respit* (from Latin),
          last syllable pronounced as English 'speed'[8]

(K)   ***Preference for English lookalikes*** (existing linguistic
      entities whose frequencies are boosted by their similarity to
      English counterparts), usually lexical items:
      Danish *kamera* (from English *camera*) ousting *fotografiapparat*;
      Danish *invitere* (supported by English *invite*) instead of *indbyde*;
      Swedish *definitivt, konversation, desperat, perfekt, speciell*, etc.

III. Code Shifts (use of English among non-anglophones)

(L)   ***Bilingual wordplay*,**
      where keywords must be interpreted in both languages:
      Danish *There is something rotten in Nyhavn* (on a campaign poster
      displaying a giant rat, protesting working conditions and hygiene in
      restaurants in Copenhagen; 'rotten' means 'the rat' in Danish)

(M)   ***Repeated shifts*** in ongoing discourse:

• Det lyder ikke så sundt!	[That doesn't sound healthy]
• Nej, men det var *the only way*.	[No, but it was the only way]
• Kan du godt lide at holde hof?	[Do you enjoy being admired?]
• *I hate it*!	[I hate it]
• Hvorfor har du så gjort det?	[Then why did you do it?]
• Det var *the only way to get the job done*.	[It was the only way etc.]

(Danish author interviewed in Danish newspaper, February 1999; my translation)

(N)   ***Quotes***, embedded in non-English discourse:
      The answer is maybe, and that's final (uttered by a Danish
      politician being questioned in Danish)

(O)   *Stand-alones*, lacking non-English discourse elements:
           Say no to hard drugs (on cigarette lighters handed out in a
           Copenhagen music club)

(P)   *Total shifts* (entire texts in English):
           Letters from Norwegian oil companies to Norwegian authorities;
           Danish hi-fi manufacturer Bang and Olufsen's Internet pages available
           in English only

As will be obvious from the examples in this typology, Scandinavians use practically all types of Anglicisms among themselves – even including the very last category, total shifts. As was the case with Latin half a millennium ago, national elites share a cross-national language, which is sometimes even used within certain domains when addressing fellow countrymen.

In modern academic and business communication in Scandinavia, the national cultures and/or languages have already ceded the vocabulary of several domains to English – plus a good deal of the prestige necessary to keep any language alive. Today, the credo 'certain things are best expressed in English' is not only heard among blasé cosmopolitans; it is often uttered by government officials and businessmen and even by schoolchildren.

Borderline cases: Intermediary –isms and dubious etymology

As can be seen in the case of pseudo-Anglicisms (category E above), not all active Anglicisms are direct imports from an anglophone source culture; they are sometimes coined in the domestic culture. Furthermore, the transfer of English language features is often relayed via a third language. In Europe, German has been very active as an intermediary language, not only between English and other Germanic languages, but also – as illustrated by the 'smoking' example above – between English and a number of Slavonic languages. In the literature, such loans are normally still considered Anglicisms; Germany and Austria are not even credited for 're-exported' pseudo-Anglicisms such as *Dressman* ('male model'), *City* ('centre of town') or *Oldtimer* ('classic car').

Especially with loan translations, it is often hard to determine from which language the item in question is calqued. Take for example the word *neboder* in Croatian. Whether this is a loan translation of German *Himmelkratzer* or English 'skyscraper' remains unanswered, according to the leading figure in Slavonic Anglicism research, Rudolf Filipović (1960: 16).

The only snag is, however, that the word *Himmelkratzer* seems to be a Croatian invention: Germans say *Wolkenkratzer*, literally 'cloudscraper', an 'inaccurate' translation of 'skyscraper'. Based on language structure rather than power, this strange mistranslation could be explained by referring to Scandinavia. In Danish, the type of building referred to is called *skyskraber*, another 'cloud-scraper', and in Norwegian the term 'skyskraper' was first entered in a dictionary in 1903 (cf. Graedler & Johansson, 1997). Hence, Danish (or Norwegian) could have copied the English original, not taking heed of the false friend 'sky', and then German could have coined a 'correct' loan translation of the Dano-Norwegian term. Keeping the mouse and the elephant image in mind, through, it is more likely that *skyskraber* and *skyskraper* are calqued (correctly) from German. If so, this could be another intermediary Germanism. However, that would still not account for the mistranslation of the American original. Why should 'sky' become 'Wolken' without looking north of the German-Danish border?

Such etymology-related questions often remain unanswered, especially in recent decades, as we are witnessing a steady growth in 'international' Greco-Latin or English-sounding neologisms that spread easily across linguistic borders in modern verbal cyberspace. One example will suffice here: pseudo-English trade marks may become generic terms, losing both their 'alien' heritage and their commercial nature. The Japanese neologism *Walkman*, a trade mark of Sony Corporation, was soon used internationally for (any) portable cassette player (although the Swedes use the pseudo-Anglicism *freestyle* instead), and the Danish product *Time Manager* (a sophisticated planning calendar for business people), registered as a trade mark in Denmark back in 1976 and now used generically in Danish, written *timemanager*, was listed as a neologism (in the UK) in 1987, but not, of course, recognised as a Danism (Jarvad, 1998: 166–7).

Finally, what appears to be a normal Anglicism may be an Anglicised English loan word. This is true of *afterskiing*, found for instance in Norwegian and Danish. Here, the English model is French: there is no 'afterskiing' in English, only *après-ski* and *après-skiing*, borrowed from French in the 1950s (Pearsall, 1998: 82). Reciprocally, *after shave* was documented in French by the end of that decade, in 1959 (Höfler, 1982: 2). To complete the picture, Swedish *after ski* is a trade mark, now used generically for a type of soft, indoor boots (Seltén, 1993: 17).

Anglicisms and Acceptability

As stated earlier, not all Anglicisms are integrated into the 'borrowing' languages. Depending on a series of factors (the type of Anglicism, the particular item's (lack of) prestige, its usage history, etc.) Anglicisms are found at different levels. This can be illustrated by the following hierarchy of Danish lexical Anglicisms, listed according to decreasing acceptability:

(a) **Integrated items** (not intuitively identified as English loans):
   (Danish *hive* < from English 'heave').
(b) **Naturalised items** (identified as English loans and commonly accepted):
   (Danish *weekend* < 'weekend')
(c) **Implants** (English-sounding, accepted by certain user groups only):
   (Danish *hænge ud* < 'hang out')
(d) **Interfering items** (often slipshod solutions, including mistranslations):
   (Danish *militære barakker* < '(military) barracks'; correct term: *kaserner*).

Extending the natural metaphors used in the four terms above, it could be said that these four categories represent not only a cline in terms of acceptability, but also a Darwinist race for survival, with many Anglicisms beginning their life as interfering items, which – as in the above example – may mislead the unsuspecting reader ('barakker' are poorly built one-storey houses). Some new, interfering Anglicisms, in written sources often marked by quotation marks or italics, reach the more advanced 'implant' stage, and out of these only a few become naturalised, or – what happens rarely now in semi-bilingual Denmark – end up as fully integrated items.

A recent example of this 'old-fashioned' full-scale development (which could still be explained within the integrational paradigm) is the lovingly derogatory term *nerd*. This word was borrowed by the Danes as late as circa 1990, but was almost immediately rewritten as *nørd*, also acquiring an all-Danish pronunciation, with a glottal stop. Soon after, the adjective *nørdet* ('nerdy') was coined, and in 1999, I noticed the first female deriva-tive, using the near-obsolete suffix '-ine': *nørdine*.

With respect to idiomaticity, the dividing line runs between types (b) and (c): to most laypeople, only items of types (c) and (d) are seen as Anglicisms.[9]

The Charm of Anglicisms

Nowadays, few – if any – European languages fail to use English words or patterns in modern communication. A generation ago, at least in some corners, a different view prevailed. In his introduction to a study of English loanwords in Croatian, a language whose literary identity was created as late as the first half of the nineteenth century, Rudolf Filipović states:

> During the formation of a language, so long as it is not yet completely mature, extraneous influences are much more powerful and more readily accepted than later, when the language has already become crystallized to such an extent that the people who use it have become sufficiently self-conscious not to feel the need or not to be willing to accept foreign elements in their language. (Filipović, 1960: 8)

What are indeed the needs or desires behind the increasing intake of English-language features in non-anglophone countries? A member of the official Danish Language Council (*Dansk Sprognævn*), Pia Jarvad, who has published several works on neologisms in Danish, lists the following reasons – or needs among language users – behind the introduction of new words (Jarvad, 1995: 36–7, my translation):

- to verbalise, i.e. to name or identify new objects or phenomena;
- to generalise and specialise;
- to express attitudes, emotions and values, i.e. to cause reactions from other people;
- to be creative, to play with language;
- to signal group membership and to establish and maintain interpersonal contacts

A model expressing similar ideas in a less positive, yet more sophisticated fashion is put forward by Chris Pratt (1986: 361), having studied Anglicisms in Spanish. Pratt makes the following distinctions:

A. Linguistic causes for borrowing:

    1. Extrinsic causes (new phenomena are introduced) leading to

        a. adopting 'the foreign sign' (i.e. an English word)
        b. using 'pre-existing native signs'
        c. inventing 'a new sign of its own'.

    2. Intrinsic reasons (new linguistic tools are invented, for example through *affixation*, as in adding -*izar* or *anti*- to an existing stem).

B. Extralinguistic causes for borrowing (prestige):

    1. Linguistic snobbery 'out of a desire by the user to appear modern, up-to-date, well-off, well-traveled, well-read, sophisticated, etc.', as when using the spelling 'cocktail' in Spanish (instead of 'cóctel').
    2. Argotic function (for example political and business jargon).
    3. Material benefit (for example ads and technical texts with expensive-sounding English buzzwords).

Of special interest here are the 'extralinguistic causes', all related to the 'exoticness' and alleged positive connotations of English-sounding words, comprehensible or not.

In the 1990s the iconic attractiveness of English was sometimes interpreted as a postmodernist symptom. A copywriter in a Norwegian advertising agency put it this way: 'A feature of postmodern times is that sound often means more than content or meaning' (Løvfall, 1997: 13, my translation). For this reason the author believes we will witness still more ads and commercials that are 'meaningless' in the eyes of linguists, but certainly make sense from a professional advertising perspective.

However, we need not interpret the success of such 'incomprehensible' code shifts or other Anglicisms in modern, let alone postmodern, terms. A more traditional frame of reference may do the job. Just imagine children in front of a fireplace enjoying a fairy tale full of old and mysteriously sounding expressions, a Nordic woman relishing sweet nothings from her Latin lover, or a medieval sermon in Latin, almost incomprehensible to the congregation, but not without an effect on their souls.

It is my claim that as is the case with idioms and other colourful linguistic devices available to the language user, loan words – *in casu* Anglicisms – have always acted as treasured spices in the cuisine of communication. There is only one limit to the use of such devices: the threshold of cliché, above which the intended effect is lost, and innovative features become trite (Gottlieb, 1994). For this reason alone, the life expectancy of 'spicy' Anglicisms and other buzzwords is often short. In language use, visibility is vulnerability.

The Development of Anglicisms

As outlined earlier, English loans may experience one of several histories in speech communities close to the English-speaking nations. In Scandinavia, everything is open to change in the borrowing process: pronunciation, spelling, meaning – even elements of the receiving language (Gottlieb, 2002). Outside Europe, an example of how differently English 'loans' tend to develop over time is found in Hong Kong Chinese and Japanese, respectively (Chan & Kwok, 1986; Ishiwata, 1986). In Chinese as spoken in Hong Kong, the situation prior to the integration of the ex-English Crown Colony was typically as follows:

> The new word appears once, usually in the media. It takes hold of the popular imagination and is propagated. If it survives the test of time it ultimately acquires a permanent place in the vocabulary by being sanctioned by inclusion in an accepted dictionary. *Some loan words may enjoy a brief popularity and are gradually replaced by terms which are more meaningful.* . . . this movement towards 'meaningful' names seems to be a tendency not just confined to the Hong Kong population. Take the example of 'laser'. It entered the Chinese lexicon as [lœy se]; today it is being replaced by the descriptive [gik gwong] or 'piercing ray'. (Chan & Kwok, 1986: 415, emphasis added)

Expressed in structural terms, what happens with the 'laser'-type Anglicisms in Chinese is that what was launched as an incomprehensible phonetic loan (an overt lexical borrowing) ends up as an all-Chinese neologism, immediately comprehensible to the speaker. Thus, in Chinese, not only loan translations offer themselves as successors to pioneering English-sounding terms; quite often the original Anglicisms yield to words that cannot by any standards be termed Anglicisms.

In Japan, the opposite tendency – more in line with the penchant for 'exotic' buzzwords mentioned in the previous section – seems to have beeen at work for more than a century. Whereas, prior to the Meiji restoration in 1869, Japanese coined its own translations of (scientific) terms of English origin, 'it has become more and more common to adopt the western terms as they are without any attempt at translation' (Ishiwata, 1986: 459).

As indicated earlier, this is exactly the situation in several European speech communities today. While for instance, fifty years ago, in German the Greco-English compound 'television' became *Fernsehen*, decades later 'telefax' was taken over as *Telefax*. Along the same lines, in Denmark, cinema 'thrillers' were named *gysere* (a literal translation of the term) as this genre was introduced to Danish cinema audiences in the early 1930s, but today's Danish DVD buyers exclusively use the term *thriller*. In the passing years, the word *gyser* has increasingly been used metaphorically: in recent press reportage, the term typically refers to sporting events, political and financial scandals, and the like. This wedging in of a new term (ironically, in this case, the original English term) allows the existing word to obtain a new meaning, or at least new connotations. If the old term is not lost in the process, we have a case of language enrichment. This issue is discussed at length in Gottlieb, 2004.

Still, many observers are not amused. As if there were any kind of licence required for new loanwords to gain access to Danish tongues and ears, a Danish professor in English phonetics, in discussing the demands one could justly make of a new loan word, somewhat naively states: 'First of all, it has to be *pronounceable*. The fact that Danes find it difficult to pronounce a word like *thriller* (with an unvoiced *th*-sound followed by a rolled –*r*) can be witnessed daily on television. Here, the indirect loan *gyser* (from circa 1935) is preferable.' (Davidsen-Nielsen, 1998: 84, my translation.) Alas, the author misses the point here: his advice is neither asked nor needed. Especially when dealing with contemporary audiovisual material, people simply prefer *thriller*, however correct his verdict on their pronunciation 'difficulties' might be.

In contemporary Western society, purist arguments just do not work. Foreign words travel without passports, and as in politics, power is in the hands of laypeople, not experts. Regrettable or not, this is the state of affairs in countries like Denmark, suburbs of the anglophone megalopolis of the twenty-first century.

A mitigating aspect of this scenario is the fact that, for everyday communication, the individual speaker of a non-English language still often prefers using words that sound 'native' rather than foreign. As one of Scandinavia's leading figures in empirical research on Anglicisms has put it: 'On the whole, then, speakers of Swedish are more willing to use translation loans than direct lexical loans' (Ljung, 1986: 376).

A Danish study of attitudes toward Anglicisms among average language users showed general acceptance of (direct) English loans that refer to 'new things and phenomena', while words that compete with well-established Danish terms are less accepted, and calques of English phrases – of the type *at ryste hænder* for 'to shake hands' – score even lower (Jarvad, 1995: 135). This finding might suggest a rather conservative stance toward (new) Anglicisms in the Danish speech community. However, the success of English-sounding neologisms is supported by the interesting fact that most subjects in Jarvad's study are more inclined to accept other people's use of Anglicisms than to use such words and expressions themselves (Jarvad, 1995: 127).

A final note on English-inspired neologisms, perhaps comforting to some: in due course, many of them fall out of use. A striking example is Danish *slacks*, an integrated loan word in the 1950s and early '60s, used of ladies' trousers (before unisex jeans eroded the usefulness of the term, which is now becoming obsolete). Sophisticated searches in the Danish DDO corpus, which covers the years 1983–92, reveal that in this period the term *slacks* was still used, but only by people born between 1930 and 1950. Together with lexemes such as *well* and *all right*, it has lost its appeal to the generations of today, in Denmark at least. No longer 'modern' and 'up-to-date' (see Pratt's 'prestige' category B1, above), such ex-neologisms are brutally discarded by the children of the baby boomers. As all elements of language, Anglicisms are mortal.

The Role of Anglicisms

Once they have gained ground, often helped by the 'poetic licence' of media personalities and other linguistic role models, 'young' Anglicisms tend to fall into one the following categories:[10]

Additions

Quite often, Anglicisms refer to new phenomena in the world outside the speech communities adopting them: in many Germanic languages, the overt lexical borrowing *AIDS* (or *aids*) came with the disease, so to speak. France managed with a loan translation of the four lexical constituents (Acquired Immuno Deficiency Syndrome), thus coming up with *SIDA*.

Replacements

In many cases, Anglicisms pop up in situations where their non-verbal referents already exist in the speech community in question: presently, Danish *sceneskræk* (a morpheme-by-morpheme translation of the English 'stage fright') is gaining ground at the expense of *lampefeber* (from German *Lampenfieber*). This replacement of a Germanism by an Anglicism is typical of the recent development in minor Germanic speech communities; ironically, in this case the two 'German' morphemes are both found in English ('lamp' + 'fever') whereas the English-inspired compound elements *scene* and *skræk* were originally borrowed from French (*scène*) and German (*Schreck*), respectively.

Differentiators

Finally, as in the case of the above-mentioned Danish neologism *thriller*, working their way in, some Anglicisms may contribute to semantic differentiation: as *rollemodel* ('role model') is slowly establishing itself in contemporary Danish usage, the existing term *forbillede* (after German *Vorbild*) seems to be getting a strictly metaphorical meaning. In other words, part of the semantic range of *forbillede* (that referring to persons) is now being taken over by *rollemodel* – which can be attested by corpus data.[11] However, an Anglicism of this sort, which in the beginning covers only a sub-sense of a domestic word, may some time take over the entire semantic field of that word. In that event, a differentiator turns into (or turns out to be) a replacement. In the case of *rollemodel* in Danish, this is not the case – yet.

The Ubiquity of Anglicisms

How many Anglicisms can one find in other languages, and how often does one find them?

How many?

When answering the first part of the question, it must be kept in mind that in any comparison between languages, the definitions and lexicographical resources in the works used often matter more than the actual differences one is looking for. So instead of rushing out with statements on the numbers, let alone the relative importance of Anglicisms in different languages, let me give an example of the problems involved in this undertaking. In the 1990s, German and each of the three Scandinavian languages got their own dictionaries of Anglicisms: German (Carstensen & Busse, 1993–96), Swedish (Seltén, 1993), Norwegian (Graedler & Johansson, 1997) and Danish (Sørensen, 1997). While Carstensen & Busse lists some 3500 items, Seltén only includes 2093 items, against Graedler & Johansson's circa 4000 entries and Sørensen's record 6180 entries (authors' own figures). Anybody with the slightest knowledge of the Germanic languages will know that Danish and Norwegian do not have three and two times as many Anglicisms as Swedish. Likewise, one would expect German – certainly at the lexical level – to display more than 57% of the Anglicism stock of Danish. Here, *lexicographical* differences – regarding theoretical criteria, aims and compilation methods – play a greater role than *lexicological* differences – regarding the languages per se (Gottlieb, 2002).

I will therefore refrain from evaluating the relative volume of Anglicisms in the different languages referred to throughout this chapter. However, an interesting yardstick may be seen in the fact that Manfred Görlach's impressive work, *A Dictionary of European Anglicisms* (Görlach, 2001) covering sixteen languages, operates with a grid of 4000 potential (active) Anglicisms, the same number as that found in the Norwegian Anglicism dictionary cited above.

In one of the first academic Anglicism studies internationally which includes a dictionary section, Norwegian linguist Aasta Stene commences her conclusion with these words: 'Numerically, the body of English loanwords in modern Norwegian is not impressive. In this material 531 loanwords have been entered . . .' (1940: 210). Stene later almost prophetically adds: 'Present-day Norwegian borrowing from English is so considerable that it is justified to say that we have entered a period of predominant English influence on the vocabulary' (210). Interestingly, the publication of this book was interrupted by the war that led to even greater anglophone (namely American) dominance than one could have envisaged back then, in the heyday of fascism in Europe.

How often?

The frequency of Anglicisms in oral and written usage may easily be overestimated. Depending on the definitions used, figures may vary a great deal, but several quantitative studies have found frequencies lower than the authors expected. Thus, as discussed in Graedler & Johansson (1995: 272–3), a study of recent English loans in Norwegian fiction only found 2 such loans per 1000 running words.

This figure happens to coincide with a minor Danish study (Jarvad, 1995: 109), in which English direct loans account for 0.2% of the total number of words in a pool of 100,000 running words of text samples, with Anglicism frequencies varying from 0.01% in a book on literary studies to 1.1% in a book on marketing, the latter source thus displaying no less than 110 times as many Anglicisms per thousand words as the former.

A study focusing on all English loans after the year 1500 in Danish text samples found higher rates: between 1% and 2% of all running words were borrowed from English. Still, the figure in itself was not judged alarming by the pro-Nordic linguist who conducted this study (Brink, 1991: 107).

But, as most observers agree, from a language-political point of view the direct loans are not the only ones to consider. The important 'undercover' types of Anglicisms which I have termed *reactive Anglicisms* are never detected in studies like the ones cited above. Yet they are always felt by the sensitive language user and deserve much more attention in future studies. They may be inconspicuous, but they play perhaps the greatest role in contemporary language change.

The Introduction of Anglicisms

As stated at the beginning of this chapter, Anglicisms may be introduced through either personal or impersonal contacts between an anglophone 'source' and a non-anglophone 'target'.

Personal contacts

The first wave of Anglicisms in the speech communities surrounding Britain originated in the eighteenth century. Mediated by sailors, English nautical terms were introduced overseas. Today, most of these loans are integrated in the 'borrowing' languages, and in Denmark nobody except etymologists realise that words as *kutter* ('fishing vessel') and *splejse*, meaning 'sharing expenses between friends' (from 'splicing' ropes) are English loan words.[12]

Even today, in most of the world's non-anglophone speech communities, personal contacts constitute a major channel through which English-language features are introduced. A poignant example is found in the influential foreign-based reporters often operating in English even when based in an area where English is not the national language, for example, in the Middle East.

Yet, since the 1940s at least, most Anglicisms have resulted from impersonal contacts. They are introduced in target languages – directly or via intermediary languages – through literature and the mass media, as dealt with in the following sections.

Impersonal contacts

Most politicians, opinion leaders and professionals in the world today depend on English-language information sources: from business executives to university professors, from news reporters to poets. Not just their ideas, but the ways they express themselves in their own language are influenced by Anglo-American language and culture. Today, impersonal contacts through the media play a more decisive role in language change than do personal contacts – which nowadays tend to stimulate foreign-language skills rather than influence the native tongues of those involved.

Cultural exports I (Original products)

A major subdivision within the 'impersonal contacts' category runs between translated and original (or non-translated) entities. Most of the original products are non-verbal, though as symbols of Anglo-American lifestyle, they have a major impact on the language in the cultures in question. Original non-verbal products include clothes, food, media technology, etc. Among the verbal products presently consumed untranslated in non-anglophone speech communities, not least by the young, are rock songs, video games, CNN-type news coverage and Internet communication in English, phenomena contributing to possible future loss of domains for the 'domestic' languages.

Cultural exports II (Translated products)

This sub-category covers translated English-language products, including books, technical documentation, films and TV programmes, often comprising a major part of the total consumption in non-anglophone countries. In Denmark, some 40% of what people read – TV subtitles included – is translated from English (cf. Gottlieb, 1997: 148–53).

In modern non-anglophone Western societies, the influence of English on the general population through people's daily contacts with translated products is enhanced by the uncoordinated, yet effective pincer movement of two disparate groups. Advancing from one side of the field, we have, as previously mentioned, the mainstream intellectual and business elite, who are all used to communicating in English. At the same time, advancing from the fringes of society are a number of American-inspired 'underdog' subcultures not (yet) part of the elite, i.e. young computer nerds, skaters, role-playing clubs, hiphop cultures, etc. The synergetic effects on the average language user of this somewhat unholy alliance, as for instance reflected in the English-sounding campaigns of the influential advertisement industry, have for some time been the object of academic studies in Scandinavia (for example Ljung, 1988; Preisler 1999a, 1999b and 2003; Johansson & Graedler, 2002).

Translations as Conveyors of Anglicisms

We will now dwell on the type of language contact presented in the previous subsection. Although no empirical studies have yet tested the relative importance of translations in the Anglification of languages, there is no doubt that translations – not least those found in the popular media – constitute a driving force in what certain critics have seen as the corruption of domestic languages.

The polysemiotic media: Anglicisms every minute

All over the world, the audiovisual, or polysemiotic, media – television, video, DVD and film – are instrumental in introducing language change. The first study to focus on Anglicisms on the screen (Sajavaara, 1991) highlighted the role of TV subtitles in the ongoing English influence on Finnish – a language which does not even belong to the Indo-European language family.

In Spain, one of Europe's major dubbing countries, critical observers have long talked about 'the effect that English is having on the Spanish speaker at home as a result of the vast quantities of badly translated material flooding the spheres of journalism, radio, television and advertising' (Lorenzo, 1996: 18, quoting A. Gooch, *Spanish and the Onslaught of the Anglicism*).

A phenomenon often mentioned in this context is the all-pervading morphosyntactic calques (Anglicism category F in the taxonomy above). Certain types of calque are more representative of *dubbing*, in which the translated lines should fit the rhythm of the original dialogue, often leading to unidiomatic and English-sounding versions (Herbst, 1994 and 1995 on German dubbing, Gottlieb, 2001a on dubbing in Denmark). Other types have become almost second nature to *subtitling* from English, in which viewers hear – and very often understand – the actors' original lines. An often-cited example of this is the transfer of the English 'negative question plus affirmative answer' sequence in dialogue situations where many other languages use the opposite pattern to express the same verbal exchange. In subtitling, the idea of viewers hearing a 'yes', but reading a *nej* (= 'no') seems to terrify most translators. This is corroborated in one of my recent studies on screen translation (Gottlieb, 2001a), in which five out of six translated video versions displayed Danish calques of the 'Are you okay?' + 'Yes!' model – which on Danish TV have nearly ousted the idiomatic model, in which the answer *nej* is expected if everything is all right.

Even in dubbing countries, the transfer of such questions-cum-answers seems to be a problem. In order to avoid Anglicisms, the Catalan *Televisío de Catalunya* dubbing style book (1997: 62) urges translators to render the lines

  – Because you didn't want to be a witness, right?
  – Yes.
as
  – Perquè vostè no volia fer di testimoni, oi?
  – No.

As in Danish subtitling, the idiomatic solution often sounds 'wrong' – by English standards, which may prevail if morphosyntactic calques continue to appear as frequently as now.

That such calques and other 'indirect' Anglicisms are indeed common in contemporary film and TV translations, both in dubbed and in subtitled versions, is documented in a study (Gottlieb, 1999) looking at unincorporated and unidiomatic Anglicisms (language-political types (c) and (d): 'implants' and 'interfering items', see p. 168), as they appeared in the subtitles of two American films broadcast by Danish public-service TV. It turned out that the film selected for its many blatant overt English loans (*Falling Down*) displayed Anglicisms in 5.2% of its TV subtitles, a considerable figure. However, the other film, *Ghostbusters* – chosen for comparison because of its more conservative subtitling strategies – turned out to have just as many implants and interfering Anglicisms (5.1%), although mostly of a more 'latent' nature. These two films contained an average of 0.43 and 0.57 Anglicism tokens per minute, respectively.

Similarly, in the previously mentioned follow-up study comparing six dubbed and subtitled video versions of three American family films (Gottlieb, 2001a), the subtitled versions displayed Anglicism densities of 0.50, 0.57 and 0.73 tokens per minute, while the dubbed versions contained more than twice as many Anglicisms: 1.04, 1.77, and 1.85 tokens per minute. In conclusion, both screen translation methods seem to play a very active role in the Anglification of the target languages involved. Present and future scenarios are outlined in Gottlieb (2004b).

The monosemiotic media: Anglicisms gaining ground in the originals

Turning to the realm of books and other monosemiotic media, there is a scarcity of empirical work comparing Anglicisms in translations and original non-anglophone texts. However, one major Swedish study needs mentioning. In the 1980s, lexicologist Martin Gellerstam compared the vocabulary in 27 novels translated from English with 29 'native' Swedish novels. On the vocabulary differences between these two text corpora, Gellerstam concludes (1986: 91): 'Many English words seem to trigger a standard translation in Swedish although the Swedish translation differs stylistically from the English original' (see also Gellerstam, this volume).

In a recent pilot study on active and reactive Anglicisms in Danish, comparing late 1990s book translations from English with parallel, untranslated texts in Danish (Gottlieb, 2000), the following comparative conclusions could be drawn:

- *English loan words* are not significantly more frequent in translations than in Danish originals (unlike Gellerstam's findings a generation earlier).
- What Gellerstam terms *international words* are found just as often in the Danish originals as in the translations; the more metaphorical

senses of such lexical items have long ago entered the Danish language, inspired by English. (This is also in contrast to Gellerstam's findings.)

- Local _colloquialisms_ (for example swear words and other emphatic elements) are significantly more common in non-translated texts than in translations (this time in accordance with Gellerstam's findings).
- The perhaps most surprising translational feature in our Danish study was that certain phenomena found by Gellerstam to be culture-specific no longer seemed to be so. For instance, Gellerstam (1986: 90) noticed that in the Swedish translations 'there seems to be more dialogue . . . at least judging from the mass of dialogue expressions like "she said smiling" and more indirect expressions like "he shrugged his shoulders" . . .' (see Gellerstam, this volume).

This illustrates that back in 1976, Swedish translations from English differed fundamentally from original Swedish novels, simply because they depicted another reality. Whether this was truly culture-specific or merely a literary device is not relevant here: anglophone novels made people do things they tended not to do in Swedish novels.

With Swedish and Danish cultures being just as alike as the two sister languages, we thought Danish (writing) habits, even by the late 1990s, would produce texts that also differed from anglophone fiction in translation. We were wrong. There were just as many instances of 'English' gestures in our comparable corpus as there were in our translations, and 70% of all Danish instances of 'shrugging' – as in _Han trak på skuldrene_ ('He shrugged') – were found in original Danish texts.

Anglification Beneath the Surface

In certain ways, the Danes are now more English than the anglophones, it seems. Not only in translated texts – which make up a significant part of present-day mass communication in any minor speech community – are language systems like Danish changing nowadays, owing to massive English influence. In 'original' discourse also, English language features make themselves at home, as the personae we create in fiction and the world view we express in non-fictional genres often emulate British and American role models. In speech communities like Denmark, lexis, phraseology, semantics, syntax and morphology are in a state of flux: some established domestic words resembling their English synonyms achieve boosted frequencies (cf. the 'Preference' category (K) in the typology), and even the phonemic system is undergoing changes, with English phonemes getting a foothold in standard pronunciation.[13]

In quantitative terms, Anglicisms may not seem so conspicuous in European languages today. Yet, a considerable part of the present growth and development of Western languages is triggered by English. In Danish, for instance, according to Jarvad (1995: 135), the vocabulary is being reshuffled, and not only are a substantial share – between 10% and 67%, depending on the defining criteria (Gottlieb, 2004a: 49) of all new words of English origin, these loans – typically nouns – tend to carry significant semantic weight. 'Those are the words that are instrumental in creating our world view, . . . and this means that to an increasing extent we let another culture with its language govern our reality' (Jarvad, 1995: 135, my translation).

In the same vein, Finnish linguist Paavo Pulkkinen notices that since World War II, the number of new semantic loans in Finnish has increased more than the number of loan translations. He suggests that the reason for this shift (from active to reactive Anglicisms) is that 'numerous Finns have recently begun thinking partly along Anglo-American lines' (Pulkkinen, 1989: 92, my translation).

As can be seen, the notion of Anglicism has major implications, nationally as well as internationally. However, instead of issuing a warning against Anglicisms as unwanted linguistic immigrants, I intend to conclude on a rather optimistic note: with English as a modern *lingua franca*, the more international communication, the more Anglicisms in the world's languages, the more easily people will understand each other. This may imply that 'real' English be changed in the process. Especially in Europe, non-native speakers of English sometimes understand each other better if their English contains shared 'un-English' syntactic or semantic features transferred from their individual languages (Wilkinson, 1990).

The danger is, of course, that the world is reconceptualised in Anglo-American terms. But again, in a politically and economically lopsided world – with anglophone cultures setting the agenda more than ever – getting rid of Anglicisms in defence of linguistic purity would only be possible with draconian measures. Paradoxically, in modern society the steady Anglification of domestic languages is a litmus test of their viability. In our day and age, a 'pure' language is a fossilised one.

Notes

1. In Denmark, whereas in 1975 48% of all translated book titles were in English, this figure had risen to 66% by 1994 (Gottlieb, 1997: 16), and by 1993, the average Dane watched (subtitled) English-language TV programmes and films for 42 minutes a day, while Danish programmes accounted for 100 minutes, and non-English imports for a meagre 10 minutes of daily watching (based on Gottlieb, 1997: 151).
2. The figures – based on *Random House Webster's* (1999) and *Gyldendals Tibinds Leksikon* (1977) – include all inhabitants in the United Kingdom, Ireland, New Zealand, Australia and the United States plus the entire non-French-speaking population of Canada and the English (10%) minority in South Africa.

3. In this context, I mean 'the first foreign language that pupils are taught after having learned the dominant national language, if this is not their actual mother tongue'. I here refer not only to immigrants in non-anglophone speech communities, for example Kurds in Germany, but also to the more numerous groups of indigenous people not speaking their national idiom, as for instance Tibetans in China, Indians in Peru and Sami people in Lappland (in northern Sweden).

4. This is reflected in dictionary definitions. The 1995 *Longman Dictionary of Contemporary English* defines an Anglicism as 'an English word or expression that is used in another language', while the 1998 *New Oxford Dictionary of English* (a larger work) surprisingly puts the word in a local context: 'a word or phrase that is peculiar to British English' and cites 'lorries' as an example of an Anglicism.

5. And even in 'exotic' languages under the spell of English, the common practice of code shifting overrules the potential gaps in language systems blocking a direct transfer of English language norms.

6. Although laissez-faire in terms of vocabulary and syntax, the official Danish Language Council is rather prescriptive when it comes to spelling and word morphology. In a Danish corpus of 36 million running words (the *Danish Dictionary* corpus, see Norling Christensen & Asmussen 1998), the 'illegal' plural *interviews* turns out to be three times as common as the only 'legal' plural form, *interviewer*, (315 occurrences vs 109). Most of the latter tokens are not even plural forms; they refer to an *interviewer*, spelled the same way in Danish.

7. This type of Anglicism is dealt with in Gottlieb, 2001b.

8. We are dealing with a modern version of folk etymology here. Such changes in pronunciation are caused by (erroneous) identification of 'rare' words as being of English origin. In a Danish context, new generations no longer save English phonemes for English loan words; English diphthongs and certain consonants (r and w) are becoming default sounds when encountering unknown words in print. In this way, pseudo-Anglicisms are created in retrospect, so to speak.

9. This is reflected in my first empirical study of Anglicisms in translations (Gottlieb, 1999), where the only phenomena considered are those found unidiomatic by language users; etymology is not the only defining factor.

10. As these are based on semantic development, they cover all active as well as reactive Anglicisms. Yet, for the sake of clarity, the examples used are all lexical items.

11. The Danish *Korpus 90*, with 28 million running words, which covers the period 1988–1992, displays only 3 tokens of the lemma *rollemodel*, against 477 tokens of *forbillede*. The *Korpus 2000*, also with 28 million words, and covering the years 1998–2002, yields 67 tokens of *rollemodel* – all referring to persons – while forbillede (with its wider semantic range) produces 533 hits. Thus, the 'semantic share' of *rollemodel* increased from 0.63% to 11.17% in one decade. (The twin corpora can be accessed at www.korpus2000.dk).

12. Before the post-WWII wave of Anglicisms mediated by impersonal contacts, an interesting 'class distinction' of English loan words was suggested by a Danish linguist (Møller, 1933: 49). He had noticed that recent non-technical English loans, for example 'high life', 'garden party', 'lunch' and 'flirt', were predominantly introduced – in their English guise – by the higher classes in society, while the working classes had coined expressions like *med det vons* ('at

once'), *tjans* ('chance') and *nejs* ('nice') through personal contacts, not least with British seamen in Danish ports.
13. One recent example will illustrate this: in Danish, 'rap' (music) is pronounced with an English 'r', thus creating a minimal pair with the Danish homograph *rap* – which already has four different meanings:
   (1) (Interjection by ducks) = quack
   (2) (Noun) = flick, rap (i.e. quick blow)
   (3) (Adjective) = swift
   (4) (Adjective) = cheeky

References

Brink, L. (1991) 'Nordens folkesprog i fare?'. In J. Normann Jørgensen (ed.) *Det danske sprogs status år 2001 – er dansk et truet sprog?* (pp. 107–110). Copenhagen: Danmarks Lærerhøjskole.

Carstensen, B. and Busse, U. (1993–96) *Anglizismen-Wörterbuch. Der Einfluß des Englischen auf den deutschen Wortschatz nach 1945.* Band 1 1993 (A–E), Band 2 1994 (F–O), Band 3 1996 (P–Z). Berlin/New York: Walter de Gruyter.

Chan, M. and Kwok, H. (1986) The impact of English on Hong Kong Chinese. In W. Viereck and W. Bald (eds) *English in Contact with Other Languages* (pp. 407–31) Budapest: Akadémiai Kiadó.

Davidsen-Nielsen, N. (1998) Fordanskning af engelske låneord – Kan det nytte? In E. Hansen and J. Lund (eds) *Det er korrekt. Dansk retskrivning 1948–1998* (pp. 79–93) Copenhagen: Hans Reitzels Forlag.

Filopović, R. (1960) *The Phonemic Analysis of English Loan-words in Croatian.* Zagreb: Institute of Phonetics, University of Zagreb.

Gellerstam, M. (1986) Translationese in Swedish novels translated from English. In L. Wollin and H. Lindquist (eds) *Translation Studies in Scandinavia* (pp. 88–95) Lund: Lund University Press.

Görlach, M. (ed.) (2001) *A Dictionary of European Anglicisms.* Oxford: Oxford University Press.

Gottlieb, H. (1994) Idioms in Corpora: Types, Tokens, Frequencies, and Lexicographical Implications. In K. Hyldgaard-Jensen and V. Hjørnager Pedersen (eds) *Symposium on Lexicography VI* (pp. 85–91) Tübingen: Niemeyer.

Gottlieb, H. (1997) *Subtitles, Translation & Idioms.* University of Copenhagen: Center for Translation Studies.

Gottlieb, H. (1999) The impact of English: Danish TV subtitles as mediators of Anglicisms. *Zeitschrift für Anglistik und Amerikanistik* 47/2, 133–53.

Gottlieb, H. (2000) *Sample chapters on the Web as a basis for empirical studies of trans-lationese.* Research paper, English Dept, University of Copenhagen.

Gottlieb, H. (2001a) In Video Veritas: Are Danish voices less American than Danish subtitles? In F. Chaume and R. Agost (eds) *La traducción en los medios audio-visuales* (pp. 193–220) Castelló de la Plana: Publicacions de la Universitat Jaume I.

Gottlieb, H. (2001b) Misse. In H. Galberg Jacobsen and J. Schack (eds) *Ord til Arne Hamburger* (pp. 94–7) Copenhagen: Dansk Sprognævn.

Gottlieb, H. (2002) Four Germanic Dictionaries of Anglicisms: When Definitions Speak Louder than Words. In H. Gottlieb, J.E. Mogensen and A. Zettersten (eds) *Symposium on Lexicography X* (pp. 126–45) Tübingen: Max Niemeyer Verlag.

Gottlieb, H. (2004a) Danish Echoes of English. *Nordic Journal of English Studies* vol. 3, no. 2, 39–65.

Gottlieb, H. (2004b) Language-political implications of subtitling. In P. Orero (ed.) *Topics in Screen Translation*. Amsterdam/Philadelphia: John Benjamins Publishing.

Graedler, A. and Johansson, S. (1995) Rocka, Hipt and Snacksy: Some aspects of English influence on present-day Norwegian. In G. Melchers and B. Warren (eds) *Studies in Anglistics* (pp. 269–87) Stockholm Studies in English. Stockholm: Almqvist & Wiksell International.

Graedler, A. and Johansson, S. (1997) *Anglisismeordboka. Engelske lånord i norsk*. Oslo: Universitetsforlaget.

Herbst, T. (1994) *Linguistische Aspekte der Synchronisation von Fernsehserien*. Tübingen: Niemeyer.

Herbst, T. (1995) People do not talk in sentences. Dubbing and the idiom principle. In *Audiovisual Communication and Language Transfer*. Translatio–FIT Newsletter 14/3–4, 257–71.

Höfler, M. (1982) *Dictionnaire des anglicismes*. Paris: Librairie Larousse.

Ishiwata, T. (1986) English borrowings in Japanese. In W. Viereck and W. Bald (eds) *English in Contact with Other Languages* (pp. 457–71) Budapest: Akadémiai Kladó.

Jarvad, P. (1995) *Nye ord – hvortor og hvordan?* Copenhagen: Gyldendal.

Jarvad, P. (1998) Pseudolån fra engelsk. In A. Garde, P. Jarvad and K.T. Thomsen (eds) *Elefant – se også myg. Festskrift til Jens Axelsen* (pp. 164–71) Copenhagen: Gyldendal.

Johansson, S. and Graedler, A. (2002) Rocka, hipt og snacksy. Om engelsk i norsk språk og samfunn. Kristiansand: Høyskole Forlaget.

Larsen, F. (1994) More than loan-words. English influence on Danish. *RASK. Internationalt Tidsskrift for Sprog og Kommunikation* 1, 21–66. Odense University: Institute for Languages and Communication

Ljung, M. (1986) The role of English in Sweden. In W. Viereck and W. Bald (eds) *English in Contact with Other Languages* (pp. 369–86) Budapest: Akadémiai Kiedó.

Ljung, M. (1988) *Skinheads, Hackers & Lama ankor. Engelskan i 80-talets svenska*. Stockholm: Bokförlaget Trevi.

Lorenzo, E. (1996) *Anglicismos Hispánicos*. Madrid: Editorial Gredos, Biblioteca Románica Hispánica.

Løvfall, J. (1997) Bruk av norsk og engelsk språk i norsk reklame. *Språknytt* no. 3, 1997, 11–14. Oslo: Norsk Språkråd.

Møller, C. (1933) *Zur methodik der Fremdwordkunde. Acta Jutlandica* V. 1. Copenhagen: C.A. Reitzels Forlag.

Norling Christensen, O. and Asmussen, J. (1998) The corpus of the Danish Dictionary. *Lexikos* 8, Afrilex-reeks/series 8, 223–42. Woordeboek van die Afrikaanse Taal. South Africa: Stellenbosch.

Pearsall, J. (ed.) (1998) *The New Oxford Dictionary of English*. Oxford: Oxford University Press (Clarendon).

Picone, M. D. (1996) *Anglicisms, Neologisms and Dynamic French*. Amsterdam/ Philadelphia: John Benjamins Publishing Company.

Pratt, C. (1986) Anglicisms in contemporary European Spanish. In W. Viereck and W. Bald (eds) *English in Contact with Other Languages* (pp. 345–68) Budapest: Akadémiai Kiadó.

Preisler, B. (1999a) Engelsk ovenfra og nedenfra: sprogforandring og kulturel identitet. In N. Davidsen-Nielsen, E. Hansen and P. Jarvad ('ɘds) *Engelsk eller ikke engelsk – that is the question* (pp. 39-64) Copenhagen: Gyldendal.

Preisler, B. (1999b) Functions and forms of English in a European EFL country. In Tony Bex and Richard Watts (eds) *Standard English: The widening debate*. (pp. 239–67) London: Routledge.

Preisler, B. (2003) English in Danish and the Danes' English. *International Journal of the Sociology of Language* 159, 109–26.

Pulkkinen, P. (1989) Anglicismerna i finska språket. In Else Bojsen *et al.* (eds) *Språk i Norden 1989* (pp. 89–93) Nordisk Språksekretariats Skrifter 10. Oslo: J.W. Cappelens Forlag.

Sajavaara, K. (1991) English in Finnish: Television subtitles. In Vladimir Ivir and Damir Kalogjera (eds) *Languages in Contact and Contrast. Essays in Contact Linguistics* (pp. 381–90). Berlin/New York: Mouton de Gruyter.

Seltén, B. (1993) *Ny svengelsk ordbok*. Lund: Studentlitteratur.

Sicherl, E. (1999) *The English Element in Contemporary Standard Slovene. Phonological, Morphological and Semantic Aspects*. Ljubljana: University of Ljubljana.

Sørensen, K. (1997) *A Dictionary of Anglicisms in Danish*. Copenhagen: The Royal Danish Academy of Sciences and Letters.

Stene, A. (1940) (printed 1945). *English Loan-words in Modern Norwegian. A study of linguistic borrowing in the process*. London and Oslo: Oxford University Press and Johan G. Tanum Forlag.

Televisió De Catalunya (1997) *Criteris Lingüístics sobre traducció i doblatge*. Barcelona: Edicions 62.

Viereck, W. and Bald, W. (eds) (1986) *English in Contact with Other Languages*. Budapest: Akadémiai Kiadó.

Wilkinson, R. (1990) Translating into European English: Evolution and Acceptability. In Marcel Thelen and Barbara Lewandowska-Tomaszczyk (eds) *Translation and Meaning, part I* (pp. 323–35) Maastricht: Euroterm.

Chapter 12
Anglicisms in Norwegian: When and Where?[1]

STIG JOHANSSON and ANNE-LINE GRAEDLER

Introduction

In Norwegian as well as in other Germanic languages, English influence is particularly strong at the lexical level. In this chapter, we examine the presence of English loan words in Norwegian, by no means a recent phenomenon. What is new is the spread into new domains and everyday discourse.

To decide how common English loan words are in Norwegian is not an easy task. Should all words be included without considering when they were borrowed and whether they have become fully integrated and do not differ from ordinary Norwegian words (for example *jobb* 'job')? Should direct loans as well as English-inspired usage of words already existing in Norwegian, for example, *familiær* in *være familiær med* ('to be familiar with'), be included? Should all compound words incorporating a loanword be viewed as independent lexical items as in *folkerock* ('folk rock'), *storbyrock* ('big city rock'), *rockesanger* ('rock singer/rock vocalist') or should the loan word alone be included? How should words be viewed that may have found their way into Norwegian via English but which have their roots in another language, for example, *jungel* via English 'jungle', originating from Hindi *jangal* ('uninhabited wilderness')? And what about international words such as *frustrasjon* ('frustration') and *signifikant* ('significant')? And, in what type of text are they found? For an understanding of how Anglicisms are used in Norwegian an answer to these questions is crucial.

English Loan Words in Dictionaries

One answer may be obtained from dictionaries. About 2200 or 3.4% of the words in *Bokmålsordboka*, an authoritative Norwegian dictionary, derive from English, representing just over 10% of the total number of words derived from foreign languages. However, if we focus on more recent loan words, the percentage is much higher. According to one estimate,[2] about 80–90% of all words deriving from a foreign language that were imported into Norwegian after World War II come from English, now the main source of new vocabulary in modern Norwegian.

English Loan Words in Running Text

Quite a different story emerges from analyses of running text: here the percentage of English loan words is much lower, because among the most commonly used words there is a limited number of English loans. If we open a newspaper and read the news, editorials or letters to the editor, we have to look hard to find a single English loan word.

Some research has been conducted by Anne Kristin Eriksen on the occurrence of English loan words in novels which were chosen because the genre (crime novels) or main characters (young people) would make it natural for English loan words to be used. However, on average there were only 1.9 English loan words per thousand words of running text. The highest number was just over four English loans per thousand, found in Kim Småge's detective story *Nattdykk* ('Night Diving') set among Norwegian divers.

Visibility

If English loan words are not commonly found in running text, why do many people think that they are so frequent? There are many reasons for this impression. Firstly, English loan words are content words: and because they carry a lexical load, they are more salient than grammatical words. Secondly, they often have a different form and, as a result, greater visual impact: *crazy, drawback, establishment, groovy, freestyle*, etc. English words are often used in order to attract the attention of readers, for example, in headlines or in advertisements. Many of these words are new and denote objects or phenomena which are much debated: *headhunting, reality TV, web design*, etc. But the most important reason is that within particular subject areas, the English influence is considerable.

English-Dominated Areas

Table 12.1 compares the frequency of English words in a number of different genres of text. Only direct loans are included and only more recent loans (dating from the last few decades). The comparison shows that there are great differences between the different genres.

Pop Music

Music is an area where for centuries external influence on Norwegian has been considerable, as reflected in, for example, loan words from Italian: *adagio, andante, largo, cello, cembalo, piano, opera, arie, solo, tempo, virtuos*, etc. In texts discussing classical music we have to search for a long time to find any English loan words (one example is *recital*, used for solo

Table 12.1 Frequency of English words in different genres[3]

Type of text	Newer English loan words per 1000 words in running text
Novels (Eriksen, 1992)	1.9
Articles related to fashion in newspapers and magazines (Valberg, 1990)	12.0
Newspaper articles about football (Kobberstad, 1999)	19.2
Articles on pop music in newspapers and magazines (Devenish, 1990)	23.0
Electronic chat rooms (Nordli, 1998)	34.3

concerts). Vocabulary related to music is drawn mostly from Italian, French and German. However, in the field of modern music, there are many examples of English loans, encompassing a range of music genres (for example *jazz, rock, pop, acid house, house, techno*), numerous compounds involving *rock* (such as *anglo-, heavy-,* and *punk-*), instruments and playing (for example *backing, CD, jukeboks, keyboard, remiks, unplugged*), and pop-music culture (for example *discoteque, evergreen, gig, groovy*).

Aasta Stene's research dating back to the 1930s outlines the start of this development (Stene 1945: 189):

> Modern dance-music and dancing have many E[nglish] terms. Some of them are short-lived, and have come into, and gone out of use in this century. Current and, mostly, well established terms are: *band, foxtrot, foxtrotte, jazz, jazze, jazzband, onestep, quickstep, quicksteppe, steppe. Reel* and *bagpipe* are exotica [that is, used to refer to foreign objects or conditions]. Types of songs are *sjanti, negro spiritual*.

In Stene's work, however, words related to music comprise only a small part of the total material, the big surge in English loans occurring after World War II. A recent article about a pop group illustrates how loan words in the field of music are mixed with an abundance of other English words and expressions:

> – *We are Addis Black Widow. This song goes out to all you folks out there. Okay? rapper* det mannlige medlemmet av [raps the male member of][4] Addis Black Widow, Pigeon. *Freestyling* kalles det på *hip-hop*-språket når man *rapper* om det som faller en inn [Freestyling in hip hop language is rapping about whatever comes into your mind]. Duoen har en veldig sterk *hip hop* attityde, kan du si. '*Loose*' gange og *kul* gate*kredibilitet*

[The duo has a very strong hip hop attitude, one might say. Loose walk and cool street credibility].
('We are Addis Black Widow. Okay?' *Norsk Telegrambyrå (NTB)*, 1 March 2001)

English influence is also noticeable in the imaginative names of Norwegian pop groups: *The Black Rockets, Crowtown, Eclipse* etc., but above all in the English lyrics.

'If everyone sings in English, we will never get a new Prøysen.'[5] This was the heading of an article in *Aftenposten*, the Norwegian broadsheet, of 5 May 1999, arguing in favour of Norwegian music being performed in Norwegian. But English is the language of rock and pop: those who wish to reach an audience abroad prefer to sing in English. Moreover, it is easier to disguise a bad lyric in English clothing. English lyrics are safe: it is easier to say 'I love you' than the Norwegian *'jeg elsker deg'*. Yet, the mother tongue speaks most directly to Norwegians, and it is no coincidence that Norwegian singer Herborg Kråkevik has had a big hit with her new recording of traditional Norwegian songs. The choice is not between English and Norwegian. There is room for both, but if there is a danger that Norwegian will be silenced, it is time for us to think: diversity or global jukebox? The multicultural element has to be protected. And wouldn't we love to see a new Prøysen?

> *We'll sleep together in my single bed*, ville jeg si [I would say]. På engelsk [In English]. Jeg måtte jo si det på engelsk [I had to say it in English]. Jeg visste jo at jeg ikke torde å si sånt på norsk [I knew that I wouldn't dare say anything like that in Norwegian]. ('Is this love', Odd Børretzen)

Fashion

Some English loan words belonging to this category go far back in time. *Fashion, fashionable* and *dandy* were included in Maurits Hansen's foreign-word dictionary as early as the middle of the nineteenth century. Fabrics and clothes are also listed such as: *buckskin, calico, jersey* etc.; *kilt, plaid, shawl*. According to Carl W. Schnitler, at the beginning of the nineteenth century 'anglomania' made itself clearly felt. In his list dating from the turn of the twentieth century, Otto Jespersen (1902) includes words related to dress but also other examples such as *dandy* and *snob*. Stene mentions adjectives such as *smart* and *up-to-date*, noting that 'E[nglish] words now seem to have much of the same magic appeal to personal vanity that French used to have' (discussed in Stene, 1945: 186).

Nevertheless, it is only in the last few decades that English has become the main exporter of loan words denoting fashion and clothes. Valberg (1990) compares loan words from English, French and other languages in texts from newspapers and magazines. Of the approximately 2600 examples identified, 44% originated from English and 37.5% from French, with proportions varying according to the type of text. In *Aftenposten* and the women's magazine *Kvinner og Klær*, French words dominated, while the magazines *Tique* and *Natt & Dag* showed an abundance of English words. Valberg comments:

> My impression is that AP [*Aftenposten*] and KK [*Kvinner og Klær*] describe the fashion of women above say the age of 30, while TIQ [*Tique*] and N&D [*Natt & Dag*] write about fashion for teenagers and those below the age of 35; [. . .] there is a connection between the present youth fashion and the continuous flow of English words into the field of fashion and beauty in Norwegian. French words seem to occur in more 'old-fashioned' contexts. (Valberg, 1990: 86–7)

While the English loan words are more recent and more varied, most of the French words are established loan words that are used regularly. English dominance among more recent loan words is conspicuous in newspaper reports from the fashion centres of the world, but fashions change and what is in vogue one year may be out the next. One example will illustrate the point:

> Det meste er tillatt i form av farger, pynt og *miks*. Bare du *ender opp* med å være veldig *sexy*, veldig romantisk eller rent ut elegant, sier *trendmakerstylisten*. Som ikke anbefaler å gå høsten i møte uten *bomber*jakke, vide bukser, vest, *cardigan*, trang skjorte, belte og pynteskjerf [Almost anything is allowed when it comes to colours, accessories and combinations. As long as you end up being very sexy, very romantic or elegant, says the trendsetter stylist, who declares that, this autumn you cannot be without a bomber jacket, wide trousers, vest, cardigan, tight shirt, belt and decorative scarf.] (*Aftenposten*, 18 February 2000)

Nevertheless, the way in which fashion is discussed is firmly established: in Norwegian, clothes are *designet* ('designed') and shown at *fashion shows*; the models walk on the *catwalk*, even if *trendene* ('the trends') are changing.

Sport

Sport is a phenomenon dating back to time immemorial, but sport as we now know it, began in England in the middle of the nineteenth century. Maurits Hansen included in his dictionary words relating to sport such as *boxe*, *jockey* and *sportsman*. Otto Jespersen's list dating from 1902 and Aasta Stene's material from the 1930s provide more information. Stene comments that sports and games account for the largest group of loan words in her material; examples include general terms: *sport, match, team*; results: *champion, rekord, cup*; behaviour: *bad loser, fair play, sporty*; athletics: *heat, sprinter, pacemaker*; boxing: *bokser, groggy, infighting, knock-out*; riding: *race, paddock, handicap*; tennis: *single, set, volley*; rowing: *cox, outrigger, stroke*; swimming: *crawl*; winter sports: *hockey, bobsleigh*; football: *wing, centre forward, keeper*.

Most of the words from Stene's list are still in use, and many more have been added, in particular, terms related to new sports: *golf, badminton, squash, basket (ball), volleyball, sandvolleyball, curling, windsurfing, rafting, snowboard(ing), boardercross, freestyle, halfpipe, speed-skiing, speedway, motocross, dragracing, hanggliding, paragliding, kickboksing*, etc. There is a considerable difference in the frequency of use of English loan words depending on the type of sport. The terminology of golf is mostly English, for example:

> '*Pitching-green* skal bare brukes til trening på *chipping, pitching* og *bunker-slag*' [The pitching-green should only be used for practising chipping, pitching and bunker-play] (quoted from *Språknytt*, 1990:3, p. 19).

Athletics, on the other hand, has mostly Norwegian words such as: *løpsøvelser* ('track events'), *stafett* ('relay race'), *kulestøt* ('shot-put'). For obvious reasons, there are few loan words in winter sports, although ice hockey has borrowed generously from the USA and Canada: *back, forward, blueline, redline, offside, icing* (see *Anglisismeordboka* (1997)).

Let us take a closer look at developments in the terminology of football, probably the most popular and influential sport in Norway.

Football over 100 Years

Kobberstad (1999) has analysed the language in newspaper articles discussing football from three periods: the month of June in 1938, 1968 and 1998. In 1938 Norway played its legendary match against Italy, 1998 saw the football World Cup in France with Norway as one of the participating teams, and 1968 falls in between these dates. Football came to Norway from England via Sweden at the end of the nineteenth century, and English terminology was used from the start, with some Norwegian additions. In the beginning it was even called *Football* in Norwegian. Kobberstad gives an example from the beginning of the twentieth century (the terms for the players are italicised):

> Har vært medlem av 'Lyn' i 4 aar [. . .] dels som *forsvarer*, dels som *løper* [. . .] han har alltid vært medlem av *løperrekken* [. . .] Har spillet: *maalmand, centerløper* og *halfback* [. . .] [has been a member of the foot-ball team *Lyn* for four years [. . .] both as a defender and as a forward [. . .] has always been one of the forwards [. . .] has played as goal-keeper, centre forward and half-back.] (*Fotball nr. 6*, 1911: 22)

The Norwegian term *målvakt/målmann* was dominant in the beginning, but later *keeper* was established as an alternative, and is today the most commonly used word. *Back* is still used for the defenders closest to the goal, but with the Norwegian plural ending (*backer* instead of *backs*).

In addition to the terms for the players on the pitch, there are many more English words related to football, and articles about football often contain more general English words: *bag, booke, charter, cruise, gamble*, etc. According to Kobberstad, the number of loan words in the selected articles from *Aftenposten* and *Dagbladet* has risen considerably since 1938, and in the material from 1998 there were on average 19.2 English loan words per 1000 words of running text. One of the most important observations is that the balance in the articles between football terminology and other loan words has changed since 1938: the main part of the material from 1998 is more general, reflecting the fact that sports articles have changed in character, now extending beyond the event itself. This is also a reflection of the increasing influence of English culture in Norway in general.

Winter Olympics in Lillehammer

When the President of the International Olympic Committee, Juan Antonio Samaranch, announced that Lillehammer had been invited to host the Winter Olympics in 1994, this choice had many consequences. With respect to the language, the impact of English on Norwegian has been analysed by Kristensen (1995) in her study of newspapers from two different years: 1988, the year the decision to hold the Olympic Games in Lillehammer was taken; and 1993, one year before the Olympics took place. The research focuses on journalism and does not include advertisements.

During the five-year period there was a marked increase in the number of non-established loan words (and pseudo-loans). Most of them had no connection to sport: *big spenders, fancy, far out, talkshow, wonderboys*, etc. There are many examples of code-switching, for instance, in headings:

> *The Soft Drink of Europe. One Europe – one Coke.* (*Dagningen*, 8 February 1993)

> *'The LOOC of Success'* [. . .] (*Gudbrandsdølen / Lillehammer Tilskuer*, 26 March 1993)

In the last example, LOOC plays on the English word *look* and the acronym for Lillehammer Olympic Organizing Committee. Other examples of English influence are found in names, for example *Pizza Driver, M-Burger, Kvitfjell Booking, Lillehammer Sponsor Partner, Shop Reklame A/S*.

The Norwegian Language Council (*Norsk språkråd*) provided linguistic advice on texts produced by LOOC, including the recommendation to use Norwegian expressions rather than English. Nevertheless, there was an obvious increase in the internationalisation of the language around this time, judging by Kristensen's study of English influence during the planning period for the Winter Olympics.

Sport is an important channel of English influence. Terms originating from sports are now in more general use, as the following journalistic examples show:

> Latterliggjøringen av direktøren og den underforståtte mistenkeliggjøringen av Museet kan vanskelig betegnes som '*fair play*' eller seriøs journalistikk. [The ridiculing of the Managing Director and the implied criticism of the Museum can hardly be termed 'fair play' in professional journalism.] (*Aftenposten*, 6 February 2001)

> Lederkurs, mentoring og *coaching* er veier til bedre ledelse. [. . .] En *coach* kan være sjefen din, eller en som sjefen leier inn som sin egen samtalepartner eller for å *coache* sine medarbeidere. [Management courses, mentoring and coaching are the means to better management. A coach can be your boss or somebody whom your boss hires to act as his own conversation partner or to coach his staff.] (*Dagbladet*, 2 March 2001)

English expressions imported through sport can in this way influence the language, but it is hard to know whether it is sport that provides a gateway to the general language or whether such language use within the field of sports is a reflection of the increased influence of English on culture in general.

Films

Film and TV are media that exercise considerable impact on modern society and both have been important channels for influence from English-speaking countries, especially the USA, both culturally and linguistically. The word *film* originates from English, and is recorded in Stene's material from the 1930s, together with *filme*, *filmatisere* and *filmatisk* (Stene, 1945: 188). Indeed, a great deal of the vocabulary relating to films is from English or based on English, including for example: *B-film*, *dokumentar* ('documentary'), *road movie*; *animation, flashback, koproduksjon* ('co-production'), *storyline, leading lady, stand-in* and *stuntmann* ('stuntman'). But the most important influence is on a different level. Through American films, Norwegian audiences have become familiar with *cowboys, sheriffs, gangsters, hippies, entertainers, rock stars*, etc, who have all influenced the view Norwegians have of the USA, and, at the same time, how Norwegians view themselves.

According to Lystad (1994), by 1992 the percentage of American films on the Norwegian market reached 60%. The total percentage of English-speaking films is even higher. Films in Norway are not generally *dubbed* (another English loan word), so there are numerous opportunities to listen to the English language, which contributes to the English-speaking environment in Norway. Another source of English influence comes from the many English film titles. During the period 1952–92, the percentage of untranslated film titles increased dramatically (Lystad, 1994), from less than 3% in 1952 to over 30% in 1992, including for instance, *Basic Instinct*, *Sister Act*, and *The Player*, despite pleas by the Norwegian Language Council for the use of Norwegian titles.

In advertisements for films, English and Norwegian are often used in combination, making a strong connection between films and the English language. For example:

> *In 1979 it came from within. In 1986 it was gone forever. In 1992 our worst fears have come true. It's back. ALIEN III.*
> Norgespremiere i September [Norwegian national premiere in September]

There are even cases of new English titles being used instead of the original ones. In April 2001, Per Haddal, film critic of *Aftenposten*, wrote about a new American film with the title *Miss Congeniality*, which was being shown at Norwegian cinemas under the title *Miss Undercover*. In the last couple of years there has been a debate about whether Norwegian films have to be in Norwegian. The film *Aberdeen* was recently made in English for financial reasons by a Norwegian director with a Swedish actor, Stellan Skarsgård, playing one of the main parts. But at the same time, the homegrown Norwegian film, *Heftig og begeistret* [Cool and Crazy], Knut Erik Jensen's documentary about a male choir in Berlevåg, became a great success, evidence that there is a future for films in Norwegian too.

English on Television

English programmes, which are becoming increasingly numerous on Norwegian TV channels, now form part of everyday life for most Norwegians. According to research carried out a decade ago (Sjåheim, 1994), a clear majority of such programmes were produced in the USA, followed by the UK and Australia. On average there were 20 English programmes a day. Even Norwegian TV productions were reported (Sjåheim 1994) to contain English words and expressions, particulary in programmes aimed at young people, to a lesser degree in sports and entertainment programmes and even less in debates, documentaries and news programmes. Some examples follow.

News:
Den såkalte *babyboomen* fra 80-tallet ser nå ut til å være over. [The so-called 'baby-boom' from the 1980s now seems to be over.]
(Einar Lunde, 'Dagsrevyen', NRK, 4 March 1993)

Sports:
Det *fightes* i alle dueller [. . .] Det er bare en del av *gamet*, så det får vi bare ta med oss. [There is fighting in all duels [. . .] That's just a part of the game and something we just have to live with.]
(Nils Johan Semb, Football Norway-England, NRK, 2 June 1993)

Young people:
Here we go, baby. (Jon Skolmen, 'À la Skolmen', TVNorge, 30 July 1993)

However, relatively few English words and expressions were used in the TV programmes studied by Sjåheim compared to advertisements on the commercial channels. In advertisements for foreign products, which constituted two thirds of the 225 advertisements in Sjåheim's corpus, English was used in one form or another on a frequent basis. In some advertisements English was used throughout, others drew on a mixture of Norwegian and English. English catch phrases were common, for example 'Pepsi – the choice of a new generation', but English was also evident in the main body of the text, as in the following example from Sjåheim (1994):

> Advertisement for Lux Wash and Scrub: … dusjsepe og kropps*peeling* i ett. De små *scrub*kornene renser og stimulerer huden din. *New Lux two-in-one skin expert – a difference you can feel, a beauty you can see.* [… shower soap and exfoliate in one product. The tiny scrubbing grains clean and stimulate your skin].

Even advertisements for Norwegian products were shown to use a mixture of English and Norwegian, and in some cases they were exclusively in English. Some of the Norwegian products such as different types of frying pans were shown with pseudo-English names, for example *Høyang Handypan* and *Høyang Wingpan*.

In conclusion, English plays an important role in TV advertisements aimed at Norwegians, according to Sjåheim's findings, and there is little reason to believe that the situation has changed dramatically since 1994. Sjåheim showed that English was used most in advertisements aimed at young people, that is the group most receptive to English. Since TV advertisements are shown repeatedly, they are likely to have an effect not only on our buying habits but also on the language used in Norway.

Advertisements and Advertising

Other research has shown that English has a promotional role beyond the particular area of TV advertisements. Grønli (1990) reports that English influence on advertising is most noticeable within the following areas: transport (cars, boats, etc.), technical gadgets (TVs, videos, computers, etc.) and leisure activities (exercise, disco, travel, etc.).

It is, of course, easier to use foreign words in an advertising text than in other texts, since adverts can consist of isolated words and phrases, while other texts demand a greater degree of adaptation to Norwegian morphology and sentence structure. The most important conclusion to be drawn, however, is that English sells. Some recent examples from advertisements in newspapers:

- *Heavy metal will never die* (ad for a car).
- *There is a new game in town* (ad for *wap/vapp*, a kind of mobile telephone).
- *Turn it on.* Vår suksess skal bygge på [our success will be based on]: *BEST LEARNING – BEST TRAINING – MOST CHALLENGING PROJECTS – MOST FUN* (ad for consultancy company in information technology).

English used in the above examples is transparent to English readers, while in the example below the English needs to be read with a knowledge of Norwegian and relies on wordplay between English and Norwegian:

- *A GLADMESSAGE TO ALL YOU READHORSES* (ad for an internet-based bookshop).

Glad is not used in Norwegian in the same way as in English – 'a gladmessage' can be compared to 'good news'. And *readhorse* in Norwegian has no corresponding expression in English – the closest there is may be 'bookworm'. But GOOD NEWS FOR BOOKWORMS probably would not sell as well.

The importance of English in advertising is reflected in the vocabulary used to talk about advertising, as the following examples show:

- *marketing, direct mail* (general terms)
- *art director (AD), copywriter* (positions)
- *break, spot, jingle* (TV ads)
- *layoute, promotere, konsept* (others)

For some of these words and expressions, it is not hard to find Norwegian translations. *Markedsføring* and *tekstforfatter* are more common than *marketing* and *copywriter*. Instead of *direct marketing, direct mail* and *telemarketing* we can say *direkte markedsføring, direkte reklame* and *telefonsalg*.

Compounding makes it easy to replace *break* ('reklamepause'), *spot* ('reklameinnslag') and *copy* ('reklametekst').

Many advertising companies have English names or names that include the English loan words *design* or *marketing*, sometimes pointing to the company's function, but often with no immediate link:

- Art Direction AS
- Bit For Bit Design AS
- Design Factory
- Good News Reklamebyrå AS

According to Grønli (1990) the choice of an English name is normally determined by a concern to reduce misunderstandings in international communication, the companies being well aware of linguistic choices made.

Economics, Business and Finance

Among the earliest loan words are those which reflect trade relations between Norway and Great Britain. In addition to English units of measurement and names for materials and other imported products, Maurits Hansen's (1842) dictionary includes words related to trade and finance: *invoice, stock, warrant*, etc. In Stene's (1945) material from the 1930s we find additional examples, such as: *boom, jobbe, run, debenture, holding-kompani, trust*. There are also a number of loans related to the organisation of trading/business such as *manager, partner, service*; imported products such as cars: *clutch, exhaust, gir* ('gear'); clothes: *genser* (from English 'Guernsey (shirt)'), *jersey, sweater*; food and drink: *roastbeef, bacon, gin, cocktail*.

At the end of the 1980s, the increased use of English words and expressions in business and economics magazines was discussed by Åge Lind, who attributed it to a desire for a trendy image (Lind, 1988). Lind set out to show that the use of English terminology is not necessary, pointing to Norwegian equivalents such as *overtakelsesforsøk* ('takeover bid') and *kontantstrømmen* ('cash-flow'). But more than a decade later, the business section in *Kapital* contains many examples of English terms: *an all time high* ('rekordnotering på børsen'), *bear market* ('aksjemarked preget av fallende kurser'), *benchmark* ('målestrek, referansemerke'), *bottom line* ('bunnlinjen, egentlig siste linjen i regnskapet der det framgår om selskapet går med overskudd eller underskudd'), *bull market* ('aksjemarked preget av stigende kurser'), *dotcom-company* ('nettselskap'), and so on.

The international orientation of the business world is also reflected in the decision of the Norwegian business schools to offer economics courses in English, an advantage for Norwegian students wishing to work internationally but also an encouragement to use English as the working language in industry and commerce. This observation is borne out by a study conducted by Christensen (1994) who found that in three large Norwegian companies knowledge of English was considered a crucial work requirement by 97%–100% of the employees surveyed.

The use of English job titles in job advertisements is widespread: *ad manager, product supervisor, trainee, webdesigner*, etc. In some cases, English and Norwegian words are combined into compounds but written in the English way as two words, for example *claims konsulent* and *site forvaltere*. The use of English names for firms and companies has been the main target for some of the Norwegian Language Council's campaigns. A common example of English finding its way into Norwegian is the genitive form written with an apostrophe following the English tradition, for instance *Tove's Hjemmebakeri AS*.

The domain of information technology – affecting all areas of business – has incorporated many English terms as direct loans into Norwegian: *logge inn/ut, online, offline, printe(r), skanne(r), megabyte, diskett, CD-ROM, PC, modem, server*, etc. In other cases, Norwegian words have acquired a new sense, for example, *katalog* ('file directory'), or new Norwegian words have been formed to reflect the English terms, for example *e-post* ('e-mail'). Considerable work has been invested in promoting Norwegian terminology, among others by the Norwegian Language Council's Committee for Computer Terminology, but there is still a constant and steady stream of new English-based terminology relating to computers: *dotcomselskap* ('nettselskap'), *e-business* ('e-handel'), *voice mail* ('stemme-post'), *palm pilot* ('håndholdt maskin'), *WAP* ('wap/vapp' and the verb 'wappe, vappe') etc.

Chat-Chat-Chat and Slang

During the last few years young people have increasingly started to *chat* on the Internet in so-called *chat rooms*. In a survey of members of two such chat rooms, most of them teenagers, Nordli (1998) established that a lot of English was used, i.e. the medium in itself is seen as English, despite the fact that most of the participants were Norwegian. Even their nicknames showed a significant English influence, such as *Cool Girl* and *Leopard Woman*.

In communicating in this way, participants often switch between Norwegian and English using many set expressions, for example to establish contact or to start or end a conversation: *alright then, buzz off, forget it, have fun, how is life, I am lost, I have no idea, just kidding, long time no see*. They also quote from films and song texts, for example: *My heart will go on and on* (Titanic), *Everything's gonna be alright* (Bob Marley).

If we include both the use of loan words and code switching, approximately 6% of the words used were English, including many playful innovations which are typical of this type of communication, pitched between speaking and writing, for example *please, pleas, pleace, plis, pliiiii-iis, pleeeez.*

Reflecting a pre-technological era, the word *slang* itself is an English loan word that entered Norwegian through the vocabulary of sailors. While earlier English loans (see Tryti, 1984) came through the spoken language, later developments such as English teaching in schools prepared the ground for further loans. Norwegian slang related to the use of drugs is an interesting example originating from the Anglo-American hippie culture of the 1960s, and hence greatly influenced by English (see Eifring, 1985): *høy* ('high') and *stein* ('stoned').

A recent research project looked into the use of slang used by pupils in secondary schools in the Nordic countries. In Norway, eight schools in Oslo, Bergen and Tromsø participated between 1997 and 1998. More than 400 pupils filled in a questionnaire in which they were asked to write down as many slang words as they could think of in association with 55 general words, including words for people, body parts and money, as well as evaluative adjectives, exclamations and insults. Overall, there was evidence among young Norwegians of a rich selection of loans based on English (www.slang.no) for common Norwegian words such as: *gutt* ('boy') – *babe, dude, guy, boy, hønk, pimp, player, sexy* and *jente* ('girl') – *babe, bitch, chick, bimbo, girl.* Variations in spelling were also noted, for instance *cool, kul* (most common), *kuul, kewl* etc.

A Final Note on Attitudes

In conclusion, perhaps we should ask how the widespread use of English loan words in Norway is viewed. Unsurprisingly, attitudes vary according to social and geographical groupings. Simonsen and Uri (1992) found that many school children in Oslo are positive towards English loan words. In another study Masvie (1992) found a more positive attitude to English influence among young people, men, and urban informants. A larger study by Pettersen (2000) established more positive attitudes among men and Norwegians living in the south, who had more opportunities to come into contact with English. When asked to choose between Norwegian and English words with the same meaning, for example *kontanter* versus *cash* and *fest* versus *party*, the informants in Pettersen's study who chose the English words felt their choice to be more 'international' and 'modern', while for those who preferred the Norwegian words the fact that 'the word is Norwegian,' seemed sufficient justification in itself. That is, a word from the mother tongue gained a value in itself, an attitude that would seem to provide some reassurance that the battle against the English lexical onslaught is not yet lost.

Notes

1. This is a translated and abbreviated version of Chapter 4 in Johansson and Graedler (2002), based on the research project 'English in Norwegian Language and Society'. For information on the integration of English loan words in Norwegian, see Graedler (1998) and the dictionary of Anglicisms by Graedler and Johansson (1997).
2. See the preface to *Nyord i norsk, 1945–1975.* 1982. Oslo: Universitetsforlaget.
3. It is important to remember that there is an element of error in all comparisons of this kind. There are differences in the size and analysis of the material. The figures are therefore to be treated with caution.
4. All translations by Gunilla Anderman and Helena Fagerström.
5. Alf Prøysen, Norwegian author, songwriter and singer, very popular in Norway. Alf Prøysen was born in Ringsaker, Norway and often wrote in his native dialect.

References

Christensen, N.B. (1994) *The Use of English in Three Major Norwegian Companies.* MA thesis. Department of British and American Studies, University of Oslo.

Devenish, I.A. (1990) *English Influence on Norwegian Pop Music Language.* MA thesis. Department of British and American Studies, University of Oslo.

Eifring, H. (1985) *Høy eller stein? Narkotikaslang i Norge.* Oslo: Universitetsforlaget.

Eriksen, A.K. (1992) *English Loanwords in Some Recent Norwegian Novels.* MA thesis. Department of British and American Studies, University of Oslo.

Graedler, A.-L. (1998) *Morphological, Semantic and Functional Aspects of English Lexical Borrowings in Norwegian.* Acta Humaniora 40. Oslo: Universitetsforlaget.

Graedler, A.-L. and Johansson, S. (1997). *Anglisismeordboka.* Oslo: Universitetsforlaget.

Grønli, G. (1990) *The Influence of English on Norwegian Advertising.* MA thesis. Department of British and American Studies, University of Oslo.

Hansen, M.C. (1842) *Fremmed-Ordbog eller Forklaring over de i det norske Skrift- og Omgangs-Sprog almindeligst forekommende Ord og Talemaader.* Christiania: Chr. Tønsbergs Forlag.

Jespersen, O. (1902) Engelsk og nordisk. En afhandling om lånord. *Nordisk tidskrift för vetenskap, konst och industri.* 500–514.

Johansson, S. and Graedler, A.-L. (2002) *Rocka, hipt og snacksy. Om engelsk i norsk språk og samfunn.* Kristiansand: Høyskoleforlaget.

Kobberstad, N. (1999) *The Influence of English on Norwegian in the Football Columns of Two Norwegian Newspapers: A Synchronic and Diachronic Study.* MA thesis. Department of British and American Studies, University of Oslo.

Lind, A. (1988) Engelsk i norsk – eller norsk i engelsk? *NHH silhuetten* 2, 26–27.

Lystad, M. (1994) *The Americanization of Norwegian Culture and Language Through American Films.* MA thesis. Department of British and American Studies, University of Oslo.

Masvie, I.L. (1992) *English in Norway: A Sociolinguistic Study.* MA thesis. Department of British and American Studies, University of Oslo.

Nordli, L.T. (1998) *English Influence on Norwegian Chat Room Language.* MA thesis. Department of British and American Studies, University of Oslo.

Pettersen, K.D. (2000) *English in Norway: Attitudes Among Military Recruits and Teacher Trainees.* MA thesis. Department of British and American Studies, University of Oslo.

Schnitler, C.W. (1911) *Slegten fra 1814. Studier over norsk embedsmandskultur i klassi-cismens tidsalder 1814-1840. Kulturformene*. Kristiania: Aschehoug.
Simonsen, D.F. and Uri, H. (1992) Skoleelevers holdninger til anglonorsk. *Norsklæreren* 1, 27–34.
Sjåheim, A.E. (1994) *The Use of English on Norwegian Television*. MA thesis. Department of British and American Studies, University of Oslo.
Stene, A. (1945) *English Loan-words in Modern Norwegian: A Study of Linguistic Borrowing in the Process*. London & Oslo: Oxford University Press & Johan Grundt Tanum Forlag.
Tryti, T. (1984) *Norsk slang*. Oslo: Universitetsforlaget.
Valberg, I. (1990) *'The Perfect Look'. A Study of the Influence of English on Norwegian in the Area of Fashion and Beauty*. MA thesis. Department of British and American Studies, University of Oslo.

Chapter 13

Fingerprints in Translation

MARTIN GELLERSTAM

Introduction

English is fast becoming the world's leading international language. It is not the language with the greatest number of native speakers (that is Chinese) but, if the population of countries where English is an official language is considered, it is the most frequently used language. By many, this is viewed as an important development as, in today's world there is an increasing need for an international language. Others, however, view English as a threat to the continual existence of the language and culture of nations with smaller numbers of speakers. Words such as *franglais* and the Swedish equivalents *svengelska* and *Svenglish* illustrate that the dominance of English leads to the mixing of languages and other types of influence. This is perhaps most clearly demonstrated by the steady stream of loan words from English into other languages that have become incorporated into the morphology and phonology of the receiving language, in this case Swedish. The influence is, however, also visible at other levels, for example the meaning of words and phrases, even if this may go unnoticed and does not create the same type of problem for the language user.

The English influence is occasionally met by determined opposition. The French, for instance, have plans to use legislation to prevent their language being 'contaminated' by English. Some concern has also been expressed by speakers of other languages regarding the role of English as the standard-bearer of cultural dominance, particularly in spheres such as the business world, the entertainment industry, television and music, sport, science, and more recently the Internet – perhaps the most obvious influence. One possible way of getting a feel of the cultural dominance of English is by studying the translation of books and films into less well known European languages. Eighty per cent of all books translated into Swedish in the 1990s were originally written in English. This well-documented phenomenon is observed in many countries.

Throughout the twentieth century there have been translations from English into Swedish. For many Swedes growing up during the post-war era, translations of English books for children and teenagers were required reading. The translations allowed young readers to experience a different world; books about children at boarding school, a type of institution unfamiliar to most Swedish readers; books set in an English country village, populated by children who lived in a world of church fêtes and angry farmers; books about foolhardy pilots and their adventures in foreign parts of the world. All were books set in a cultural environment that seemed both exciting and slightly exotic. And the differences were not just cultural. Linguistic differences also contributed to the exoticism: there was a considerable amount of dialogue and the reader learned new verbs of diction; people 'remarked' on things, 'exclaimed', 'added', not to mention 'groaned' and 'muttered' and of course 'smiled' and 'laughed', all descriptions of the manner in which the dialogue was conducted. Such constructions were seldom found in books written in Swedish such as Astrid Lindgren's *Pippi Longstocking* (which already existed at the time). What's more, people speaking in the translated books ended their sentences with expressions seldom found in Swedish literary works, such as the equivalents of 'don't you?' and 'isn't it?'

Childhood experiences are often remembered later in life when translations are studied from a more professional perspective. The corpus of translated novels from the 1970s, which is one of the sources on which this chapter draws, makes it clear that the main characters are in the habit of 'adding', 'exclaiming' and 'remarking' in their dialogue to a far greater extent than characters do in original Swedish novels. The first type of influence can hardly be laid at the translator's door, while in the latter case more natural means of expression are available in Swedish. In such cases we talk about *translationese*, or, it has been suggested, 'översättningssvenska', translational Swedish. This type of Swedish usually has negative connotations: it is a poor translation if there are clear traces of the source language. This view may, however, be called into question and above all there are different degrees of influence affecting the translator (invisible/unconscious) and the reader (visible/conscious). Instead, I am choosing the more neutral concept of 'leaving fingerprints in translation', that is all forms of translation which can in some way be viewed as having been influenced by the original text, without the term implying any value judgement. It is not just a case of one translator's idiosyncrasies, but all traces of translation. Such traces may result from the transference of the English rhetorical tradition, as in the structure of dialogue for example, as well as from less successful methods of translating tag questions.

Corpus

For some time, 'translational Swedish' has been the subject of research (Gellerstam, 1986, 1989, 1996) through the use of a corpus of novels comprising approximately 4 million running words. This amounts to some 30 novels translated into Swedish from English plus a corresponding amount of text from novels originally written in Swedish. The corpus itself is a selection from an even larger collection of novels published by Bonniers during 1976–7 (for a more detailed description, see Gellerstam, 1986). The novels are stored in Språkbanken (The Language Bank), a linguistic reference database in the Swedish Department at Gothenburg University (Språkbanken is accessible at http://spraakbanken.gu.se).

The texts are mainly from the same period. The authors represent a relatively broad spectrum, from the literary elite including writers such as Saul Bellow and Nadine Gordimer – and in the original Swedish – novelists such as Kerstin Ekman and Göran Tunström – to those referred to as popular authors, for example, writers of detective novels. The translators are all professionals, in most cases with many years of experience. Thus it is not a parallel translation corpus of source texts and their translations, but rather a 'comparable corpus' comparing 'authentic' and 'translated' Swedish texts. In this chapter, reference will also be made to a translation corpus of EU texts from the mid-1990s which has been used for the discussion of syntactic transfer. The material forms part of a smaller (or 'parallel') translation corpus available at Språkbanken.

For the section on lexical transfer, reference is made to an unpublished paper written by one of my students (Helgesson, 2001).

Lexical Transfer

Change in lexical meaning

Swedish vocabulary is currently undergoing a period of strong English influence. This influence was noticeable throughout the latter part of the twentieth century, and is a natural consequence of the growing Anglo-American cultural influence. The dominance of English is manifested by a large number of loan words, especially within the particular subject areas in which British and American English play an important cultural role.

In addition to the loan words that introduce new concepts and new words, there is also a clear influence on the meaning of existing Swedish words. While these changes have been taking place throughout the period of English influence on Swedish, it has become more and more obvious with time. The trend has attracted criticism and debate due to the poor adaptability of English loan words to the Swedish morphological inflection patterns – the English s-plural, for example – while on the other hand changes in meaning have taken place without attracting undue interest. Occasionally, semantic shifts have been commented on, often with a certain element of surprise, but, on the whole, changes in meaning are more anonymous and easily acceptable. It is debatable whether these changes are merely the result of translation. It is, of course, perfectly possible for a

Swede with good bilingual competence to simply start using a Swedish word with a new meaning taken from the corresponding English word. Nevertheless, it could be argued that the new meaning does not become part of the Swedish semantic system until it appears in print and an important way of introducing new meanings in texts is through translation. Once the word has gained a foothold in the Swedish lexicon it gradually starts to appear in original Swedish texts.

Translation loans of this kind are likely to crop up in words that are common to both the lending and the receiving language, international words that often occur in several languages but may have a number of slightly different meanings. One method of signalling mistranslations caused by polysemy is to refer to these words as 'false friends', a term implying that the reader thinks he/she recognises the word. In reality, however, the word has a different meaning than first thought and, as a result, is translated incorrectly.

The words that are presented in Table 13.1 as examples of semantic loans fulfil the requirement that they appear in their original Swedish meaning in an early *Språkbanken* corpus from 1965, as well as in a Swedish dictionary from that time; they also appear in a corresponding corpus from 1997 with a new meaning, the same as in English, the donor language. The examples are taken from Helgesson (2001). Additional examples of new lexical meanings can be found, for example, in the most recent dictionary from *Svenska språknämnden*, the Swedish Language Council, listing new words (Moberg, 2000).

Standard translations

The type of 'fingerprint' referred to in this chapter found in standard translations is the effect caused by the combination of two different factors. The first factor is a case of early language acquisition, which means that at some time, the learner has started to associate one word in English with a particular word in Swedish. Since many words do in fact have a direct equivalent in another language, there is a clear tendency to look for one single standard translation for a word, even if a number of synonyms are available as is frequently the case. The reason for this could be the early age at which learners acquire foreign languages, often in the form of word lists that frequently provide no more than a single translation equivalent. For instance, Swedes learn that *emellertid* is the Swedish equivalent of the English 'however', despite the fact that the Swedish *men* ('but') is often an idiomatic alternative. In the case of the English adverb 'completely', the usual translation is *fullständigt*, although the translation *helt* ('fully') is just as idiomatic. When gradually, it becomes apparent that translation is not just about translating word for word – a belief frequently supported by the creation of bilingual dictionaries – but also longer

Table 13.1. Lexical changes in Swedish resulting from English language influence

English meaning	New Swedish meaning
address (*a person, a problem*)	adressera (*ett problem*)
affair (*love affair*)	affär (*kärleksaffär*)
agent (*'manager'*)	agent
alternative (*alternative energy*)	alternativ (*energi*)
buy ('accept')	köpa (*jag köper inte det argumentet*)
comfortable ('relaxed')	komfortabel (*vinst* 'a comfortable win')
concept ('idea')	koncept (*ett nytt koncept* 'a new concept')
condition ('state')	kondition (*i dålig kondition* 'in bad condition')
conservative ('safe')	konservativ (*en konservativ uppskattning* 'a conservative estimate')
dated ('old-fashioned')	daterad
freeze (*wages, prices*)	frysa (*löner, priser*)
given (that)	givet (*att*)
initiate ('take initiative')	initiera (*en undersökning* 'an investigation')
kick (*get a kick from something*)	kick (*få en kick av något*)
local (*our local shops*)	lokal (*våra lokala affärer*)
maximise ('make as big as possible')	maximera
minimise ('make as small as possible')	minimera (*risker* 'risks')
motivate ('provide motivation')	motivera (*någon att göra något* 'someone to do something')
must (*it's a must*)	måste (*det är ett måste*)
opening ('possibility, chance')	öppning
package (*a package solution*)	paket (*paketlösning*)
segment ('section')	segment (*marknadssegment* 'market segment')
single ('not married')	singel (*jag är singel* 'I'm single')
spend ('to spend time')	spendera *ett veckoslut med barnen* ('a weekend with the children')
soap (*soap opera*)	såpa (*såpopera*)
volume ('amount, degree')	volym (*arbetsvolym* 'volume of work')

stretches of text, the use of the same standard translation equivalents still continues.

The second factor is related to the absence of more than one translation alternative reinforcing the trend towards drawing on one and the same translation equivalent. Asked for the Swedish translation of the English word 'arrive', a Swedish speaker would invariably give the answer *anlända*. This could be a combination of the factors which we have discussed or quite simply that Swedes have learned how the word should be translated and hence do not consider any other choices. However, the word 'arrive' can also be translated in other ways:

- The train will arrive at 11 o'clock
  Tåget *kommer* kl. 11
  (The train comes at 11 o'clock)

- The train arrived at 11 o'clock
  Tåget *kom in* kl. 11
  (The train got in at 11 o'clock)

- When will we arrive?
  När *kommer* vi *fram*?
  (When will we get there?)

In all of the above examples, the Swedish word *anlända* may also be used. However, unlike the English 'arrive', this word is stylistically marked. It is not what a Swedish speaker would say or write spontaneously. Still, it remains the standard choice when translating from English, partly due to the power of habitual use, partly due to the translator failing even to consider other alternatives.

The same applies to the Swedish *tillbringa*, the standard translation of the English 'spend' in the sense of 'passing a certain amount of time in one place', for example 'I spent a week in Spain': *jag tillbringade en vecka i Spanien*. This word is also stylistically marked and a more idiomatic way of expressing it would be the Swedish equivalent to 'I *was* in Spain for a week'.

This process of 'Pavlovian translation' which excludes consideration of more than one alternative has, to my knowledge, not as yet been studied in depth. An interesting observation concerns the possible impact of morphological structure which somehow appears to influence the choice of word sought in the target language. Why is it that the Swedish word *anmärkningsvärd* is usually translated into English as 'remarkable' (the first equivalent given in dictionaries) and the English 'remarkable' is usually translated as *anmärkningsvärd*, in both cases words of approximately the same length, despite the fact that numerous other possible but shorter equivalents exist in both directions?

Head nouns in predicative phrases

In English predicative phrases it is often crucial to use a noun as in adjective + noun whereas Swedish requires only an adjective. The English 'she is a nice person' is naturally translated into Swedish as *hon är trevlig* ('she is nice'). Another example is the English 'when I was a little boy', *när jag var liten* ('when I was little') in Swedish. This is also the case with Swedish adjectival nouns that are equivalent to the adjective + noun construction in English (Svartvik & Sager, 1986): the head word can be a person or an object as in 'the long-haired boy', *den långhårige* ('the long-haired'), 'the annoying thing was . . .' *det fatala var* . . . ('the annoying was . . .'). Words describing people, such as 'man', 'woman', 'boy', 'girl' and object words, such as 'thing', 'fact', are the most frequently occurring examples of this type of head word in English.

These structural differences are obvious in translations from English into Swedish because of the way that English nouns (normally not required in Swedish) are over-represented. In the translated novels examined we find: *han är en charming person* ('he is a charming person') instead of *'han är charmig'* ('he is charming'), and *en fånig sak hände* ('a silly thing happened') instead of *något fånigt hände* ('something silly happened'). Some further examples from the translated novels are shown below:

- *Han är en förtjusande person att leva ihop med.* ('He is a *charming person* to live with').
- *Sarah är en mycket god person* ('Sarah is *a very good person*').
- *Hon var en mycket pålitlig flicka, dotter till biskopens hushållerska.* (She was a very *reliable girl*, daughter of the bishop's housekeeper').
- *Nu är du en snäll pojke* ('a *good boy*') *i fortsättningen, för annars . . .* ('Now you are a *good boy* in the future or else . . .').
- *Jag har en allvarlig sak* ('a serious thing') *att bekänna.* ('I have *a serious thing* to confess').

It is worth pointing out that the sentences cited here are not impossible in Swedish; as in other cases of influence from the source language, the result is not normally sentences that break Swedish rules – but it would be unusual for them to be used in writing by Swedish authors. A look at some figures gives us an idea of the ratio of use of the head word in translations and in original Swedish novels (the first set of figures refers to translations, the second to Swedish original novels): *kvinna* (woman) 1185/367, *flicka* (girl) 806/310, *pojke* (boy) 405/183, *person* (person) 374/140, *sak* (thing) 1021/493, *faktum* (fact) 274/70.

Syntactic Transfer

Modality and tag questions

Typical markers of modality in English include the use of tag questions such as 'haven't you?' and 'isn't it?' Modality is also expressed by phrases such as 'I suppose' and 'I should think'. Yet another way is to use adverbials such as 'probably' and 'presumably'.

The way to express this type of modality in idiomatic Swedish is to use the adverbs *ju, nog, väl, visst* and *säkert* in sentences such as the following:

- *Jag måste **nog** gå nu* ('I have to leave now, I think').
- *Han är **ju** bara ett barn* ('He is just a child, isn't he?').
- *Du gillar honom **visst** inte* ('You don't like him, do you?').

- *Jag får **väl** ringa till rörmokaren* ('I'll have to call the plumber, I suppose').
- *Han är **säkert** här när som helst* ('He will be here in a minute, I'm sure').

In translation, the English way of expressing modality is frequently transferred into Swedish, resulting in sentences such as:

- *Dr Livingstone, förmodar jag* ('Dr Livingstone, I presume').
- *Han har åkt till London, antar jag* ('He has gone to London, I suppose').
- *Du känner en massa folk där, eller hur?* ('You know a lot of people there, don't you?')

In the last sentence, *eller hur* is used as a tag modality marker. This phrase is found approximately twice as often in the translation corpus from 1976–7 as in the corresponding 1980–1 corpus containing only Swedish authors.

Other markers of modality are adverbs like 'probably'. Although the nearest idiomatic equivalent in Swedish is *nog* ('He is probably in his office' *Han är nog på kontoret*), an adverb like *antagligen* is clearly preferred by translators; 305 cases in translation, whereas the Swedish originals have only 147 cases. Although a possibly English-inspired translation variant in Swedish, the choice is nevertheless strikingly less frequent in novels written by Swedish writers.

The subject rule

The gist of the Swedish subject rule is as follows: if the syntactic context of a sentence does not clearly point to a definite subject of a contracted clause, it is assumed that the subject of the main clause is also the subject of the contracted clause. In for instance: *Han åkte till stan för att träffa sin kusin* ('He went to town to meet his cousin'), the subject of *för att träffa* ('to meet') is the subject of the main clause, *han* ('he').

A commonly found violation of the subject rule is linking a contracted clause to a passive rather than an active clause, which means that what would have been the subject of the main active clause is no longer explicit. An example of this type of sentence is *Kylan måste utestängas för att skydda instrumenten* ('The cold must be kept out to protect the instruments'). Contracted clauses often follow the pattern *för att* + INFINITIV ('in order to' + INFINITIVE). In Swedish, Erik Wellander has been the foremost contributor of entertaining examples of violations of the subject rule, such as *Efter att ha satt sig i vagnen föll hästen åter i sken* ('After sitting down in the wagon, the horse bolted again').

Views on the violation of the subject rule seem to have changed in the last few decades – violations are becoming increasingly commonplace.

This kind of development is not unique. If violations of the subject rule are seen as one of many linguistic changes indicating that content is more important than structure, for example *polisen är tacksamma för allmänhetens tips* ('the police [singular] are grateful [plural] for tip-offs from the public'), it may be argued that the understood subject is there in spirit if not in body. This is certainly the case when the contracted clause is linked to a passive clause.

Similar problems exist in English with respect to the subject rule. It is not good practice to write: 'When driving at night, pedestrians may turn up unexpectedly'. In certain cases there are stock participle phrases – ('considering . . . considering the circumstances, speaking of, strictly speaking', etc.) in which the subject rule is not usually followed. Similar phrases also appear in Swedish, such as *det är svårt att, det är lätt att förstå*, etc. – 'it's difficult to understand, it's easy to understand', etc. For example, *Det är svårt att ransonera superlativerna efter att ha sett Älvsjö besegra Karslund med 4-1* ('It's difficult to ration the superlatives after having seen Älvsjö beat Karlslund 4-1').

The Swedish construction *genom att + INFINITIV* often corresponds to *by + VERB + ing* in English, for example *The Commission has played an important role by removing* ('genom att ta bort') *many of the privileges*. In the event of the main clause containing a passive verb, the resulting translation will not be as good: *Reduction of SO₂ emissions can be achieved by lowering the sulphur content in bunker fuel oils*. Still, the English construction seems more acceptable than the Swedish equivalent: *kan åstadkommas genom att sänka svavelinnehållet*. This is probably linked to the fact that the English –ing construction is considerably closer to being a noun than the Swedish infinitive, which is a verb form. In other words, it is also grammatical to say *genom sänkning av svavelinnehållet* ('by a lowering of the sulphur content').

The current hypothesis is that the English –ing construction is not only translated in most instances using the Swedish infinitive as would be expected, but also in instances where the real subject of the main clause is hidden, for example when the passive is used. As a result, through the medium of translation, violation of the subject rule has gained acceptance in Swedish. In the EU texts studied – or rather the *by + VERB+ ing* phrases studied – there are 30 cases of violations of the Swedish subject rule in the form of the standard translation *genom att* ('by') + *INFINITIV*. This number should be considered only against the total number of these phrases in the corpus, approximately 200. While it may be viewed as a general reflection of a decreased awareness of the subject rule, it also constitutes a translational phenomenon, a 'fingerprint' left in the Swedish translations.

Rhetorical Transfer and Patterns of Dialogue in Translated Texts

There are various ways of presenting dialogue in fiction. It is, for instance, possible to allow the speakers involved to say something without informing the reader who is speaking; it is assumed that the context makes it obvious. If it becomes impossible to remember whose turn it is to speak and there is not much in the way of clues this method may result in ambiguity.

Another method is for the author to employ clear markers describing the speaker and also the manner in which this person speaks. The markers can be positioned differently:

- 'You don't fool me', she said laughing.
- She laughed: 'You don't fool me'.

In the second example, there is no longer a verb of diction, rather a general description of the circumstances in which someone says something:

- She shook her head/She shrugged her shoulders/She furrowed her brow

In the English novels translated into Swedish, these markers are commonplace, considerably more frequent than in the original Swedish texts.

Let us now take a closer look at markers using verbs of diction and compare the translations from English with original Swedish texts. As an exhaustive study of all forms of dialogue is not possible in the present discussion, I have chosen to look at only one type, as exemplified in the construction *'No', she said calmly*. One reason is that this type may prove to be interesting as an example of cross-linguistic differences in the use of narrative forms, and possibly also reveal something about the literary quality of a given text.[1] The grammatical construction looks like this, DIRECT SPEECH, he/she said + MANNER ADVERBIAL

- 'Don't try', she said with disdain. (Sundberg, *Victory*)
- 'It doesn't matter', he said calmly. (Shaw, *Nightwork*)
- 'And now you must go to sleep', he said in a tone that was friendly but authoritative. (Adams, *Shardik*)

This twofold message of the identity and the manner of the speaker reveals a few odd features. Male speakers are more likely to be associated with adverbs such as *shortly* and *with a broad grin*, while female speakers will figure in contexts such as *she said and smiled* and various varieties of *trembling lips*. If the distribution of the constructions between the translated and the original texts is examined, the findings show 484 cases in the translations with only 64 instances in the original Swedish texts.

In order to find an explanation for this noticeable difference, let us take a closer look at the distribution of the figures for both groups. This makes it apparent that, far from all the English translations contain this type of construction, barely more than 50% do. There are none at all in novels by Saul Bellow and Joyce Carol Oates, Bellow's book consisting mainly of the author's reflections and containing very little dialogue. Nor does Agatha Christie use this type of construction. On the other hand, we find many incidences in Irwin Hall (93), Anne Rice (79), Judith Rossner (67) and Hammond Innes (54), all writers who fall more or less into the genre of detective novels or can be categorised as writers of 'thrillers'. The pattern is not, however, really that clear-cut. As an author like Nadine Gordimer uses this construction relatively often (34 times), it is obvious that it is not just a characteristic of 'low brow' fiction.

Significantly, Richard Adams (*Shardik*), who is considered a good writer of fiction, albeit perhaps not a potential Nobel Prize candidate, uses the construction:

. . . he said abruptly
. . . he said jealously
. . . he said authoritatively
. . . he said smiling
. . . he said in a low voice
. . . he said with an uncertainty he hadn't shown before
. . . he said with a sort of unspoken delight
. . . he said in a tone that was friendly but authoritative
. . . he said with clenched teeth

We have also studied occurrences of the construction 'No, said Frank calmly' where the absence of a subject pronoun allows inverted word order – as in 'DIRECT SPEECH, said somebody, + MANNER ADVERBIAL. Random examples of this construction do present an overall similar picture – even in this category authors such as Saul Bellow and Joyce Carol Oates, are conspicuous by their absence, while the authors who appear committed to using the construction discussed above also figure here.

What happens then in the case of the Swedish authors who, on the whole, are very sparing in their use of this construction? Three authors who use it more than just sporadically may be mentioned here: Dagmar Edqvist (16 times), Barbro Hall (18) and Rita Tornborg (10). As far as Dagmar Edqvist is concerned, she is representative of a somewhat older narrative style. She has been included in the corpus material, as has Björn Höijer, because their work has been published in new editions alongside a younger generation of authors who form the corpus of novels from 1976–7.

There are two explanations for the remarkable fact that a particular construction occurs much more frequently in translation from English.

First the material is different, that is the English corpus contains text types different from those in the Swedish corpus. This is a plausible explanation as the ratio of detective novels in the English corpus is greater. This could also be the reason why it contains twice as much dialogue as the Swedish corpus, although it should not be taken as given that detective novels automatically contain a great deal of dialogue, since this might imply that the English corpus contains a kind of fiction expected to employ the type of stereotypical speech constructions that have been studied. It is, however, difficult, if this is the case, to explain the very significant difference in frequency distributions between the two corpora as it might also be expected that the construction would be found in the crime novels of the Swedish corpus. This is not so.

There is, however, a different way in which to account for the phenomenon. Let us assume that the construction *she replied calmly* is a tried and tested construction used in popular English fiction, recognisable, for instance, from books of that genre. This is a narrative type of fiction that has been widely translated into Swedish and devoured by a large number of readers. As a result, the construction has been incorporated into the verbal consciousness of many Swedes, at the same time as the genre of the fiction in which it is found has made the construction appear slightly doubtful. It has become the hallmark of 'pulp fiction', well known from publications such as short stories and serial weeklies focusing on topics of violence, excess and enjoyment, all translated from English. It has, in short, a construction studiously avoided by 'good' Swedish writers.

At the same time, it is clear that the construction is not ruled out in English fiction. It is, for instance, difficult to understand its frequent use by Nadine Gordimer and Richard Adams unless it is more accepted in English literary style than in Swedish.

Final Comments

One issue currently under debate in Sweden, as well as in many other countries, is the role of the national language in a world in which English is used uniformly as the international language. Swedish is at the receiving end of growing competition: first, from industry where English is the in-house language of several companies; then, education is now offered in English-language sixth-form colleges, and research in many subject areas now results in papers and articles written in English. This phenomenon is referred to as 'loss of domains of usage' and points to the potential danger that, in times to come, certain subjects will not be discussed in Swedish because the language will no longer be in possession of the appropriate terms.

The problem of loss of domains of usage remains an issue for experts. For the general public, the influence of English is, above all, visible in the quantity of English loan words, more or less incorporated wholesale along with their English inflection and pronunciation. In addition, and this is the main point of my contribution, there is a continuous influence on a more subtle level, an influence that may have longer-term implications for Swedish. This is an impact that makes itself known through semantic loans and established translation practice on the level of grammar, syntax and rhetoric. In this discussion I have chosen to highlight this type of influence by avoiding the word *translationese*, which is, on the whole, viewed as having derogatory connotations – it should not be obvious that what is being read is a translation. I have chosen instead the more neutral concept of *fingerprints* – a concept that should be handled with care, in the same way as the style of an individual author should be.

Contrastive studies, most of which now make use of parallel texts, are an important source of information on differences between the source and the target language encountered through the process of translation. These differences can often lead to surprising revelations about the researcher's own mother tongue, facts which only come to light in the meeting of one language with another language. In this contribution I have attempted to show that, in the search for such differences, it is well worth digging a bit deeper.

Notes

1. Novels referred to:

    Sundberg, K. (1976) *Seger*. Stockholm: Bonnier.
    Shaw, I. (1975) *Nightwork*. New York: Delecorte.
    Adams, R. (1976) *Shardik*. New York: Avon.

References

Gellerstam, M. (1986) Translationese in Swedish novels translated from English. In L. Wollin and H. Lindqvist (eds) *Translation Studies in Scandinavia* (pp. 88–95) Lund: Gleerup.
Gellerstam, M. (1989): Om svenskan i översättningar från engelskan. In S. Allén, M. Gellerstam and S.G. Malmgren (eds) *Orden speglar samhället* (pp. 105–17) Stockholm: Allmänna förlaget.
Gellerstam, M. (1996) Translations as a source for cross-linguistic studies. In K. Aijmer, B. Altenberg, and M. Johansson (eds) *Languages in Contrast* (pp. 53–62) Lund: Lund University Press.
Helgesson, E. (2001) *Frysta hyror och konservativa uppskattningar. En undersökning av betydelselån från engelskan mellan 1965 och 1997*. Unpublished undergraduat paper. University of Gothenburg.
Moberg, L. (2000) *Nyordsboken: med 2000 nya ord i 2000-talet Stockholm*. Svenska språknämnden: Norstedts ordbok 12.
Svartvik, J. and Sager, O. (1996) *Engelsk universitetsgrammatik*. Stockholm: Almqvist & Wiksell.
Wellander, E. (1982) *Riktig svenska* (4th edn). Solna: Esselte studium.

Chapter 14

Translation and/or Editing –
The Way Forward?[1]

EMMA WAGNER

Introduction

New niches are opening up for translators, especially English translators. There is a growing demand for editing of texts written in English
by non-native speakers. English translators may also be asked to revise
translations produced by 'two-way translation' (translation out of the
translator's mother tongue into English). In this chapter I shall discuss the
reasons for these developments and some of their implications.

In the first section I shall look at what is happening to English and ask
whether the rise of English as a global language is leading to a standardised form of international English. I shall introduce the concept of so-
called 'sub-English', with examples, and suggest some causes and some
solutions, including editing.

Then I shall briefly outline what is happening to languages in the EU
institutions, where the policy of multilingualism will be maintained, but
has to be tempered with pragmatism. Translation activity in the EU institutions will depend on text types and purposes, and also on the type of
EU institution and its language needs.

The final section will draw some conclusions about the changes these
developments may bring for translators: they must learn to challenge and
improve originals; they may be asked to provide two-way translation
which other translators will then edit. I mention some of the problems
encountered when editing, and suggest some ways of dealing with them.

What is Happening to English?

In an article entitled 'Communicating in the Global Village: On
Language, Translation and Cultural Identity', Mary Snell-Hornby gives
one view of what is happening to English (1999: 109):

> . . . we can say that the world language English can be viewed from
> three different perspectives. Firstly, there is the free-floating lingua

franca ('International English') that has largely lost track of its cultural identity, its idioms, its hidden connotations, its grammatical subtleties, and has become a reduced standardised form of language for supra-national communication – the 'McLanguage' of our globalised 'McWorld' or the 'Eurospeak' of our multilingual continent. Then there are the many individual varieties, by and large mutually intelligible, but yet each an expression of a specific cultural identity with its own idioms, metaphors and cultural allusions (Indian English, for example, or British English as demonstrated by any feature article in the *Daily Mail*). And finally, there are the literary hybrid forms as demonstrated in postcolonial literature, forging a new language 'in between', altered to suit its new surroundings.

In this triple-group scenario Mary Snell-Hornby claims that the *lingua franca* function of English is fulfilled by a 'reduced standardised form of language' – a language which appears to be an impoverished relation of the much richer carriers of culture in the second group (varieties expressing a specific cultural identity) and the third group (post-colonial hybrid forms of English). In this chapter, I shall be looking at the first of the three types: English as a *lingua franca*. I shall give some examples of this form of English, questioning the claim that it is a reduced standardised form of English. I shall introduce the term 'sub-English', to describe the defective but by no means standardised or impoverished English that is often used for international communication. I shall explain where sub-English comes from and why it is relevant for translators: because there is an increasing market for editing sub-English in certain circumstances, and translators are well placed to develop the editing skills required.

International English and sub-English

In the extract quoted above, Mary Snell-Hornby calls international English a 'McLanguage for a McWorld' – a neat and superficially convincing concept. But is it really true that international English is *reduced* and by implication impoverished? Is it really *standardised*? Below I give some examples of international English and Eurospeak texts, which suggest that in reality the situation is a little different.

It could be argued that it is tolerance of non-standard usage that makes a language particularly suitable as a *lingua franca*, especially for informal communication between individuals as opposed to official communications and legislation. On 30 June 2000, the following text was used in a quarter-page advertisement for Smartgroups, published in *The Times*. It is deliberately written in defective English. It may shock purists, but that is the point of the advert – to show that communication is possible even when you use non-standard English.

Computer make amazing thing happen!!!!
If you have hobbies or member of club, now is very easy for comunicate! For make new friends of make some arrangement of work.

Sometime communication is difficult. But computer make amazing thing happen!! Now you can make smartgroup and join with friend in many country.

The world is our common house. Let's not forget that it's given us to use in a good way. We can change the world. We can make it happen!

www.smartgroups.com

The advert uses the idioms of personal websites, e-mails and chat rooms, complete with typing errors, to direct readers to the Smartgroups site, which turns out to be written in standard English (and in several other languages). One is tempted to ask: if defective international English is being used deliberately in adverts, could it be that this type of language reflects a cultural identity after all?

Language is both a means of communication and a badge of cultural identity. In his book *English as a Global Language*, David Crystal calls these two functions 'intelligibility' and 'identity' (1997: 18–9):

> The need for mutual intelligibility, which is part of the argument in favour of a global language, is only one side of the story. The other side is the need for identity – and people tend to underestimate the role of identity when they express anxieties about language injury and death. Language is a major means (some would say the chief means) of showing where we belong . . .

The Smartgroups advert quoted above demonstrates that standardisation is not a prerequisite for intelligibility and that a degree of linguistic laxity may actually promote communication. My experience in EU institutions confirms that this is the case, and that there is no such thing as 'standardised' international English or Eurospeak. However tempting it may be to believe in the rise of a 'McLanguage', it does not exist. The various forms of English used in various types of international context are, by definition, not standardised. Instead, there seem to be many types of what I would prefer to call 'sub-English'. In the next section I give some examples, with sources and comments. My examples are all written texts; in oral use, even greater linguistic laxity may be tolerated in the interests of communication. But in certain types of writing, especially published writing, linguistic laxity can lead to problems. These problems may range from downright incomprehensibility to the projection of an ignorant or insensitive image which may damage the credibility of the author or the organisation responsible (as does Eurospeak). That is why it is sometimes advisable to edit sub-English texts, rewriting them in standard English and/or altering them in other ways to make them more effective. Editing is not always necessary: sub-English can often be left unedited in ephemeral, personal and non-official contexts. But in other cases, as indicated after each example below, editing is advisable.

The Causes of sub-English

There are many factors contributing to the proliferation of sub-English (or perhaps one should say 'sub-Englishes', given their diversity). The main causes seem to be as follows (there may be some overlap between them). I give examples of each below, with further explanation and comments.

In original writing (not based on a foreign-language original):

• writing in English by non-natives;
• International English.

In translations:

• translation into English by non-natives;
• machine translation.

Cause 1. Writing in English by non-natives

'Non-natives' is shorthand for authors whose mother tongue is not English. The following example comes from an international organisation; in such places, drafting in English by non-native speakers is particularly prevalent. The source of Example 1 is an official Commission press release written by a non-native author and published in this form in June 2001.

Example 1

The Commission today adopted a Communication suggesting a new framework for co-operation on the information and communication activities of the European Union. It explains how inter-institutional co-operation, particularly between the Commission, the European Parliament and the Council should take place; the framework is open for participation from the Council, the other institutions and the authorities of Member States. New forms of co-operation will be established where relations with Member States, National Parliaments, Local Authorities and the Civil Society are concerned.

The Communication adopted at the initiative of the Commissioner Antonio Vitorino invites to an open debate where all would have their word to say.

Comments:

This Communication on communication is a particularly unfortunate piece of what is commonly derided as 'Eurospeak'. Defects in this text include the over-use of initial capital letters, an inward-looking obsession with arcane procedure, Gallicisms ('all would have their word to say') and the soporific effect of so many abstract nouns ending in '-ion'.

Is editing needed?

Yes. This is the type of text that would achieve its purpose better if it were edited. If, as is usually the case, it is to be translated into several languages, it should be edited before translation, or the defects may be reproduced in the other language versions. If the translations are all supposed to match, editing should remove any ambiguous expressions. Otherwise the translators will have to guess what is meant and may guess differently, leading to non-matching translations.

Cause 2. International English

By this I mean English overtly used as a *lingua franca* to reach the largest possible number of people, often tourists, travellers and business people of many different nationalities. It is often found at airports, in tourist information and in advertising, where clarity and impact are more important than linguistic correctness. In Example 2, the source is an advert at Copenhagen Airport, June 2003.

Example 2

Going outside the EU? Save up to 60% on liquor. Up to 60% savings when compared to city prices.

Comments

British English would refer to 'wines and spirits' rather than 'liquor', and to 'high-street prices' rather than 'city prices'. American English would not refer to 'city prices' either. However, 'liquor' is perfectly clear as well as short, and 'city prices' is in fact clearer to non-British readers than 'high-street prices'.

Is editing needed?

No. The text is clear and effective.

Cause 3. Translation into English by non-natives

That is, by a person who is not of English mother tongue (often because there are not enough translators available who are native speakers of English). In this case in the first example (3A) the source for the text is a leaflet enclosed with sweets purchased in Greece, May 2003. The Greek text was included on the same leaflet. The translation into English was produced by a non-native speaker.

Example 3A

Akanes (traditional Greek sweet) – history

When, during the Turkish enslavement, the local lords asked the servant who lived in Serres to make them something sweet, they used to produce a think mush from sugar came mixed with nuts and fresh aromatic butter, coming from the local mountain Lailia.

The mush used to boil in large boilers, over strong fire, whereas someone was continually stirring the mixture with a big label. The lord overlooking the procedure used to order the servant from Serres, telling him 'AKA' (which means stir) and the servant answered 'NE' (which means yes). That's how the modern word 'AKANE' came out.

Comments

Some additional errors have been introduced by a careless printer ('think mush' should be '<u>thick</u> mush'; 'sugar came' should be 'sugar <u>cane</u>'; 'big label' should be 'big <u>ladle</u>'. Note: a spell-checker would not pick up these errors; a proof-reader would.)

Is editing needed?

The printer's errors need to be removed, because they distort the meaning, but otherwise the text has – in my opinion – a charming Greek flavour that would be lost if it were converted into correct English.

The next example is a translation of part of a newspaper article published in Finnish in Finland's national daily *Helsingin Sanomat*, 12 September 2001. Again, the translation into English was produced by a non-mother tongue speaker.

Example 3B

The Cutts version of the Toy Directive will be translated into all EU languages during the autumn. The objective is to show that the English language is not the only one suffering from complexity. EU has already asked Mr. Cutts for a permission to quote the new version when the Toy Directive will be updated the next time.

The EU lawyers have fought against the language reform. They estimate that the reform will complicate the work of the Court of Justice. They also fear that the preciseness will disappear. The lawyers feel that the directives are addressed to the Member States and the experts of law in the first place and not to the citizens.

'Our aim is that the directives would be written to the literate and curious citizens, not just for special groups of people', Wagner concludes. (Helsingin Sanomat, 12 September 2001)

Comments

The translation was done rapidly, for one person's information, not for publication. It can be understood without referring to the Finnish original.

Is editing needed?

Yes, but only if the translation has to be published. It is quite acceptable in its present form for the intended purpose.

Cause 4. Machine translation

The final text illustrating sub-English is taken from a Systran machine translation, quoted in *Can Theory Help Translators?* by Chesterman and Wagner (2002: 20).

Example 4

The terminological information retrieval

Research almost is necessary for each document, but they depend most obviously on its period, on its degree of technicality, of its size, and also of its destination: indeed, as well as all the documents do not have inevitably to be translated into ten languages, similarly, research will be less pushed for a document to classify in a file, while they are probably important for a text intended for the publication.

Comments

The translation contains many mistakes of grammar, terminology and word order and is impossible to understand without referring to the French original, which is as follows:

Les recherches documentaire et terminologique

Des recherches sont nécessaires pour presque chaque document, mais elles dépendent évidemment de son délai, de son degré de technicité, de sa taille, et également de sa destination: en effet, de même que tous les documents ne doivent pas forcément être traduits en dix langues, de même, les recherches seront moins poussées pour un document à classer dans un dossier, alors qu'elles seront vraisemblablement importants pour un texte destiné à la publication.

Is editing needed?

Editing is not enough here. If the translation is to be made comprehensible, it must be corrected by a translator able to understand the French original, a process known as post-editing.

In the examples above, the texts for which editing is recommended are the press release written in English by a non-native (Example 1) and the translation into English, also by a non-native (Example 3B), if it is to be published.

What is Happening to Languages in the EU Institutions?

Despite fears to the contrary, it seems clear that the EU's policy of multilingualism – equal rights for all official languages – will remain unchanged.[2] It is firmly anchored in a legal basis which is confirmed in the draft European Constitution currently under discussion. However, as EU enlargement adds to the number of official languages, the policy of multilingualism will have to be combined with pragmatism. Full multi-lingualism may have to be reserved for important texts such as legislation, official documents and certain types of public information.

Translation purposes and 'two-way translation'

It was with this pragmatic approach in mind that the European Commission's Translation Service introduced a breakdown into translation types in 2001 (Wagner, 2001: 265).

Translation type	Definition
Legislation	Translation in accordance with the Commission's rules for legislative documents
Basic understanding	Rough translation, usually for one person, to permit understanding of content. Will not be published.
For information	Accurate translation for internal information purposes. Will not be published.
For publication	High-quality translation to be published and/or distributed to specialists or the general public (client should specify which)
For EU image	High-quality polished translation that is important for the Commission's image

Legislation will always have to be translated into all the official languages of the EU, and carefully revised, but more pragmatic approaches can be taken with other text types. Some texts may not need to be translated at all; others may be translated only into English and/or French. Machine translation into a *lingua franca* could be used for 'Basic understanding'. When a translation is required 'For information' it will normally be translated into a widely-understood language such as English. In such cases it may be more efficient to abandon the revered principle of translation only *into* the translator's mother tongue, and to use what is called 'two-way translation' (translation *out of* the mother tongue). In practice this means that if a text is written in a less widely understood language such as Finnish or Polish, and has to be translated 'For information', not for publication, it may be preferable or necessary to ask translators to translate out of their mother tongue (in this case Finnish or Polish) into a *lingua franca* such as English. The result may sometimes even be better if the translator is working out of her/his mother tongue – s/he can scan the text much faster, and is more sensitive to nuances of meaning in the original language. Naturally care must be taken to build in safeguards such as careful selection of translators, checks on the way translations are used, and revision by a native speaker in some cases. Two-way translation should not be used to produce translations 'for publication' and 'for EU image'; these should be done by native speakers of the target language.

Language use and types of EU institution

It is sometimes mistakenly assumed that the EU institutions translate everything into all official languages. They do not. The number of languages used in-house and the volume of translation depend on the type of EU institution, its staff and its functions. They also depend on the relative volume of *inbound texts* (written outside the institution, and sent to it) and *outbound texts* (written by the institution, for outside consumption). In the examples of sub-English given above, Example 3B is an inbound text (Finnish newspaper article) and Example 1 is an outbound text (press release).

There seem to be three basic patterns:

Pattern 1:
European Parliament – must cater for Members of the European Parliament (MEPs) not elected for their language skills
Inbound texts – may arrive in any language, may need to be translated into any language.
Outbound texts – written by Eurocrats but also by MEPs, often in their mother tongue; may need to be translated into all languages.
(all languages > all)

Pattern 2:
European Commission – executive of Eurocrats
Inbound texts – may arrive in any language, will be translated into English or French
Outbound texts – written by Eurocrats in English or French; may need to be translated into all languages.
(all > English / French > all)

Pattern 3:
European Central Bank – specialist body
Single working language: English. Some texts written in-house are edited by the English translators.
Translation of outbound material and legislation.
(English only, some translation > all)

What This Means for Translators

The developments described above suggest that translators should prepare for certain changes, some of which may challenge entrenched beliefs.

Correcting the original text

The first change entails developing a more critical attitude to the texts to be translated and abandoning the belief that the original is sacrosanct. The breakdown into translation types given above shows that texts – and their translations – may have different functions or purposes. Translators are there to help the text achieve its purpose. In some cases, therefore, when texts have been written for a certain purpose and are clearly unfit for that purpose, translators should intervene. They should have the courage to tell authors that if the original text is not edited, it can lead to:

- a bad public image for the organisation in whose name the text is published;
- non-concordance between the translations into other languages.

Given that so many authors are obliged to write in a language (English) that is not their mother tongue, they should be willing to accept that their text can be improved or corrected. In practice, however, this may entail breaking down some psychological barriers. It is also worth pointing out at this stage that many native speakers of English are poor drafters too; they may be specialists in other areas and never have received any training in clear communication.

There are two ways of improving the quality of original texts: training and editing. Ideally, the two should be combined and based on the same principles. Editing has an educational effect that can reinforce the messages of training or, for authors too busy to attend training courses, it can demonstrate the principles of clear writing in practice. One example of an attempt to train authors and translators in the principles of clear writing was the Fight the Fog campaign at the European Commission. The website at http://europa.eu.int/comm/translation/en/ftfog includes an on-line 'Teach Yourself Fog-Fighting' seminar.

In some organisations there is a special editing department; in others, editing is done by translators who are native speakers of the language required (usually English) in addition to translation. Because of the psychological barriers mentioned above, the editors' corrections are not always accepted by authors. Some authors (but by no means all) see any form of correction as an insult. The editors at an international law firm that systematically edits its English texts have even suggested that authors go through three stages in their reactions to editing: (1) outrage; (2) modesty; (3) co-operation. Sparks can fly at the first stage, but the second stage of excessive humility is unproductive too. The ideal, for both author and editor, is to arrive at the third stage and to co-operate in making the text as effective as possible.

A particular problem for translators who edit is their lowly status. Authors are unlikely to accept correction by translators if they do not respect translators in the first place. However, repeated attempts and co-operation will usually lead to a better understanding on both sides.

Some people find correction by computer software easier to accept than correction by a human editor. Editing software such as Stylewriter (http://www.editorsoftware.com/stylewriter) is available and can, if used judiciously, help authors to improve their texts without the embarrassment of implied criticism by a human editor.

Editing is rather a vague concept; if it is to be provided as a service, it must form part of a clear document flow, with agreed procedures for marking editing changes and explaining why they are necessary. It also needs an agreed terminology so that clients can specify the purpose of the text and the level of editing required. To specify the text purpose, the typology above may provide a starting point. To define types of editing, it may be useful to follow the breakdown proposed by Brian Mossop (2001: 11).

Copy-editing. This is the work of correcting a manuscript to bring it into conformance with preset rules: the generally recognised grammar and spelling rules of a language community, rules of 'good usage' and 'house style'.

Stylistic editing. This is improving work, to tailor vocabulary and sentence structure to the readership, and to create a readable text by making sentences more concise, removing ambiguities, and so on.

Structural editing. This is the work of reorganising the text to achieve a better order of presentation of the material, or to help the readers by signalling the relationships among the parts of the message.

Content editing. This is the work of suggesting additions to or subtractions from the coverage of the topic. The editor may (perhaps with the assistance of a researcher) personally have to write the additions if the author for some reason cannot or will not do so. Aside from such 'macro-level' work, content editing also includes the 'micro-level' tasks of correcting factual, mathematical and logical errors.

Abandoning the 'mother-tongue principle'

The second change facing professional translators is the 'decriminalisation' of two-way translation, defined as translation *out of* the translator's mother tongue into a *lingua franca* such as English. This entails abandoning the sacrosanct principle according to which professional translators only translate *into* their mother tongue. In fact two-way translation has been common for many years in the less professional sector of the translation profession, and in countries where there are simply not enough professional translators of English mother tongue to meet the demand for translation into English. In most cases a less-than-perfect translation is better than none at all. The problem is how to sell the idea to professional translators, and the key to that is ensuring that two-way translation is used only for certain text purposes, or with safeguards. In Section 1 of this chapter I give two examples of translation into English by non-mother tongue speakers of English: Examples 3A and 3B. In my opinion, as stated in my comments on those examples, both texts are fairly effective in their present form, though the first could be improved by proof-reading corrections. The second would need editing if it were to be published, but could in my opinion be corrected by a person who has no knowledge of Finnish. This process, the *editing of sub-English translations* is not the same as revision. A reviser would have to understand the Finnish original text and align the translation with it; an editor would treat the sub-English translation as a text in its own right, and would use knowledge of the subject matter, rather than knowledge of Finnish, to correct the translation. This process is similar to revising a translation without an original and is also, therefore, dangerous if misused. It will not be accepted by professional translators unless there are built-in safeguards. But demand for translation into English is such that this method (translation by a non-native plus editing by a native speaker of English) is already common in commerce and industry, though it has not yet arrived in international organisations.

Instead of wringing their hands over this development, professional translators should acknowledge the existence of the trend. They can then help to define best practice, devising the safeguards needed to ensure that such methods are confined to the translation types for which they are acceptable. Translators can also benefit from the trend by promoting their own high-quality services as a better product than sub-English translations – there are plenty of poor translations to use as dire warnings to clients. Or finally, they can go with the trend and develop the editing skills needed in this new market situation. Many translators have a natural aptitude for editing and enjoy combining it with translation, as it makes for a more varied career, promotes greater interaction with authors and ultimately leads to higher status and self-esteem.

To sum up, opportunities will arise for:

- editing of sub-English originals;
- editing of sub-English translations;
- two-way translation (out of the mother tongue into English).

There are niches here for linguists with inside knowledge, i.e. translators, but they must be prepared to follow special training courses and agree on best-practice methods and techniques.

Notes

1. Chapter based on a talk given at the University of Surrey, 17 June 2003.
2. The policy and legal basis of multilingualism are explained in Chapter 1 of *Translating for the European Union Institutions* by Emma Wagner, Svend Bech and Jesús M. Martinez, published by St Jerome, Manchester (2002).

References

Chesterman, A. and Wagner, E. (2002) *Can Theory Help Translators?* Manchester: St Jerome.
Crystal, D. (1997) *English as a Global Language*. Cambridge: Cambridge University Press.
Mossop, B. (2001) *Revising and Editing for Translators*. Manchester: St Jerome.
Snell-Hornby, M. (1999) Communicating in the global village: On translation and cultural identity. *Current Issues in Language and Society* 6/2, 1–18.
Wagner, E. (2001) Translation in the EU machinery. *Perspectives* 9/4, 263–70.

Chapter 15

Translating into a Second Language: Can We, Should We?

BEVERLY ADAB

Introduction

Translators are normally expected to translate into their mother tongue for many well-documented reasons, including native-speaker language competence, familiarity with the cognitive mapping of conceptual referents and a high level of inter-textual reference acquired through repeated exposure over time (see Neubert, 1981). For Chesterman, there exist some quasi-universal perceptions about translation, which he calls *translation memes*. A meme is a 'unit of cultural transmission' which 'encapsulates concepts and ideas about translation itself' (1997: 5–7). We would argue that the view that translators should work into their mother tongue is a meme which is fast becoming unenforceable and impractical in this era of globalised communications and intercultural exchanges.

Why Translate into a Second Language?

On a practical level, translating into the mother tongue may not always be possible, due to lack of native speakers of the target language who have a similar competence in the source language. We shall, for the purpose of this chapter, understand the concept of a second language as being that which is perceived as consciously learned, as opposed to that being inductively acquired, usually from birth and/ or through socialisation within the family. We will not enter into discussion of bilingualism here. We will further assume that the language of initial socialisation, in which nursery rhymes are learned and first communicative competence is acquired, is the primary language of cognitive modelling and conceptualisation (first language). Admittedly, for many people, particularly in former colonies where the colonial power is the origin of a major world language, such as the UK or France, the language of schooling may replace this first language as that of habitual use (for example in Algeria, Tunisia, Morocco). However, this is not a universal and does not necessarily entail the internalisation of the cognitive model of the true native speaker. Campbell supports this view: 'it is probably wise to assume at the outset that perfectly balanced bi-linguals are so rarely found that virtually all human translation activity falls into one of the two categories – into or from the second language' (1998: 57).

Campbell (1998: 23) also discusses translation needs in Australia, from the 1990s onwards, listing the following as areas in which translation activity and the demand for translators are increasing: immigration, also cultural, political and commercial interaction in particular with Asian countries. He notes, 'Australian translators . . . must be prepared to translate almost anything and in either direction' (1998: 25). This is becoming increasingly true, not only within multicultural societies and trade organisations consisting of nations trading internationally, but also within a given region of the globe, for whom a *lingua franca* is a *sine qua non* of successful communication.

A somewhat similar situation exists in Finland, where the lack of native speakers of foreign languages who are competent in Finnish means that native speakers also have to be prepared to translate in both directions (see Gambier, forthcoming, and also Garant participating in the 2001 EST training group discussion on directionality in translation and translator training organised through the European Society for Translation Studies (EST)): 'a Finn with a high English level is the only option'. Likewise, in many of the former Communist countries working towards candidacy for EU membership, translation from, for example, Romanian into English or French was undertaken by Romanians working into their second language. In the same 2001 EST discussion, Brian Mossop (York University, Canada) comments on expectations of directionality for translatorial performance, noting that in Canada, a country which many might perceive as being at least partially bilingual:

> a very common phrase in job offers for salaried translator positions have wording along the lines 'will translate mostly from English into French but occasionally from French into English'. This means the employer does not have enough work in the French-to-English direction to warrant hiring a special translator, so English-to-French translators (practically all native French speakers) do it. (In Canada, there is about 10 times as much work into French as into English).

Mossop also raises an interesting point with regard to expectations of translation into the second language in the Canadian situation:

> When French speakers do translate into English, the quality of their work does not always have to be as high because, in Canada, translations into English are often for information only (whereas translations into French are more often published).

Emma Wagner, formerly of the European Commission Translation Service (see also this volume), notes in a further contribution to the same EST discussion group a different situation:

> Here at the European Commission we have in the past always insisted on translation into the mother tongue only, as a guarantee of quality. This is still the official policy. In our context, most translation requiring a high-quality product (legislation, **'for publication'** and promotional stuff) is translation out of French and English. It must still be done by native speakers of the target language. However, translation out of languages other than French and English is often **'for information'** and is not published. It is for in-house information only, so it is translated into one language only – English or French, the in-house *linguae francae*. L1-into-English is fine 'for comprehension' or 'for information'. We plan to recruit people with this ability in future, but they must still be excellent into-L1 translators. For information, the term we have coined here is 'two-way translation' (French: traduction aller-retour), meaning out of L1 and into L1.

We shall now consider the role of addressee expectations in determining the acceptability of a text which has been translated into a second language.

Accountability and other professional norms

Other contexts in which translation into a second language may be required, not only in Australia but around the world, comprise legally binding documentation and situations, for example court cases (immigration, asylum), in any country having a multicultural composition (for instance the UK, and Germany and France among our near neighbours), as well as business interactions, contracts, sales, promotions and marketing.

Dissemination of knowledge also accounts for much translation activity. Scholars of a mother tongue other than English, particularly in the sciences, may find it hard to gain widespread recognition of their work if this is not published in English, for example for cutting-edge research in medicine on aspects such as genome research. Here too, translators will often work into their second language albeit in highly domain-specific contexts.

One key factor in this type of translation is the need for reliability and the concomitant *accountability* attached to the performance of the translator. Chesterman (1997: 67–8) raises the question of the role of professional norms; firstly that of *acceptability* (see Toury, 1995), seeing this as being determined by other translators within the target society, as much as by those who use the finished products. *Accountability* is another higher-order professional norm discussed by Chesterman, where the translator takes into account the needs and demands for loyalty of the text commissioner, the text user, the source text writer, and the translator him/herself, an ethical norm relating to standards of professional integrity. Perceptions of these two norms may vary by consensus among the addressees of a target text. Several factors contribute to the development of perceptions of *acceptability*, of which *a*, if not *the*, major one is the role of enculturation in shaping expectations.

Acceptability and Expectations: Shaping Factors

Cognitive frameworks and the role of metaphor in conceptualisation

According to Marmaridou (1996, 49–73), 'Translation is an instance of conceptual metaphors. Linguistic meaning is a reflection of conceptual structure.'

For an author such as Marmaridou, language expresses perceptions of experienced reality through a framework of metaphor (see Lakoff & Johnson, 1980). For example, in anglophone cultures, *up* is good – better, desirable: build *up a business*; *down* is worse, less desirable – *put someone down*, *let down*, *bring down*. These authors also discuss how, from Fillmore's perspective (1977), language patterns are frames which evoke associated scenes of experience. Hence experiential meaning may be framed, expressed and understood differently across cultures and languages; furthermore, the translation process requires a cognitive interpretation of the underlying framing metaphors as much as of the other intra- and extra-textual features (see Nord, 1991) normally associated with this process. The question here is whether the translator, as a member of the source language community, is able, when mapping source language concepts into target-language frames, to adopt the target language perspectives or whether there is still some degree of interference from his/her own mother tongue and source culture which will impede successful completion of the cognitive aspects of the process. These reservations are shared by Jakobsen (1993: 158): 'Cultures not only express ideas differently, they shape concepts and texts differently.' Marmaridou concludes that, 'the translator primarily functions in terms of the conceptual structures of his or her mother-tongue and categorizes the world according to these structures' (1996: 54). Similarly, Nord asserts that 'translation involves comparing cultures' and 'translators perceive the foreign culture by means of comparison with their own culture of primary enculturation' (1997: 34). How then does the translator into a second language compensate for or overcome this potential for interference, given the description by McCracken (1988: 73) of how cultural categories of time, space, nature and person serve to 'divide up the phenomenal world', creating a system which organises and underlies the perception of the world by the individual, so that the perceptions held by one culture are not necessarily appropriate and relevant as a frame of reference for interpretation of another culture.

On the subject of the role of metaphor in conceptualisation and hence in translation, Gentzler (2000: 3) comments that metaphors are culturally bound, but that the Western, logocentric languages exert tremendous influence on how images and figures of speech are configured, relating this to issues of balance of power between languacultures (Agar, 1991) in contact. Gentzler claims that the '[gender of the author] and his or her world view cannot be separated from the semantic content', suggesting that 'our view of reality has become dependent on metaphorical associations', so that 'language is no longer conceived as a tool through which reality is reflected but is viewed instead as a medium through which our conceptions of reality are formed'. Translation, he says, can also become a 'site to enlarge' semantic and conceptual space. On this basis we could expect translators working into their second language to bring new perceptions and conceptual mapping to the second language, realised by hybrid constructs in which influences of the (translator's) first language are observable in the second-language/target text.

The process of hybridisation

The concept and the nature of hybridity are discussed in Schäffner and Adab (2001: 167–80), with hybridity (a positive quality) being distinguished from *interference* (due to lack of competence). Note that the discussion does not take a view as to directionality:

> A hybrid text is a text that results from a translation process. It shows features that somehow seem 'out of place'/'strange'/'unusual' for the receiving culture, i.e. the target culture. These features, however, are not the result of a lack of translational competence or examples of 'translationese', but they are evidence of conscious and deliberate decisions by the translator.

This process of *hybridisation* can be the result of several factors, including:

> the increasing internationalisation of communication processes breaks down text type areas, with hybrid texts being created in a multi- or supra-cultural environment; or socio-political changes in a given culture, which create the need for new or modified text types. Hybrids reflect specific textual features (vocabulary, syntax, style, etc.) which may clash with target language conventions.

And:

Acceptance (of a hybrid text) is in general due to the fact that all cultures are open and adaptive systems. Once a text is accepted, it is no longer a hybrid text. Thus, hybrid texts are a transitional and historical phenomenon.

Price (2000: 27) reflects on a 'tendency to dichotomise', to differentiate clearly in translation between source and target languages, arguing that 'multiplicity of voice' can be a positive attribute which can restore the 'in-between',[1] highlighting shared features of language and reminding us that the translator himself inhabits a 'hybrid space' of understanding. True hybridity of language and textual features are, of course, to be differentiated clearly from what Kussmaul describes, with reference to translation, as 'interlanguage' (1995: 5).

We might need at this point to consider what factors would enhance or encourage acceptance of a text, in the second language, which may well have a hybrid nature. This also raises the question of who the addressees are.

Addressees and other factors

It is clearly not the case that translation into a second language, especially when working into a language of global use such as English, French or Spanish, is always going to target native speakers of that language.

This situation (addressees for whom the target language is not their first language) arises, for example, in the EU, where addressees may be native speakers of one of the key 'official' languages, or they may be speakers of another community language, for whom English or French is a second or third language. It also happens on the Indian subcontinent where, due to the proliferation of national/province-based languages, English is often the preferred language for communication among the different provinces and users consider themselves to be virtually bilingual (but not bicultural). Somewhat similarly, translators in former French colonies in North Africa may consider themselves to be bilingual, French-Arabic, although, from the perspective of conceptual mapping, one or the other language and its cognitive structures will most probably dominate. Hence problems arise when mapping French cultural concepts into Arabic for non-speakers of French (who are also by definition less well educated and therefore less able to compensate for, or take into account, any interference at the levels of language or conceptual mapping and world views).

Where, however, the concept of shared culture is supported by (*restricted*) shared experience and domain-specificity of reference, addressees are more likely to find a translated text *acceptable* and *adequate* for the intended purpose (see Nord, 1997: 34–7). Conversely, 'cross-cultural differences can and do produce conflicts or inhibit communication' (Williams, 1992: 179).[2]

Most situations in which translators are required to translate into a second language are ones involving pragmatic (informative, operative) texts, rather than literary (expressive or poetic) texts. This should help to reduce the potential for ambiguity or misinterpretation.

It may also be that addressees who are using the target language as second language, a *lingua franca*, may themselves not possess a full range of native speaker competences (linguistic, cultural, textual) but may instead share domain-specific expertise (see also Thelen, this volume). Part of that expertise may involve knowledge of a restricted form of the target language as a second language, so that any features which might appear strange to the native speaker of the target language will be more readily accepted by the former group. Thus domain expertise is one major levelling factor which can ensure effective communication through translation into the second language. Reliance on domain-specific expertise and use of approved terminology can also help to enhance acceptability by maximising communicative impact.

A further factor is the existence of some fairly standardised working practices, at least among multinational companies, which also lend commonality of experience to the communicative situation. The greater the number of shared experiences, the fewer the potential problems of transfer and acceptability (see Chesterman, 1997: 12). The concept of 'culture' in the business context can therefore be redefined on the basis of a reduced (restricted) set of behaviour patterns and experience held in common by the addressees. This is largely the result of the process of *globalisation*, sometimes described in a more derogatory manner as 'MacDonaldisation' (De Mooij, 1998; Ritzer, 1998). In these contexts the following definition could obtain: 'Culture is a normative system of symbolic order which conditions social organisation, including role relationships, values etc' (Williams, 1992: 202).

Other factors may also be important in determining acceptability. The purpose of the translated text may be a factor: it may be that translation into the second language occurs within a workplace/company communications structure, for information only, not for publication. Hence expectations of conformity to second language norms may be less stringently applied, provided that any deviations from these do not obscure the informative content of the message. However, what happens in situations where translation into a second language has to take place, for reasons already discussed, in the context of officially or professionally accountable communicative interactions?

Enhancing Acceptability

Miriam Schlesinger (in a contribution to the 2001 EST discussion) raises the question of how to define an acceptable finished product in professional situations, querying whether in fact the translator working into second language can, as a general rule, be expected to generate a product (target text) which will satisfy client needs and fulfil professional accountability norms. Her answer is negative, although she does wonder, together with Emma Wagner, whether translator trainers should accept the existence of dual standard qualifications, where translators might be recognised as fully competent for work into their first language and having limited 'near-native' competence (i.e. producing work which still needs some editing by native speakers) for work into a second language. In this context, Schlesinger argues that there might be scope for some kind of special training for native speakers in the skills of 'revision' and 'editing' of work produced by non-native speakers of that language.

It would appear, however, that ,for communication to be successful in these situations, either expectations have to be changed or else few translators working into a second language, even those who have studied relevant text type conventions, will be likely to produce a text that would need no editing by a native speaker, unless, perhaps, the documents in question are to be produced in a *restricted* form of the second language.

Using a restricted (controlled) language

What is meant by a *restricted*, or *controlled*, form of a language? Briefly, one which avoids potential for ambiguity and misinterpretation through a limiting of available forms of expression.

Ambiguity can arise from:

- Linguistic/syntactic problems: polysemy, incorrect word order, logical connectives, incorrect collocations, use of quantifiers, articles, number, synonyms, use of tenses, speech act conventions.
- Conceptual definition: conceptual vagueness or lack of correspondence.
- Metaphorical frameworks: the importance of these has already been discussed.

Ambiguity is often compensated by:

- Native speaker subconscious disambiguation, using contextual, inter-textual and language systemic information.
- Reader assumptions based on known facts/factors of communicative event (this may be accurate or misguided/erroneous).

(Rupp & Götz, 1997)
What are the desirable features of a restricted (or controlled) form of a language?

- Explicitness is highly desirable, so that there is no assumption of background, situational knowledge other than that which is domain-specific and the conceptual content of each reference or term will be unambiguous and can be expected to be interpreted in only one way by the addressee (see Neubert & Shreve, 1992, *situationality, informativity*).
- The use of domain-specific, standardised terminology will be underpinned by clear, unequivocal referents, with a clearly defined taxonomy and range of concepts.
- The use of conventionally accepted language structures (overt, explicit rather than implicit or indirect) to realise speech acts will also facilitate clear communicative impact.
- A reduced vocabulary will ensue from domain-specificity, with few or no synonyms to confuse interpretation.
- Collocations will usually be predictable.
- In stylistic terms, elegant variation is not the aim of pragmatic texts, the primary communicative functions being informative and/or operative (instructional) although for persuasive texts such as advertising, translation into second language is not recommended unless the translator also has marketing expertise acquired through the medium of second language. However, working into first language is not always sufficient: for example, it is not recommended practice, even when working into first language, to have a translator without marketing expertise translate an advertising text (Adab, 2000).
- Available syntactic forms will be fewer, and text type conventions for a specific domain are already a restricted set.
- Use of domain-specific terms will also generate repetition, thus enhancing *cohesion* (see Neubert & Shreve, 1992: 108).

If translators working into second language can operate within the parameters of a restricted form of a language, there is every reason to suppose that what they produce should be acceptable to all addressees, whether native or non-native speakers of the second language.

However, there are other tools which can enhance acceptability of translated text, not only, but perhaps more importantly, those produced into second language.

Tools Available for Enhancing Acceptability of the Target Text

The use of corpora of authentic texts

With the explosion in use of the Internet, including e-mail, for access to authentic exemplars of texts, the use of corpora in translation has evolved rapidly from an ideal to a fact of contemporary translation activity (Adab forthcoming). One of the principal advantages of corpora of parallel texts in the target language is the opportunity to identify norms as evidenced in practice and to apply these to one's own translation performance. The translator into second language cannot help but find other, previously produced documents, whether translated or written by native speakers in the second language, against which to measure translation decisions and revise/evaluate the finished product.

Avellis & Laviosa (2000) describe how corpora can be used as 'a tool for increased acceptability' as follows:

> Experimental research and classroom practice in translator training show that the use of bilingual comparable corpora and monolingual corpora in translating into and out of the mother tongue leads to the production of higher quality translations. The improvements have been noted in particular with regard to subject field understanding, correct term choice, and idiomatic expression (Bowker, 1998) as well as an enhanced understanding of the source language text and the ability to produce fluent target language texts (Zanettin, 1998) with more appropriate and naturally sounding collocations (Stewart, 2000). The body of evidence is consistent enough to justify the creation of monolingual corpora as aids to translation practice, particularly in specialized subject domains such as legal, scientific, technical, commercial texts where the understanding of the subject field is a crucial factor in achieving accuracy and fluency.

Machine translation and translation memories – another tool

According to Hutchins (1995), the term 'machine translation' (MT) refers to computerised systems responsible for the production of translations with or without human assistance. He notes:

> Although the ideal goal of MT systems may be to produce high-quality translation, in practice the output is usually revised (post-edited). It should be noted that in this respect MT does not differ from the output of most human translators which is normally revised by a second translator before dissemination.

Also:

The translation quality of MT systems may be improved either, most obviously, by developing more sophisticated methods or by imposing certain restrictions on the input. The system may be designed, for example, to deal with texts limited to the sublanguage (vocabulary and grammar) of a particular subject field (for example biochemistry) and/or document type (for example patents). Alternatively, input texts may be written in a controlled language, which restricts the range of vocabulary, and avoids homonymy and polysemy and complex sentence structures.

Without being reductionist, it could be argued that making machine translation less open to ambiguity or misrendering depends to some extent on similar factors as those described for enhancing acceptability of translation by a translator working into a second language.

Hutchins goes on to assert that:

> Since 1990, various groups (at UMIST (Manchester), the University of Brussels, Grenoble University and the Science University of Malaysia) have experimented with 'dialogue-based' MT systems where the text to be translated is composed or written in a collaborative process between man and machine. In this way it is possible to construct a text which the system is known to be capable of translating without further reference to an author with no knowledge of the target language, who cannot revise the output and therefore needs assurance of good quality output. The most obvious application is the fairly standardised messages of business communication.

This highlights the additional importance of source-language technical writing and careful production of a source text which will lend itself more easily to translation. Finally, in explaining the role of machine translation and translation tools in today's translation market, Hutchins notes:

> Before the 1980s it was often assumed that the aim of MT research was the (partial) replacement of human translation. Now the aim is focused on special domain-restricted mass-volume systems and on systems for non-translators – areas where professional translators have not been active. It is quite clear from recent developments that what the professional translators need are tools to assist them: provide access to dictionaries and terminological databanks, multilingual word processing, management of glossaries and terminology resources, input and output communication (for example OCR scanners, electronic transmission, high-class printing). For these reasons, the most appropriate and successful developments of the last few years have been the translator workstations (for example IBM's Translation Manager, the TRADOS TWB, the STAR Transit systems, and the Eurolang Optimiser, and PTT from the Canadian Translation Services.)

The points raised are equally relevant for translation into a second language. As a tool, machine translation is most commonly held to be useful, without requiring major editing work, in texts whose informative content is conveyed through few, fixed syntactic structures and a standardised terminology, as for example, in:

- Software localisation of computer products, using a translation workbench.
- Gist information for reviews/information gathering/internal communications – this can be achieved through the use of a commercially (Systran) or freely available (Babelfish) translation software programme.
- E-mail messages.
- Standard communications such as reports, circulars etc.

However, such programs and tools are not always available in all commercially active languages: it is the lack of engineers' familiarity with a language, or the difficulties posed by writing systems and language systems, rather than the number of users which determine how easily machine translation systems can be produced to work into and out of a given language.

Translation memory programs, such as TRADOS, do require interaction between translator and software, however much of the repetitive work is automated; when decisions have to be taken, suggestions are proposed based on a corpus of previously translated documents for the same domain and/or type, to assist the translator. These programs are most useful for high volume, domain-specific translation of legal or commercial documents, particularly where the translation is of a source text which has been only partially revised. Hence they are to be recommended, cost and hardware permitting, for use in translation into the second language for treaties, instruction manuals and other very lengthy texts, to ensure standardisation of style, terminology and text type conventions. Translators working into a second language should not, therefore, be at a significant disadvantage when using such systems.

Revision and editing – native speaker or another second language speaker

Processes of this kind may also contribute to improving conformity of a text to addressee expectations, provided of course that such revision or editing is undertaken by someone resident in or highly familiar with the 'culture' of the addressees, however this concept may be defined in the specific translation situation. Discussion on the EST-IT list focused on whether or not a non-native speaker could fill this role, with some contributors (for example Ubaldo Stecconi) expressing the view that the importance of native speaker status can often be over-inflated, while others (for example Emma Wagner) suggested that revision and editing are best undertaken by native speakers. Particular contextual and situational factors will operate in favour of translators working into a second language, under the right conditions, with appropriate tools.

Conclusion

In this chapter I have touched, albeit briefly, on problems facing the translator working into second language; on factors and tools which might influence or enhance the acceptability of texts produced by such translators; on situations in which working in this direction could more readily lead to functional adequacy; and on the importance of clearly defined expectations of such texts.

In the light of these considerations, and in the face of the real-life situations facing translators who are non-native speakers of highly used languages, I would recommend the adoption of a controlled form of the target language and use of relevant tools as the keys to achieving communicative functionality. Translation into a second language can be done, it is being done, it should be done to the best of the translator's ability.

Notes

1. For further discussion of the concept of the space 'in-between', see Sherry Simon and Mary Snell Hornby in C. Schäffner and B. Adab (eds) (2001), 'Hybrid Texts in Translation', special volume of *Across Languages and Cultures*.
2. Williams, G. (1992) discussing the work of J.J. Gumperz and D. Hymes (eds) (1972), *Directions in Sociolinguistics: The Ethnography of Communication*. New York: Holt Rinehart and Winston.

References

Adab, B. (2000) The Translation of Advertising Texts: Towards a Set of Guidelines. In A. Beeby (eds) *Investigating Translation* (pp. 225–37) Amsterdam: Benjamins.

Adab, B. (2002) The Internet and other IT Resources: Tools For Translators within a Translation Programme. Proceedings of the conference on: Translation And Information Technology, Chinese University of Hong Kong, 2000.

Agar, M. (1991) The Biculture in Bilingual. *Language in Society*, 20, 167–81.

Avellis, G. and Laviosa, S. (2000) A COMIC Multimedia Resource for Translating into and out of Business Italian. Paper presented at conference held at the Scuola Superiore di Lingue Moderne per Interpreti e Traduttori, Universita di Bolognà on Corpus Use and Learning to Translate (CULT2K). Bertinoro, Italy, 3–4 November 2000.

Berry, D.M. (2001) Natural Language and Requirements Engineering. CSD & SE Program, University of Waterloo, Canada. http://www.ifi.unizh.ch/groups/req/IWRE/papers&presentations/Berry.pdf

Bowker, L. (1998) Using Specialized Monolingual Native-Language Corpora as a Translation Resource: A Pilot Study. In S. Laviosa (ed.) L'Approche Basée sur le Corpus/The Corpus-based Approach. *Special Issue of Meta* 43(4), 631–51.

Campbell, S. (1998) *Translation into the Second Language*. London: Longman.

Chesterman, A. (1997) *Memes Of Translation. The Spread of Ideas in Translation Theory*. Amsterdam: Benjamins.

De Mooij, M. (1998) *Global Marketing and Advertising: Understanding Cultural Paradoxes*. London: Sage.

Featherstone, M. (2000) *Understanding Culture: Globalisation, Postmodernism and Identity*. London: Sage.

Fillmore, C.J. (1977) Frames and the Semantics of Understanding. *Quaderni di Semantica* 6:2, 222–53.

Gaddis Rose, M. (ed.) (2000) *Beyond the Western Tradition. Translation Perspectives XI*. Center for Research in Translation. State University of New York, Binghamton.

Gambier, Y. (forthcoming) Traduire l'Europe. Keynote paper, conference on Translating Europe, University Babes Bolyai, Cluj Napoca, Romania, 8–10 March 2001.

Gentzler, E. (2000) Translating Metaphor: Beyond the Western Tradition. In M. Gaddis Rose (ed.) *Beyond the Western Tradition. Translation Perspectives XI* (pp. 3–22) Center for Research in Translation. State University of New York, Binghamton.

Hutchins, W.J. (1995) Machine Translation: A Brief History. In E.F.K. Koerner and R.E. Asher (eds) *Concise History of the Language Sciences: From the Sumerians to the Cognitivists* (pp. 431–45) Oxford: Pergamon Press.

Jakobsen, A. L. (1993) Translation as Textual (Re)Production. *Perspectives: Studies in Translatology* 2, 155–65.

Lakoff. G. and Johnson, M. (1980) *Metaphors we live by*. Chicago: University of Chicago Press.

Marmaridou, S. (1996) Directionality in Translation: Processes and Practices. *Target* 8:1, 49–73.

Martenson, R. (1987) Is Standardisation of Marketing Feasible in Culture-bound Industries: A European Case Study. *International Marketing Review*, Autumn, 7–17.

McCracken, G. (1988) *Culture And Consumption: New Approaches to the Symbolic Character of Consumer Goods and Activities*. Bloomington: Indiana University Press.

Neubert, A. (1981) Translation, Interpreting and Text Linguistics. *Studia Linguistica* 35 (1–2), 133–45.

Neubert, A. (2000) Competence in language, in languages, and in translation. In C. Schäffner and B. Adab (eds) *Developing Translation Competence* (pp. 3–18) Amsterdam: Benjamins.

Neubert, A. and Shreve, G.M. (1992) *Translation as Text*. London: Kent State University Press.

Nord, C. (1997) *Translating as a Purposeful Activity: Functionalist Approaches Explained*. Manchester: St Jerome.

Ritzer, G. (1998) *The MacDonalisation Thesis*. London: Sage.

Rupp, C. and Götz, R. (1997) Sprachliche Methoden des Requirements Engineering (NLP). In PROFT #CONQUEST-1 First Conference on Quality Engineering in Software Technology, N?rnberg, Germany (25–26 September 1997).

Schäffner, C. and Adab, B. (2001) The Hybrid Text in Translation. Guest editors – *Special Edition of Across Languages and Cultures* 2 (2). Budapest: Académiai Kiadó.

Stewart, D. (2000) Supplying Native Speaker Intuitions or Normalising Translation? Translating into English as a Foreign Language with the British National Corpus. Paper presented at Research Models in Translation Studies, 28–30 April 2000. UMIST, Manchester, UK.

Toury, G. (1995) *Descriptive Translation Studies and beyond.* Amsterdam: John Benjamins.

Van den Broeck, T. (1986) Contrastive Discourse Analysis as a Tool for the Interpretation of Shifts in Translated Texts. In J. House and S. Blum Kulka (eds) *Interlingual and Intercultural Communication: Discourse and Cognition in Translation and Second Language Acquisition Studies* (pp. 37–47) Tübingen: Narr.

Williams, G. (1992) *Sociolinguistics: A Sociological Critique.* London: Routledge.

Zanettin, F. (1998) Bilingual Comparable Corpora and the Training of Translators. In S. Laviosa (ed.) L'Approche Basée sur le Corpus/The Corpus-based Approach. *Special Issue of Meta* 43(4), 616–30.

Chapter 16

Translating into English as a Non-Native Language: The Dutch Connection

MARCEL THELEN

Introduction

Translating into a speaker's second language has long been the subject of international debate. According to the Nairobi UNESCO Declaration of 1976:

> . . . a translator should, as far as possible, translate into his own mother tongue or into a language of which he or she has a mastery equal to that of his or her mother tongue

and to the Charter of the International Federation of Translators (Fédération Internationale des Traducteurs, FIT):

> The translator shall possess a sound knowledge of the language from which he/she translates and should, in particular, be a master of that into which he/she translates.

From the time that they were formulated, these guidelines have become known as the so-called 'mother tongue principle' for translating and have been the leading principles for translation companies, translation schools, and court procedures for swearing in translators. Their validity appears to be undisputed; it still seems to be common practice to translate into one's mother tongue, and translation into a non-native language is undertaken only in very exceptional cases. But is this true and is the mother tongue principle still tenable in all situations? The debate now seems to have been reopened. Campbell (1998, 2001 and elsewhere in this volume), for example, sheds new light on this principle when discussing translation into English in Australia and Laos, respectively.

What is clear is that, while the Nairobi Declaration is rather strict regarding the requirements for a translator working into another language, the Charter of the FIT is somewhat vaguer. However, in both cases it is far from clear what the exact level of competence should be for a translator to be allowed to work into a non-native language: what are the criteria for viewing the translator's mastery of a non-native language as 'equal' to that of her/his mother tongue and when can a translator be said to have mastered the language into which s/he translates? I will leave the answers to these questions to further research, as they fall beyond the scope of this chapter. Instead, I will focus on the mother tongue principle itself, and the notion of 'native speaker', in particular in relation to the translation situation in The Netherlands. My focus will be on translating specialised not literary nor general-language texts into English as a non-native language. I will argue that the mother tongue principle is too rigid, that the concept of the native speaker needs revision, and that the Nairobi Declaration and the Charter of the FIT can easily be neutralised, clearing the way for translating into English as a non-native language. This presupposes the adoption of a new framework for translating which I have called General Subject-Field-Specific Language Studies (General SSL Studies) (see Thelen 2001, 1999/2001 and forthcoming).

English in The Netherlands

General

Almost since time immemorial, the Dutch have been known for their command of languages other than Dutch, even to such an extent that foreigners visiting The Netherlands and wishing to practise their newly acquired proficiency in Dutch do not get the slightest opportunity to do so. Instead, they are usually addressed in their own native language, provided this is either English, French or German; of these English scores best. As a result, one is inclined to believe that the Dutch are very good at languages and that the teaching of languages within the educational system must be near perfect. A closer look reveals something different.

Despite the fact that at secondary school level English is now a compulsory subject, and that other languages such as German, French, Spanish, and Italian (along with Latin and ancient Greek) are offered as options, the foreign language proficiency of the average Dutchman does not go beyond that needed for general communication at a very basic level. It is a fact that at secondary level, at least in the case of modern languages, a number of books in the foreign language have to be read (but this is very often done with the help of summaries in Dutch) and that much attention is given to communicating in the foreign language. However, one of the most essential elements for learning a language (that is grammar) is almost completely neglected. The situation changes somewhat at university level, in that, although not as a general rule, books very often have to be studied in the original foreign language. Thus, a richer vocabulary and higher level of proficiency may be acquired.

Of course, there are many variations not only in content and number of years of training, but also in regional attitudes towards foreign languages, as for instance in the case of the Dutch living near the German and Belgian borders and especially the French-speaking part of Belgium. On the whole, however, the level of proficiency of those who discontinued their formal education after secondary school is, for obvious reasons, generally lower than that of those who attended university; it is really the people who studied a language at university who can be said to master a foreign language at higher levels of communication. Bilinguals and natural talents present exceptions to this situation.

The above applies to English as a foreign language, a subject to which I will return.

As for the interest in studying a foreign language in The Netherlands, a drastic change can be detected in comparison with the situation pertaining a decade ago. While at secondary school, there is a relatively small degree of freedom – depending on the particular type of school and educational package chosen – for students to choose whether they will take up foreign languages other than English, which is compulsory, and if they do, what language(s) this/these will be. More and more students opt not to study languages, choosing instead subjects such as science, business and administration, information technology (IT) or IT-related studies. This pattern is also apparent at university level. Fewer students are choosing languages, and even fewer are deciding to study translation (see Thelen, 2001). This pattern seems to be international.

As a result of this development, more and more educational institutions are placing increasing emphasis on subjects other than languages, no longer offering straight foreign language programmes. Instead, as a form of compensation for this loss, language modules are often introduced in newly designed courses in other subject areas. English is not an exception here.

Accordingly, the number of Dutch speakers who master English sufficiently well enough to communicate at a more advanced and sophisticated level is decreasing and, overall, the level of proficiency in English is declining. This certainly holds true for standard English; global English or European English may be the exception since the number of speakers of global English is probably higher, but the question is whether this global English will be able to retain the depth and richness of standard English or whether it will develop into a superficial language that is used as a mere tool for communication. A distinction between general language and special language is relevant here, since there are a number of pertinent differences. I return to this below.

The influence of English

For many years, English has been growing in importance as a global language strengthening and consolidating its impact on other languages. This can be seen in many areas, notably computer-related fields, marketing, science, technology, business, administration and advertising. English has become such a global language, that there are already noticeable differences between this global type of English and standard English. European English is a good point in case, see, for example, Wilkinson (1990) who describes this type of global English and its differences from standard English based on three studies carried out among international management students (written), final-year students of translation (Dutch-English translation projects), and European companies (advertisements).

The influence of English on Dutch is also noticeable: English has left, is still leaving and undoubtedly will continue to leave numerous traces in Dutch. As a result, there are for Dutch, as for other languages, dictionaries of neologisms (for example Kolsteren, 1999, Timmers, 2000) and books on new types of Dutch and jargon (for example Kuitenbrouwer, 1993, Lemmens, 1994). Traces of English show up in neologisms which have already been accepted (or 'assimilated') in items that still look foreign, are perceived as such and still interrupt the regular flow of thought, reading or speaking. Assimilated neologisms can be found, described and explained in dictionaries of neologisms, and items belonging to the second category may be found, for example, in authentic and spontaneous newspaper chapters:

> *Wij willen een statement maken tegen het schandalige succes van dit soort rotzooi'* (*de Volkskrant*, Wednesday 18 April 2001). 'We want to make a statement against the outrageous success of this type of rubbish' (translation: Marcel Thelen (MT).

According to Gellerstam (see this volume) traces of the influence of English can also be found in translationese. From his analysis, it becomes clear that by translationese he means neologisms or loans that have developed and grown in another language as a result of translations, where these translations were correct from a lexical, syntactic and rhetorical point of view of the target language, but were at the time of their first use still 'strange' in the target language. I do not think that this is what is generally understood by translationese (or 'translatorese' as Peter Newmark calls it) when the translation is too close to the source text or is violating one or more rules of the target language (see also Shuttleworth & Cowie, 1997). As a result, I do not include translationese here.

In addition to these traces of the influence of English, what Gellerstam calls 'fingerprints', English leaves yet other traces in Dutch that cannot readily be classified as belonging to one of the two above categories. This third type I would call 'apparent mental traces', that is constructions that have nothing to do with translation but are used in spontaneous oral or written communication by a Dutch native speaker. In such a case, the native speaker uses a perfectly correct Dutch syntactic construction but 'thinks English' in terms of an English conceptual structure. In order to convey the intended meaning, s/he uses an English word from this English conceptual structure as an item to fill a particular gap in the intended Dutch syntactic structure with which the English conceptual structure is associated. Schematically presented this would look as indicated in Figure 16.1.

Figure 16.1 Structures in Dutch and English

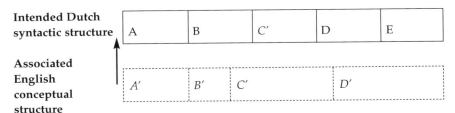

Intended Dutch syntactic structure

| A | B | C′ | D | E |

Associated English conceptual structure

| A′ | B′ | C′ | | D′ | |

Examples can be found in abundance in Dutch national newspapers: for example *commitment*:

> *Zelfs als je nog niet precies weet wat je eigenlijk wilt gaan doen, moet je nu je commitment uitspreken* (*de Volkskrant*, n.d.). 'Even if you do not yet know what exactly you want to do, you should express your commitment now' (MT);

or *shakeout* in:

> *Er lijkt zich naast de e-commerce shakeout van de afgelopen maanden ook een afvalrace in de webjournalistiek te gaan voordoen* (*de Volkskrant*, Friday 21 July 2000). 'In addition to the e-commerce shakeout of the previous months competitive elimination in web journalism also seems to be taking place' (MT);

or *cashen* in:

> *Hij incasseerde 22,2 miljoen gulden, vooral door het cashen van opties ter waarde van 15,5 miljoen gulden* (*de Volkskrant*, Saturday 2 June 2001). 'He received 22.2 million guilders, especially by cashing options worth 15.5 million guilders' (MT).

In other ways too, English leaves traces, most clearly evidenced by whole English sentences, phrases and expressions used without any clear or noticeable reason in an otherwise completely Dutch textual environment:

> *We rule this city* (title of an article in *de Volkskrant*, Friday 15 June 2001).

> *Maar ik vind je alleen competitive in spelletjes, want je vloekt altijd als ik pingpong met je speel en ik sla raak* (*de Volkskrant*, Friday 27 April 2001). 'But I find you competitive in games, only because you always swear when I play table tennis with you and I return the shot' (MT).

> *Getting things done* (catch phrase in a university advertisement in *de Volkskrant*, Saturday 23 June 2001).

Many similar traces of English can be found in Dutch. In itself this is nothing strange or extraordinary; like any other contemporary language, Dutch is alive and changes constantly. However, these changes, at least changes like the ones above, put the notion of native speaker under further pressure: standard English is developing away from its roots into a global type of English among 'other speakers', and Dutch is assimilating more and more of this global type of English, arguably paving the way for a gradual convergence of the two languages and disappearance of language-specific characteristics. This situation may give rise to questions like: 'who is native speaker of what?' and 'what is a native speaker anyway?' It would be very difficult and would fall far beyond the scope of this chapter to try and find a suitable answer to a question like the first; the second will be discussed in the following section.

The Notion of the 'Native Speaker'

In education, the notion of 'native speaker' is used to denote a person who masters a language as her/his first language and who is therefore entitled (and much preferred over non-native speakers) to give proficiency training in this language. Ideally, language training institutions have at least one native speaker for each language; sometimes such a person comes directly from abroad (either from his native country or from another country) and sometimes s/he has stayed in the country for some time before taking up the position. In translation, a native speaker is a person who has mastered the target language as his native language and is therefore entitled and preferred to translate from another language into his native language.

This may seem very straightforward but it is not. Someone with English as her/his mother tongue is a native speaker of English. This certainly holds for someone coming directly from the UK having lived there from birth, or from any other country where English is the language of habitual use. However, someone with English as her/his mother tongue who has lived in The Netherlands for more than 30 years can hardly be

called a full native speaker of English any longer: there is too much interference between her/his mother tongue English and Dutch (see also the
possible impact of developments outlined in section 1). These are obviously two extremes on a scale of 'native-speakerhood'. This means that
the concept of 'native speaker' is not clear-cut, but rather fuzzy. The most
important question here is: can language proficiency criteria be developed
to demarcate non-native speakers from a range of near-native speakers
and full native speakers on a sliding scale? This is hardly possible, and
therefore it is my view that the notion of 'native speaker' is out of date
and should no longer be used to stipulate who should translate into
English as a non-native language.

One could argue that, if taken as prototypical, the notion of 'native
speaker' could well be defined and demarcated on a scale, but since it is
used in actual practice as a criterion to allow individuals to translate into
a non-native language or deny him/her this option, and since money and
possibly also a career is involved, there should and can only be very
precise distinguishing and not prototypical or fuzzy criteria.

With technological developments moving ever faster, the growing use
of the Internet, and increasing globalisation, physical boundaries between
countries and languages as criteria for the distinction between translation
into one's mother tongue and into a non-native language are bound
to weaken and will therefore no longer be valid criteria for 'native-
speakerhood': no longer are languages or native speakers confined to
particular geographical areas.

What then about the emergence of global or European English? It is
a blend of standard English and other languages. Who would be called a
native speaker of this type of English? The person who masters standard
English or the person who has learned the global type of English?
Apparently, the notion of native speaker still denotes the 'old' type of
native speaker and not the native speaker of global English. The lexicographer, Vincenzo Lo Cascio, in a recent lecture on a new bilingual Italian-
Dutch/Dutch-Italian dictionary, introduced the notion of the 'real
speaker' (as opposed to the 'ideal speaker'). It would perhaps be better to
use this dichotomy instead of native versus non-native.

General Language versus Special Language

Clearly, a distinction should be drawn between general language and
special language (language for specific purposes) in order to refine the
arguments presented in earlier sections.

The examples cited in section 1 pertain to general language which is
what I would call an 'open class' variety of language, where there is no
limit on the number of expressions, sentences, etc. General language is the
type of language that – *mutatis mutandis* – every human masters to some

degree. It is different with special language, which is the type of language that is used by a restricted number of people for communication within a discourse community and is used to describe specific subject fields. This type of language has more or less the character of controlled language; it could be called a 'closed class' type of language. Examples of special languages are the languages of economics/business/administration, law/politics, medicine/biology, science/technology/IT, media and the arts, leisure and tourism, and so on. Special language is coupled with/tied to knowledge of specific subject fields. Someone learning about a particular subject field is in a position to learn about the special language of that particular subject field. Students who learn more about a specific subject field in English will thus be able to learn more about the special language features of the English in this field.

Would it then be justified to say that, once students have learned about a specific subject field, they automatically become experts in the special language of this subject field and that they would thus be excellent candidates for translating into English as their non-native language in this specific subject field? The answer has to be no. Although a student may become expert with respect to the subject matter of their specific subject field, they will not have been trained to explore in a systematic way the relationship between the subject matter, the organisation of the subject field and the English special language of the subject field. Besides, English special language is more than just fixed terms and expressions. Even for English LSPs, mastery of English general language is necessary.

As in the case of proficiency in English general language, proficiency in English special languages can also be improved with the help of proper and appropriate translation training and practice. Hence, Dutch speakers who are trained to combine proficiency in English general language with proficiency in English special language would be capable of translating into English as their non-native language. Evidence in support of this claim can be found in the daily training of translation students at the Maastricht School of Translation and Interpreting. It is certainly not uncommon for students to translate better from Dutch into English, their non-native language, than from English into Dutch, their mother tongue. With sufficient practice and training students are able to make considerable progress. The situation might improve even further if the notion of global/European English is taken into consideration. Due to the growing influence of English as a global language, a derived international variety of English, the number of translation jobs requiring translation into global/European English (be it general language or special language) is increasing in comparison with the number of translation assignments involving standard English. I would even claim that there are no truly native speakers of this global European English and that mastery of this variety of language can be taught and learned. Consequently, the traditional notion of native speaker of English should be abandoned in the context of modern global communication, and in particular, modern professional translation.

While it is sometimes argued that subject field specialists make plausible candidates for translating into English as a non-native language, they may still lack proficiency in English general language as well as an overall language awareness. In other words, they may be more subject focused than language focused. A concomitant problem is the limited availability of such experts, such that demands for translation into a non-native language may not be matched by the supply of experts in the particular field.

Translation in The Netherlands

Translation companies in The Netherlands adhere strictly to the mother tongue principle, preferring to commission native speakers of English to work into English, that is, English-speaking translators who are either living in The Netherlands or who can be contacted via the Internet, often using translation agencies or a freelance 'supplier' belonging to a translation company's network. Only in extreme circumstances and under pressure to meet tight deadlines would translation companies agree to using non-native speakers of English to translate into their non-native language.

Applying the mother tongue principle seems to have become a sort of quality assurance, part of a guarantee of specialisation. Sticking to the native speaker rule is, however, not necessary in many cases, especially since clients do not all require the same quality of translations depending on the envisaged purpose (see Wagner, this volume, in relation to the European Commission). In addition, with the implementation of technology and different kinds of translation tools, it becomes increasingly 'easy' for non-native speakers to produce good English through post-editing. Many translation companies already make use of translation memories and terminology management systems that take over much of the translation work (see Adab, this volume). The latest development in this area is illustrated by the Translation Service of the European Commission in combining machine translation, translation memories and terminology management systems into one system that leaves very little work to be done by the human translator in the post-editing phase (see Taes, 2001).

Very often, translation companies seem to use native speakers as a form of protection against dissatisfied clients; it gives the companies an additional form of authority. A good system of client education would, however, help to render such a stance redundant.

From the above discussion, it should be clear that, in my view, there are no native speakers of global/European English special languages, and that, as a result, there is no need for a translation company to engage only

English-speaking translators for translation into English. Furthermore, there are sometimes simply not enough English-speaking translators in particular specific fields thus forcing companies to resort to non-native speakers in any case. Under these circumstances, it is reassuring to know that translation schools do in fact train their students in translating into English as a non-native language. In the next section I would like to argue that what is called for is a completely different perspective on translation: translation as one of the many options of what I have called 'General SSL Studies'.

General SSL Studies

General Subject-Field-Specific Language Studies (General SSL Studies) was formulated for the first time as a new and independent discipline in Thelen (2001), and discussed further in Thelen (1999/2001 and forthcoming). Its structure is shown in Figure 16.2.

Figure 16.2 Inputs to General SSL Studies (adapted from Toury, 1995: 15)

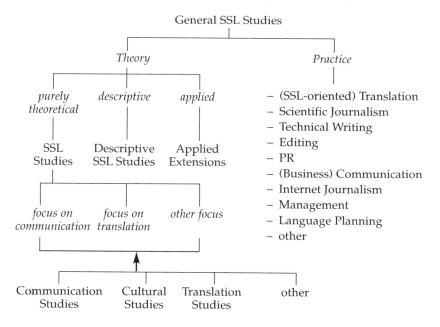

Originally designated Subject-Field-Specific Language Studies, it was subsequently renamed in order to distinguish it from 'SSL Studies' (Thelen, 2001). General SSL Studies is informed by Communication Studies, Cultural Studies, Translation Studies and, possibly, also other disciplines.

Figure 16.3 Elements of General SSL Studies

General SSL Studies	Terminology	LSP
scope • terms and larger chunks of language such as phrases, paragraphs and sentences	• terms and phrases • the epistemology and ontology of specialist subject fields • the way concepts are related to terms	• all levels specific to languages and text
focus • the transfer of linguistic data within or between levels of communication within one and the same language or between languages • how subject-field specific language actually functions in communication	• the epistemology and ontology of specialist subject fields • the way concepts are related to terms • the standardisation of terms • terms without a translation or communication context	• the acquisition and practical use of language that is specific to a particular specialist subject field
other • attempts to acquire an insight into the relation between language and the internal organisation of a specialist subject field		

General SSL Studies focuses on the typical type of language of specialist subject fields and differs from Terminology on the one hand and LSP on the other in a number of respects as shown in Figure 16.3.

The characteristics of General SSL studies are as follows:

- they deal with the language of a particular specialist subject field;
- they include not only linguistic, but also psycholinguistic, sociolinguistic and pragmatic aspects of the special language in question;
- they function in a contrastive way with an eye open to the possible mutual influence of the LSP of a particular subject field as realised in different languages and cultures;
- they are concerned with a variety of aspects involved in language and languages such as translation, communication or culture.

The expert in General SSL Studies may eventually act as a translator (software ~, web ~), a terminologist, a technical writer, a communication specialist, a (scientific) journalist, etc. In other words, translation is not the only focus and possibility of General SSL Studies.

Since the General SSL specialist has learned

- what the phenomenon of special language is,
- what characteristics of it are realised in different languages and cultures and the underlying triggers for these realisations,
- what differences there can be between languages, cultures and levels of communication for a particular type of special language of a particular specialist subject field,
- what translation is and what is involved in terms of, for example, translation procedures,
- what translation tools are available (translation memory systems and terminology management systems), how to work with them, and what benefits may be derived from machine translation systems,

s/he may very well translate between any pairs of languages in which s/he is proficient regardless of whether s/he is a native speaker in a particular target language. In this way, the notion of native speaker and the mother tongue principle will be neutralised and made superfluous.

Conclusions

In this chapter I have argued that the notion of 'native speaker' and the mother tongue principle are no longer valid for these times, especially not in The Netherlands where Dutch and standard English both seem to be moving in the direction of a global type of English that does not yet have its native speakers. The availability of a range of translation tools and changing translation requirements seem to support the claim that native speakers of the target language are no longer the sole professional option. Unlike in Laos, specialist knowledge on any subject is readily available in The Netherlands; by contrast, in the situation that Campbell describes in Laos (see this volume), the Lao translators not only have no subject knowledge of new developments necessary for their translations, they also do not have a sound knowledge of English, especially the ASEAN variety of English discourse.

In addition, the concept of 'native speaker' and the mother tongue principle cannot be precisely characterised such that translating into English as one's mother tongue can be clearly set apart from translating into English as a non-native language. Despite the fact that in many countries, language awareness and proficiency seem to be decreasing, there remains a potential that can be developed further, for example through

General SSL Studies, which has the capacity to neutralise the concepts of mother tongue and native speaker. Experts in General SSL Studies would arguably even make better translators for working into English than current native speakers of English without specific training.

Therefore there does not seem to be any reason for translation companies to adhere to the concept of native speaker and to the mother tongue principle other than for reasons of self-protection against potentially difficult clients and of marketing. For the latter substitutes can easily be found, and the former can be made superfluous by proper client education. Allowing Dutch natives to translate into English as a non-native language would be a recognition of their translation potential and give them a chance to gain further experience to become experts in an area for which they may have a natural feeling and talent. It is to be welcomed that schools offering translation training still train students in translating into English as a non-native language. I hope that this chapter is also understood as a plea for including General SSL Studies in the curriculum of translation schools.

References

Campbell, S. (1998) *Translation into the Second Language*. Harlow, Essex: Addison-Wesley Longman Limited.

Kuitenbrouwer, J. (1993) *Neo-turbo. Van yuppie-speak tot crypto-mumble*. Amsterdam: Prometheus.

Larson, M. (1984, 1998) *Meaning-Based Translation. A Guide to Cross-Language Equivalence*. Lanham/New York/Oxford: University Press of America, Inc.

Lemmens, M. (1994) *Tot straks na de reclame! Het Nederlands in beweging*. The Hague: Sdu Uitgevers.

Lo Cascio, V. (2001) De echte spreker: overwegingen bij het totstandkomen van een tweetalig woordenboek Italiaans-Nederlands/Nederlands-Italiaans The real speaker: considerations on the occasion of the completion of a biligual dictionary Italian-Dutch/Dutch-Italian]. Unpublished farewell lecture. Amsterdam, 27 March 2001, University of Amsterdam.

Shuttleworth, M. and Cwie, M. (1997) *Dictionary of Translation Studies*. Manchester, UK.: St Jerome Publishing.

Taes, A. (2001) Introducing CAT at the Translation Service of the European Commission. In R. Temmerman and M. Lutjemans (eds) *Proceedings of the International Colloquium 'Trends in Special Language Technology'*, *Brussels, Flemish Parliament, 29 and 20 March 2001* (pp. 27–9). Antwerp: Standard Editions Ltd.

Thelen, M. (1999/2001) Present issues in teaching specialised translation: a new perspective on translation. Paper read at the conference, 'Aspects of Specialised Translation', London, 26-7 November 1999. In L. Desblache (ed.) *Aspects of specialised translation* (Langues des Métiers/Métiers des Langues, collection dirigée par Daniel Gouadec) (pp. 15–25) Paris: La Maison du Dictionnaire. Published as 'Present Issues in Teaching Specialised Translation: a practice-oriented MA programme.'

Thelen, M. (2001) Subject Field Special Language Studies (General SSL Studies): towards a new discipline. In M. Thelen and B. Lewandowska-Tomaszczyk (eds) *Translation and Meaning, Part 5. Proceedings of the Maastricht Session* of the 3rd International Maastricht-Lodz Duo Colloquium on 'Translation and Meaning.' Held in Maastricht, The Netherlands, 26–29 April 2000. Maastricht: Hogeschool Zuyd, Maastricht School of Translation and Interpreting.

Thelen, M. (2002) Translation Studies in the year 2000: the state of the art. Part I: Terminology in theory and practice. In B. Lewandowska-Tomaszczyk and M. Thelen (eds) _Translation and Meaning, Part 6. Proceedings of the Lodz Session of the 3rd International Maastricht-Lodz Duo Colloquium on 'Translation and Meaning'_ (pp. 21–39). Held in Lodz, Poland, 22–24 September 2000. Maastricht: Hogeschool Zuyd, Maastricht School of Translation and Interpreting.

Timmers, C. (2000) _Faxen, faxte, gefaxt: De juiste spelling van ruim 1500 oorspronkelijk vreemde woorden._ The Hague: Sdu Uitgevers.

Toury, G. (1995) _Descriptive Translation Studies and Beyond._ Amsterdam: John Benjamins Publishing Company.

Wilkinson, R. (1990) Translating into European English: evolution and acceptability. In M. Thelen and B. Lewandowska-Tomaszczyk (eds) _Translation and Meaning, Part 1. Proceedings of the Maastricht Session of the 1990 Maastricht-Lodz Duo Colloquium on 'Translation and Meaning'_ (pp. 323–35). Held in Maastricht, The Netherlands, 4–6 January 1990. Maastricht: Euroterm Maastricht.

Chapter 17

Native versus Non-Native Speaker Competence in German-English Translation: A Case Study

MARGARET ROGERS

Introduction

The status of English as a global language raises important questions about ownership and authority which in turn have implications for translation as a profession. If we accept that there are now many Englishes, the traditional dividing line between native speakers and non-native speakers of English is becoming increasingly blurred. But as moves to intensify the professionalisation of translation have progressed, one of the issues which has arisen is that of translation direction in relation to native or non-native speaker competence. In other words, is it good professional practice to translate out of as well as into your mother tongue? In this chapter I would like to make some of the assumptions associated with this question explicit and to put it into a context which takes account of a number of translational factors. In the first section, the notion of native speaker competence is discussed, followed by a consideration of translation competence in the context of UK higher education and its relevance to native speaker and non-native speaker translators. Some data are then presented in the form of a case study of the translations of two native speakers of English and two native speakers of German working from German into English. One of the criteria which will be considered is that of 'naturalness', an elusive yet intuitively important aspect of target text creation. Finally, some conclusions are offered, supporting the view that 'professionalism' does not necessarily proscribe translation out of the mother tongue.

Native Speaker Competence

For understandable reasons, professional organisations attempt to set standards for the behaviour of their members. This has the dual purpose of ensuring a certain quality of service to clients while also developing a sense of group identification, in order to distinguish those whose competence marks them as a member of the 'profession' from those whose competence does not. According to the profession concerned, this may be achieved in different ways. In some, the title is protected, for example 'solicitor' and 'general practitioner' in the UK, barring those without the appropriate academic and/or professional qualifications from practising. Protection of the title 'translator' has been an issue of some contention, particularly in certain countries (for example Belgium, Italy). In most countries, however, the title is not protected, meaning that anyone can call him- or herself a 'translator'. All the more reason then, to try to define the in-group through other means, one of which is a reference to 'mother tongue or native speaker competence' in the target language. A common definition of a 'professional' as opposed to a 'non-professional' translator is one who only translates into their mother tongue or 'equivalent', as, for instance in the UK-based Institute of Translation and Interpreting's Code of Conduct, section 4 (Standards of Work) (http://www.iti.org.uk/indexMain.html).

4. STANDARDS OF WORK
4.1 Translation
4.1.1 Subject to 4.4 [Contractual arrangements] and 4.5 [Exception] below, members shall translate only into a language which is either (i) their mother tongue or language of habitual use, or (ii) one in which they have satisfied the Institute that they have equal competence. They shall translate only from those languages in which they can demonstrate they have the requisite skills.

A previous version was less explicit:

Section 4.1 Standards of Work, Languages:
4.1 Languages
. . . a Member shall translate only into a language in which he has a mother-tongue or equivalent competence, or interpret only between languages in one of which he has mother-tongue or equivalent competence.

The addition in the later version of 'language of habitual use'[1] adds some clarification, but still leaves open the interpretation of what is now called 'equal competence'. Related concepts such as 'mother tongue', 'native speaker' and 'bilingual' are also often taken to be self-evidently clear, particularly in majority-language cultures such as the monolingual English speech community in the UK. Campbell (1998: 5) has pointed out that the model which is often assumed for the translator is that of the 'ideal bilingual'. However, in practice, there are many different types of bilingualism as well as sociolinguistic factors which blur the boundaries between 'native' and 'non-native speaker'. Barbour & Stevenson, for example, discuss the situation of immigrant children in Germany, whose bilingualism ranges between 'equilingualism' and 'semilingualism' (1990: 194–5). In addition, there are legal and economic factors which further contribute to a weakening of the native speaker/non-native speaker distinction as it is traditionally understood. The European Union, for instance, encourages, through its various programmes and legislation, the mobility of labour, as well as of students and teachers, meaning that EU citizens may spend a considerable part of their working lives and/or their education outside their country of birth. Changing ways of working, such as teleworking or telecommuting, and the internationalisation of large companies also mean that the preferred language of use may not be the language of the surrounding locality.

Furthermore, in some parts of Europe, most notably the Nordic countries, translation out of the mother tongue – particularly into English – is an accepted practice, typically because the demand for translation out of that language exceeds the supply of native speaker translators. Indeed, in those countries, training curricula often reflect this reality (cf. for instance, McAlester, 1992; Mackenzie, 1998; see also Thelen, this volume, for The Netherlands). Professional practice in the former German Democratic Republic (in the state-run Intertext agency) was similar: where English was the target language, the resulting translations were revised by an English native speaker, although not necessarily a trained translator. In Australia, translation out of the mother tongue is also 'a regular and accepted practice', according to Campbell (1998: 12).

So, there are many factors which relativise any strong claims about professionalism and translating into the native language, whether they have to do with the relativity of the notions of 'native language', 'mother tongue' and 'bilingual' or with social and economic conditions. That is not to say that translators working out of their mother tongue or language of habitual use are not capable of producing 'the worst translationese' (Newmark, 1991: 21), but when discussing non-native speaker translation it is easy to forget that working into the mother tongue or language of habitual use may also produce work of an unacceptable standard.

Translation Competence

Those wishing to become professional translators may be forgiven if they detect a certain ambivalence of purpose in the translation exercises which they are set as part of their undergraduate degree programmes in modern languages in UK universities. Their first introduction to translation for professional purposes as opposed to language proficiency often requires some radical rethinking. The debate about translation for language teaching versus translation for professional purposes is a long-standing one (see for instance, Cook, 1998; Rogers, 2000), which during the 1990s began to show some signs of resolution (cf. Sewell & Higgins, 1996;

Malmkjær, 1998). 'Translation competence' may nevertheless be defined in different ways, depending on pedagogical purpose, a factor which is potentially confusing for students, such as those whose work is reported in the case study below. Consider, for instance, the following sentences which a student with English as mother tongue has been asked to translate into German and English respectively:

(1)   The children were recommended to go to bed early.
(2)   Heute ist mit den Bauarbeiten begonnen worden.

If the point is to test or practise aspects of the foreign language, i.e. German, in production and reception respectively, a structurally close translation is normally required in any mark scheme:

(1a) Den Kindern wurde empfohlen, früh ins Bett zu gehen.
(2a) Today, building works were begun.

In the case of example (1), the production of a passive structure with an intransitive verb (*empfehlen* + Dative 'to recommend (to) someone') is at issue; in example (2), the point is to recognise that the German structure is passive. Hence, answers such as (1b) and (2b) would be less acceptable in these contexts:

(1b) Man hat den Kindern empfohlen, früh ins Bett zu gehen.
(2b) They began building today.

Sentences for translation such as example (1) typically occur in grammar exercises, and example (2) in tests of reading comprehension,

Table 17.1 Characteristics of translation into non-native language and into native language in the traditional language-teaching curriculum

Translation direction	Characterised by
Into non-native language	• Objective: non-native language production; accuracy training
	• Focus on form (syntax and morphology)
	• Lexical knowledge as a test of memory
	• Linguistic encoding
Into native language	• Objective: non-native language reading comprehension; structural and lexical recognition
	• Focus on form (syntax and morphology)
	• Lexical knowledge as a test of memory
	• Linguistic decoding

often as part of a text. To a large extent such translation exercises are still foreign-language focused, even though the non-native language is the source language and not the target language in this case. We can try to summarise the traditional role of translation in the proficiency-based language-teaching curriculum as in Table 17.1.

By contrast, translation which is understood as 'source-text induced target-text production' (Neubert, 1985: 18), in which the source text is translated for a particular situation and purpose, can no longer be perceived primarily as a linguistic encoding or decoding exercise which is a test of the translator's knowledge of grammar and vocabulary. As Kussmaul succinctly states (1995: 1), '[t]ranslation is not just an exchange of words and structures, but a communicative *process* that takes into consideration the reader of the translation within a particular situation within a specific culture' (*emphasis added*). Procedural knowledge (know how to) is therefore as important as declarative knowledge (know that).

Figure 17.2 presents a view of translation competence which is centred around three intersecting components: cultural competence, linguistic competence and subject field competence.

Figure 17.2 Competences relevant to translation

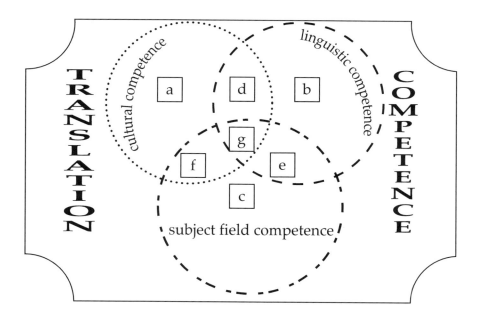

The different sets and their intersections can be glossed as follows:

(a) cultural competence, for example historical, geographical, institutional, religious, media-related, literary knowledge, *inter alia*, which is in many cases bound up with linguistic knowledge through the use of terms, expressions and the representation of meaning; ability to research cultural information and expectations;

(b) linguistic competence which has to do with the system of each language of the translation pair and its use in communicative situations, for example the grammar and lexicon, text creation and text understanding;

(c) competence in a specific subject field which presupposes training and/or experience, for example knowledge of laser optics, stamp collecting, contract law, theoretical linguistics, machine tools, and so on; ability to research new subject fields;

(d) the intersection of cultural competence and linguistic competence relates to those areas such as the realisation of specific genre conventions in particular languages and the existence of culture-specific genres;

(e) the intersection of linguistic competence and subject field competence relates to the knowledge and use of special languages, including their terminologies, typical syntactic patterns and subject-specific genres;

(f) the intersection of subject field competence and cultural competence relates to culture-specific aspects of particular subject fields; these may be more or less culture bound, ranging from law and social administration (highly culture bound) to pure sciences (more universal);

(g) the central point of intersection indicates a specific translation assignment which draws on the three sets of competences indicated in the overall context of general translation competence, including the ability of the translator to assess his or her own limits with respect to subject matter, time limits, language direction, etc.; also the ability to take translation decisions based on the specified translation assignment and to justify these decisions, for example to clients

If we now consider these aspects of translation competence in relation to native speaker and non-native speaker translators, we can arrive at some notion of their relative strengths. These are summarised in Table 17.3, according to whether native speakers or non-native speakers may typically be assumed to have an advantage.

The view presented in Table 17.3 is, of course, a simplification: deficits in both mother tongue and non-native language competences can be and are addressed in translator training curricula through, for example, the study of contrastive genre conventions, terminology, specialised subject fields, and so on, as well as through the development of research skills.

Table 17.3 Some translation-relevant competences in a professional context showing probable strengths of native speakers and non-native speakers of the target language

Aspects of translation competence	Native speakers of target language	Non-native speakers of target language

(a) cultural competence
    i) of target language culture
    ii) of source language culture
	+	+

(b) linguistic competence
    i) of target language
    ii) of source language
	+	+

(c) subject field competence	(+)	(+)

(d) genre conventions
    i) of target language
    ii) of source language
	+	+

(e) Languages for Special Purposes
    i) of target language
    ii) of source language
	+	+

(f) culture-bound subject-field
    competence
    i) of target language
    ii) of source language
	+	+

(g) specific translation assignment
    i) assessing own competence
       and constraints
    ii) ability to create a target text fit
       for a particular purpose and to
       justify translation decisions
	(+)
	
	+
		(+)
		
		(+)

In order to explore some of these issues further, in the following section the results of a small case study are presented, focusing on the translation texts of a small subset of a group of English-speaking and German-speaking translators of a German text into English. The subjects are all students and may therefore be considered as novice translators. The objective is to evaluate the common assumption that translation out of the mother tongue necessarily produces inferior texts.

German-English Translation: A Case Study

Approach

The approach which I have chosen for this analysis is to focus on a small number of translations produced as homework by non-native speakers of English (mother tongue, German) and native speakers of English attending a German-English translation class at the University of Surrey in the then Department of Linguistic and International Studies. Four translations were selected for close analysis: the two non-native speaker translations which were in my judgement the most successful and the two native speaker translations which were the least successful among their respective sub-groups. Other choices would also have been possible, for example most successful native speaker and least successful non-native speaker translations. But given our concern with the assumed superiority of native speaker translations, the choice of most successful non-native speaker and least successful native speaker translations seems more likely to shed some light on our question: are translations done by native speakers necessarily better than those done by non-native speakers. Furthermore, it is hoped that the data can provide some indications of how native speaker and non-native speaker translations may vary.

Background

The four-year Surrey undergraduate programmes operative at the time of the study allowed students to combine one or two foreign languages with Economics and International Business, Law or European Studies, also incorporating a number of courses concerned with social, political and economic aspects of the target culture. The curriculum entailed a high degree of integration between language studies and the chosen special subject, with, for example, students of German and Law following courses not only in English Law but also in German Law and German-English legal translation. For all language-based degree programmes, the student is required to spend around nine months in the foreign-language culture in a work or study placement. These programmes are not intended as a full training for translators, although they provide a solid basis for further specialised study. Every year, exchange students from German-speaking countries join the UK students for particular classes.

The module on which this case study is based deals with the translation of a range of German texts into English. It is the first opportunity students have to practise translation as an exercise in text creation rather than as a language-learning exercise. Topics covered include politics, society, economics, issues of current interest. The texts range from informative through instructive to persuasive in type. Students are actively encouraged both in classwork and homework to use dictionaries and any other appropriate resources to solve their translation problems. The aim of the class is to introduce students to some of the variables in translation as text creation and to explore ways in which translation decisions can be seen in relation to the text type, as well as the purpose and situation of the translation task.

The source text for the translations on which the analysis is based is 'Die Kirchensteuer bleibt', from the *Frankfurter Rundschau*, 4 January 1994 (see Appendix A below). The text is anonymous and informative, and reports on a disagreement within the German government about the continuation of 'church tax', levied by state tax offices on behalf of the two biggest churches. The second half of the text, which was the homework set, describes the historical origins of church tax. The translation brief was to produce a target text for the European page of an English (UK) broadsheet to appear in the following week's edition. The item would be of particular interest to a British audience, since church tax is not payable in the UK; the article could therefore add to the knowledge of the reader about a different culture.

The UK-registered students in the class (all native speakers of English) were in their third and penultimate year of undergraduate study and had spent one three-month period in a German-speaking country as a part of their degree programme. They were joined in the class by a number of German native speakers from German and Swiss institutions of higher education, all native speakers of German and studying at a British university as a part of their studies in their home institution. Let us start with an overview of successful and less successful translations in both groups, before moving on to a discussion of particular translations. The four translations selected for more detailed discussion (the two least successful native speaker translations and the two most successful non-native speaker translations) are presented in Appendix B below. Success is defined here as suitability for publication in a broadsheet English-language newspaper in the UK, as specified in the assignment.

Overview of all translations

Church tax is not a concept in the UK, and was unfamiliar to the English native speakers, leaving them without a clear frame of reference for translation problems at both the conceptual and the terminological level. While the non-native speakers of English had a conceptual grasp of the topic, their knowledge of related English terminology was largely lacking.

The least successful native speaker translations are characterised largely by serious mistranslations of the source text at the level of sentence structure, tense errors, and spelling and other orthographic errors. While individual sentences often read rather fluently, they make little sense in relation to the whole text, thereby endangering its coherence.

By contrast, the successful non-native speaker translations are characterised not by misleading translations but by what might be called a lack of 'naturalness' (see Newmark, 1988: 24–9). The 'unnaturalness' in such translations is often the result of lexical transfer from the source text (arguably from the source language), resulting in odd collocations, too many abstract nouns or infinitives instead of gerunds, as well as cognates from an inappropriate register. But the danger of the source text syntax being mistranslated to such a degree that the proposition is misrepresented is avoided. The basic message of the text is intact in the successful non-native speaker translations, but not so in the least successful native speaker translations where a reassuring fluency can be misleading.

The least successful non-native speaker translations are characterised by a choice of terminology in the target text which is semantically remote enough from acceptable choices that the sense is obscured. One student, for example, wrote the following (italics indicate incorrect terminology):

- 'Church tax was guaranteed *lawfully* in Weimar's constitution of 1919' ('legally').
- 'In it was said, *denominations* [. . .] would be justified to levy the tax . . .' ('religious societies').
- 'The tax is levied on the basis of laws of church tax which [. . .] *declared* by the federal states' ('enacted').
- 'The tax rates are *associated with* income taxes . . .' ('linked to').
- 'The general public has different attitudes' ('Public opinion is split').

The successful native speaker translations are characterised by an absence of serious mistranslations (as in the successful non-native speaker translations) and by a degree of naturalness which is present to only a limited degree in the least successful native speaker translations.

Moving on to the more detailed analysis, we will start with the native speaker translations (Student M and Student C) before going on to the non-native speaker translations (Student Cl and Student A).

Least successful native speaker translations

Bearing in mind the brief for the target text to be published in a national newspaper, student M's translation immediately creates a bad impression on the reader before any incoherence emerges, through numerous orthographical errors: 'empirial' ('imperial'); 'Weimar republic' ('Weimar Republic'); 'basic law' ('Basic Law'); 'west-germans' ('West Germans'); 'abolishion' ('abolition'); 'recieves' ('receives'). More serious – in so far as it concerns the information transmitted by the text – is the mistranslation of the second sentence of the source text extract, where M has failed to identify an item of reported speech. In German, reported speech can be marked solely by a subjunctive verb form – in this case, *seien* from *sein* ('to be') – and not necessarily by a *that*-type subordinate clause as in English. As a result of his missing this clear grammatical clue (the corresponding indicative verb form is *sind*), M's translation makes little sense. In particular, we can note the opening of the second sentence, which raises false expectations of a cleft sentence ('There, it was in the form of religious societies which . . .'):

> *Die Kirchensteuer wurde in der Weimarer Verfassung von 1919 reichsrechtlich garantiert. Dort hieß es, Religionsgesellschaften, die Körperschaften des öffentlichen Rechts sind, seien berechtigt, aufgrund der bürgerlichen Steuerlisten nach Maßgabe der landesrechtlichen Bestimmungen Steuern zu erheben.*

> The church tax was guaranteed by empirial law in the 1919 constitution of the Weimar republic. There, it was in the form of religious societies which were religious bodies. These bodies had the right to raise taxes based on the civil tax lists as determined by the law of the province.

Another curious aspect of M's translation, which was repeated by many other native speaker translators, is his use of the definite article in the phrase 'The church tax . . .' (for, *Die Kirchensteuer* . . .). In English no definite article is required in this context; analogous English expressions with a generic reference also require no such article: 'income tax', 'capital gains tax', and so on. It seems that on this occasion the source text structure outweighed target language analogues, producing translationese. A feasible explanation of this is the absence of a 'frame' of knowledge to which the concept of *Kirchensteuer* could be referred. The parallels with other types of personal taxation in the UK were therefore not apparent.

M's translation also fails the naturalness test in places. For instance, his translation of the last sentence formally reflects the prepositional phrase *für das Inkasso* as 'for collection of the tax', using a noun where a gerund would be more natural: 'for collecting the tax', reflecting the verbal style more typical of English.

By contrast with M's translation, C's translation contains fewer orthographical and lexical errors (for example 'affect' for 'effect'; 'continuance' for 'continuation'), but a larger number of misunderstandings of the source text. C's translation starts with an interesting error of functional sentence perspective which fails to acknowledge the thematic status of *Kirchensteuer*, which is not only the theme of the sentence in question but also the hypertheme of the text.

> *Die Kirchensteuer wurde in der Weimarer Verfassung von 1919 reichsrechtlich garantiert.*

> As of 1919, the Church Tax was guaranteed legal status throughout the German Reich.

C's translation reads instead like the continuation of a chronological narrative, in which time is the theme (what happened then, and then, and then . . .), whereas it is this section of the text which actually starts the description of the historical origins of church tax. The translation therefore disorientates the reader who might be forgiven for thinking that s/he has missed a previous date in the history of church tax.

What could be the origin of such an error? It is common in English for declarative sentences to begin with an adverbial sentence adjunct of time, for example 'On one occasion, one of the prisoners escaped.' However, in this case, C has failed to recognise the significance of the grammatically and contextually dependent nature of the German time phrase *von 1919* which is attached as an attribute to the prepositional phrase *in der Weimar Verfassung*. It is therefore not free to be placed sentence-initially in English as a sentence adjunct. In fact, student C not only misinterprets the relative communicative importance of the information in the sentence, he actually omits the crucial reference to the Weimar Constitution altogether.

Just as M experienced difficulties with the reported speech structure of the second sentence (*Dort hieß es* . . .), so does C, but in a different way. C's translation sounds almost feasible.

> As of 1919, the Church Tax was guaranteed legal status throughout the German Reich. That is to say, it was justifiable to levy taxes to raise revenue for religious societies, which are open to everyone and fulfil the stipulations of regional legal requirements, appearing on civil tax lists.

However, the cohesive function of *dort* ('there') establishing the Weimar Constitution – which does not even get a mention – as the source of the right to levy church tax, has been entirely missed. Instead of pursuing the outstanding question of what *dort* ('there') could co-refer with in the previous sentence and thereby discovering his error of omission, C incorrectly moulds his second sentence to accommodate the error. Successful native speaker translations overcame the cohesion problem posed by *dort* by using a relative clause to combine the first and second sentences: '. . . in the Weimar Constitution of 1919 which stated that . . . '. This avoids the awkwardness of expressing the cohesive link which is explicitly represented in the German at the beginning of the sentence, but which commonly results in an unnatural effect in English if not structurally modified.

A further mistranslation in C's work concerns the relationship between the churches and the federal states in levying the tax. The source text states that the tax is levied on the basis of church tax laws, which are enacted by the federal states based on agreements *with* the two biggest churches. However, in his translation, C not only mistakes the tense, using the past instead of the present thereby implying that the laws are no longer valid ('was levied' for *wird . . . erhoben*; 'were based on', for *basierend auf*), he also mistakenly states that the agreements are 'between the two largest churches' even though the German clearly states *mit den großen Kirchen*. This error was repeated by other native speaker translators. The student's incorrect solution not only runs counter to the explicit linguistic evidence of the text, it is also hard to imagine what gave rise to the hypothesis in the first place, since the paragraph has been concerned with the relationship between the federal states and the churches, not with the relationship between the churches. No non-native speakers made the same error.

Further tense errors occur in C's second paragraph, using the past tense instead of the present: 'were linked' (*sind . . . gekoppelt*), 'accounted for' (*machen . . . aus*), 'was divided' (*ist geteilt*). While it is clearly by no means the case that verb tenses are always neatly transferable from source text to target text, in the text under discussion there are no syntactic or semantic reasons for using a past tense in the English translation, since church tax was still in operation at the time of writing, as clearly indicated in the last sentence of the said paragraph, in which the results of a referendum on the issue are reported. Other native speaker students made the same set of tense errors. One possible explanation has to do with coherence, i.e. with the attempt to interpret the source text and its various parts as a whole. It seems that the frame has been set as 'past', since the first paragraph of the section translated describes the historical origin of church tax. The student then fails to perceive the shift to present circumstances, possibly because the changeover does not coincide with a paragraph break. No German-speaking students made such tense errors, suggesting that even explicit linguistic signals in the form of a tense change may be insufficient to trigger a reinterpretation in the *second* language, i.e. to counter the assumptions of a frame which has been previously set.

At a pragmatic level, student C's translation contains some interesting features which support the view that native speakers also need explicit training in target language genre conventions and style. First, C uses double exclamation marks in his heading: 'Church Tax to Stay!!', an unusual feature for a broadsheet newspaper and reminiscent of a more dramatic tabloid style. Secondly, C uses a footnote to add rather misleadingly presented information for the English readership, a convention which is not normally used in reportage, although it may occasionally occur in feature articles. Thirdly, the style of the footnote is more reminiscent of marketing language ('was created exclusively for') than journalistic prose dealing with fiscal and constitutional matters.

Most successful non-native speaker translations

The most successful non-native speaker translations, while lacking any evidence of source text misunderstandings, are characterised by a greater number of lexical errors of various kinds than are present in the native speaker translations. Cl, for instance, writes of 'legal public corporations' ('public corporations'), 'tax rates are coupled on both kinds of income tax' ('tax rates are linked to both kinds of income tax'), 'of all taxes to be paid' ('of all taxes to be levied'), 'Public opinion splits' ('Public opinion is split'). Student A has fewer errors of this kind, although there are a couple of odd collocations: 'Tax rates are linked to the income taxes forming eight or nine percent of the tax owing' ('Tax rates are linked to income tax accounting for 8% or 9% of the tax liability'); 'The attitude in public is divided' ('Public opinion is divided'). In contrast to most of the native speakers of English, both Cl and A understand the cohesive nature of the link between the first and second sentences of the extract set, but fail to express it naturally in English. Both use the expression: 'There it was said' (*Dort hieß es*), which is nevertheless comprehensible.

The most obvious and arguably only grammatical error made by Cl (and also A) in the English target text occurs in the last sentence of the text and is one of syntax, namely word order, in which transfer from German is evident:

> *Laut Hammerschmidt erhält der Staat für das 'Inkasso' durch die Finanzämter pro Jahr rund 500 Millionen Mark Gebühren.*

> According to Hammerschmidt, every year the State gets for collecting the tax through Tax Offices 800 [*sic*] million Marks of charges.

This error reflects the tendency in German to place direct objects as near the end of the clause as possible, whereas English prefers the post-verbal slot: 'According to Bishop Hammerschmidt, the state gets about 500 million marks every year for collecting the tax through its tax offices'. While the word order error might disturb the reader, it is not fatal: the sentence survives. Much more serious is the editing slip which allows the incorrect transcription of '500' as '800' to remain, an error which could, however, just as easily have been committed by a native speaker as by, as in this case, a non-native speaker.

One relatively minor orthographical error was noted for Cl and for A, both concerning the translation of the compound adjective and noun 'westdeutsche Bürger' ('west-Germans' and 'West-German citizens' respectively for 'West Germans').

Summary

In conclusion, we can say that the native speakers translations discussed are less fit for purpose in certain crucial respects than the successful non-native speaker translations. The results of the case study are summarised in Table 17.4.

The results suggest that competent non-native speaker student translators can outperform native speaker student translators in some respects, although neither group satisfactorily fulfilled the translation brief of producing a text suitable for publication in an English broadsheet newspaper. Possible explanations of the native speaker/non-native speaker differences should be approached with caution, given the limited nature of the data. However, a contributing factor may have been the fact that the two student translators with German as their mother tongue were training specifically to be translators, meaning that their translation competence is likely to have been more developed than those of the English-speaking students, whose curriculum was less specialised with regard to translation.

Table 17.4 Main characteristics of selected native speaker and selected non-native speaker translations

Unsuccessful native speaker translations	*Successful non-native speaker translations*
• are inefficiently proof-read	• are more efficiently proof-read on the whole
• seem focused on low-level translation units	• produce a coherent target text
• indicate misinterpretation of some source-text structures, i.e. some mistranslations	• do not indicate misinterpretation of source-text structures, i.e. no mistranslations
• show some lack of coherence suggesting the adoption of inappropriate frames	• coherent but sometimes lacking surface cohesive markers or using cohesive devices which are not target-like
• do not show evidence of relevant source-language cultural knowledge (or background research)	• show evidence of relevant source-language cultural knowledge
• show occasional target-language syntax error	• show occasional target-language syntax error
• demonstrate limited naturalness in parts	• contain unusual lexical choices, showing a lack of naturalness

Conclusion

We started this chapter by considering the issue of professionalism in relation to the direction of translation into or out of the mother tongue. The question was argued to be less straightforward than might at first appear, owing partly to the difficulties of defining the concept of 'native speaker' for a variety of social and economic reasons and partly to the range of competences required for successful translation. The case study data have shown that solutions produced in the selected competent non-native speaker student translations were informatively more reliable (with the exception of the number slip) than those produced in *some* native speaker translations, in this case, the weakest. Where the successful non-native speaker translations may have lacked a degree of naturalness (compared, for instance, to successful native speaker translations), the absence of mistranslations and the acceptable level of comprehensible English suggest that non-native speakers trained in translation may be perfectly competent translators in certain situations, particularly where the purpose of the task is to provide information only. It could reasonably be argued that the present data do not support a global proscription on the use of non-native speakers as professional translators, but rather that their work be subject to certain conditions. These would include subsequent revision by a native speaker translator (in my view, revision of the two successful non-native speaker translations by a competent native speaker translator would present fewer problems than revision of the chosen native speaker translations), or restriction to certain translation tasks such as translation for information purposes only. By contrast, fluent but inaccurate translations by native speaker translators can be counter-productive.

As far as translator education is concerned, the results of the present study support the provision of courses in translation out of the mother tongue in particular contexts and suggest that results for non-native speakers could be further improved by training in terminology research (see Adab, and Thelen in this volume).

For native speakers whose translations are unsatisfactory in the ways described in the present case study, proof-reading and mother tongue training could be beneficial. There is also a specific need for more source-language cultural and linguistic training, and for more practice in applying translation strategies so that apparent contradictions, inconsistencies or non sequiturs which emerge during translation can be identified, systematically pursued and hopefully resolved by conducting further background research and reanalysing the source text. A reorientation away from a sentence-focused approach to a text-based approach to translation through the study of text grammar on a contrastive basis would be one way of tackling problems of coherence and cohesion. Related to this is the change in perspective which has to occur when making the shift from proficiency-based translation, which is largely form-oriented, and in a sense contextless, focusing on accuracy of grammar and vocabulary, to translation as text creation. Learning to understand translation as an interaction between form and content is an important step towards developing translation competence in a professional context.

Note

1.   Newmark (1991: 21) attributes the term 'language of habitual use' to Anthony Crane.

References

Barbour, S. and Stevenson, P. (1990) *Variation in German*. Cambridge: Cambridge University Press.

Campbell, S. (1998) *Translation into the Second Language*. London & New York: Longman.

Cook, G. (1998) The Use of Translation in Language Teaching. In M. Baker (ed.) *Routledge Encyclopedia of Translation Studies* (pp. 117–20) London & New York: Routledge.

Kussmaul, P. (1995) *Training the Translator*. Amsterdam/Philadelphia: John Benjamins.

Mackenzie, R. (1998) The place of language teaching in a quality-oriented translator's training programme. In K. Malmkjær (ed.) (pp. 15–19).

Malmkjær, K. (ed.) (1998) *Translation and Language Teaching, Language Teaching and Translation*. Manchester: St Jerome.

McAlester, G. (1992) Teaching Translation into a Foreign Language – Status, Scope and Aims. In C. Dollerup and A. Loddegaard (eds) *Teaching Translation and Interpreting* (pp. 291–9) Amsterdam/Philadelphia: John Benjamins.

Neubert, A. (1985) *Text and Translation*. Leipzig: Verlag Enzyklopädie.

Newmark, P.P. (1988) *A Textbook of Translation*. New York: Prentice Hall.

Newmark, P.P. (1991) *About Translation*. Clevedon: Multilingual Matters.

Rogers, M. (2000) Translating as a professional occupation and its relevance for language teaching/learning. In M. Byram (ed.) *Routledge Encyclopedia of Language Teaching and Learning* (pp. 635–8). London & New York: Routledge.

Sewell, P. and Higgins, I. (eds) (1996) *Teaching Translation in Universities*. London: AFLS & CILT.

Appendix A: Source text (paragraphs 1 and 2 were translated in class; the remainder were set for homework)

['Die Kirchensteuer bleibt']

Regierungssprecher Vogel widerspricht Minister Blüm

BONN, 3. Januar (dpa/FR). Die Kirchensteuer, die von den staatlichen Finanzämter [sic] im Auftrag der Kirchen eingezogen wird und den beiden großen Kirchen derzeit jährlich je acht Milliarden Mark bringt, bleibt nach

Regierungsauffassung so, wie sie ist. Die Bundesregierung habe nicht die Absicht, an ihren Modalitäten etwas zu ändern, versicherte Regierungssprecher Dieter Vogel am Montag vor der Presse in Bonn. Er reagierte damit auf die von den Kirchen heftig kritisierten Äußerungen von Arbeitsminister Norbert Blüm (CDU), der gesagt hatte, das Kirchensteuersystem in Deutschland sei nicht so sicher, wie manche Bischöfe glaubten.

Vogel bewertete die Überlegungen Blüms, die dieser im Zusammenhang mit dem Streit um die Finanzierung der Pflegeversicherung und als Reaktion auf den Widerstand der Kirchen gegen die geplante Streichung von zwei Feiertagen gemacht hatte, als persönliche Meinung des Ministers. In der Bundesregierung sei über das Thema niemals beraten oder diskutiert worden. 'Da wird sich nichts ändern', betonte er. Der Sprecher der katholischen Deutschen Bischofskonferenz, Rudolf Hammerschmidt, verwies darauf, daß die Kirchensteuer grundgesetzlich verbrieft sei. Wer daran rütteln wolle, müsse das Grundgesetz ändern.

Die Kirchensteuer wurde in der Weimarer Verfassung von 1919 reichsrechtlich garantiert. Dort hieß es, Religionsgesellschaften, die Körperschaften des öffentlichen Rechts sind, seien berechtigt, aufgrund der bürgerlichen Steuerlisten nach Maßgabe der landesrechtlichen Bestimmungen Steuern zu erheben. 1949 wurden die Kirchenartikel der Weimarer Verfassung in das Grundgesetz, Artikel 140, übernommen. Die Steuer wird aufgrund von Kirchensteuergesetzen erhoben, die – basierend auf Verträgen mit den beiden großen Kirchen – von den Bundesländern erlassen werden.

Die Steuersätze sind an die Lohn- und Einkommensteuern gekoppelt und machen je nach Bundesland acht oder neun Prozent der Steuerschuld aus. Die Haltung in der Öffentlichkeit ist geteilt. Im Frühjahr 1992 plädierten 47 Prozent der westdeutschen Bürger für die Abschaffung der Kirchensteuer, 49 Prozent für deren Beibehaltung.

Laut Hammerschmidt erhält der Staat für das 'Inkasso' durch die Finanzämter pro Jahr rund 500 Millionen Mark Gebühren.

Frankfurter Rundschau 4 January 1994

Note: *The text has been reproduced with original errors.*

Appendix B: Target texts

Student M (native speaker of English)
['The Church Tax Is To Stay']
The church tax was guaranteed by empirial law in the 1919 constitution of the Weimar republic. There, it was in the form of religious societies which were legal bodies. These bodies had the right to raise taxes based on the civil tax lists as determined by the law of the province. In 1949 the church tax articles of the Weimar constitution became part of the basic law, article 140. The tax is levied due to the church tax laws which, based on contracts with the two big churches, are declared by the individual federal states.

The rate of the tax is set in conjunction with income tax and adds up to about eight or nine percent of the tax burden of each federal state. Public opinion is divided on the issue. In the Spring of 1992, 49 percent of west-germans were in favour of the tax whilst 47 percent called for its abolishon. According to Hammerschmidt the state recieves around 500 million Marks commission every year through its tax offices for collection of the tax.

Student C (native speaker of English)
[Church Tax to Stay!!]
As of 1919, the Church Tax was guaranteed legal status throughout the German Reich. That is to say, it was justifiable to levy taxes to raise revenue for religious societies, which are open to everyone and fulfil the stipulations of regional legal requirements, appearing on civil tax lists. In 1949, the Church article of the Weimar Constitution took affect as article 140 under the new German Basic Law.[1] The tax was levied according to the Church Tax Laws, which were based on agreements between the two largest churches and enacted upon by the Federal Länder (Regional Assemblies).

The tax rates were linked directly to the wage and income tax levels and according to the state accounted for 8 or 9% of the total tax collected in Germany. Public opinion about this tax was divided. In spring 1992, 47% of the population of West Germany argued for the abolition of the Church Tax system, whilst 49% fought for its continuance. According to Hammerschmidt the German government receives through the tax offices around 500 million Deutschmarks as a charge for the collection of the tax.

1. The Weimar constitution was abolished and a new constitution known as the Basic law was created exclusively for the Federal Republic of Germany.

Student CI (non-native speaker of English)
In 1919 church tax was guaranteed in the Constitution of Weimar according to the law of the (2nd) Reich. There it was said that religious societies, which were legal public corporations, were allowed to raise taxes on the basis of civil tax lists authorized in accordance with federal regulations. In 1949 the articles of the Constitution of Weimar concerning church tax were integrated into the new constitution, article 140. The tax is raised on the basis of church tax legislation based on contracts with both churches and enacted by the lander.

Tax rates are coupled on both kinds of income tax and represent, depending on each federal land, eight or nine percent of all taxes to be paid. Public opinion splits. In spring 1992 47 percent of all west-Germans plead for abolishing the church tax, 49% for keeping it.

According to Hammerschmidt, every year the State gets for collecting the tax through Tax Offices 800 million Marks of charges.

Student A (non-native speaker of English)
[Church tax to stay]
Church tax was legally guaranteed in the Weimar Constitution of 1919. There it was said that religious societies, which are public corporations, were entitled to levy taxes owing to the urban tax lists in accordance with the legal requirements of the Land. In 1949 the ecclesiastical articles of the Weimar Constitution were adopted in the Basic Law, article 140. Tax is levied because of laws concerning church taxes which are enacted by the federal states based on contracts with both big churches.

Tax rates are linked to the income taxes forming eight or nine percent of the tax owing depending on the federal state. The attitude in public is divided. In spring 1992 47% of West-German citizens pleaded for the abolition of church tax. 49 percent pleaded for its retention. According to Hammerschmidt the state receives by the collection through the tax offices about 500 million Deutschmark per year.

Chapter 18

À l'anglaise or the Invisible European

GUNILLA ANDERMAN

In order to reach English language audiences, the work of many European writers must be mediated by translation. More often than not, this process will not work to the advantage of the original writer:

> Compared to composers, poets are at a great disadvantage: their music does not cross linguistic frontiers. (Weightman, 1997)

As a result, anyone with the ambition of becoming a writer will have drawn the short straw if they happen to have been born in a smaller nation where a less widely used language is spoken. The dilemma of having to be translated in order to enter the world arena as a writer has been summed up by Joseph Skvorecky, Czech writer and translator: What would have happened, for instance to Mark Twain, Skvorecky asks, if his mother tongue had not been English, if he had been born in Bohemia instead of the US? (see Anderman, 1988). Unlike Mark Twain, American writer of world repute whose stories can be enjoyed in translation in a number of different languages, the course of the international career of his European counterpart would to a large extent have been determined by the availability and skill of translators.

The fate of Skvorecky's hypothetical Czech writer is by no means unique. While in many countries in Europe high value is placed on literary works written in English and new novels by established English-speaking writers appear in translation within months of their publication, the status of European literature in English translation is considerably less exalted.

In a study of the critical responses to books in English translation from another, little known European language, Ria Vanderauwera has shown reviews of translated books from Dutch to be disappointingly short, with scant information about the original author and source literature often safely copied from the publisher's blurb. Instead, the great masters of the Low Countries, such as Dutch and Flemish painters, showed a tendency to find their way into review articles. In one case, the protagonist in a Dutch novel reviewed is described as (1985: 131):

. . . a hapless fellow . . . tenderly delineated by the author . . . a self portrait, as realistic as one of Rembrandt's . . .

Soon the reviewer also finds occasion to allude to another, well known Dutch painter:

. . . the dark forces of life . . . are important for the writer, who creates surrealistic passages that remind us of Breughel.

For many English-speaking readers the knowledge of Dutch painters of the past is superior to that of present-day art and literature in The Netherlands. The work of Dutch writers, however, is only available to the outside world through translation, and the number of translators with a knowledge of Dutch who are able to reflect accurately in English the style and content of the original literary work is likely to be few and far between. In addition, there is the comparatively much greater number of novelists and dramatists who, in recording their experiences directly in English, offer fierce competition in vying for the attention of potential buyers in the bookshops in English-speaking countries.

Vanderauwera's findings relating to the English reception of Dutch literature in English translation also hold true of many other writers who are speakers of one of the little known languages in Europe. Still, while limited knowledge of the culture or social structure of the country where a literary work originates may account for some of the reluctance to accept 'foreign imports' in translation into English, there are other factors pointing to a situation of greater complexity than a simple lack of familiarity with different cultures and societies. The resistance to foreign works in translation is not confined to the literature of smaller European nations; the German-speaking countries play a sufficiently important part in Europe for an English-reading public to have easy access to information about German and Austrian culture and social customs enabling a novel or a play to travel in translation. Nevertheless, the plays of German playwright Bertolt Brecht do not sit comfortably in translation with many British actors (Anderman, 2004). And, although the Vienna of the *fin de siècle* is not unfamiliar to the English-speaking world, British playwright David Hare nevertheless preferred to set *The Blue Room*, his version of Arthur Schnitzler's *Reigen*, or *La Ronde*, in an unspecified English-speaking metropolis. Thus, English 'literary colonialism', the grudging acceptance of foreign 'imports' in English translation, seems to befall work written in well known as well as little used European languages. A look at the situation in reverse – at what happens when English literature is translated into other European languages – will highlight the asymmetry even further.

English Literature in Translation

One of the Royal Shakespeare Company's most successful plays of the early 1980s, later turned into a full feature film version, was *Educating Rita*. British playwright Willy Russell's play about Rita, the Liverpool hairdresser who enrols at the Open University to read English and American literature, has been translated into a large number of languages. During her tutorials with Frank, her tutor, Rita discusses a number of the books on her prescribed reading list, which features many of the classic works of Anglo-American literature. Figuring prominently in their discussions is E.M. Forster's *Howard's End*, a work frequently referred to in a number of different contexts throughout the play. While, in translation into English, the frequent allusion to a European writer whose work is unfamiliar to theatre audiences might cause problems of comprehension, such is the awareness of English language and English literature globally that in some countries the use of the title of Forster's novel could be retained in English without translation (see Anderman, 1988). Further reinforcement of the worldwide awareness of literary works in English is provided by the film industry. For those unfamiliar with E.M. Forster's novel, the release of the Merchant Ivory screen version of *Howard's End* brought additional increased familiarity with the English writer's work.

The advantages of a writer being born into an English-speaking community are clearly more than of a purely linguistic nature. At the present moment, English is not only the language of global communication but also the language of a leading literary tradition. As a result, for a literary work to be fully accepted in translation into English, more often than not it needs to conform to the postulates of prevailing Anglo-American poetic norms in addition to meeting necessary linguistic requirements. Fiction or drama written in a markedly different literary tradition are noticeably less likely to be accepted in English translation, a fact that may help to explain the frequently raised eyebrows in the English-speaking world at the choice of the annual recipient of the Nobel Prize for Literature, a decision arrived at by a committee of speakers of a little known European language, long accustomed to translated literature written in accordance with a variety of poetic norms. The willing acceptance of literature in translation shown by the Swedish Nobel Prize Committee is indicative of a country where translated literature holds a primary position.

Within a national literary system, literature in translation may hold different positions; it can hold either a primary or a secondary position:

> We have no choice but to admit that within a group of relatable national literatures, such as the literatures of Europe, hierarchical relations are soon established, with the result that within this macro-polysystem some literatures take more peripheral positions. (Even-Zohar, 1978: 121)

Even-Zohar points out that while what he calls 'stronger' literatures, with long established positions, have the choice of adopting novelties such as literary works in translation, literatures with less strong traditions often depend more heavily on imports in the form of literature in translation. As an example, Even-Zohar mentions the situation of French literature, which he describes as much more rigid than many other systems. This, combined with the long, traditional central position of French literature within a European context, has resulted in literary works translated into French assuming a clear secondary position. The situation with respect to Anglo-American literature is rather similar, Even-Zohar points out, while the Russian, German and Scandinavian literary systems seem to show different patterns of behaviour (Even-Zohar, 1978: 124; see also the contribution by Rollason in this volume which relates the presence of Anglicisms in French to the currently 'weaker' position of French vis-à-vis English).

Even-Zohar's observation, that in languages with 'strong' literary traditions, translated literature is bound to hold a secondary position, leads to a further consequence. Because of the implicit requirement in countries with 'strong' literary traditions that foreign literature conform to already existing poetic norms, literary works in translation into English are usually required to be target-language oriented. In the case of literary works translated into the languages of smaller nations where translated literature plays a primary role, on the other hand, the literary tradition of the language of the original work is more easily acknowledged. This in turn makes the translation more likely to be source-language oriented, showing more clearly the roots of the country of origin of the literary work. Expressed in different terms, the text itself may be said to hold priority over its readers, which in the case of translation from a leading language such as English presents few problems to European readers steeped in Anglo-American culture. If, however, this approach is used in translation from other European languages into English, translated literature becomes the exclusive prerogative of a cultural and educated elite. Summed up, the two approaches have been described as: 'Either the translator leaves the author in peace as much as possible and moves the reader towards him; or he leaves the reader in peace as much as possible, and moves the author towards him' (Lefevere, 1977: 41).

In more recently used terminology, the choice has been viewed as that between a 'domesticating' and a 'foreignising' approach (see Venuti, 1995). In the case of translation out of English into other less well-known European languages, familiarity with Anglo-American culture and society makes possible an approach where the author is left in peace as far as possible and the reader is moved towards him/her. In contrast, when translating in the other direction, an English-speaking readership is more likely to want to be left in peace and have the foreign author moved within closer proximity of their own experience. This preference, which has perhaps most clearly manifested itself in the need for adaptations, rewrites and new versions of European plays for performance on the London stage, is, however, not a unique prerogative of speakers of English. When in the past, the position now held by the English language and the Anglo-American literary tradition was occupied by French and Gallic culture, literature in translation from other languages was subjected to similar constraints including the work by English writers imported from across the Channel.

The Hegemony of Prevailing Literary Traditions

The period of time that France ruled as the leading political and literary power in Europe amply illustrates the fate of works in translation into a language holding the position of a prevailing literary tradition. In order to conform to the strict French requirements of neoclassicism, the eighteenth century saw large-scale rewritings of Shakespeare's plays as part of the translation process. For the first stage production, in 1769, of Ducis's translation of *Hamlet* for the Comedie Française, Ducis altered and rearranged the plot, cut down the list of players and the relationships between the main characters. The action solely took place in Elsinore, within a 24-hour period. The sub-plots of the original, the play within the play, the death of Ophelia, the gravediggers' scene, and Hamlet's 'Alas poor Yorick' meditation, were all discarded in order to ensure that the unities of time, place, and action were observed. In Ducis's translation, Shakespeare was 'naturalised'; it is what Shakespeare would have written had he been a contemporary and compatriot of Racine. It was the French saying to themselves 'Ah yes, if only he had been French' (Heylen, 1993: 28–30). A similar fate seems to have befallen *Julius Caesar* in translation by Voltaire, who omitted two and a half acts of the play in order to ensure that it ended with Caesar's death and not with the later course of events related to Brutus and the other conspirators (van den Broeck, 1988: 61).

Primary Position of Translated Literature in English

The nineteenth century saw continued French literary and cultural dominance in Europe. In England, French influence in the theatre peaked in the period 1850–70 to the extent that *Ours*, the title of a play by T.W. Robertson, an English playwright of gently satirical comedies, was systematically referred to in the press as *L'Ours* (Hale, 2000: 220–4).

An important reason for the dearth of original works written for the English stage in the nineteenth century can be related to the less than auspicious financial conditions for English playwrights. For a one-act farce, the going rate was ten shillings a night, while comic pieces in two or three acts brought the playwright ten shillings per act per night; provincial rates were even lower. Not surprisingly a number of writers found it an easier and more attractive solution to simply turn the latest popular play lauded on the Parisian stage into an English-speaking version. With English playwrights keeping an eager eye on the outpouring of success-ful plays on the other side of the Channel, it was not unusual for an orig-inal French play to give rise to more than one version or adaptation. In the case of, for instance, *Les Pauvres de Paris*, by Eduard Brissebare and Eugene Nus, there appear to have been as many as four English-speaking versions (Hale, 2000: 226). In fact, it was not uncommon for the complete oeuvre of some British playwrights at the time to consist almost exclu-sively of adaptations of French plays. The influence of French theatre during the Victorian period was lasting, owing its origin to Eugene Scribe (1791–1861), the most popular playwright of the nineteenth century whose work appeared in translation throughout Europe and remained in vogue for nearly half a century. Scribe restructured French drama and, while freeing it from the sterility of neoclassic theory, moved it toward a concept of living theatre still practised today. Through Scribe, with almost 400 plays to his name but whose total output may never be known because of his frequent use of pseudonyms, French theatre dominated European drama. Scribe also had some legal training, which enabled him to introduce contractual changes ensuring that playwrights as well as theatre managers benefited financially from the success of their creative efforts. As a result, playwriting became remunerative, generating a keen interest among aspiring French writers to write for the stage.

While the middle of the nineteenth century saw French playwriting holding a 'strong' position in relation to other European traditions, English playwrights enjoyed less favourable working conditions, one of the reasons for the 'weaker' position held by the English drama tradition. As a result, translation in England at the time assumed a primary position and the import of translated French plays was an ongoing process, leading to a lasting influence on the development of English drama. Through translating and adapting the French *pièce bien faite*, 'the well-made play', playwrights of the Victorian period acquired the technique of plot construction, learning to put down on the page what was likely to work on the stage. Overall, the effect of the assimilation of French litera-ture during the nineteenth century has been viewed as setting English literature on the course in which it was later to develop (Hale, 2000: 234–6).

As the external circumstances which had been instrumental in creating the power relation between the French and the English playwriting system changed, so did the unrestrained influx of French plays in English translation and adaptation on the London stage. New copyright legisla-tion and an improvement in the remuneration of English playwrights both contributed towards British writers looking with renewed interest to writing for the stage. Following the Berne Convention of 1866, international copyright law provided protection of the property of playwrights for a period of 50 years following their death. Writing in 1900, Sutherland Edwards comments on the new working conditions that make 'every novelist desire [. . .] as in France, to present his work on stage'.

By this point in time, however, change had long been in the air. The latter part of the nineteenth century saw the writer turned into a detached observer of the processes of society in a role designed to match that of the scientist. As a reaction to the wit and *esprit* of earlier French writing, the subjects being aired by the new school of naturalist writers from across the Channel took Victorian England by shocked surprise, resulting in an initial, strong reaction to the new literary imports in translation. In 1888, the publisher Henry Vizetelly was convicted and fined £100 for the publication of Zola's *La Terre* in English translation and the following year, having renewed their efforts, the Vigilance Association managed to haul Vizetelly into court again, this time for publishing Flaubert, Bourget and Maupassant, which resulted in a sentence of three months' imprisonment. Other controversial literary events followed; on 7 June 1889, a performance of *A Doll's House* by Henrik Ibsen was staged at the small Novelty Theatre in Great Queen Street in London, marking the first significant outburst of Ibsen-mania. This staging of *A Doll's House* shows the first sign of a grudging acceptance of foreign imports on the English stage different in kind from the previous customary French lightweight fare in varying degrees of adaptation. When Ibsen's play arrived in England, mainland Europe had taken up for debate the issue of women's rights to self-fulfilment, now aired on stage in *A Doll's House*. From this moment in time, continuing until 1897 when *John Gabriel Borkman* was staged by the New Century Theatre, the production of Ibsen's plays was to constitute the single most important influence leading away from French-influenced popular plays to the Shavian theatre of the early twentieth century. English drama was set on its course, the start of a development from a 'weak' into a 'strong' tradition, gradually freeing itself from the shackles of the previous supremacy of the French reign.

Twentieth Century Literary and Linguistic Hegemony

The end of World War II saw the beginning of a gradual transition of power from French language and culture to English and American mass culture. Still, traces of the historically firmly rooted Gallic 'imperiousness' vis-à-vis foreign literature in translation resurfaced as late as the 1960s. Published by Hachette, the three books about Pippi Longstocking by Swedish writer Astrid Lindgren appeared in French translation during that decade. The first of the three books appeared in Swedish in 1945, the year that saw the introduction of children's laws that legislated against corporal punishment in Sweden. The freckle-faced, ginger-haired protagonist lives all on her own except for the company of her horse and her monkey. No evil, however, befalls Pippi because of her enormous strength, which enables her to ward off any attempt at interference from representatives of the adult world. When translated into French, however, Pippi (as Fifi) appeared in two, rather than three volumes. Overall, changes to the original seem to have resulted from attempts to modify the anti-authoritarian behaviour of Astrid Lindgren's young heroine in order to make her fit more easily into the prevailing norms of a French adult world and, it would appear, into more conventional and authoritarian attitudes towards child rearing and children's literature.

The French translator seems to have been most inclined to cut when 'Fifi's' behaviour towards adults threatened their authority or presented them in an undignified light (Heldner, 1993). As a result, a chapter where Pippi engages in a game of 'tag' with two policemen, showing French representatives of law and order in a less than flattering light, was omitted altogether. Another chapter, where Pippi is the guest at a coffee party and, in spite of valiant efforts, does not succeed in behaving 'properly' and fails to comply with the rules of social etiquette, similarly disappeared. Evidence that the changes in translation into French were not solely motivated by the need for an abridged publication seems irrefutable in that additions also succeeded in finding their way into the French version. For instance, when the source text does not show Fifi to be sufficiently remorseful because of some misdemeanour, as when she answers the teacher back, the translator springs into action with an appropriately apologetic addition: ' "Don't be angry", Fifi begged her. "I'm sorry I made you unhappy. I'm insufferable but, you see, when you live all on your own you get to be a bit different from others" ' (discussed in Heldner, 1993: 57–61).

Perhaps most telling is the publisher's decision to question Pippi's strength, her most powerful weapon. As a result, French Fifi is not allowed to pick up and carry her horse which instead is replaced by a pony. French children, it was explained, who had been through a world war would be too realistic to be taken in by a horse but might accept a pony! (Stolt, 1978: 135)

It is, however, not only social and cultural aspects of Astrid Lindgren's original that emerged transformed in French translation, changes also occurred of a more linguistic nature. Given the problems facing the translator trying to transfer non-standard speech into French, it is perhaps not surprising to find French Fifi's language bereft of the highly personal mixture of idiolect and sociolect characterising the original. In translation between English and French, the problems of dialect translation have now been more widely documented. In 'Scottish horses and Montreal trains: The translation of vernacular to vernacular', Martin Bowman reports on the project of staging a dramatised version of *Trainspotting* in French-speaking Canada. Standard French being too elevated a linguistic variety for the dramatisation of Irwin Welsh's novel, the target language vernacular chosen for the translation was 'joual', a regional dialect of Montreal (Bowman, 2000). In translation into French, sociolectal works tend to run into a roadblock created not by an inherent deficiency in the French linguistic system but rather by the linguistic void within its literary normative system (Brisset, 1989: 19). This has also resulted in difficulties in translating into the French spoken in France the European canon, including the works by Brecht and Strindberg, which require the use of dialects or less elevated forms of standard language. As in the case of the translation of *Trainspotting*, Brisset points to the use of a more proletarian vernacular such as the French of Quebec as a solution to the problem, which allows the translator a wider range of linguistic possibilities.

In its present role as European *lingua franca* and the upholder of a long established literary tradition, English, in its different forms across the world, would seem to safeguard against the threat of an overemphasis on correctness and prescriptiveness. Instead, a greater danger may be the threat of a recurrence of the attitude to 'the other' as expressed in 1851 by Fitzgerald, writing during the heyday of British colonial power:

> It is an amusement to me to take what liberties I like with these Persians, who (as I think) are not poets enough to frighten one from such excursions, and who really want a little art to shape them. (Quoted in Bassnett, 1991: 3)

The Might of Global English

It has been suggested that the ascent of the English language to its present omnipotent position is at least partly the result of its hybrid nature, its unique linguistic history that for long has entailed borrowing freely from other languages, allowing a development unrestrained by forces attempting to safeguard its purity. More uncompromising and less open-minded is the concern with adherence to the poetic norms in operation within the trendsetting Anglo-American literary tradition. More recently, however, doubts have been expressed about the continued influence of the literary voice of America (Burn, 2003). Arguably the first major novel written in American rather than in English, with its juxtaposition of vulgar slang and high style, was written now over fifty years ago. Saul Bellow, the author of *The Adventures of Augie March*, started work on his third novel while on a Guggenheim scholarship in Paris in 1948. Bellow hated Paris, but the more he detested France, the more he loved America. And as an expatriate living in Europe it was the common American vernacular that Bellow felt desperate to recreate in writing. Rebelling against what he saw, Bellow created a voice for where he wanted to be. At the present time, however, around half a century later, 'the fast-talking, high-energy, American novel that has dominated English literature seems stale and wearisome' (Burn, 2003). Not impervious to domestic and external events, literary traditions come and go. Is it the increasing isolationism, the way a deeply entrenched America now positions itself in relation to the rest of the world, in many ways the result of recent events, that has made the 'voice that the history of the last half-century has been told in, all of a sudden sound so pale, so stale, and grating'? (Burn, 2003)

Recent London theatre productions point to a similar void in the English drama system, as manifested in the number of European classics in translation or new versions in the commercial theatre sector. The theatre season of 2003 saw productions of August Strindberg's *Dance of Death* and *After Miss Julie*, Patrick Marber's English reworking of *Miss Julie*, Henrik Ibsen's *The Lady from the Sea* and *Brand*, Luigi Pirandello's *Absolutely (Perhaps)* as well as *Three Sisters* by Anton Chekhov at the National Theatre. Suddenly, European playwrights, whose work was previously more frequently associated with the non-commercial theatre sector, were making their appearance in the West End.

> So often a blessing can become a curse if it stifles curiosity. (Tonkin, 1997)

At this point in time, looking to Europe could be the means of providing a 'strong' literary system with the injection of energy that might be needed in order to safeguard the strength and continued supremacy of the position now held by Anglo-American language and literature.

Special note

Some of the issues discussed here are also mentioned in Anderman, G. (1999) European literature in translation: A price to pay? In D. Graddol and U.Meinhof (eds) *English in a Changing World. Aila Review* 13.

References

Anderman, G. (1988) Translation or version: some observations on translating drama. In G. Anderman and M. Rogers (eds) *Translation in Teaching and for Professional Purposes*. Proceedings of the BAAL Conference held at the Centre for Translation Studies, University of Surrey, 1986, II, 69–81.

Anderman, G. (2004) *Europe on Stage: Translation and Theatre*. London: Oberon Books.

Bassnett, S. (1991) *Translation Studies* (revised edition). London: Routledge.

Bowman, M. (2000) Scottish horses and Montreal trains: The translation of vernacular to vernacular. In C.A. Upton (ed.) *Moving Target* (pp. 25–33). Manchester: St Jerome Press.

Brisset, A. (1989) In search of a Target Language: The politics of theatre translation in Quebec. *Target* 1(1), 9–27.

Burn, G. (2003) After the Flood. *Guardian Review* 15 November.

Even-Zohar, I. (1978) The position of translated literature within the literary polysystem. In J.S. Holmes, J. Lambert and R. Van den Broeck (eds) *Literature and Translation. New perspectives in literary studies* (pp. 117-27) Louvain: Acco.

Hale, T. (2000) The imaginery quay from Waterloo Bridge to London Bridge: Translation, adaptation and genre. In M. Salama-Carr (ed.) *Translating French Literature and Film II* (pp. 219–38) Amsterdam: Rodopi.

Heldner, C. (1993) Pippi Långstrumps äventyr i Frankrike. *Opsis Kalopsis* 3, 57–61.

Heylen, R. (1993) *Translation, Poetics, and the Stage. Six French Hamlets.* London: Routledge.

Lefevere. A. (ed. and trans.) (1977) *Translating Literature: The German Tradition From Luther to Rosenzweig.* Assen and Amsterdam: van Gorcum.

Skvorecky, J. (1985) A translator spills the beans. *New York Times Book Review*, 17 May.

Stolt, B. (1978) How Emil becomes Michel – on the translation of children's books. In G. Klingberg, M. Ørvig and S. Amor (eds) *Children's Books in Translation. The situation and the problems* (pp. 130–46) Stockholm: Almqvist and Wiksell International.

Sutherland Edwards, H. (1900) *Personal Recollections.* London: Cassel and Company.

Tonkin, B. (1997) *Independent Saturday Magazine*, 1 November.

Van den Broeck, R. (1988) Translating for the theatre. In J.T. Ydstie (ed.) *Festschrift for Patrick Chaffey on His 50th Birthday* (pp. 54–68) Oslo: University of Oslo.

Vanderauwera, R. (1985) *Dutch Novels Translated into English: The Transformation of a 'Minority' Literature.* Amsterdam: Rodopi.

Venuti, L. (1995) *The Translator's Invisibility.* London: Routledge.

Weightman, J. (1997) The huge ego of Victor Hugo. *Sunday Telegraph*, 26 October.

Chapter 19

Intercultural Dialogue: The Challenge of Communicating Across Language Boundaries

ANNE IFE

Introduction

When a significant proportion of the world's population functions on a daily basis in a language that is not its mother tongue, this inevitably has implications both for those involved and for any outcomes of their inter-actions. Successful communication across cultures requires more than mastery of the basics of language learning, as represented by the learning of words and grammar, as well as the development of a good accent: the challenge does not stop there. The specific focus of this contribution deals with what it means to communicate across cultural boundaries in a second language, and what the implications are, both for those who need to use a second language and those mother tongue speakers who have dealings with second language speakers. It further examines some of the consequences for communication when both parties are using a second language or, as it is often called in this context, 'a *lingua franca*' or 'language of wider communication': in other words, a language used as a common language by speakers whose mother tongue it is not. Our focus here will be English, but it should be borne in mind that, in specific contexts, any language can be used as a *lingua franca*[1] if it is a shared tongue in which a group of people choose to communicate. The chapter considers what is known of the specific characteristics of communication in such contexts. Finally, we conclude by reflecting on the roles and responsibilities of the various participants in cross-cultural communication, and on the role language teachers and other educators have to play in ensuring that cross-cultural communication is as effective as possible.

Communication between mother tongue and second language

When using a second language the first priority is of course *intelligible* communication: little meaningful interaction will occur unless speakers master to a reasonable degree of proficiency the syntax and vocabulary and the phonetic system of the second language. However, once we begin to communicate in a second language new challenges arise of which, as speakers, we may be only dimly aware or completely unaware. When functioning as second-language speakers, or as participants in second language interactions, we may sometimes transfer elements of our own language, or expectations from our own mother tongue, that we are not conscious of. This can lead to our being perceived by others in ways that might surprise us. On occasions this can contribute to wrong impressions being formed and even to ill-feeling or misunderstanding or a failure to get on with another person and can ultimately lead to national stereotyping. Because of this there is a need, in the cross-cultural or intercultural context, for heightened language awareness. It should be stressed, though, that this is needed on both sides, whether participants are speaking their mother tongue (as English mother tongue speakers often are) or whether they are speaking a second language, and whether they are involved in mixed mother tongue/second language conversations or *lingua franca* (second-language only) conversations.

One aspect of linguistic competence that may be transferred is pragmatic competence, the dimension of language knowledge that leads to language being used appropriately in different contexts and that allows us to understand the true force of the words we hear spoken (Grundy 1994, Yule, 1996). Native speakers of a language know, without necessarily being aware of it, that language is not just the literal sum of the words spoken – we know *how* to say things to convey a particular meaning and to achieve a particular response. Adult mother tongue speakers in their own cultural context have, in Yule's words, knowledge of 'how more gets communicated than is said' (Yule, 1996: 3). Moreover, they have an understanding of what it is appropriate to say and to whom, and indeed how it is appropriate to speak to a particular individual.

Pragmatic competence has received considerable attention in the cross-cultural context as awareness has grown that different cultures have different pragmatic norms and that transferring the norms of the mother tongue into the second language could lead to misunderstandings. Thomas (1983) suggested that problems could arise on two fronts. She predicted that 'pragmalinguistic failure' would occur when speakers transfer the rules for the linguistic formulation of utterances from their mother tongue into the second language, while 'sociopragmatic failure' would occur when speakers have 'cross-culturally different perceptions of what constitutes appropriate linguistic behaviour' (Thomas, 1983: 99). As an example of 'pragmalinguistic failure' Thomas (1983: 101) cites the example of Russian students who, when asked 'Would you like to read?', responded 'No, I wouldn't' because they did not understand that this apparent request about their preferences in English has the pragmatic force of an instruction to act and expects compliance. An unaware mother tongue listener might interpret the reply as unco-operative and deliberately obstructive. Conversely, Thomas notes (1983: 102) that Russian speakers would typically ask directions by using a direct command form – the equivalent of 'Tell me how to get to . . .' rather than as in English 'Excuse me, please, could you tell me how to get to . . .'. 'Sociopragmatic failure', on the other hand, would involve using inappropriate linguistic behaviour in a specific context because of a failure to recognise different social norms. This could include, for instance, being over-deferential to a person who does not command such respect in the target culture (or vice versa); or speaking openly about a topic that in the target culture is taboo or semi-taboo (sex, death, money, etc.). Sociopragmatic competence is closely tied with social and cultural behavioural norms and with an individual's identity and may, in Thomas's view, be more resistant to modification than pragmalinguistic competence. Indeed, she suggests that it is not the role of a teacher to correct any sociopragmatic failure since it is 'a reflection of the student's system of values and beliefs, and should not be "corrected", but only pointed out and discussed' (1983: 109).

Central to the notion of pragmatic competence are speech acts such as requests, apologies, complaints and compliments, which are crucial in interpersonal communication. There are, in all languages, conventions about how to formulate speech acts and these appear to vary from language to language. By way of example, in some languages it is perfectly normal to use a command form to ask another to do something while other languages prefer more indirect formulations. On the other hand, too much couching of a request in moderating phrases could in some languages seem peculiar and even over-deferential. As a consequence, if second-language speakers take their own mother tongue pragmatic norms and carry them into another language, there is a danger that they may at times be misunderstood or misperceived because they give an impression other than the one they intend. A number of studies have explored speech acts such as complaints, requests and apologies in cross-cultural contexts, several of them reviewed by Anderman (1992) in her discussion of the need for pragmatic awareness in the successful translation of drama texts (see also, for example, Blum-Kulka & Olshtain, 1984; House & Kasper, 1978; Kasper & Blum-Kulka, 1993).

From the studies reviewed, Anderman concludes that, in comparison with other European languages, English is more indirect. The English way of couching requests, for instance, is often oblique and indirect with much use of so called *softeners* or *downgraders* (for a full analysis, see Blum-Kulka & Olshtain, 1984). The function of phrases like 'would you mind' 'would you like to' and 'would you do me a favour' is precisely to soften the force of the fact that the speaker wants someone else to do something for him/her. What the speaker is doing is preserving the 'face needs' of the hearer by trying not to appear as if (s)he is imposing his/her will on the addressee and thus denying the addressee's right to independence (on face-threatening acts see Brown & Levinson, 1987: 61–8). Languages may vary in the emphasis they place on either negative or positive face needs, but English native speakers appear to rate negative face needs high, leading to a form of politeness that reflects a wish not to impose on others. When this is carried over into contexts where more explicit instructions are expected, it can lead to strange perceptions by others.

Béal (1998) demonstrates this vividly through a detailed linguistic study of the contact between Australian English native speakers and a group of French second language English speakers who went to work for a time in an Australian company. She observed their interaction over a long period and discovered that the two groups were developing particular perceptions of each other, in part because of the way they used language. The Australians, she found, when giving instructions in the workplace, used lots of 'softeners' of the kind discussed above in relation to British English. The French, however, had other expectations deriving from their mother tongue, both from the way requests tend to be formulated in French (pragmalinguistic norms) and because of the different sociopragmatic norms in French. The French expected from their managers more direct instructions and found the Australians' oblique question-type requests, together with the use of the addressee's name and other downgraders, rather indecisive and unauthoritative. Among examples of language used to an employee, the following is not untypical: 'Can you just give Barbara a bit of a hand on sorting the memory on that machine? You wouldn't mind?' (Béal, 1998: 12), where words and phrases show the inserted 'softeners' used to mitigate the impact of the request. The Australians, on the other hand, found some of the directness transferred from French into English (including requests in the form of direct commands) rather bossy: 'No, no! I want an explanation before.' Because of their own sociopragmatic norms, the French workers openly expressed negative feelings about, for example, a task in hand: the Australian workers were said to be disconcerted by this (for them) unusual show of negative feeling (Béal, 1998: 18).

Obviously, speakers who achieve a high level of proficiency in a second language begin to understand the way the pragmatic dimension works in that language, but it requires sophisticated linguistic knowledge and in-depth cultural awareness, and not all cross-cultural exchanges take place between highly proficient second language speakers. It is also the case that not all mother tongue speakers are language aware, and they may not realise that a second-language speaker is not, for instance, being intentionally rude but simply carrying over pragmatic norms from his or her own mother tongue. To give a simple example: second-language

English speakers often do not say 'please' and 'thank you' when using English because it is not the norm in their mother tongue to use such expressions with such frequency as they are used in English. Indeed, there may not even be equivalent terms. English native speakers can react badly to this omission because they simply do not know the norms of the second-language speaker's own mother tongue. Conversely, when English speakers transfer their 'please' and 'thank you' into other languages, they may be perceived as too deferential or insincere. English learners of Spanish are often warned not to overuse *por favor* and *gracias* in Spanish, but actually putting this into practice can require a psychological adjustment that does not come easily. Equally, if a French or Spanish speaker is offered food in an English-speaking home they may refuse by saying 'thank you', thereby transferring mother tongue norms. They may find, however, that their host/hostess in fact thinks they have accepted what is offered because that is what it means to respond with 'thank you' in such a context in English.

Differences of the type outlined above reflect only a fraction of the many ways in which languages can differ. Diverging expectations deriving from mother tongue norms cover all areas of interpersonal communication, including all (potentially face-threatening) speech acts, such as requesting, apologising, complaining, disagreeing, accepting, refusing, expressing gratitude, paying and receiving compliments. The pragmatic dimension covers the management of conversation and interaction, including when to talk and when to be silent: Finnish culture famously permits much longer silences than do other cultures, while Spanish culture (and perhaps other Mediterranean cultures) are uncomfortable with long silences. It involves when to interrupt, how to interrupt, how to change topic, and how to begin and end not just a whole conversation but also conversational turns. Béal (1998: 19) cites the example of French speakers who often start a conversational turn in French with *Mais*, which is unexceptional in the French context, but transposed into English by 'But' it can sound aggressive and confrontational, as if the speaker is about to disagree with, or contradict, their conversational partner. The unspoken conversational rules of English would suggest a more gentle, less contrastive word, such as 'Well' or, if the desire is to make a counterpoint, to introduce it gently as in 'I'm not sure about that', or 'You may be right but'.

The very substance of conversation in terms of what it is safe or acceptable to talk about (personal circumstances? death? money? etc.) may also vary from culture to culture, as may what is expected of both listeners and speakers by way of bodily behaviour. This can be a question of how close to each other conversants are expected to stand or sit, or a question of eye contact: while some cultures expect a steady gaze from a listener to show attention, others do not. The latter example is cited by Tannen (1984: 192), who offers a more detailed review of some of the areas of cross-cultural difference mentioned above.

We have confined our discussion thus far to mixed mother tongue/ second language conversations. Before considering what might be done to facilitate understanding across language boundaries by averting some of these potential points of conflict, we should consider the issue of what happens when neither speaker knows the language of the other – a situation increasingly found in the world today as vast numbers of people communicate in English as a *lingua franca* (Graddol, 1999).

The lingua franca context

When both or all speakers in an interaction are second language speakers, then two or more sets of linguistic norms make contact and it is possible or even likely that neither speaker knows the other's language or culture. It could be argued that the situation is here more equal, in that neither person is an authority on the language being used. This certainly ties in with research results that suggest that second-language speakers are more at ease if no native speakers are present (House, 2002a; Meierkord, 2000). It ties in also with informal comments made by international students who suggest that *lingua franca* conversations feel more comfortable, and are more supportive, since second-language speakers can help each other out in ways that are not so feasible with mother tongue speakers present. This is especially true if they feel some sort of cultural kinship that lets them understand where others are 'coming from' in terms of attitude towards linguistic interaction. In my own context, Greek students have said this about their Spanish peers, for instance.

Nonetheless, whenever we use language we have pragmatic expectations deriving from our mother tongue, so it would seem that the chances of misunderstanding in *lingua franca* conversations are much greater and perhaps more likely than in mother tongue/second-language ones. Research into this area is beginning to grow (see, for example, Knapp & Meierkord, 2002) – although it is revealing that it is mostly second-language English speakers, who themselves frequently function in *lingua franca* contexts, who see the greatest need for this, rather than mother tongue speakers of English. House (2002b: 247), based in Germany, speaks of 'large-scale neglect' of *lingua franca* interaction by the research community and urges more research to be undertaken for a real understanding of how English is being used in the global sphere. Seidlhofer (2002: 198–217) similarly argues for the need to study in detail the nature of the language being used in English *lingua franca* conversations and is engaged in a research project to collect a corpus of samples of English in use in this context.

As regards the increased potential for misunderstanding in *lingua franca* interaction, where neither side knows the pragmatic norms of the other, both House (2002a) and Meierkord (2000) have conducted empirical studies. Contrary to expectations, early research has suggested that misunderstanding among *lingua franca* speakers is not as great as supposed, and probably less significant than that observed between mother tongue and second-language speakers (House, 2002b: 260), although Seidlhofer (2002: 211) cites metaphorical language use and use of idiom as (not surprisingly) aspects of language that cause problems between speakers using English as second language.

On the other hand, it often seems that the level of communication achieved is not great either, as both House (2002a) and Meierkord (2000) have demonstrated, and conversations may sometimes operate to the lowest common denominator when it becomes apparent that one or more participants have comprehension difficulties. This suggests that *lingua franca* speakers do appear, as suggested above, to be mutually supportive of each other, keen not to highlight an individual's lack of comprehension and sensitive to their face needs. Thus many conversations continue even when it is evident that one person has not really understood the other, perhaps by ignoring an obvious misunderstanding, or perhaps by a sudden change of topic to allow the conversation to continue. Meierkord has also observed a reduced range of 'safe' topics, which participants tended to deal with fairly superficially. She notes, however, that many *lingua franca* conversations occur between participants who are aware of each other as language learners so they may make allowances for each other and perhaps lower their pragmatic expectations. Certainly, as indicated above, we would expect language learners to have a greater understanding of the challenges of crossing linguistic boundaries than people who have not learned a second language. Firth (1990: 277) suggests that 'What seems feasible is that the requirements of accountability will be relatively more relaxed in "*lingua franca*" settings, with the participants allowing for greater "latitude" in judgements of pragmatic appropriacy, directness etc.'.

In mother tongue to second-language conversations we might assume that the pragmatic norms are probably those of the mother tongue/target language. Above, we suggested that both learners and mother tongue speakers must share some responsibility for making such conversations work, the second-language speaker aiming for target language pragmatic norms, the mother tongue speaker being tolerant of differences and aware that the second-language speaker has different mother tongue norms. In the true *lingua franca* context, however, there are no mother tongue speakers present and a major question surrounds what the pragmatic norms are. Even when mother tongue speakers are involved, they may be a minority, so it is debatable whether theirs should be the norms to prevail.

Meierkord (2000) suggests that, in the context of informal *lingua franca* conversations in English, where speakers may also be conscious of their status as language learners, a combination of linguistic uncertainty and lack of knowledge of their interlocutor's norms for linguistic behaviour in, for example, greeting and leaving, may lead to their clinging for security to what they know to be acceptable in British or American English: '. . . they will prefer not to experiment during these phases. Using only those routine formulas they know to be acceptable in either BrE or AmE gives them certainty about not violating any rules' (Meierkord, 2000: Section 3.2.3). While this principle may turn out to be demonstrated in informal conversations that are in effect transitory, different principles may apply when *lingua franca* interaction continues among stable groups. Firth, referring to interaction in the international trading context, suggests that what Meierkord calls an 'inter-culture' may grow up, with its own pragmatic norms:

> What we must allow for and consider is that when persons are involved in ongoing, long-term international communications, as is the case with international (trading) personnel, the persons concerned create their own 'network' . . . Within such a network, norms, standards and interpretive procedures are likely to be developed, becoming collectively recognizable as a 'style' peculiar to, or at least characteristic of, the specific network . . . the use of English among specific 'networks' of individuals may become 'internationalized', with emergent norms or 'styles' that transcend cultural and, indeed, linguistic boundaries. (1990: 277)

If much work to date has found fewer misunderstandings than expected in *lingua franca* conversations, House (2002a, 2002b) introduces a note of caution. In work with more advanced English learners she similarly found evidence of supportive behaviour in *lingua franca* discussions, generating an overall impression of consensus. She further notes, however, a tendency to engage in 'parallel monologues', whereby individuals pursue their own agendas and do not engage in interwoven discourse in the way native speakers would be expected to. This is further highlighted by a notable absence of discourse markers available in English, so that participants give no impression of registering or reacting to another's contribution. Interestingly, in subsequent reflection with participants she found that they could sometimes indicate points in the conversation when they were conscious of deeper misunderstandings and linguistically cultural differences. She reports a German speaker who, after engaging in discussion with three Asian participants, noted that the Asian speakers appeared not to operate with the same conversational rules as she was used to. Instead they preferred to 'ignore potentially confrontational remarks' and to resist 'any seriously argumentative talk, in which interactants' viewpoints might be challenged and conflicts explicitly stated and negotiated' (2002a: 258).

Whereas House, rather like Firth, had earlier suspected the existence of a kind of 'intersociety' in *lingua franca* interaction, where both mother tongue and second-language pragmatic norms were irrelevant, she now interprets what she sees happening in *lingua franca* interaction rather differently. The co-operative behaviour noted in most such interaction, whereby speakers help each other out of linguistic difficulty by supplying words or completing sentences, House sees as operating at a local linguistic level, demonstrating concern for the other participants (2002b: 260). On the other hand, the pursuit of individual topic agendas, resulting in parallel monologues, is taken as evidence of both a self-centred conversational approach and a 'let-it-pass' principle deriving from participants' unwillingness to destroy an appearance of consensus. The latter was noticeable especially in participants of Asian origin and may indeed reflect a cultural pragmatic norm whereby face needs have to be protected though consensual feeling in conversation.

Discussion

Since so much communication takes place these days across language boundaries, whether between mother tongue and second-language speakers or between second-language speakers only, it is important to try to enhance the chances of successful communication and to minimise the risk of misunderstanding or non-communication. What can be done, beyond teaching the basics of the language, to prepare individuals in their interpersonal interactions with speakers from other language communities?

Some would say that it is the task of the language teacher to ensure that the second-language speaker knows the pragmatic norms of the target language community. Leaving aside for the moment the inadequacy of this principle in the true *lingua franca* (second-language/second-language) context, this throws the onus on to the language learner, rather than on all participants in the interaction. But it can also be argued that mother tongue speakers need to be aware of the linguistic norms of their own language, partly to be more comprehending of the breaking of linguistic norms by second-language speakers, but also to understand the perceptions that might be provoked in outsiders by their own use of language. For English mother tongue speakers there may be a particular responsibility here, since they very often find themselves dealing with English second-language speakers whom it is vital to meet half way. Frequently this does not happen: English radio journalists, for instance, interviewing foreign people on their radio programmes regularly treat them as if they are native speakers and make no concessions to suggest an understanding of how difficult it is to function at near-native level as a second-language speaker.

It is essential, without being patronising, to temper one's own language to an appropriate level. This might include avoiding excessive idiomaticity or choosing vocabulary likely to be understood by the speaker (which does not necessarily involve simplifying vocabulary, since speakers of Romance languages frequently understand Latinate words better than words of Anglo-Saxon or Germanic origin). It would also involve avoiding excessive syntactic complexity, such as multiple subordinate clauses or even the double negatives much beloved of public speakers. There is an example of this in the following reply by the British Prime Minister, Tony Blair, to a question from a Chinese university student (printed in the *Independent*, 23 July 2003):

> Chinese student: 'Newspapers have called the UK the 51st state of the US. I want your views on that comment.'
>
> Tony Blair: 'It is not true to say that we don't have our disagreements with the US . . .'.

Blair's reply may be deliberately oblique, but to a non-native speaker it becomes doubly so because of the double negative which adds to comprehension difficulties. On the other hand, bearing in mind the earlier discussion of English politeness, it could be argued that Blair may subconsciously not have been well disposed to the questioner because of (to English ears) the very direct and inappropriately dogmatic and imperious formulation of the request ('I want your views on that comment' rather than 'Could you give me your view on that comment?')!

Understanding these subtleties requires some sophistication on the part of the mother tongue speaker. Béal's recommendation (Béal, 1998: 22), in the context of her Australian case study, is for the receiving community, as well as the visiting community, to receive some preparation in the form of awareness of the pragmatic rules of their own language. However, where the receiving community is resolutely monoglot, as many English-speaking communities still are, surely such preparation can be only partially successful without any personal experience of attempting to learn and use a foreign language. This is perhaps one of the best arguments why English speakers must continue to learn foreign languages, even though the need may not always seem apparent. Bassnett (2002), lamenting the recent decline in language learning in Britain, notes that an increase in intercultural training in the business world is now frequently serving in the English-speaking context as a substitute for language learning. We return to the topic of intercultural training below, but while increased intercultural awareness is vital and to be widely encouraged, we would argue that this alone cannot impart a true understanding of what it means to communicate in a language other than one's own. Unless individuals have attempted to articulate, or recode, their own perception of reality in terms of another language, they will never truly understand the experience of someone who is having to do just that.

In the case of 'true' *lingua franca* (second-language/second language) interaction, of course, both parties have an understanding of the necessity of such recoding. The problem we are now facing is a different one, as already discussed: it is a question of what the prevailing pragmatic norms are. As it is likely that neither party knows the mother tongue pragmatic norms of the other, the second-language pragmatic norms may come into force to some degree. Since each party will be less familiar with those norms, they are unlikely to be so sensitive to any failure to observe them, which may well help to explain the apparent lack of misunderstanding that has been found in *lingua franca* interaction. However, the issue still arises of each party approaching the interaction from a different cultural background and a different set of norms. Thus the need for individuals to be aware of their own norms is equally applicable. If *lingua franca* speakers are indeed 'talking past' each other in the way that House suggests (2002b), it indicates a need to encourage them to reflect on their use of the second language in the light of their own linguistic and cultural norms. House recommends (2002b: 263) 'self observation' as the best way of doing this, whereby *lingua franca* participants listen to and reflect on their own oral production and that of others and become aware of ways in which they can develop some features of 'pragmatic fluency', which will both respond to their own needs and those of others.

House's 'self-observation' can be linked to the ethnographic principle that is an essential part of the intercultural training mentioned above, whereby individuals learn to observe the Self as well as the Other. Intercultural training has indeed flourished in professional contexts in recent years and Bassnett's view, that it has in part compensated for low levels of language learning in the English-speaking world, may to some extent be true. This is not an accusation that can be levelled at the mainland European context, however, where intercultural studies have become increasingly respected and increasingly widespread in recent years and have been introduced in several European universities. These are communities inhabited by precisely the people who have to live the reality of second-language use, in both the mixed and the true *lingua franca* mode; and the value of intercultural awareness is not lost on them.

Conclusion

Language is but one part of intercultural communication and it goes beyond the scope of this discussion to broach other aspects such as non-verbal behaviour, communication styles, cultural assumptions and values. Equally, in discussing pragmatic norms, we have been able to focus only on a small area of language competence that can vary from language to language. A detailed discussion of language variation that is culturally determined, as well as the wider scope of interculturalism can be found in Bennett (1998). While sharing Bassnett's reservations about the dangers of replacing language study, we would argue that the growing emphasis on Intercultural Studies is to be welcomed. In this respect Britain is now following the US and mainland European lead; and the subject Intercultural Studies is now being introduced in some universities, as well as in business training contexts.

Béal (1998: 23) laments that the Australian and French participants in her workplace study had not been better prepared for their intercultural experience and alerted to the ways in which their linguistic behaviour might prejudice them in their dealings with colleagues of the other nationality. Arguably, such preparation should not be confined to the workplace: to alert people generally to the potential dangers and difficulties, as well as the immense benefits, of interacting meaningfully in the international community, we should ensure that an emphasis on awareness in cross-cultural interaction becomes even more widespread. We should also ensure that we do not leave it to those who have to function in a second language to make all the effort. It is as vital for the mother tongue English speakers in today's world to be conscious of the way their language works as it is for those learning it to know how it differs from their own. It is also clear that such insight will be immensely more effective if awareness goes hand in hand with experience of trying to communicate in a second language. This means both language learning and intercultural awareness, not one or the other. As workers increasingly work, and students increasingly learn, in cross-cultural contexts, even in their home country, the opportunities for such a combined approach have never been better. With the continuing rise in global interaction, and the increased communication in one language predicted by Graddol (1999) for the coming decades, and to minimise the risks of failed communication or misunderstanding, we must hope that such opportunities are seized.

Note

1. Although the term *lingua franca* has various more specific meanings in linguistic terms (see for example Edwards, 1995: 217), we shall here use it in the way in which it is increasingly used to refer to English in its 'wider communication' role in the global context.

References

Anderman, G. (1992) Translation and speech acts. In Y. Gambier and J. Tommola (eds) *Proceedings of the 4th Scandinavian Symposium on Translation Theory, Translation and Knowledge. Vol 14* (pp. 377–87) Turku: Centre for Translation and Interpreting, Turku University.

Bassnett, S. (2002) Opinion. *Guardian Education* 12 March 2002, 13.

Béal, C. (1998) Keeping the peace: A cross-cultural comparison of questions and requests in Australian English and French. In P. Trudgill and J. Cheshire (eds) *The Sociolinguistics Reader, Vol 1: Multilingualism and Variation* (pp. 5–24). London: Arnold.

Bennett, M. (1998) Intercultural communication: a current perspective. In M. Bennett (ed.) *Basic Concepts of Intercultural Communication: Selected Readings* (pp. 1–34) Yarmouth, Maine: Intercultural Press.

Blum-Kulka, S. and Olshtain, E. (1984) Requests and apologies: A cross-cultural study of speech act realization patterns (CCSARP). *Applied Linguistics* 5(3), 196–213.

Brown, P. and Levinson, S. (1987) *Politeness: Some Universals In Language Usage*. Cambridge: Cambridge University Press.

Edwards, J. (1995) *Multilingualism*. London: Penguin.

Firth, A. (1990) '*Lingua franca*' negotiations: Towards an interactional approach. *World Englishes* 9 (3), 269–80.

Graddol, D. (1999) The decline of the native speaker. In D. Graddol and U. Meinhof (eds) *English in a Changing World. AILA Review* 13, 57–68.

Grundy, P. (1995) *Doing Pragmatics*. London: Edward Arnold.

House, J. (2002a) Communicating in English as a *lingua franca*. In S. Foster-Cohen, T. Ruthenberg, and M.L. Poschen (eds) *EUROSLA Yearbook, Volume 2 (2002)* (pp. 243–62). Amsterdam/Philadelphia: John Benjamins Publishing Company.

House, J. (2002b) Pragmatic competence in *lingua franca* English. In K. Knapp and C. Meierkord (eds.) *Lingua franca communication* (pp. 245–67) Frankfurt/Main: Lang.

House, J. and Kasper, G. (1978) Politeness markers in English and German. In *Actes du 5ème Congrès de l'Association Internationale de Linguistique Appliquée* (pp. 157–85). Québec: Les Presses de l'Université Laval.

Kasper, G. and Blum-Kulka, S. (eds) (1993) *Interlanguage Pragmatics*. New York: Oxford University Press.

Knapp, K. and Meierkord, C. (eds) (2002) *Lingua franca Communication*. Frankfurt/Main: Lang.

Meierkord, C. (2000) Interpreting successful *lingua franca* interaction. An analysis of non-native/non-native small talk conversations in English. *Linguistik Online5*, 1/00, www.linguistik-online.de/1_00/ (accessed 25 April 2003).

Seidlhofer, B. (2002) *Habeas corpus* and *divide et impera*: 'Global English' and Applied Linguistics. In K. Spelman Miller and P. Thompson (eds) *Unity and Diversity in Language Use* (pp. 198–217). London, New York: BAAL/Continuum.

Tannen, D. (1984) The pragmatics of cross-cultural communication. *Applied Linguistics* 5 (3), 189–95.

Thomas, J. (1983) Cross cultural pragmatic failure. *Applied Linguistics* 4 (2), 91–112.

Yule, G. (1996) *Pragmatics*. Oxford: Oxford University Press.

Index